The Theory and Practice of Representative Negotiation

Colleen M. Hanycz • Trevor C.W. Farrow • Frederick H. Zemans

2008
EMOND MONTGOMERY PUBLICATIONS LIMITED
TORONTO, CANADA

Emond Montgomery Publications Limited
60 Shaftesbury Avenue
Toronto ON M4T 1A3
http://www.emp.ca

Printed in Canada.

We acknowledge the financial support of the Government of Canada through the Book Publishing Industry Development Program (BPIDP) for our publishing activities.

Acquisitions and developmental editor: Mike Thompson
Marketing director: Dave Stokaluk
Copy editor: Claudia Forgas
Proofreader: Diane Gula
Production editor: Jim Lyons, WordsWorth Communications
Indexer: Paula Pike, WordsWorth Communications
Text designer: Tara Wells, WordsWorth Communications
Cover designers: Stephen Cribbin & Simon Evers

Library and Archives Canada Cataloguing in Publication

Hanycz, Colleen, 1966-
    The theory and practice of representative negotiation / Colleen Hanycz, Frederick Zemans, Trevor Farrow.

Includes index.
ISBN 978-1-55239-264-5

    1. Negotiation—Textbooks.   I. Zemans, Frederick H.   II. Farrow, Trevor C.W.
III. Title.

HD58.6.H36 2008   658.4'052   C2007-904534-0

Contents

PART III Negotiation Process

Chapter 3 *Introduction to the Negotiation Process Model*
Colleen M. Hanycz

Chapter 4 *Strategic Negotiation: Moving Through the Stages*
Colleen M. Hanycz

Part IV   Ethics

Chapter 5   Representative Negotiators of Integrity

Frederick H. Zemans

PART V   Perspectives, Lenses, and Issues Pertaining to Legal Negotiation

Chapter 6   Shapeshifters and Synergy: Toward a Culturally Fluent Approach to Representative Negotiation

Michelle LeBaron

Chapter 7   Power and Negotiation

Michael Coyle

Chapter 8   Gender and Negotiation

Delee Fromm

Chapter 9   Emotion in Negotiation

Delee Fromm

Chapter 10   The Essential Role of Communication in Negotiation

D. Paul Emond

Chapter 11   *Critiques of Settlement Advocacy*

Andrew Pirie

Preface

Much of our work in this book has been guided by the aphorism, attributed to W.B. Yeats, that "education is not the filling of a bucket, but the lighting of a fire." We hope that this book will inspire more questions than it answers, as students and practitioners of representative negotiation from all walks of life examine our views on the subject and test our ideas for soundness.

Our aim has been to expand the rich body of literature on negotiation theory by focusing on the unique nature of representative negotiation. Adding another dimension to the already complex process of bringing together people with often conflicting interests, needs, and goals proves quite challenging at the best of times. What we hope to offer in the pages that follow is a new way of thinking about negotiating on behalf of others, complete with a variety of lenses through which to view that task.

Our process in writing this book has been a satisfyingly collaborative and integrative one. Much of the writing has been done by the three of us, and the remainder has been contributed by an exceptional team of leading dispute resolution scholars. Through new writing of their own and comments on existing negotiation literature, these authors have added a significant amount of original thinking to the scholarship in this area. We think that you will agree that the result is a fresh look at representative negotiation, with a uniquely Canadian perspective, that will not only supply educators with a useful and convenient teaching tool but also provide negotiation scholars and practitioners alike with ideas for meaningful new areas of study and practice.

This process has been uniquely rewarding for all of us as we have shared the rare opportunity of learning about representative negotiation from existing scholars, from our contributing authors, and, of course, from each other. This is most certainly one of those equations where the whole is greater than the sum of its parts, and we are grateful to have been given the opportunity to help educators and practitioners in teaching negotiation and gaining insight into its complexities.

This book could not have been completed without the assistance and inspiration provided by numerous people. We would like particularly to thank our contributing authors, each one of whom brought to this project an energy, excitement, and commitment that bolstered our own. It has been our distinct pleasure to undertake this project with such a gifted group of scholars.

Thanks are also due to the instructors, interns, and students of Lawyer as Negotiator, an upper-year undergraduate course offered at Osgoode Hall Law School, for inspiring this book from the beginning and for allowing us to test our theories over the years.

We are grateful to the professionals at Emond Montgomery Publications, especially our copy editor, Claudia Forgas, for her tireless efforts and enlightening creativity, and our acquisitions and developmental editor, Mike Thompson, for helping us realize our aspirations in this project.

Finally, we thank our families, who continue to support us with their ideas, their encouragement, and their inspiration and who regularly provide us with testing grounds for our emerging thoughts and theories around negotiation in all of its many forms.

Colleen M. Hanycz
Trevor C.W. Farrow
Frederick H. Zemans

About the Authors

Michael Coyle teaches Negotiation and Mediation at the University of Western Ontario Faculty of Law. Prior to joining the faculty in 2000, he spent 10 years as director of mediation at the Indian Commission of Ontario. He has extensive experience in multi-party negotiations, negotiation training, and dispute resolution process design.

Paul Emond is a professor at Osgoode Hall Law School, York University, where he teaches in the dispute resolution field. He is the co-director and program coordinator of Osgoode's part-time LL.M. (ADR). In addition to courses at Osgoode Hall, he conducts negotiation and mediation workshops for private law firms, governments, native organizations, and public interest groups.

Trevor C.W. Farrow joined the faculty of Osgoode Hall Law School in 2006, prior to which he was on faculty at the University of Alberta Faculty of Law. Professor Farrow was previously a litigator at the Torys law firm in Toronto, the Ames Fellow at Harvard Law School, and a teaching fellow at Harvard College.

Delee Fromm is both a lawyer and a psychologist. She has taught various negotiation courses at the University of Toronto for both law and MBA students, and currently teaches at York University. Through her consulting firm, Fromm & Goodhand, she trains and coaches in the areas of negotiation, gender dynamics, leadership, and conflict resolution.

Colleen M. Hanycz joined the faculty of Osgoode Hall Law School in 2003, following several years in practice as a litigator in Toronto. Professor Hanycz teaches courses in Civil Procedure, Dispute Resolution, and Lawyer as Negotiator, and is the convenor of the curriculum stream known as Litigation, Dispute Resolution and the Administration of Justice.

Michelle LeBaron is a professor at the University of British Columbia Faculty of Law, and is director of the UBC Program on Dispute Resolution. Prior to her work at UBC, Michelle taught for ten years at George Mason University in Virginia. She has published widely in cross-cultural dispute resolution, has practised as a lawyer and clinical counsellor, and teaches and practises internationally. Her current work focuses on the arts as resources for working across cultures.

Andrew Pirie was appointed to the University of Victoria Faculty of Law in 1981, and is a former executive director of that university's Institute for Dispute Resolution. Professor Pirie's teaching and scholarship focus on alternative dispute resolution (ADR), with principal interests in the theory and practice of negotiation and mediation.

Frederick H. Zemans is a Senior Scholar and Professor Emeritus at Osgoode Hall Law School and his teaching and research focus on negotiation, mediation, and social justice. He is a founding member of Osgoode Hall's Graduate Programme in ADR, where he developed both the Practicum and Ethics and Professional Responsibility courses. He was a member of the Evaluation Team of the Ontario Mandatory Mediation Pilot Project between 1999 and 2002.

PART I

Introduction

CHAPTER 1

An Introduction to Representative Negotiation

Colleen M. Hanycz, Trevor C.W. Farrow, and Frederick H. Zemans

A Week in the World of Representative Negotiators

An Ottawa Real Estate Deal

On Monday afternoon, Samantha Jones calls Partha Kumar, an Ottawa real estate agent, and tells him that she is interested in buying the house owned by another woman who is moving to Nova Scotia to take on a new job. Samantha had been trying to purchase a house in Ottawa without the assistance of a real estate agent; however, she was having a tough time finding a house that was reasonably priced and in one of the centrally located neighbourhoods in which she wanted to live. Finally, she found a house she wanted to buy. Late last week, Samantha had a number of cordial discussions with the owner, who was selling her house on her own. The owner indicated that she hadn't had much serious interest in the house and that, as of Friday, only one firm offer had been made.

Samantha phoned the owner this morning and found out that nothing had changed over the weekend. However, by midday, as Samantha was getting ready to call the owner back and make an offer, she received a call from the owner's real estate agent. He indicated that there are now two offers on the house, one of which is $15,000 higher than the other offer that Samantha and the owner had discussed last week and again earlier today.

The call from the agent and the information about the second offer took Samantha completely by surprise. She immediately called the owner, who confirmed that she is now represented by the agent. When asked about the second offer, however, the owner hesitated and then tried to hide from Samantha her obvious surprise about the information. Samantha is convinced, after her discussion with the owner, that the "second offer" is only a bluff and that the agent is simply trying to drive up the price in order to maximize the selling price and the agent's commission.

Samantha asks Partha whether he thinks it would be helpful for him to represent her, particularly given her strong interest in this house and the potential bluff that the other agent may or may not be making. What should Partha say? On what considerations should he base his assessment? If he agrees to represent Samantha, how should he proceed?

A British Columbia Labour Dispute

On Wednesday evening, after three long days of unsuccessful and inflammatory discussions between representatives of management and labour at a timber mill in British Columbia, employees have gathered to discuss the possibility of walking off the job early the next morning. They are fed up of what they describe as poor working conditions, a poor mill safety record, and uncertainty about an outstanding pension dispute that has not been resolved for the past six months.

This week, the mill is completing a large shipment that is set to leave by rail on Friday morning to a long-standing customer in the United States. At the meeting, everyone is certain that a threatened job action at this point would be very disruptive for the mill and the purchaser and would, therefore, likely be an effective means of pressuring their employer for some kind of immediate concession. However, a number of employees are concerned about job action at this point. They have heard rumours about potential layoffs at the mill due to a slow US housing market that is having a ripple effect on the home-building sector. The shipment they are currently working on will certainly be lucrative for the mill and will likely maintain good relations with the US purchaser who, notwithstanding current slowdowns, seems poised to purchase further lumber from the mill in the near future.

After a long evening of discussions, employees agree to try to talk to management once more before walking off the job. However, given the previous three days of unsuccessful and acrimonious discussions, it is also agreed that negotiations should only proceed with the assistance of a representative negotiator. Even though it is late, the group decides to call Dina Williams, a friend of one of the employees and a long-time union-side negotiator. During the call, Dina is briefed about the situation. Before the end of the conversation, she is asked whether she thinks there is value in bringing a representative into the negotiations at this stage of the dispute. And, if she thinks there is value, Dina is asked to give an overview of the strategy she would use in the negotiation if she were to take the case. Dina says that she will think about the questions over night and get back to the group early the next morning.

Assuming that she agrees to take the case, what should Dina say about the value she would add and the strategy she would use? What considerations might influence her thinking?

Agent Orange Litigation

On Friday afternoon Jim LeBlanc, a partner at an established Montreal law firm, receives a call at his office from the CFO of a large Quebec chemical manufacturing company. The company—a market leader that has been in business for over 60 years—is a significant client of the firm in terms of its annual billings.

During the 1950s and 1960s, the company was involved in a number of different herbicide projects. It produced a chemical component that became an essential ingredient in the defoliating compound known as Agent Orange, which was used primarily in the late 1960s by the American armed forces in the Vietnam War. After the war, widespread reports of dioxin-related health problems stemming from the use of Agent Orange began to emerge. An estimated 3 million Vietnamese suffered physical problems as a result of the use of Agent Orange during the war. Countless others, including American war veterans, also had severe negative effects from the chemical.

Ultimately, legal action by victims, their families, and others is being taken on several fronts, including suits against a number of US chemical companies. There are various thorny legal issues at stake in the litigation, including disputes about causes of action, limitation periods, evidence, and jurisdiction. There are also significant political issues at stake. Vietnam is currently going through major social, political, and economic reforms and is increasingly seeking acceptance into the global economic community. At the same time, the US government and others are actively engaging with Vietnam on both political and economic levels. There is therefore significant interest in finding some kind of resolution to this difficult issue.

The Quebec company's CFO informs Jim that until recently the company has not been part of the litigation. However, given its involvement in the production of a component of Agent Orange, and further, given the wide-ranging jurisdictional issues that are at stake in the US litigation, the company has been recently brought into the dispute. The Canadian government has been informed of the situation and is sending a representative to Washington next week to discuss the situation with US authorities. At the moment, no one is certain how the situation will play out. While it seems in everyone's interest that a diplomatic resolution be reached, one does not seem to be forthcoming. As such, all of the litigants involved are both preparing for litigation as well as looking at ways of potentially negotiating a settlement.

A colleague of Jim's has been asked to lead a litigation team. Jim, however, is being asked to lead a separate settlement team on behalf of his Quebec client—alongside the litigation efforts—to see if the company can somehow either be let out of the litigation or at least play only a minor role in any kind of financial settlement. Jim agrees to take the brief. When approaching the negotiation, what considerations will inform Jim's negotiation strategy?

Representative Negotiation

These kinds of disputes, and countless others involving all aspects of social, political, and commercial relationships and endeavours, occur every day across Canada and around the world. They invariably involve very different individuals and organizations with very different problems and interests. What they all have in common, however, is the potential to become disputes that form the basis of a representative negotiation.

Negotiation is a dispute resolution process that has been around as long as disputes themselves. More recently, however, negotiation has become the subject of intense academic study and practical training. Scholars and practitioners—influenced by a wide range of research in areas such as sociology, economics, psychology, political theory, law, communication, and media studies—have over the past half century, and particularly over the past 25 years, made significant advances in the way that negotiation is thought about, taught, and practised.

Surprisingly, negotiation conducted *on behalf of* disputing parties—third-party, or "representative," negotiation—has been much less studied and is less understood as compared with basic direct negotiation and its tools and processes. It is this important landscape that we sketch and depict in *The Theory and Practice of Representative Negotiation.*

This Book

This book examines the influences on and the issues related to representative negotiation. Unlike direct negotiation, when representatives are added to the negotiation mix, a number of other opportunities and challenges emerge.

A threshold decision is whether to use a representative in a negotiation. Will adding Partha to the Ottawa real estate negotiation, for example, assist Samantha in successfully dealing with a potentially difficult real estate agent? Adding Partha to the mix will certainly bring another set of interests to the negotiation—those of the representative—beyond the direct interests of the principal disputants. Deciding whether to add a representative, and then understanding, managing, and capitalizing on the extra interests of the representative—such as, self-interests, professional interests, and public interests—are all matters taken up in chapter 2.

The Process Model of Negotiation

In chapters 3 and 4, we introduce a novel negotiation framework that we advance throughout this book: the process model of negotiation. Usually, negotiation models are based on a particular strategic approach, such as distributive bargaining or integrative bargaining. Often these models focus primarily on disputants' "positions" or "interests." The process model of negotiation, on the other hand, is neither solely distributive nor integrative, and it is based neither solely on positions nor interests. Rather, our model is driven primarily by an assessment of the "value climate" of a negotiation: essentially an assessment of what is at stake in a potential negotiation settlement and what is available to satisfy the various divergent interests around the negotiation table. The assessment of what we are calling the negotiation's "value climate" determines the strategic approach that should be adopted. For example, if there is value to be generated or revealed, then the model urges representative negotiators to adopt an integrative framework (that is, an approach that *creates* or identifies value). If, however, an assessment of the value climate indicates that there is little or no additional value to be generated—a point that, we argue, arrives in every negotiation—then the model urges representative negotiators, acting in the best interests of their clients, to shift to a distribute negotiating framework (that is, an approach that *claims* value).

So when Sandra is considering her approach to the BC labour dispute, one of the factors she will need to address is the value climate that is at stake in the negotiation. Clearly the dispute is not just about wages. Additional issues—mill safety, pension security, long-term employment security, and future contracts—are also at play. All of these factors provide moments for value realization and creation. The hybrid model of negotiation—which combines strategic frameworks and is based primarily on the assessment of a negotiation's value climate—is one that will assist negotiators like Sandra to approach the various stages of representative negotiation. The hybrid model is also, in our view, one of several unique and exciting offerings of this book.

Chapter 5 takes up the issue of ethics in representative negotiation. Ethics is a surprisingly understudied and underregulated area of negotiation. In our view, ethics and professionalism are central to any discussion of negotiation, including representative negotiation. And it is in chapter 5 that we address this issue head on. Is making a "bluff" offer, for example, by the Ottawa real estate agent ethical? Is it professional? If no, what should Partha do about it when acting on behalf of Samantha? Should he "fight fire with fire"? What is at stake for Samantha? For him? For others?

In the next five chapters (chapters 6 to 10), we examine a number of lenses through which to view representative negotiations, lenses that serve to further influence our approach to strategic negotiation. Culture, power, gender, emotion, and communication all play a significant role in the representative negotiation process at all levels: between representative and principal, between representative and representative, and often also—directly or indirectly—between principal and principal. Without seriously considering the role that these various factors play, representative negotiators risk impoverishing the potential for success in a given negotiation. For example, if Jim does not take seriously the culture, power, emotion, communication, and possible gender-related issues that are likely at stake in the Agent Orange dispute, he will have a severely limited understanding of the potential challenges of the negotiation, as well as the potential range of resources that might affect the value climate of that negotiation and its settlement. By contrast, if Jim is to look at this negotiation from as many different angles as possible, he will enrich not only his understanding of the matters in issue, but also the strategic gains that he is able to achieve using this process.

Finally, in chapter 11, we take a critical look at settlement advocacy. Sometimes, there are many good reasons why disputes should not settle, at least not in private with the use of informal negotiation tools. It is important to consider when representative negotiation should be used and when more formal, traditional, or public tools—such as litigation—should be used. This calculus is important both at the micro level (the client) as well as at the macro level (society). For example, would the private resolution of the Agent Orange dispute be to the benefit of Jim's client? Likely so, given that reputational and other financial interests often motivate the desire to keep a lid on the client's involvement in the dispute. However, from society's perspective (which potentially comprises the views of members of various national and international communities), having the matter resolved in public—through traditional court-based tools that are the subject of attention and scrutiny by the media and non-governmental organizations—might address broader public interests regarding corporate and regulatory behaviour modification, public vindication, monetary compensation, etc. So depending on your—and your client's—perspective, the choice to resolve cases by direct or representative negotiation engages significant public policy considerations.

As we know from the scenarios above and from our own daily lives, representatives are central to our negotiation culture. By examining the nature of the relationship between representatives, as professionals, and principals, we are better able to think about negotiation strategically. And by thinking about negotiation strategically, as representatives, we are able to optimize the interests of our clients.

We offer one model for thinking about negotiation, a model that is centred on the availability of value and resources to satisfy the needs and interests of the principals to a negotiation.

We also highlight some of the many other factors that should be considered by a representative when planning a negotiation strategy in order to achieve the best possible gains on behalf of someone else. And throughout this, we emphasize the crucial role played by ethics and professionalism in representative negotiation. Whether you represent your client as a lawyer, a business person, a real estate agent, or otherwise, you must continually be aware of your own distinct ethical position as you navigate the challenges posed by negotiating for someone else. You must also recognize that some disputes may not be best served by informal resolutions that tend to occur in private and without review.

In the pages that follow, we offer many bits of information and suggested perspectives that we believe should inform your approach to negotiation. We ask that you think about all of them as you begin to understand the inner workings of representative negotiation.

PART II

Representative Negotiation

CHAPTER 2

Representative Negotiation

Trevor C.W. Farrow

Introduction

The Unique Role of Representative Negotiators

While much of the literature on negotiation deals with the tools and strategies of negotiation in general, this book deals with those tools and strategies in a specific context: representative negotiation. The role of representative negotiator is different from the role of direct negotiator, and brings with it a significant number of additional opportunities and challenges that need to be considered in order to understand its potential fully.

This chapter will introduce some of the unique and defining aspects of the role of representative negotiator. It will also set out some of the challenges that representative negotiators face—challenges that are discussed in detail elsewhere in this book. The introductory section of this chapter discusses various contexts of representative negotiation, with a particular emphasis on legal negotiation. The next section of this chapter examines various merits and drawbacks of the representative's role, and looks at the threshold question of whether to engage a representative to assist with a negotiation. The following section of this chapter looks at the nature of representative negotiation, with a particular focus on the role of the representative and the competing interests that are potentially involved in a representative negotiation. Finally, for readers interested in pursuing these and related issues further, a list of selected sources is included in the last section of this chapter.

Various Contexts of Representative Negotiation

We see the role of representative negotiator in all aspects of human interchange. Put simply, it is "everywhere."[1] Starting with intimate or personal relations, sometimes family members or friends are asked to help deal with particularly important, thorny, or sensitive issues. More publicly, representatives are engaged to assist with the creation or transition of relationships and the resolution of disputes in almost all sectors of society involving almost all types of issues: commercial transactions, investment decisions, real estate deals, labour disputes, plea bargaining in criminal law, family disputes, immigration issues, education issues, etc. Finally, representatives are almost always used when relationships and disputes require a negotiated arrangement or settlement at government, regulatory, and international levels as well.

Legal Representatives

The relevance of representative negotiation in the context of law cannot be overstated. Because lawyers are often significantly involved in many if not most negotiated arrangements, negotiation plays a significant part in almost every lawyer's career. Put simply, it is a lawyer's "bread and butter." As Charles Wiggins and L. Randolph Lowry have commented,

"We should've just dropped off our lists and taken our chances. But no, you had to bring a lawyer into the negotiations."

Figure 2.1

Source: CartoonStock.com, cartoonist–Baldwin.

Lawyers are a distinctive subclass of negotiators. They are members of a profession that exists to act as an intermediary between others involved in activities requiring bargaining. As such, they should be experts in managing the negotiation process. Virtually all transaction planning activities require lawyers to negotiate on behalf of clients. Likewise, over ninety five per cent of all adjudicated disputes are resolved by some process other than courtroom proceedings.[2]

As such, this chapter largely examines the role of the representative negotiator in the specific context of legal representation.

---

1   R.H. Mnookin, S.R. Peppet & A.S. Tulumello, *Beyond Winning: Negotiating to Create Value in Deals and Disputes* (Cambridge, MA: Belknap Press, 2000) at 70.

2   C.B. Wiggins & L.R. Lowry, eds., *Negotiation and Settlement Advocacy: A Book of Readings*, 2d ed. (St. Paul, MN: Thomson, 2005) at 497.

Deciding on When to Use Representative Negotiation

Direct Versus Representative Negotiation

In the context of a negotiation, a threshold decision is whether to use a representative. To make this decision, clients should weigh the various merits and drawbacks of hiring a representative for a specific negotiation. The following article by Jeffrey Rubin and Frank Sander takes a closer look at some of the considerations involved in choosing direct vs. representative negotiation.

Jeffrey Z. Rubin and Frank E.A. Sander

"When Should We Use Agents? Direct vs. Representative Negotiation"

(1988) 4 Negotiation Journal at 395-401, footnotes omitted

Although we typically conceive of negotiations occurring directly between two or more principals, often neglected in a thoughtful analysis are the many situations where negotiations take place indirectly, through the use of representatives or surrogates of the principals. A father who speaks to his child's teacher (at the child's request), two lawyers meeting on behalf of their respective clients, the foreign service officers of different nations meeting to negotiate the settlement of a border dispute, a real estate agent informing would-be buyers of the seller's latest offer—each is an instance of negotiation through representatives.

In this brief essay, we wish to build on previous analyses of representative negotiation to consider several key distinctions between direct and representative negotiations, and to indicate the circumstances under which we believe negotiators should go out of their way either to choose *or* to avoid negotiation through agents.

The most obvious effect of using agents—an effect that must be kept in mind in any analysis of representative negotiation—is complication of the transaction. If we begin with a straightforward negotiation between two individuals, then the addition of two agents transforms this simple one-on-one deal into a complex matrix involving at least four primary negotiations, as well as two subsidiary ones. In addition, either of the agents may readily serve as a mediator between the client and the other agent or principal. Or the two agents might act as co-mediators between the principals. At a minimum, such a complex structure necessitates effective coordination. Beyond that, this structural complexity has implications—both positive and negative—for representative negotiation in general. Let us now review these respective benefits and liabilities.

Expertise

One of the primary reasons that principals choose to negotiate through agents is that the latter possess expertise that makes agreement—particularly favorable agreement—more likely. This expertise is likely to be of three different stripes:

Substantive knowledge. A tax attorney or accountant knows things about the current tax code that make it more likely that negotiations with an IRS auditor will benefit the client as much as possible. Similarly, a divorce lawyer, an engineering consultant, and a real estate agent may have substantive knowledge in a rather narrow domain of expertise, and this expertise may redound to the client's benefit.

Process expertise. Quite apart from the specific expertise they may have in particular content areas, agents may have skill at the negotiation *process*, per se, thereby enhancing the prospects of a favorable agreement. A skillful negotiator—someone who understands how to obtain and reveal information about preferences, who is inventive, resourceful, firm on goals but flexible on means, etc.—is a valuable resource. Wise principals would do well to utilize the services of such skilled negotiators, unless they can find ways of developing such process skills themselves.

Special influence. A Washington lobbyist is paid to know the "right" people, to have access to the "corridors of power" that the principals themselves are unlikely to possess. Such "pull" can certainly help immensely, and is yet another form of expertise that agents may possess, although the lure of this "access" often outweighs in promise the special benefits that are confirmed in reality.

Note that the line separating these three forms of expertise is often a thin one, as in the case of a supplier who wishes to negotiate a sales contract with a prospective purchaser, and employs a former employee of the purchaser to handle the transaction; the former employee, as agent, may be a source of both substantive expertise *and* influence.

Note also that principals may not always know what expertise they need. Thus, a person who has a dispute that seems headed for the courts may automatically seek out a litigator, not realizing that the vast preponderance of cases are settled by negotiation, requiring very different skills that the litigator may not possess. So, although agents do indeed possess different forms of expertise that may enhance the prospects of a favorable settlement, clients do not necessarily know what they need; it's a bit like the problem of looking up the proper spelling of a word in the dictionary when you haven't got a clue about how to spell the word in question.

Detachment

Another important reason for using an agent to do the actual negotiation is that the principals may be too emotionally entangled in the subject of the dispute. A classic example is divorce. A husband and wife, caught in the throes of a bitter fight over the end of their marriage, may benefit from the "buffering" that agents can provide. Rather than confront each other with the depth of their anger and bitterness, the principals may do far better by communicating only *indirectly*, via their respective representatives. Stated most generally, when the negotiating climate is adversarial—when the disputants are confrontational rather than collaborative—it may be wiser to manage the conflict through intermediaries than run the risk of an impasse or explosion resulting from direct exchange.

Sometimes, however, it is the *agents* who are too intensely entangled. What is needed then is the detachment and rationality that only the principals can bring to the exchange. For example, lawyers may get too caught up in the adversary game and lose sight of the underlying problem that is dividing the principals (e.g., how to resolve a dispute about the quality of goods delivered as part of a long-term supply contract). The lawyers may be more concerned about who would win in court, while the clients simply want to get their derailed relationship back on track. Hence the thrust of some modern dispute resolution mechanisms (such as the mini-trial) is precisely to take the dispute *out* of the hands of the technicians and give it back to the primary parties.

Note, however, that the very "detachment" we are touting as a virtue of negotiation through agents can also be a liability. For example, in some interpersonal negotiations, apology and reconciliation may be an important ingredient of any resolution (see, e.g., Goldberg, Green, and Sander, 1987). Surrogates who are primarily technicians may not be able to bring to bear these emphatic qualities.

Tactical Flexibility

The use of agents allows various gambits to be played out by the principals, in an effort to ratchet as much as possible from the other side. For example, if a seller asserts that the bottom line is $100,000, the buyer can try to haggle, albeit at the risk of losing the deal. If the buyer employs an agent, however, the agent can profess willingness to pay that sum but plead lack of authority, thereby gaining valuable time and opportunity for fuller consideration of the situation together with the principal. Or an agent for the seller who senses that the buyer may be especially eager to buy the property can claim that it is necessary to go back to the seller for ratification of the deal, only to return and up the price, profusely apologizing all the while for the behavior of an "unreasonable" client. The client and agent can thus together play the hard-hearted partner game.

Conversely, an agent may be used in order to push the other side in tough, even obnoxious fashion, making it possible—in the best tradition of the "good cop/bad cop" ploy—for the client to intercede at last, and seem the essence of sweet reason in comparison with the agent. Or the agent may be used as a "stalking horse," to gather as much information about the adversary as possible, opening the way to proposals by the client that exploit the intelligence gathered.

Note that the tactical flexibility conferred by representative negotiations presupposes a competitive negotiating climate, a zero-sum contest in which each negotiator wishes to outsmart the other. It is the stuff of traditional statecraft, and the interested reader can do no better than study the writings of Schelling (1960) and Potter (1948), as well as Lax and Sebenius (1986). To repeat, the assumption behind this line of analysis is that effective negotiation requires some measure of artifice and duplicity, and that this is often best accomplished through the use of some sort of foil or alter ego—in the form of the agent. But the converse is not necessarily true: Where the negotiation is conducted in a problem-solving manner (cf. Fisher and Ury, 1981), agents may still be helpful, not because they resort to strategic ruses, but because they can help articulate interests, options, and alternatives. Four heads are clearly better than two, for example, when it comes to brainstorming about possible ways of reconciling the parties' interests.

Offsetting—indeed, typically *more* than offsetting—the three above apparent virtues of representative negotiation are several sources of difficulty. Each is sufficiently important and potentially problematic that we believe caution is necessary before entering into negotiation through agents.

Extra "Moving Parts"

Representative negotiations entail greater structural complexity, additional moving parts in the negotiation machinery that—given a need for expertise, detachment, or tactical flexibility—can help move parties toward a favorable agreement. Additional moving parts, however, can also mean additional expense, in the form of the time required in the finding, evaluating, and engaging of agents, as well as the financial cost of retaining their services. And it can mean additional problems, more things that can go wrong. For instance, a message intended by a client may not be the message transmitted by that client's agent to the other party. Or the message received by that agent from the other party may be very different from the one that that agent (either deliberately or inadvertently) manages to convey to his or her client.

At one level, then, the introduction of additional links in the communication system increases the risk of distortion in the information conveyed back and forth between the principals. Beyond that lies a second difficulty: the possibility that eventually the principals will come to rely so extensively on their respective agents that they no longer communicate directly—even though they could, and even though they might well benefit from doing so … Consider, for example, the case of a divorcing couple who, in explicit compliance with the advice of their adversary lawyers, have avoided any direct contact with each other during the divorce proceedings. Once the divorce has been obtained, will the parties' ability to communicate effectively with each other (e.g., over support and custody issues) be adversely affected by their excessive prior reliance on their attorneys?

Yet another potentially problematic implication of this increasingly complex social machinery is that unwanted coalitions may arise that apply undue pressure on individual negotiators … Greater number does not necessarily mean greater wisdom, however, and the pressures toward uniformity of opinion that result from coalition formation may adversely affect the quality of the decisions reached.

In sum, the introduction of agents increases the complexity of the social apparatus of negotiation, and in so doing increases the chances of unwanted side effects. A related problem should be briefly noted here: the difficulty of asymmetry, as when an agent negotiates not with another agent but directly with the other principal. In effect, this was the case in 1978 when Egypt's Sadat negotiated with Israel's Begin at Camp David. Sadat considered himself empowered to make binding decisions for Egypt, while—at least partly for tactical purposes—Begin represented himself as ultimately accountable to his cabinet and to the Israeli parliament. While this "mismatched" negotiation between a principal (Sadat) and an agent (Begin) *did* result in agreement (thanks in good measure to President Carter's intercession as a mediator), it was not easy. The asymmetry of role meant that the two sides differed in their readiness to move forward toward an agreement, their ability to be shielded by a representative, and their willingness/ability to guarantee that any agreement reached would "stick."

Different dynamics will characterize the negotiation depending on whether it is between clients, between lawyers, or with both present. If just the clients are there, the dealings will be more direct and forthright, and issues of authority and ratification disappear. With just the lawyers present, there may be less direct factual information, but concomitantly more candor about delicate topics. Suppose, for example, that an aging soprano seeks to persuade an opera company to sign her for the lead role in an upcoming opera. If she is not present, the opera's agent may try to lower the price, contending that the singer is passed her prime. Such candor is not recommended if the singer is present at the negotiation!

Problems of "Ownership" and Conflicting Interests

In theory, it is clear that the principal calls the shots. Imagine, however, an agent who is intent on applying the *Getting to Yes* (Fisher and Ury, 1981) approach by searching for objective criteria and a fair outcome. Suppose the client simply wants the best possible outcome, perhaps because it is a one-shot deal not involving a future relationship with the other party. What if the agent (a lawyer, perhaps) *does* care about his future relationship with the other *agent*, and wants to be remembered as a fair and scrupulous bargainer? How *should* this conflict get resolved and how, in the absence of explicit discussion, *will* it be resolved, if at all? Conversely, the client, because of a valuable long-term relationship, may want to maintain good relations with the other side. But if the client simply looks for an agent who is renowned for an ability to pull out all the stops, the client's overall objectives may suffer as the result of an overzealous advocate.

This issue may arise in a number of contexts. Suppose that, in the course of a dispute settlement negotiation, a lawyer who is intent on getting the best possible deal for a client turns down an offer that was within the client's acceptable range. Is this proper behavior by the agent? The Model Rules of Professional Conduct for attorneys explicitly require (see Rules 1.2(a), I.4) that every offer must be communicated to the principal, and perhaps a failure to do so might lead to a successful malpractice action against the attorney if the deal finally fell through.

Another illustration involves the situation where the agent and principal have divergent ethical norms. Suppose that a seller of a house has just learned that the dwelling is infested with termites, but instructs the agent not to reveal this fact, even in response to specific inquiry from the buyer. How should these tensions be fairly resolved, keeping in mind the fact that the agent may be subject to a professional code of conduct that gives directions that may conflict with the ethical values of the client? There may, of course, be artful ways of dealing with such dilemmas, as, for example, slyly deflecting any relevant inquiry by the buyer. But preferably these problems should be explicitly addressed in the course of the initial discussion between agent and principal. To some extent, the problem may be resolved by the principal's tendency to pick an agent who is congenial and compatible. But, as we pointed out before, principals are not always aware of and knowledgeable about the relevant considerations that go into the choice of an agent. Hence, if these issues are not addressed explicitly at the outset, termination of the relationship midstream in egregious cases may be the only alternative.

Differing goals and standards of agent and principal may create conflicting pulls. For example, the buyer's agent may be compensated as a percentage of the purchase price, thus creating an incentive to have the price as high as possible. The buyer, of course, wants the lowest possible price. Similarly, where a lawyer is paid by the hour, there may be an incentive to draw out the negotiation, whereas the client prefers an expeditious negotiation at the lowest possible cost.

While these are not insoluble problems, to be sure, they do constitute yet another example of the difficulties that may arise as one moves to representative negotiations. Although in theory the principals are in command, once agents have been introduced the chemistry changes, and new actors—with agenda, incentives, and constraints of their own—are part of the picture. Short of an abrupt firing of the agents, principals may find themselves less in control of the situation once agents have come on the scene.

Encouragement of Artifice and Duplicity
Finally, as already noted, the introduction of agents often seems to invite clients to devise stratagems (with or without these agents) to outwit the other side. Admittedly, there is nothing intrinsic to the presence of representatives that dictates a move in this direction;

still, perhaps because of the additional expense incurred, the seductive lure of a "killing" with the help of one's "hired gun," or the introduction of new, sometimes perverse incentives, representative negotiations often seem to instill (or reflect) a more adversarial climate.

Conclusion

It follows from the preceding analysis that, ordinarily, negotiations conducted directly between the principals are preferable to negotiation through representatives. When the principals' relationship is fundamentally cooperative or informed by enlightened self-interest, agents may often be unnecessary; since there is little or no antagonism in the relationship, there is no need for the buffering detachment afforded by agents. Moreover, by negotiating directly, there is reduced risk of miscoordination, misrepresentation, and miscommunication.

On the other hand, representative negotiation *does* have an important and necessary place. When special expertise is required, when tactical flexibility is deemed important and—most importantly—when direct contact is likely to produce confrontation rather than collaboration, agents *can* render an important service.

Above all, the choice of whether to negotiate directly or through surrogates is an important one, with significant ramifications. It therefore should be addressed explicitly by weighing some of the considerations advanced above. And if an agent *is* selected, careful advance canvassing of issues such as those discussed here (e.g., authority and ethical standards) is essential.

Figure 2.2 sets out a number of factors— including those discussed above by Rubin and Sander—that should be considered when deciding whether to engage a representative for a given negotiation.

Notes and Questions

1. In addition to the list of merits and drawbacks set out in figure 2.2, can you think of other factors that should be considered when deciding whether to engage a representative in a given negotiation? Could any of the factors listed as merits also be listed as potential drawbacks, or vice versa? In what circumstances?

2. The factors discussed by Rubin and Sander—as identified and added to in figure 2.2—contemplate a relatively dichotomous approach to choosing whether to engage a representative. It may be, however—particularly for more complex negotiations—that this either/or approach to representation is inadequate as both a descriptive and normative approach. Clients may want to be involved in a very engaged way for all or part of the negotiation process, even one that involves the active participation of a representative. For an approach that challenges the dichotomous approach of Rubin and Sander—one that contemplates more of a continuum of authority between principal and agent—see Neil E. Fassina, "Direct and Representative Negotiation: A Principal-Agent Authority Continuum" (Paper presented at the IACM 15th Annual Conference, June 2002) online: SSRN <http://ssrn.com/abstract=304973> or DOI: 10.2139/ssrn.304973. See also the additional considerations regarding the interests of representatives discussed in the next section of this chapter.

Figure 2.2   Some Potential Merits and Drawbacks of Using
Representative Negotiators

Some Potential Merits	Some Potential Drawbacks
1. Expertise 　　• Knowledge 　　• Process Skill 　　• Special Influence 　　• Experience 　　• Resources 2. Detachment 　　• Clear Thinking 　　• Protection of Relationships 　　• Encouragement of Cooperation 3. Tactical Flexibility 4. Validation/Support	1. Complexity 2. Conflicts 　　• Ownership 　　• Conflicting Interests 　　• Different Incentives 3. Escalation 　　• Encouragement of Client Artifice 　　• Encouragement of Duplicity 　　• Encouragement of Competition 4. Loss of Control 　　• Lack of Client Engagement 　　• Lack of Accountability 5. Lack of Shared/Perfect Information 6. Cost (Time and Money) 　　• Retaining an Agent 　　• Monitoring an Agent

Source: This figure is based—in part—on considerations discussed in J.Z. Rubin & F.E.A. Sander, "When Should We Use Agents? Direct vs. Representative Negotiation" (1988) 4 Negotiation Journal 395; R.H. Mnookin, S.R. Peppet & A.S. Tulumello, *Beyond Winning: Negotiating to Create Value in Deals and Disputes* (Cambridge, MA: Belknap Press, 2000) at 69-96; Hon. George W. Adams, Q.C., *Mediating Justice: Legal Dispute Negotiations* (Toronto: CCH, 2003) at 78-84.

3. Does a lawyer's ethical obligation to "advise and encourage the client to compromise or settle a dispute … and … discourage the client from commencing or continuing useless legal proceedings"[3] include an obligation to consider whether such compromise is done directly or with the services of a lawyer? What, if any, conflict-of-interest issues does this question raise? For further ethical discussions of representative negotiation, see the following section of this chapter as well as chapter 5.

Nature of Representative Negotiation

Let's assume that the decision is made to retain a representative negotiator. What is the representative's role in a negotiation? What potentially competing considerations must a representative face? We look at the models that seek to answer these questions next.

---

3 See *e.g.* Canadian Bar Association, *Code of Professional Conduct*, c. III. 6.

The Basic Role of the Representative Negotiator[4]

The basic role of the lawyer is "to do something on behalf of someone else: typically the client."[5] In the context of a representative negotiation, "what is typically being sought is a negotiated deal or settlement that is to the benefit of the client, not the representative lawyer."[6] The resulting lawyer–client relationship is one that is often characterized—like the typical lawyer–client relationship—as one located in principals of agency. As a starting point, this characterization is helpful. The negotiator's reason for being, in the eyes of her client, is largely to negotiate a deal that is seen as favourable based on a calculus of the client's specific positions and interests, often (although certainly not always) as they relate to positions and interests of the other side.

The problem with this binary principal–agent vision of the role of the representative negotiator is that it almost invariably provides an inadequate understanding of what is actually going on, and what potentially could or should be going on, in the mind of the representative negotiator and between the representative and her client.

A more nuanced description of representative negotiators starts to build on this agency vision by proposing that the representative's role is largely (or almost exclusively) character-ized by two interests: those of her client and those of her bargaining opposite. For example, according to Wiggins and Lowry, "As representative negotiators, attorneys always have two negotiations occurring simultaneously: One with their bargaining opposite and one with their own client."[7]

According to this more nuanced view, representative negotiators are said to occupy a "boundary-role position," in which they, as Dean Pruitt comments, "can be thought of as intermediaries whose job is to reconcile the interests of their own and the opposing organ-ization. They must represent the interests of their constituents to the opposing representative *and* represent the views of the opposing representative to their constituents."[8]

An expanded description of the interests at stake in representative negotiation—beyond the agency model that focuses almost exclusively on the interests of the representative's cli-ent—helps to articulate more accurately the role of the representative negotiator. However, by primarily focusing on two interests—those of the client and those of the representative's bargaining opposite—the boundary-role position model still fails to account fully for what is typically going on inside the representative's mind. As such, although an improvement

---

4   This section of this chapter is largely based on arguments presented in T.C.W. Farrow, "The Negotiator-as-Professional: Understanding the Competing Interests of a Representative Negotiator" (2007) 7:3 Pepperdine Dispute Resolution Law Journal (forthcoming), part of which is excerpted below.

5   *Ibid.* at 3.

6   *Ibid.*

7   Wiggins & Lowry, *supra* note 2 at 498 (commenting on arguments presented in "When Should We Use Agents?"). But see also *ibid.* at 497.

8   D.G. Pruitt, *Negotiation Behavior* (New York: Academic Press, 1981), cited in Wiggins & Lowry, *supra* note 2 at 500.

over the simple agency model, the boundary-role position model still does not provide an adequate view of the role of the representative negotiator, both in terms of the role's responsibilities, challenges, and potential opportunities. The next section of this chapter expands on these models.

Competing Strategic, Ethical, and Societal Considerations

This section of this chapter—through the following article excerpt—provides a more expansive view of the role of the representative negotiator that attempts to address potential deficiencies in the agency and boundary-role position models. To appreciate fully the role of the representative negotiator, it's important to have a broad understanding of the competing interests and considerations it must manage.

Trevor C.W. Farrow
"The Negotiator-as-Professional: Understanding the
Competing Interests of a Representative Negotiator"
(2007) 7:3 Pepperdine Dispute Resolution Law Journal
(forthcoming), footnotes omitted[9]

…

III. Negotiator-as-Professional
To address these deficiencies, I advance an alternative, expansive model of the representative negotiator that I call the "negotiator-as-professional" model. It is a model that sees the role of the representative negotiator as being defined not simply by the client's interests or by the two interests that are identified by the boundary-role position models, but rather by at least four sets of interests: client interests, a broad understanding of the representative's self-interests (that may include, but are not limited to, interests vis-à-vis the representative negotiator's bargaining opposite), ethical interests, and the public's interests.

A. *Client Interests*
1. *Interests of the Representative's Client*
In any lawyering model, the representative's client maintains one of, and typically the primary set of interests in the relationship. This is the defining characteristic of the lawyer-client relationship in the adversary system. In the context of negotiation, as Rubin and Sander point out, lawyer representatives bring to the table a particular "expertise" and a "tactical flexibility" to be used to the benefit of the client. Further, according to Pruitt, the "essence of the representative effect" under the boundary-role position in negotiation

---

9   Many of the sources noted in the omitted footnotes for the following article can be found in
the list of selected further reading at the end of this chapter.

"is trying to please one's constituent" (a task that is obviously directly dependent on the client's interests). Therefore, as Pruitt further argues, "[i]t follows that bargainers who are representatives will usually be less conciliatory than those who are negotiating on their own behalf" and, subject to contrary instructions from the client, "representatives tend to view their constituents as desiring a tough, nonconciliatory approach to bargaining of the kind that is produced by a win/lose orientation." Here we see ourselves largely back to the "zealous advocate" tendency that foregrounds the interests of the client typically to the exclusion of essentially everything else.

This model is further articulated in the negotiation context by Robert Cochran, who argues that not only should representatives tend to "please" the client, they should also afford a significant amount of deference to the client's choices in all aspects of the lawyering process. When looking at the question of "what choices the client should make," Cochran answers by advocating that "courts [should] require lawyers to allow clients to make those choices which a reasonable person, in what the lawyer knows or should know to be the position of the client, would want to make." Here again we see a strong preference for the client's interest as the keystone to the relationship.

So any model of the role of lawyer-as-negotiator must find a central position for the client's interests. However, the problem with models that focus essentially exclusively on the client's interests is that they are not accurate or honest in their description of what is in reality actually at play in the minds of representative negotiators, nor do they account for the fact that representative negotiators do not, and often should not, necessarily align their interests with those of their clients (or forgo their or other interests) in the spirit of zealous advocacy. I can say with first-hand experience—as a litigator and negotiator turned academic—that as a conceptual matter, there are more interests at play than only those of the client. And as a practical matter, privileging the interests of the client does not always sit well with representative negotiators.

An example from a recent negotiation class illustrates these concerns. In an animated debrief portion of an in-class mock negotiation that I recently conducted involving the intellectual property rights to artistic materials of the negotiating parties, a student of mine—after reflecting on the difficulty of maintaining a negotiation relationship with the other side as well as maintaining any sense of personal integrity vis-à-vis a very difficult position she was being asked to advance on behalf of her client—stated in shear frustration: "we started from a ridiculous position: our client simply wanted too much. Her position was […] crazy." The student's frustration resulted in a significant discussion about the role of the lawyer generally, and the lawyer-as-negotiator in particular. The easy response to her concerns was that she was her client's agent, and she could either conduct the negotiation or get off the file. However, that model—the simple agency model of lawyering that essentially backgrounds all other interests in favour of strong client autonomy—did not sit at all well with her. Advancing instructions that in her view were "ridiculous" and "crazy" did not leave my student with either a good feeling about the specific case or about her general role as a representative negotiator. For her, notwithstanding her role as a lawyer-negotiator, there was clearly more at stake.

Overly client-centric visions of the role of representative negotiator, like the model advanced by Cochran, do not help with this frustration, which belies interests at play other than those of the client. So the question then becomes: Do we need to live with that frustration? Is the zealous advocate view of the world the right (or only) one, particularly in light of concerns that leave the representative feeling frustrated, inadequate and perhaps hamstrung regarding potential alternative approaches and solutions? Because there are clearly interests other than those of the client that need to be recognized, the answer to this question, must be no. Before getting to some objections to this position, and further, to a set of interests involving the various potential self-interests of the representative negotiator that were at stake in my student's role-play example, I briefly (below) identify another set of client interests: those of the opposing client.

2.   *Other Client's Interests*
Because this article deals with the mindset of the representative negotiator (and not specifically the mindset of principles), I do not spend much time here on the interests of the other side. Thinking about the interests of negotiation principals—by identifying, maximizing and/or minimizing mutual interests, creating space for mutual gains, value creating and value claiming, etc.—are important tools that are discussed elsewhere. However, it is obviously important—when thinking about the competing interests at stake in the mind of the representative lawyer—to make sure that the other side's interests, in addition to interests vis-à-vis the bargaining opposite, are on the table.

The typical lawyer-client relationship militates against any responsibility of the lawyer for the interests of the other side. Further, zealous advocacy models expressly reject such concerns. And my point here is not at all to say that the lawyer negotiator is now responsible for the other side's interests, particularly when he is also represented. However, to the extent that alternative negotiation models are considered—for example strong cooperative models that actively include the other side's interests in the spirit of maintaining future relationships and mutual gains or hybrid models that contemplate the balance of value creation and value claiming—consideration for the other side's interests must at least be considered and discussed with the representative's client. And in any event, regardless of which negotiation model one follows, modern ethical codes are increasingly mandating consideration of the other side in the context of truth-telling and fair play.

B.   *Representative Negotiator's Self-Interests*
Separate from client interests, there are a number of potential sets of self-interests at play for the representative in the negotiation process. When thinking about these interests, it seems to me that there are two questions that need to be addressed: What kind of negotiator is the representative (hard, soft, principled, etc.)? And what pecuniary and other self-interests are at stake? While the representative's ethical interests could also be considered here, they are instead treated in a separate part of this article.

1.   *Representative Negotiation Style*
On the first question, negotiators must decide if they have the interest and skill to proceed with one or more negotiation styles, and if so, whether negotiation style is a topic open for discussion with his or her client. Some negotiators are of the view that they are unable to wear different negotiation "faces." Again turning to examples from my teaching, several students have recently indicated to me—in the context of role-plays that require experimentation with different negotiation styles—that they feel very uncomfortable putting

on a face or playing a role (the competitive negotiator, the cooperative negotiator, the bad cop, the tough guy, etc.) and that, in their view, their skills are maximized when they present themselves as an authentic and principled representative in all cases. Drawing on personal practical experiences as a litigator and settlement counsel, these concerns resonate not only in the classroom but also amongst practicing representatives.

These threshold concerns are typically and ultimately dealt with on a calculus of competence and context. To the extent that the lawyer representative and the client think that the lawyer's chosen approach renders them competent for the negotiation, then all is well: proceeding on the basis of the lawyer's preferred style, as discussed with the client, is the chosen course of instruction. To the extent that is not the case, codes of conduct typically require the lawyer to get off the case and recommend another representative. Further, in line with scholars who argue that some contexts—typically including one-off personal injury cases—often lend themselves better to one negotiating style over another (competitive negotiation for example), it may be that the context of a certain case determines the required level of competency with a given style. Again, choices will be made at this threshold stage regarding the approach and the continued retainer.

If the representative is competent to proceed with one or more of a variety of different styles, the issue then becomes one of ownership. Who gets to choose with which style to proceed: the representative or the client? Here we see the potential of an obvious conflict. As Rubin and Sander discuss, there is often a potential conflict with a client's instruction (for example to achieve the best possible outcome in a one-off negotiation through the use of a competitive approach) and the interest of a representative negotiator (who would prefer, for example, to retain a relationship with the negotiator's bargaining opposite by using a cooperative approach). Similarly, Gifford and Pruitt's descriptions of both the "boundary role position" and the lawyer-as-negotiator position result in the same potential competing interests between the representative and the client.

Now before I get into further discussion of this potential conflict, it should be recognized that even though the potential of competing interests exists, there does not necessarily need to be a conflict. Clearly a good relationship between the representative negotiator and the bargaining opposite can militate to the benefit of both the representative lawyer and the client. As Gifford recognizes, negotiating fairly with the other side does not mean a "selling-out" of the client's interests. Similarly, Pruitt argues that developing relationships with the other side can help both with the client's immediate outcome as well as potentially with future negotiations: "Because they communicate with one another over a period of time and share similar organizational positions, representatives often develop ties to one another. These ties can contribute to the reconciliation of conflicts that would otherwise be intractable."

However, when interests do not align, the potential of conflict between the representative and the client is real and very typical. In these circumstances, the client-centered "zealous advocate" model advocates for the backgrounding of the representative's interests in favor of the client's preferences. This view of the negotiator's role fits Robert Cochran's model. For Cochran, if the representative lawyer viewed that a cooperative approach was appropriate, but the client preferred a competitive approach (perhaps in the context of a one-off real estate purchase for the client who does not anticipate being in a similar market position again), the client's preferences should prevail. According to Cochran, regardless of the lawyer's preference vis-à-vis the bargaining opposite, the client has a "right to choose the negotiating style."

On the traditional lawyer-client relationship model, this view is not controversial. In fact, it is still largely the dominant view. The lawyer's role is to carry out the wishes of the client—period. As the argument goes, any other view of the role of the lawyer usurps a meaningful sense of client autonomy; and further, particularly given the virtual monopoly of power that lawyers have over the provision of increasingly essential legal services, any other view would essentially create an all-powerful oligarchy of lawyers. The problem with this unsubtle view of legal representation, however, is that it is not fully supported in the literature or in codes of conduct, and further, it ignores the daily reality of the negotiation process. Of course representatives will have interests. And so the question becomes: Why should those interests always take a back seat, particularly in cases—like the one involving my student—in which a client's position is "ridiculous"? In these circumstances, should a lawyers be obligated to ignore their own views and interests and advance a "ridiculous" position? My view is that such an argument disingenuously ignores the reality of what actually goes on in the world of negotiations. Such an argument conveys an impoverished view of lawyering that does not make room for a representative's own views, interests and experiences in a given situation that may, at the end of the day, work to the benefit of the client's cause. This ultimately cheapens the overall negotiation process to one that alienates negotiators—like my student—who are looking for a meaningful place to practice their skills in a professional, reasonable and fulfilling way. Further, to the extent that codes of conduct prohibit the advancement of "frivolous" or "useless legal proceedings," query whether advancing a "ridiculous" position amounts to unprofessional conduct.

The boundary-role position approach described by scholars like Pruitt and Gifford allows for the reality of potentially competing interests in the mind of the representative negotiator that zealous advocacy models tend to ignore. So when thinking about the potential interests at stake when preparing for a negotiation, the boundary-role position approach paints a more realistic landscape for the representative negotiator. At least now the tension in my student's mind has a voice and a place in the dialogue of negotiation preparation. And by actively recognizing these potentially competing interests, the lawyer can strategize about how to resolve them. In a purely zealous advocacy model, these considerations are left off the table (or are at least the elephants in the room that no one is meant to talk about).

So far we have identified the client's interests and the representative's self-interests largely relating to negotiation styles vis-à-vis the bargaining opposite. It is with these interests that the current boundary role position schools of thought leave us. And because they consider all of these interests, and not simply the client's interests, they are an improvement on the typically one-dimensional client-centered views of the zealous advocate. However, there are other interests at stake that still need to be considered as part of the representative's self-interests as well as other interests involving ethics and the public.

2. *Pecuniary and Other Self-Interests*
In addition to style and the representative's reputation vis-à-vis the bargaining opposite, there are other potentially thorny self-interests at stake—particularly when negotiating

settlements in the context of litigation—that should be identified and put on the table as issues to be acknowledged and considered when preparing for a representative negotiation. So the second question that needs to be asked under this discussion of the representative negotiator's self-interests is: What pecuniary and other self-interests are at stake and what is the client willing to do about them?

Wiggins and Lowry have articulated that negotiating attorneys and their clients "are like allies in warfare. Outwardly they may have an identity of goals and are bound together by professional obligations; yet internally they may have divergent interests and inconsistent long term objectives." A number of potential conflicting interests arise in these circumstances. For example, to the extent that a piece of litigation is worth much more to the lawyer as a going concern as opposed to a settled case, there are incentives to keep the case alive and advise against settlement. Along these lines, the lawyer-as-potential-settlement-negotiator may also be much less risk averse when it comes to recommending trial over settlement, given potential desires for trial experience, exposure to the press, significant contingency fee rewards (which admittedly can cut both ways), and internal firm or community respect for being a tough, court-ready litigator (that also may be based, at least in tournament discourse, on the desire to be thought of as "partnership material"). The choice of payment structures—for example percentage of outcome vs. hourly rate—may also impact a representative's interests vis-à-vis approaching a negotiation.

The underlying interests that raise these concerns are real and should be put on the table and considered in the context of full, sophisticated negotiation preparations. And typically there are solutions. Unlike self-interests based on the representative's reputation, purely financial self-interests are relatively easy to deal with. Codes of conduct typically paint rather bright conflict of interest lines in these areas that allow (or require) the lawyer, after recognizing the issues, to background his or her financial interests in the spirit of the very notion of lawyering itself. When it comes to some of the other, more personal or subtle concerns—undiluted focus on the trial process, a need to maintain a tough and ready litigation pose, etc.—there are other solutions, in addition to codes of conduct that require attorneys to consider settlement, which assist with potentially competing interests. For example, the use of parallel settlement counsel as a way not to distract the focused litigator from his or her endgame is a process—based on the literature and on my first-hand experience with the use of settlement counsel in complex civil litigation settlements—that can work quite effectively.

Complicating (and clouding) these potential conflicting interests is the lawyer's inability to understand, or willful blindness to, what the client's interests (and other interests) actually are at the outset, as opposed to what the lawyer assumes (or wants) them to be. As Leonard Riskin recognized, the traditional zealous advocate tendency—based on the "lawyer's standard philosophical map"—blinds the lawyer to a number of things including the potential needs of the client that may not be "legally meaningful," including many non-financial issues relating to "honor, respect, dignity, security, and love …" To assist with this impoverished tendency of the traditional advocate, particularly in favor of promoting the benefits of mediation, Riskin argues in favor of expanding the traditional map. All interests, and not simply those located on the adversarial map, need to be taken into account and understood as part of the lawyer's role as a representative. As I have recently argued elsewhere, education, an open-mindset, and a shift in the adversarial culture are all already leading to these ideals becoming more of a reality.

C. Representative Lawyer's Ethical Interests

According to a March 2006 statement by Brian A. Tabor, Q.C., President of the CBA: "Standards of professional ethics form the backdrop for everything lawyers do." As such, any model of lawyering—including lawyers as negotiators—must actively embrace interests of an ethical nature. Therefore, in addition to reputational, pecuniary, and other self-interests, there are also significant (potentially related) ethical interests of the representative negotiator that need to be carefully considered in the context of developing the negotiator-as-professional model. There are two points of discussion here. The first, fundamental point deals with the relevance of the representative negotiator's own moral code. The second point deals with other ethical interests at play in a representative negotiation.

1. What Kind of Lawyer Is the Representative Negotiator?

The basic question that I am interested in here is: What kind of lawyer is the representative negotiator? Is the negotiator a zealous advocate driven solely by the client's self-interest; or is the negotiator an agent whose moral outlook also counts in the calculus of the principal-agent relationship, particularly regarding the kinds of cases taken, the results sought, and the tools used? This question—that goes to the heart of professionalism itself—has been nicely framed by Rob Atkinson:

> Should a professional always do all that the law allows, or should the professional recognize other constraints, particularly concerns for the welfare of third parties? This question divides scholars of legal ethics and thoughtful practitioners into two schools: those who recognize constraints other than law's outer limit, and those who do not.

Because I have written elsewhere on this topic relating to lawyers generally, I will only briefly develop the basic issues here as they relate specifically to the representative negotiator. As a preliminary matter, there continue to be strong arguments for following Atkinson's second school: what counts is what is legal, and non-legal considerations—including a lawyer's personal ethical interests—are not relevant in terms of the lawyer's representation of his or her client. Traditional and still dominant views of the lawyer's role as a zealous advocate—as reinforced by codes of conduct and academic literature regarding the lawyer's role in general and the negotiator's role in particular—support this school of thought.

The problem is that, notwithstanding this dominant school of thought, some representative negotiators, as a practical matter, are persuaded by Atkinson's other school of thought: that non-legal considerations—again including a lawyer's personal ethical interests—should not be irrelevant. Again drawing on examples from my teaching, many students are uncomfortable with the notion of negotiating deals, the underlying ethical consequences of which they fundamentally disagree with. For instance, going back to my original example of the negotiation student who was representing a client with ridiculous and crazy instructions in an hypothetical role-play, when pushed in the de-brief session on whether she would take that case, she responded: "I'm not sure, if I had a choice, that I would work for someone like my client in the negotiation … she's an egomaniac."

Fortunately, representative negotiators do have a choice. So the question then becomes: Why should we pursue a model of professionalism that requires representative negotiators to negotiate deals on behalf of their clients that they would never negotiate for themselves or in any event that they think are ridiculous? The answer in my view is that we should not. Clearly there are times, particularly after a retainer has been accepted and negotiations are under way, when the lawyer may be asked to take positions professionally that s/he would not take personally. But these situations aside, there are many occasions when the lawyer's interests and views should be voiced in the spirit of improving the underlying cause as well as the overall system, notwithstanding an individual client's initial desires. In this spirit, Allan Hutchinson, for example, argues for a model that does not require lawyers "to forgo moral judgment," for to do otherwise reduces them to "amoral technicians with significant drawbacks and limitations ..." What this looks like in practice is making choices about what negotiations a representative takes, and what tools and negotiation styles they are willing to use once a client is taken on. Of course this is all done with the client's knowledge and instructions. And if instructions are not forthcoming, the lawyer should get off the file.

Before we dismiss all of this as moral meandering without a sound basis in legal policy, we should also recognize that professional codes of conduct—as supported by competing academic literature—support the relevance of a lawyer's morality, sense of justice, honour, and ethics. For example, according to the preamble and scope of the *Model Rules*: "... The Rules do not ... exhaust the moral and ethical considerations that should inform a lawyer, for no worthwhile human activity can be completely defined by legal rules." The CPC states: the "lawyer should not hesitate to speak out against an injustice." Similar considerations regarding the relevance of broad notions of morality and honour obtain in various regional jurisdictions. For example, according to *The Lawyer's Code of Professional Responsibility* (*LCPR*) of the New York State Bar Association ("NYSBA"), "A lawyer should be temperate and dignified, and refrain from all illegal and morally reprehensible conduct." Further, according to the preface of the *Code of Professional Conduct* of the Law Society of Alberta ("LSA"): "... the rules and regulations ... cannot exhaustively cover all situations that may confront a lawyer, who may find it necessary to also consider ... general moral principles in determining an appropriate course of action."

Although not uncontroversial, there is therefore a tension even within the various codes of conduct between the responsibility to zealously represent a client and the potential role for the lawyer's own ethical interests, whether based on morality, a sense of honour or some other social norm. Regardless, there is clearly a basis for the relevance of—and in my view an overriding professional obligation at least to consider—the lawyer's own ethical interests in the context of his or her role as a representative negotiator.

As such, these interests—which are not recognized by either the simple client-centered models or the more expanded boundary role position models of representative negotiation—should be recognized as interests that influence the lawyering and negotiation processes and, as such, need to be on the table for discussion when the negotiator-as-professional sits down to prepare for the representative negotiation process. The end calculus becomes a discussion between the representative lawyer and the client. The final decision of whether to stay with the representative always rests with the client. But the fundamental decisions regarding whether and how the negotiation is handled are also decisions regarding which the lawyer should have determining input. Any other model, not only turns a blind eye to reality, but also impoverishes the responsibilities and possibilities of the representative's role.

2. Other Ethical Interests of the Representative Negotiator

In addition to the fundamental question of the relevance of the representative negotiator's personal moral compass, there are other ethical issues that come up all the time in representative negotiations that need to be considered and discussed with the client. Gifford, when discussing the boundary role position model, does contemplate the notion of professional responsibility in passing:

> When negotiating on behalf of the client … the lawyer is drawn in conflicting directions. On the one hand, she is obligated professionally to obtain the most favorable settlement possible during the negotiations … On the other hand … he must respond to pressures from his negotiating counterparts … and pursue settlements that are fair and just to both parties. The pressure on the lawyer to accommodate these tensions … results in part from the expectations of future contact with the other lawyers *and in part from the traditional courtesy and fair play among lawyers* [emphasis added].

While this is right, ethical considerations involve more than simply "courtesy and fair play among lawyers." Terms like "courtesy," "fair play," and—as Silver articulates, the "duty of 'good faith' towards other counsel"—are unlikely to be precise enough, or wide-reaching enough, to place adequate limits on "dishonest bargaining practices" and other such negotiation tactics. What we are therefore talking about, in addition to "fair play," etc., is a full range of ethical and professional considerations, including obligations of confidentiality, truth-telling, the avoidance of conflicts of interest, and the like. Neither the client-centered model nor the boundary role position model adequately and expressly embraces a full consideration of the representative negotiator's ethical considerations and interests.

That is because, surprisingly, the consideration of ethics continues to be a relatively new issue in negotiation theory. As Eleanor Norton comments, "[t]here has been little evidence of or interest in coherent standards or express norms for appropriate behavior in negotiations." Similarly, as Lynn Epstein comments: "[n]egotiations have always enjoyed a certain amount of protection from ethical constraints. This protection is due to a long-standing tradition of allowing parties to negotiate freely, and without restrictions that encompass other aspects of legal representation. Historically, this freedom surrounded most negotiations in a shroud of secrecy." Although there is starting to be more focus recently on ethics and negotiation, Epstein's description still largely obtains. Often when ethics are raised, it is typically done in passing, as an afterthought, or at least as a separate discussion that does not form part of the central make-up of the representative negotiator's very being as a professional.

This inadequate treatment of ethics jeopardizes the adequate training, ethical preparation and professional conduct of representative negotiators. As Wiggins and Lowry have argued, "there is a clear potential for conflict between the attorney's own values and the perceived duty of single-minded zealous advocacy on behalf of the client's interests." Shockingly, this impoverished state of affairs—that results in a "confounding [of] the boundary of professional responsibility and negotiation ethics"—apparently makes it "difficult to … make prescriptive statements about truth telling and lawyers." These acknowledgments amount, in my view, to a remarkably sad state of affairs. If lawyers cannot be counted on, or at least mandated to tell the truth, who can? What we are left with then is a relatively barren ethical terrain that leaves the representative negotiator without adequate guidance for ethical negotiation. Current practices encourage Gross and Syverud, for example, to ask questions such as: "Under what circumstances should a party make a sincere offer? An outrageous demand? An insincere threat to go to trial?" Further, for example, Holmes comments that "the concept of truthfulness in negotiation raises unique ethical questions because in most circumstances candor is not necessarily required." Silver articulates that representative lawyers "can be misleading, can bluff and can threaten action at will." Further, Boulle and Kelly argue that, even for lawyers governed by professional codes of conduct, "in negotiation … exaggeration and sheer puffery are tolerated." As such, Wiggins and Lowry question whether "the profession should attempt to police lying in negotiation" at all.

In my view, this ethically questionable state of affairs in representative negotiation should not be tolerated, particularly for representative negotiators who are also members of the bar and subject to professional obligations. The negotiator-as-professional must actively embrace ethical problems, both in preparation with the client and then during the negotiation process itself. And to the extent that a client seeks to foreground her personal interests over the ethical concerns and interests of the representative negotiator, that move must be either rejected through active discussions with the client—which often in any event work to the benefit of the client's case—or the lawyer must get off the file in accordance with principles of professionalism. In my view there is no middle ground. James White has argued that much of the difficulty in regulating negotiation behavior comes from the fact that "negotiation is a non-public behavior." That may be right as a descriptive matter. However, we do not seem to have an appetite for accepting borderline ethical behavior in law's public sphere. We should be even less accommodating of such behavior in the private sphere.

D. The Public's Interests

The fourth general set of interests at play in representative negotiations includes considerations of interests to the public. While notions of personal morality and ethical considerations are bound up with notions of the public good, particularly in the context of the regulation of lawyers, a further question also needs to be considered: should a representative negotiator consider, during deliberations with the client, the public worth of a given outcome of the negotiation process? In my view, the answer is yes for the negotiator-as-professional.

Here again traditional models of representative negotiation are either actively against these sorts of public-welfare considerations (based in zealous advocacy principles) or essentially silent. A typical example of this opposition is the following statement by Abe Krash: a lawyer's "views of the public interest are immaterial to his [or her] professional responsibility." For Riskin, the basic reason for this opposition or silence is that models of lawyering that celebrate the zealous advocate blind the lawyer to, or mandate against, a number of considerations including "the overall social effect of a given result."

In opposition to this indifference, Duncan Kennedy—on the theory that lawyers should "[t]ry … [their] best … to avoid doing harm with … [their] lawyer skills"—argues that lawyers "shouldn't take the case if … [they] think it would be better for society, or more moral, for the client to lose." Similarly, Allan Hutchinson argues for a "fresh account of legal ethics [that] would … encourage lawyers to develop a critical morality that encompasses such pressing issues as 'what kind of lawyer do I want to be?' and 'what interests am

I going to spend my life serving as a lawyer?'" Finally, at the 1971 "Excellence in Advocacy" program of the Advocacy Institute, held in Ann Arbor, Michigan, the celebrated author Martin Mayer argued that:

> [I]f lawyers cannot look at the society as a whole and say that certain aspects of their work … represent a plus for this society and for the world of our children, then they had better look to last-ditch defenses. Better yet, lawyers should try to find a way to salvage what is worth doing out of their work and be influential in the production of what is going to happen next.

Again, these are certainly not uncontroversial positions, particularly given the underpinnings of the dominant zealous advocate model located in strong notions of a freedom-seeking adversary system. But they are positions, again, that certainly find support in current codes of conduct. For example, the CBA states that the "primary concern" of the *CPC* is "the protection of the public interest." Accordingly, "the lawyer should not hesitate to speak out against an injustice." So to the extent that a representative negotiator is being asked to take a position that he considers not to be in the "public interest" or that amounts to an "injustice" (terms that are not typically defined in codes of conduct), then he is professionally encouraged to seek alternative solutions and/or to "speak out." In my view these alternatives specifically include speaking out during negotiation preparation sessions with a client who is trying to advance a cause that amounts, in the eyes of the lawyer, to an "injustice"; or in the eyes of my negotiation student, to something that is "ridiculous." This will obviously be context and lawyer specific. But that is OK. And it is certainly not a reason to shy away from the opportunity to do good, or at least to avoid doing harm, with a representative's negotiation skills. That is the opportunity and the responsibility, in my view, of the negotiator-as-professional.

E. Other Interests

I have raised four basic sets of interests that I think must be considered by representative negotiators when approaching any given client's retainer. In addition, there may be other interests, including competing interests of various constituencies within a representative's own client (like, for example, when negotiating labor issues on behalf of a trade union or land claim rights on behalf of a group of native bands), or competing public interests (like, for example, when negotiating on behalf of a coalition of community groups or public-interest NGOs) that are not easily reconciled during a representative's contemplation of a given course of conduct. Often traditional conflict of interest rules will assist with these considerations. However, in situations in which equally valid public interests are at stake, *bona fide* contextual and individual reflection may be the only available tool. Further, client or representative interests regarding race, gender, culture, and power may, and often do, significantly influence the negotiation process. Regardless of the interest or choice, the point here is that active consideration of and deliberation about all interests must occur.

IV. Potential Objections: Zealous Advocacy and Conflicting Interests

Perhaps the two biggest obstacles to my vision of the negotiator-as-professional are both the dominant zealous advocate model itself and the potential of irreconcilably competing interests. Because I have already taken up objections from the zealous advocacy model in the context of representative negotiations, I do not address them further here, other than briefly to say the following. There is no doubt that the arguments and considerations that I am advancing in this article are not supported by the still-dominant model of the zealous advocate. They are therefore neither uncontroversial nor unproblematic. However, because my vision of the lawyer-as-negotiator is supported, at least in part, from a theoretical perspective by both the literature and aspects of current codes of conduct; and further, as a practical matter, by the intuitions and experiences of both experienced and novice negotiators, there is clearly both something lacking about the current models and something appealing about my alternative model. So while I acknowledge the continued hurdles that dominant, zealous advocacy models put in the way of my arguments, because of their own problems, my view is that we need to continue to search for alternative models. The negotiator-as-professional is one such alternative model that, in my view, does a better job of capturing both theoretical opportunities and practical realities of the representative negotiation process.

Equally challenging to my arguments is a further question: what if the representative is not able to reconcile the competing interests in her mind in any given negotiation? The simple answer to this question is: just because the calculus is difficult does not mean that the lawyer should not engage in it. Resorting to the zealous advocate model for expediency reasons does not do justice either to it or to alternative models. A slightly more compelling answer comes from the realm of professional responsibility: lawyers are bound to consider a broad conception of the competing interests at stake in a negotiation, both as a competence matter and as an ethical matter. So professionally, the issue is likely closed. However, this again does not really deal with the practical—and typical—situation of competing interests. What should the lawyer do?

A typical situation involves a conflict between the interests of the representative's client and interests vis-à-vis the representative's bargaining opposite. This conflict—discussed above—is what Gifford and others identify as a "boundary-role conflict." The obvious answer is to try to work out with the representative's client—during the preparation stage—a solution that maximizes the potential of both interests. For example, clients often do not appreciate the power of a good relationship between negotiators. Alternatively, they often do not realize, as generally discussed above, that a good relationship between negotiators does not mean that their interests are being somehow inadequately protected. This initial hard work with a representative's client, with full disclosure of the representative's views and interests, will typically resolve many of these conflicts. However, if a solution cannot be worked out, one option—that I have argued against—is Cochran's preference for dominant client control. The alternative vision that I am suggesting is leaving significant control with the lawyer that may ultimately lead, in particularly tough situations, to a lawyer's withdrawal from a case. While an imperfect solution, it is a preferable solution to preferring a model that impoverishes the importance of other interests (a model that potentially forces the lawyer to check him or herself—and his or her moral compass—at the door on arrival at work every morning).

Again, the point of my model is not necessarily to solve all potentially thorny circumstances with a one-size-fits-all approach (that is one of the dangerously attractive features of the zealous advocate model). No nuanced model or code, in my view, provides such a solution. For example, as the *CPC* recognizes, "[i]nevitably, the practical application of the Code to the diverse situations that confront an active profession in a changing society will reveal gaps, ambiguities and apparent inconsistencies." The lawyer-as-professional model does not necessarily offer further comfort. What it does offer, however, is a forced nod to reality that takes into account all that is going on in the representative's mind. It also—in a real way—takes seriously ethical, public and other interests that current representative negotiation models do not. And when conflicts do arise, the negotiator-as-professional is not apologetic, when appropriate, in preferring (with full disclosure to the client) ethical and public interests over those of his or her client. This again can align with the spirit of the professional obligations of lawyers generally. As the *CPC* provides, in situations of conflict or competing ethical considerations: "the principle of protection of the public interest will serve to guide the practitioner to the applicable principles of ethical conduct ..." Again, far from irrelevant, a lawyer's "personal conscience" and "sensitive professional and moral judgment" will animate a lawyer's thinking in applying and resolving competing ethical obligations.

At the end of the day, what the model offers is hopefully a nuanced calculus of all interests that are on the table. This account should assist in situating the representative's role vis-à-vis the client and others potentially involved or interested in a negotiation. In tough cases—when representative and client interests appear to collide—the model will assist in the difficult work that is done in advance of the negotiation in the context of discussions between the representative and his or her client when contemplating a retainer or, later, when preparing for a negotiation. And finally, if conflicts persist, it is acknowledged—in these tough cases—that the model may not ultimately assist with the resolution of those conflicts. However, even then, the model will succeed in giving adequate authority and support to the representative who is trying—vis-à-vis the competing interests that are still at play—to work out what he should do, with knowledge of the client, including potentially declining to accept or continue with a retainer.

V. Conclusion

What I have tried to argue is that representative negotiation models advanced to-date, like the zealous advocacy model or the "boundary role position" model lose sight of, or only pay passing lip service to, the many (and potentially competing) interests that make up the mindset of a representative negotiator. The negotiator-as-professional model takes seriously a much more expansive view of potentially competing interests in the mind of the representative negotiator. Because the different interests will come up in different ways and may or may not compete in any given situation, the importance of this model is not that it paints bright lines in terms of resolving all tensions at all times; but rather that it assists in identifying the competing interests at play and thereby forces the representative negotiator to address and potentially resolve competing interests and conflicts ahead of time rather than simply ignoring them, being unaware of them, or being trapped by them.

At the end of the day, choices need to be made in the negotiation process. And they need to be made with the client. Should different negotiation styles be considered? If so, who has the final say? Based on whose interests, etc.? What is the desired outcome? Again, whose interests should drive this calculus? Etc. And these choices may also lead to representatives declining a given client's brief. This is all a healthy part of the negotiation process. And as I have argued, the alternative—ignoring these interests and tying the representative's hands in favor of blind zealous representation—is not a healthy (or professional) way to proceed.

Further, and in any event, representative negotiators should care about this discussion because the client's case, while clearly central to the representative's mental calculus, is only one case. The lawyer's approach and reputation as a representative negotiator in the legal community follow him or her for an entire career. And while it takes years to develop a solid reputation as a lawyer and negotiator, it takes about five minutes to destroy one. So the lawyer clearly has a personal, professional and financial stake in his or her reputation as a lawyer and negotiator—independent of the client—vis-à-vis negotiation style and the bargaining opposite. These same interests will also likely be at stake for the representative's bargaining opposite. They therefore need to be considered as meaningful aspects of the processes when preparing for a negotiation.

In my view, the negotiator-as-professional model should find favor in, or at least be potentially beneficial to, all layers of the legal community. In terms of clients, to the extent that lawyers are hired to provide expertise, not only regarding the substance of a given problem, but also on the process of how that problem should be resolved, resting significant control over that process in the hands of lawyers should, as a systemic matter, work to the benefit of clients and their causes. It is also of benefit to clients on the theory that full communication is not only professionally required but is also beneficial to their interests. The model will benefit lawyer representatives individually and the profession generally, not only in giving lawyers significant control over how they negotiate, but also in how they feel about themselves as empowered agents in the building of their client's cases and their own careers. Finally, this model will also potentially benefit society as a whole, both through increased general professional behavior as well as specific lawyering conduct that takes seriously social welfare considerations in the calculus of competing courses of conduct.

As I have readily acknowledged, there may be some cases in which competing interests do not lend themselves well to resolution, and in those cases, lawyers will need to think seriously about withdrawal from the case. But as I have argued, what we are talking about is not simply learning how to negotiate one case for one client, but rather what a lawyer—and certainly a representative legal negotiator—does during a significant portion of his day for a significant portion of his or her career. Without taking seriously all of these potentially competing interests, my view is that we proceed with a very impoverished sense of what that career has, does, can and should look like. Without taking seriously all of these interests, we do not have an adequate answer to my student who is otherwise dissatisfied and disillusioned with the potential of a career as a representative negotiator. The negotiator-as-professional model, in my view, provides us with a better sense of the lawyer's role that will help to address some of the theoretical and practical challenges and opportunities of the representative negotiation process.

Notes and Questions

1. The following excerpt is from the "The Negotiator-as-Professional" article (at p. 28): "Clearly there are times, particularly after a retainer has been accepted and negotiations are under way, when the lawyer may be asked to take positions professionally that s/he would not take personally. But these situations aside, there are many occasions when the lawyer's interests and views should be voiced in the spirit of improving the underlying cause as well as the overall system, notwithstanding an

individual client's initial desires." Do you agree, and if so, in what circumstances would you take a position that you wouldn't otherwise take? Alternatively, when might you prefer your own interests over those of your client? How and why? Does your view of the lawyer's role in the adversary system influence your views on these issues?

2. Murray L. Schwartz, in his article "The Professionalism and Accountability of Lawyers" (1978) 66 Cal. L. Rev. 669 at 671, argues, among other things, that in lawyering situations in which arbiters are not present—expressly invoking the lawyer's role as a "negotiator" or "counsellor"—the "non-advocate lawyer should be held morally accountable for assistance rendered the client even though the lawyer is neither legally nor professionally accountable." Do you agree?

3. Does the excerpt from "The Negotiator-as-Professional" article or the Schwartz quotation (above) animate how you might respond to the following two hypothetical examples (which are also excerpted from "The Negotiator-as-Professional" article at n. 62)?

> (1) A rich, speculative, private land developer asks you to negotiate a deal with a slum landlord over the purchase of a fully-functioning low income rental facility that currently houses 80 families in favour of its demolition and replacement with a high-end multi-use condo facility that would house 8 high income families. (I have been influenced by Duncan Kennedy regarding this hypothetical. See Duncan Kennedy, "The Responsibility of Lawyers for the Justice of Their Causes" (1987) 18 Tex. Tech. L. Rev. 1157 …) (2) The CEO of a large privately-held downsizing transnational security firm asks you to negotiate a deal that would result in the termination of all employees of the Jewish or Muslim faith, based on your client's unfounded occupational requirement theory that these employees, while "good people," simply pose too much of a reputational and security risk (in terms of attacks against security officers in the field) and therefore are too costly to the firm.

In each case, what would you do? Why?

4. How do professional codes of conduct apply to the roles and approaches of representative negotiators in the hypothetical scenarios set out above? See, for example, the provisions regarding settlement and negotiation in the American Bar Association, *Model Rules of Professional Conduct* (2006 ed.), online: ABA <http://www.abanet.org/cpr/mrpc/mrpc_toc.html> and the Canadian Bar Association, *Code of Professional Conduct* (adopted by council, August 2004 and February 2006), online: CBA <http://www.cba.org/CBA/activities/pdf/codeofconduct06.pdf>. For an example of more extensive provisions, see the Law Society of Alberta, *Code of Professional Conduct*, online: LSA <http://www.lawsocietyalberta.com/files/Code.pdf> at c. 11 ("The Lawyer as Negotiator").

Selected Further Reading

Hon. G.W. Adams, Q.C., *Mediating Justice: Legal Dispute Negotiations* (Toronto: CCH, 2003).

American Bar Association, Standing Committee on Ethics and Professional Responsibility, "Lawyer's Obligation of Truthfulness When Representing a Client in Negotiation: Application to Caucused Mediation" (Formal Ethics Opinion 06-439, 12 April 2006).

L.A. Bebchuk & A.T. Guzman, "How Would You Like to Pay for That? The Strategic Effects of Fee Arrangements on Settlement Terms" (1996) 1 Harv. Negot. L. Rev. 53.

P.E. Bernard & B. Garth, eds., *Dispute Resolution Ethics: A Comprehensive Guide* (Washington, DC: American Bar Association, 2002).

G.A. Chornenki & C.E. Hart, *Bypass Court: A Dispute Resolution Handbook*, 3d ed. (Canada: LexisNexis, 2005).

R. Cochran, "Legal Representation and the Next Steps Toward Client Control: Attorney Malpractice for Failure to Allow the Client to Control Negotiation and Pursue Alternatives to Litigation" (1990) 47 Wash. & Lee L. Rev. 819.

R.J. Condlin, "Bargaining in the Dark: The Normative Incoherence of Lawyer Dispute Bargaining Role" (1992) 51 Md. L. Rev. 1.

W.F. Coyne Jr., "The Case for Settlement Counsel" (1999) 14 Ohio St. J. on Disp. Resol. 367.

J.S. Docherty & M.C. Campbell, "Teaching Negotiators to Analyze Conflict Structure and Anticipate the Consequences of Principle-Agent Relationships" (2004) 87 Marq. L. Rev. 655.

L.A. Epstein, "Cyber E-Mail Negotiation vs. Traditional Negotiation: Will Cyber Technology Supplant Traditional Means of Settling Litigation?" (2001) 36 Tulsa L.J. 839.

T.C.W. Farrow, "Dispute Resolution, Access to Civil Justice and Legal Education" (2005) 42 Alta. L. Rev. 741.

T.C.W. Farrow, "Dispute Resolution and Legal Education: A Bibliography" (2005) 7 Cardozo J. Conflict Resol. 119.

T.C.W. Farrow, "Thinking About Dispute Resolution" (2003) 41 Alta. L. Rev. 559.

N.E. Fassina, "Direct and Representative Negotiation: A Principal-Agent Authority Continuum" (Paper presented at the IACM 15th Annual Conference, June 2002), online: SSRN <http://ssrn.com/abstract=304973> or DOI: 10.2139/ssrn.304973.

J. Freund, "Bridging Troubled Waters: Negotiating Disputes" (1985–1986) Litigation 43.

D.G. Gifford, "A Context-Based Theory of Strategy Selection in Legal Negotiation" (1985) 46 Ohio St. L.J. 41.

D.G. Gifford, "The Synthesis of Legal Counseling and Negotiation Models: Preserving Client-Centered Advocacy in the Negotiation Context" (1987) 34 UCLA L. Rev. 811.

R. Gilson & R.H. Mnookin, "Disputing Through Agents: Cooperation and Conflict Between Lawyers in Litigation" (1994) 94 Colum. L. Rev. 509.

S.B. Goldberg, F.E.A. Sander & N.H. Rogers, *Dispute Resolution: Negotiation, Mediation, and Other Processes*, 4th ed. (Gaithersburg, NY: Aspen, 2003).

S.R. Gross & K.D. Syverud, "Getting to No: A Study of Settlement Negotiations and the Selection of Cases for Trial" (1991) 90 Mich. L. Rev. 319.

G.C. Hazard Jr., "The Lawyer's Obligation to Be Trustworthy When Dealing with Opposing Parties" (1981) 33 S.C.L. Rev. 181.

A.C. Hutchinson, "Legal Ethics for a Fragmented Society: Between Professional and Personal" (1997) 5 Int'l J. of the Legal Prof. 175.

D. Kennedy, "The Responsibility of Lawyers for the Justice of Their Causes" (1987) 18 Tex. Tech. L. Rev. 1157.

K.K. Kovach, "Lawyer Ethics Must Keep Pace with Practice: Plurality in Lawyering Roles Demands Diverse and Innovative Ethical Standards" (2003) 39 Idaho L. Rev. 399.

A. Krash, "Professional Responsibility to Clients and the Public Interest: Is There a Conflict?" (1974) 55 Chicago Bar Rec. 31.

D.A. Lax & J.K. Sebenius, *The Manager as Negotiator: Bargaining for Cooperation and Mutual Gain* (New York: Free Press, 1986).

D.A. Lax & J.K. Sebenius, "Negotiating Through an Agent" (1991) 35 J. Confl. Resolution 474.

D.A. Lax & J.K. Sebenius, "Three Ethical Issues in Negotiation" (1986) Negotiation Journal 363.

S. Levmore, "Commissions and Conflict in Agency Arrangements: Lawyers, Real Estate Brokers, Underwriters, and Other Agents' Rewards" (1993) 36 J.L. & Econ. 503.

G.T. Lowenthal, "The Bar's Failure to Require Truthful Bargaining by Lawyers" (1988) 2 Geo. J. Legal Ethics 411.

C. Menkel-Meadow & M. Wheeler, eds., *What's Fair: Ethics for Negotiators* (San Francisco, CA: Jossey-Bass, 2004).

R.H. Mnookin, S.R. Peppet & A.S. Tulumello, *Beyond Winning: Negotiating to Create Value in Deals and Disputes* (Cambridge, MA: Belknap Press, 2000).

R.H. Mnookin & L.E. Susskind, eds., *Negotiating on Behalf of Others: Advice to Lawyers, Business Executives, Sports Agents, Diplomats, Politicians, and Everybody Else* (Thousand Oaks, CA: Sage Publications, 1999).

J.K. Murnighan, D.A. Cantelon & T. Elyashiv, "Bounded Personal Ethics and the Tap Dance of Real Estate Agency" in J.A. Wagner III, J.M. Bartunek & K.D. Elsbach, eds., *Advances in Qualitative Organizational Research*, vol. 3 (New York: Elsevier, 2001).

E.H. Norton, "Bargaining and the Ethics of Process" (1989) 64 N.Y.U.L. Rev. 493.

A.J. Pirie, *Alternative Dispute Resolution: Skills, Science, and the Law* (Toronto: Irwin Law, 2000).

D.G. Pruitt, *Negotiation Behavior* (New York: Academic Press, 1981).

L. Riskin, "Mediation and Lawyers" (1982) 43 Ohio St. L.J. 29.

R. Wasserstrom, "Lawyers as Professionals: Some Moral Issues" (Fall 1975) 5 Hum. Rts. Q. 1.

J. White, "Machiavelli and the Bar: Ethical Limitations on Lying in Negotiation" (1980) Am. Bar Found. Res. J. 926.

C.B. Wiggins & L.R. Lowry, eds., *Negotiation and Settlement Advocacy: A Book of Readings*, 2d ed. (St. Paul, MN: Thomson, 2005).

G.R. Williams, "Style and Effectiveness in Negotiation" in L. Hall, ed., *Negotiation: Strategies for Mutual Gain* (Newbury Park, CA: Sage, 1993).

PART III

Negotiation Process

CHAPTER 3

Introduction to the Negotiation Process Model

Colleen M. Hanycz

Introduction

We have become negotiation consumers. Whether planning a multi-party undertaking or sitting down with a neighbour to resolve a fence dispute, negotiation has become woven into the fabric of our daily lives. In this chapter, we focus upon building an understanding of the core lenses through which to analyze negotiation situations. We will also suggest a framework for negotiating strategically that links our desired outcomes to tangible approaches.

The art of negotiation lies not in the rounds of bargaining that occur at the table, but rather, to a large degree, in the diagnostic planning stages that are completed before the actual negotiation begins. Clearly, there are many ways to frame a negotiation strategically and, in the pages that follow, we offer one such model for conceptualizing this important process.

We propose a process model of negotiation that is shaped primarily by an analysis of the nature and scope of available resources. Our suggestion is that an accurate articulation of the "value climate" heading into a negotiation is the crucial first step that will determine the remainder of the strategic planning necessary to that negotiation. Before we can strategize about the variables of and approaches to a specific negotiation, we must correctly diagnose its key characteristics; as such, the strategic process model that we propose is built entirely upon this crucial value foundation.

And while the first step of any process falls chronologically at its outset, it is equally important to revisit this first step as the journey unfolds. Such an approach is required if we are to adopt and maintain a model of representative negotiation that is truly party-centred. By recognizing that the parties to a negotiation are autonomous, we find ourselves continually cycling back to reassess the changing value climate of a negotiation. An effective negotiator constantly realigns her strategic approach to optimize individual and systemic outcomes in a shifting negotiation landscape.

What Do We Mean by "Value Climate"?

The notion of "value climate" is relatively straightforward. Essentially, a negotiator must identify the resources that are available, or that can be generated, in order to satisfy the competing needs of the parties in a negotiation. Is this a situation with scarce resources, where the demand on resources outstrips their availability? Or is this a situation with additional resources, which might not be immediately obvious but which are potentially available to satisfy everyone's needs? Only once a negotiator has conducted this resource analysis, is she able to select the framework—either distributive or integrative—that will maximize outcomes.

Before we dissect the process of assessing the value climate of a negotiation, we need to explain what we mean when we refer to the "value available" to a negotiation. If a farmer is selling apples at a fruit stand and a buyer wants to purchase some, what "value" exists around this transaction? First of all, there is the money that will change hands as the price for purchasing a set amount of apples. The amount of money will be dictated by what the vendor is willing to accept and what the buyer is willing to pay. But is there more at play here than the price of apples? For example, what about the quality of the apples being bought and sold? Is there some value to the vendor if the buyer is willing to purchase older, perhaps bruised apples? Is there some additional value to the buyer if the vendor is willing to keep the purchased apples at the fruit stand until the end of the day and then carry them to the buyer's car? Perhaps the buyer will pay more for apples that still have some leaves attached to their stems. These are examples of potential sources of additional value.

As we will explain below, sometimes an abundance of additional resources exists that dramatically changes the value climate. Other times, there is no additional value to import into a negotiation. Have some previously available resources fallen off the table or new resources appeared that might form the basis of different settlement opportunities? Diagnosing the value climate is the first and most crucial step in the strategic planning of a negotiation. And as we have said before, a skilled negotiator continually revisits the value climate to identify any shifts in the nature and availability of additional resources or options.

Specifically, the negotiator must diagnose the *nature, scope,* and *limitations* of the value available for sharing among the negotiating parties in the form of a negotiated agreement. In this context, the concept of value can be quite complex as it includes not only the immediately obvious or "visible" value, but also the latent value that remains less visible and that requires some effort to uncover. It is that less-evident value, properly identified and utilized, that often forms the solid foundations upon which enduring agreements are constructed. By accurately assessing all available value—visible and latent—the strategic negotiator is able to design an approach that will optimize, exhaust, and distribute that value in a way that encourages agreement.

A word of caution: the value climate is not the *only* factor that an effective negotiator must consider. In fact, that same negotiator must continually juggle a number of other variables and perspectives to be able to adjust her approach to an evolving negotiation as needed. For example, a lawyer or other representative negotiator must pay careful attention to the role of both personal and professional ethics when formulating negotiation strategies. If a negotiation threatens to drift off-side into ethically grey areas of negotiator conduct, how does a negotiator—especially of the representative variety—adequately respond while maintaining the primacy of his client's interests? A negotiator should also consider the impact of power, culture, and emotion upon the negotiation as it proceeds. For example: What impact does gender have on the dynamics of a negotiation? Why are cultural and emotional sensitivities so important to the process and result of negotiated agreements? Who ever thought it could be this complicated to get a fair price for apples in a fruit market?

The next step in the planning process is to understand the way in which assessing the value climate of a planned negotiation serves to inform the negotiator in selecting the appropriate strategic approach to that negotiation. For example, the resources available to any negotiation—or stage of a negotiation—*should* have a dramatic impact on the behaviours adopted by the negotiators. This view of negotiation strategy is very different from the one suggesting that negotiators adopt, on principle, a specific and constant approach to negotiation resources.

Currently, the approach to negotiation most commonly advocated is *integrative bargaining*, made famous by Roger Fisher and William Ury in *Getting to Yes: Negotiating Agreement Without Giving In.*[1] We will discuss integrative bargaining in greater detail shortly. While the positive potential of the integrative framework is indisputable, negotiators must demonstrate versatility above all else, and an ability and willingness to move easily between both of the major orientations to resources—the integrative framework and the distributive framework—outlined below.

The best negotiator—the one who professionally achieves the best outcomes for her client—is one who recognizes that the constantly shifting landscape of negotiation demands similarly shifting approaches. What should continually inform—in fact, dictate—the approaches that we adopt in our negotiations is an unwavering focus on the needs, interests, and autonomy of the parties on behalf of whom we are negotiating. If we are able to achieve and maintain this focus, then the resultant shifts in our approaches to negotiation will be principled, strategic, fruitful, and professional.

Overview of Negotiation: Expanding and Dividing the Pie

What we are proposing amounts to a straightforward equation: a negotiator's professional assessment of the resources available to a negotiation—the value climate—dictates the strategies she utilizes in achieving the goals of her client. The value climate triggers an analysis that, in turn, largely triggers a particular set of negotiation behaviours in order to achieve the client's objectives.

Many readers will have encountered the concepts of "win–lose" versus "win–win" negotiation outcomes. This shorthand has come to represent what are actually very complex

---

1 R. Fisher & W. Ury, *Getting to Yes: Negotiating Agreement Without Giving In* (New York: Penguin Books, 1981).

frameworks for strategically analyzing and planning a negotiation. We will begin our discussion with the "win–win" model often attached to the concept of *integrative bargaining*. We will then move to a consideration of *distributive bargaining*, regularly referred to as "win–lose" (or "zero-sum game") negotiating.

Integrative and distributive bargaining each provide a framework for approaching the resources available to satisfy the goals of the participants in a given negotiation. They do not, however, indicate the ways in which negotiators ought to approach the social interaction of negotiation. Nor do the terms *integrative* or *distributive* refer to strategic tactics employed in a negotiation. Similarly, *integrative* and *distributive* are not adjectives used to describe types of negotiators. They are simply ways of thinking about value and resources when strategizing for both unfolding and future negotiations. As perceptions around values and resources often shift over the course of a negotiation, so too should the negotiators' approaches and corresponding strategies.

It should be noted that, traditionally, negotiation scholars and practitioners have used the terms *distributive* and *competitive* interchangeably. Similarly, integrative bargaining has often been referred to as *cooperative* or *collaborative* negotiation. For our purposes, it is crucial to distinguish among these terms. They are not alternative labels for the same concept. Rather, it is a layered effect best understood moving from framework approaches to a negotiation outward to the tactics adopted by a negotiator in a given situation. As is indicated in figure 3.1, a negotiator who adopts an integrative framework has at his disposal a number of both competitive and cooperative/collaborative tactics. The same choice holds true for a distributive approach to bargaining.

When we speak of the specific strategies used within a given framework, we are referring to either *competitive* or *cooperative/collaborative tactics*. At the end of this chapter we will discuss tactics, but it is important at the outset to clarify that these tactics are not the same as integrative and distributive frameworks.

Figure 3.1   The Value Climate of a Negotiation

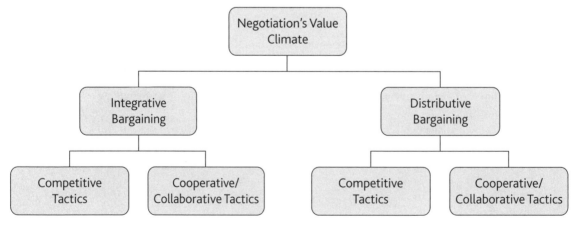

Integrative Bargaining: Expanding the Pie

When a negotiator adopts an integrative approach toward a negotiation or a stage in a negotiation, she is said to attempt to "create value" or "expand the pie." Done properly, the negotiator has assessed the value climate of the negotiation as one that will benefit from the addition of other resources not currently under consideration as a means of satisfying the needs of the parties to the negotiation. Simply put, this approach views the pool of resources available to the negotiation as expandable.

What makes an integrative approach so different from popular depictions of negotiation is its conviction that *all* parties to a negotiation can achieve their respective goals due to the capacity of the resource pool to be expanded to meet various needs. An integrative approach to a negotiation recognizes that there may be opportunities to create additional value in a phase of the negotiation that will satisfy parties in addition to the negotiator and the client.

Thinking Inside the Box...

Joe Smith lives in Ottawa, Ontario, and recently accepted a position with a large firm in Vancouver, British Columbia. The only challenge of an otherwise perfect opportunity is that Joe must relocate and start work in Vancouver within two weeks' time. One of the many items that Joe has decided not to move to Vancouver is a new 46" plasma screen television that he purchased three months ago. Joe has placed an ad in the weekend newspaper asking to sell the television for $3,000. Joe is concerned that he might be unable to sell the high-end unit before his move, recognizing that the cost of moving the TV might be greater than its value. Melia Jones saw the ad, and called Joe with an offer of $2,000. Given the replacement value of the unit, Joe is very unhappy with such a low offer. Unfortunately, Melia is not willing to spend more than $2,000 for a television. How might Joe and/or Melia *create additional value* in this scenario in order to make a deal?

In the example in the box above, Joe has advertised a television for $3,000, and he must sell it before he leaves for Vancouver in less than a week. The potential buyer, Melia, can only afford to pay $2,000 for the television. Rather than seeing this scenario as one requiring some version of a "meet in the middle" compromise, an integrative analysis would consider opportunities for creating additional value. For example, Melia might suggest as part of her offer that she could pay for the television in full and pick it up the following day. This would go some distance to achieving Joe's non-monetary need that the television be out of his hands quickly.

Alternatively, Joe might counter-offer to sell the TV to Melia for $2,500 but include the extra speakers Joe purchased to enhance the sound and agree to deliver the TV and speakers for free in his truck. Again, by creating additional value, Joe or Melia might craft an opportunity for agreement that would not have otherwise existed. These examples illustrate strategies to creating value that would flow from taking an integrative approach to this negotiation.

It is essential to recognize, however, that not *all* scenarios immediately favour an integrative approach. The phenomenal success of Fisher and Ury's *Getting to Yes* can be attributed in part to the authors' view that negotiation outcomes are *always* optimized when the negotiators retain a focus on interests instead of positions. Rather than concede that some negotiations lack the scope for creating additional value, Fisher and Ury argue that reorienting negotiation opponents to focus on interests ("negotiation ju-jitsu") is the better route.

Our suggestion, however, is that a firm adherence to an integrative framework, especially in the face of an unfavourable value climate, is not something that necessarily benefits the client. In fact, sometimes an accurate analysis of the value climate of a given negotiation reveals an absence of opportunities to create additional value in a negotiation. While negotiators should always begin their value climate analysis by looking for opportunities to create value, rigidly adhering to an integrative framework despite situational factors that do not promote the generation of added value is potentially done to the detriment of the client.

It is with this in mind that we reiterate the importance of developing *both* lenses for viewing the value climate of a negotiation. While the effective negotiator continuously monitors for changes in the evolving negotiation that might reveal new opportunities to adopt or return to an integrative framework with a focus on creating value, these opportunities do not necessarily exist in every negotiation.

Positions and Interests

Central to an integrative framework is a focus on the *interests* (or *needs*) of the parties to a negotiation, rather than on those parties' *positions*. Why not focus on positions? Often, focusing on positions reveals the absence of a "zone of agreement." In other words, if Joe is selling his television for $3,000 and Melia will only pay $2,000 for a television, there would appear to be no overlapping zone of agreement.

By automatically adopting a distributive stance that assumes no opportunities to create additional value, Joe and Melia might now launch into the conventional "haggling" that moves back and forth between price concessions until either a range of settlement is stumbled upon or one of the parties walks away.

Consider, instead, a situation where Joe's asking price for the TV is $3,000, but he is very concerned about selling the TV within a short time frame. Consider also the additional information that Melia, while unwilling to pay more than $2,000 for a TV alone, has that amount of money in cash and can pay for the TV and pick it up on short notice.

In other words, an analysis of the respective positions of Joe and Melia reveals some complementarity between their interests. If a negotiator is able both to understand her own interests and to excavate below her opponent's positions to reveal his interests as well, the opportunities for common ground—and additional value—are often increased.

In this case, the fact that Melia is able to pay a lower amount for the TV but pay immediately and pick it up on very short notice may satisfy Joe's bundle of *interests* sufficiently to warrant an agreement. Melia's willingness to pay for and pick up the TV quickly might even be of greater value to Joe than receiving his asking price of $3,000 from a different buyer, especially if that buyer was unable to move as quickly as Melia.

In chapter 4, we discuss some techniques for identifying or generating additional value in an integrative framework.

Limitations of the Integrative Framework

In a perfect world, every negotiation situation would be one in which there was sufficient existing or potential value to satisfy the needs of all parties to that negotiation. However, it must be recognized that sometimes such additional value simply does not exist and the only resource, for example, that can be generated revolves around the price set for an item.

Again, take the plasma TV example. Imagine that Joe is in no rush to sell his television and that all he wants out of the deal is as much money as he can get to upgrade to a bigger, newer unit. Melia, in this new scenario, is strictly limited to paying $2,000 for a television and, in fact, she is going to have to pay this maximum amount incrementally over time.

In a situation like this, one that is very common in everyday negotiations, a close analysis of the value climate might well reveal that there are few or no opportunities for creating additional value. Despite some literature that advocates attempting to reorient the other negotiator into looking at hidden interests and generating new value, sometimes a negotiation that claims to be just about price really is just about price. In those cases, adopting a distributive framework is clearly in the client's best interests, even if that means ultimately failing to find a zone of agreement.

Similarly, you may start with a value climate that is highly conducive to generating options and resources for agreement that are not immediately visible. Once that value is created and added to the pool, the skilled negotiator must have a plan for moving forward with the distribution of that value. This plan recognizes that the pool of available value is full and should now be distributed in a way that maximizes the client's interests.

Sometimes, the only way to maximize your client's interests is by equally satisfying the interests of all or some other parties in the negotiation. Whatever your client's interests are, you must eventually adopt a distributive framework; either from the outset, if the value climate is barren, or following a successful integrative bargaining phase in the negotiation.

Another limitation of adhering to an integrative framework arises when your opponent *does not* adopt an integrative bargaining approach, even in the context of a favourable value climate. There is little more beautiful to behold than a negotiation dance between two skilled negotiators working within an integrative framework. We see value revealed and maximized as resources appear where none existed before. Conversely, it is far less pleasant to watch the cat-and-mouse game of a negotiation where one negotiator is working integratively and the other is working distributively. In that scenario, the integrative bargainer searches for value, sometimes generating additional resources and options, only to be exploited by her opponent as he "claims" the new value to satisfy the interests of his client.

Figure 3.2

Source: cartoonresource.com.

"How did the negotiations go? Take a wild guess."

We are speaking now of the vulnerability inherent in the integrative framework. Although Ury has suggested a "breakthrough strategy"[2] to shift even the most intractable negotiation situations (or negotiators) into an interest-based frame, the negotiator who adopts an integrative framework in the face of an opponent who is operating in a distributive framework must worry about the possibility of suboptimal outcomes.

This possibility is enhanced in those situations where we are negotiating on behalf of another, be that a client, our boss, or someone else relying upon our professionalism. While the risks associated with integrative bargaining may be more easily justified by the potential gains when we conduct our own direct negotiations, such risks must be viewed through other glasses—including, in the case of lawyer negotiators, professional regulations—when negotiating on behalf of someone else.

Selecting the best approach to a negotiation must be based on the context and the situation. It cannot be predetermined or rigid. A negotiator should not have one, fixed "recipe for success" that is applied to all negotiation scenarios. Rather, the unique context of the negotiation must dictate the appropriate approaches. In chapter 2, we also discuss the impact of professional issues on the choice of negotiation approaches.

Taking this idea one step further, the specific resource context of the negotiation—its value climate—is the most appropriate filter with which to view and strategically plan a negotiation. When the value climate offers opportunities to create additional options for gain, then an integrative framework focusing on mutual interests and their overlap is best. But when that value climate does not demonstrate promise for creating additional resources, a distributive approach should be considered. The truly gifted negotiator is able both to assess the original value climate going into a negotiation and to note its changes as the negotiation unfolds, continually adjusting her operating framework to align with the shifting scenarios that she and her client face.

The Nuts and Bolts of Interests

Chapter 4 details a negotiation process model that allows the negotiator to optimize outcomes for her client by ensuring that all available value has been generated and subsequently distributed during a negotiation. Here, we limit our discussion to a few of the interests that might underlie the positions occupied in a given negotiation. By identifying the various interests at stake—the needs, the desires, the hopes, and the fears—a negotiator working within the integrative framework is able to produce options to improve the value climate of the negotiation.

While there have been various scholarly attempts to define and catalogue the types of interests or needs that parties to a negotiation may have, David Lax and James Sebenius's inventory is perhaps the most instructive and comprehensive:[3]

---

2   W. Ury, *Getting Past No: Dealing with Difficult People* (New York: Penguin Books, 1991).

3   D. Lax & J.K. Sebenius, *The Manager as Negotiator: Bargaining for Cooperation and Competitive Gains* (New York: Free Press, 1986), as summarized in Lewicki, Barry & Saunders, *infra* note 9 at 65.

1. *Process interests* are underlying needs that the negotiating parties have pertaining to the manner in which the negotiation is conducted—interests in the way a deal is achieved or a conflict is resolved. As a negotiator, it is crucial to identify that your opponent is adopting, for example, a distributive approach to a negotiation because she enjoys being able to use competitive tactics that make her feel like she has bested her opponents.

2. *Substance interests* can be defined as "outcome needs" that a party may hold. These are the interests underlying a given position that relate to the content of the negotiation. For example, by selling his television for $3,000, Joe is able to satisfy his interest in having money to buy a TV once he has relocated, and he also may satisfy a deeper need to not have been exploited in selling a TV below its value.

3. *Relationship interests* are those needs that a negotiating party has respecting his relationship with the other parties to that negotiation. A negotiator might take a softer position on an issue so as not to jeopardize his long-term relationship with the opposite party. Conversely, some history of discord between negotiating parties might drive one party to be overly rigid in adhering to unreasonable positions in order to not "lose face" in the context of that history.

4. *Interests in principle* is the final category of interests described by Lax and Sebenius and includes those interests that are deeply held by a party relating to, for example, principles of fairness, ethics, and acceptable behaviours in a negotiation. We might add to this list those interests held by an individual that derive from religious, political, or cultural principles. It is this group of interests that is often held most deeply and that is most important to reveal. If it is these interests that lie, hidden, at the heart of a seemingly unreasonable position, it is unlikely that the parties holding such interests will compromise on their position unless the interests remain satisfied.[4]

Complicating this consideration of underlying interests in a negotiation analysis is the fact that a negotiator's interests may be very different from—contrasting, in fact—the interests of her client. For example, if a corporation is interested in achieving a fair process and optimizing its substantive outcomes in an offshore manufacturing agreement, the corporation's negotiator may have very different personal and professional interests to add to this mix. She might, for example, see this negotiation as a critical opportunity to make a name for herself as a tough negotiator, a process interest that might lead her to adopt highly competitive tactics and exploit any opponents' attempts to work within an integrative framework.

As a representative negotiator, the assessment of interests must be multi-faceted. You must consider the respective interests of the parties. Then you must focus particularly on those interests of the representatives (yourself and the other negotiator)—including professional issues discussed in chapters 2 and 5—that might conflict with the parties' interests and derail a negotiation that otherwise has great potential to succeed. Many a corporate

---

4 See *e.g.* Maslow's hierarchy of needs in A. Maslow, *Toward a Psychology of Being* (New York: D. Van Nostrand, 1962), which details basic psychological needs. If a party position in a negotiation has been structured around a high-priority need, it is unlikely that such a position will be readily vacated unless the underlying need is otherwise met.

negotiator has failed to identify a counterpart's interests going into a key negotiation, such that the value climate of that negotiation was grossly miscalculated.[5]

A further warning: guard against the tendency to reduce a complicated set of inconsistent positions to a set of vague, meaningless common interests. Here's an example: Barry and Susan are engaged in a custody battle over their two young children. During one of the negotiation rounds with their lawyers, Barry claims that the children are always stressed and worried after spending time with their mother who provides them with no freedom and far too many chores. Susan claims that the children come home after a weekend spent with their father totally exhausted from staying up half the night playing video games and eating candy, with nary a green vegetable in sight! In a search for common interests, one negotiator states, "I think we can agree that both of our clients are concerned about the welfare of their children." While such common ground might, in fact, exist, if the shared interest is so vague, obvious, and universal as to be meaningless, its trite identification may serve to harm the negotiation rather than to help it.

Negotiators must search for interests held in common that are *meaningful* in the context of the negotiation, and avoid the reductivist approaches that might seem favoured by interpersonal communication skills emphasized in negotiation training, such as reframing. Otherwise, they run the risk of oversimplifying and miscasting complex conflict and thereby forcing the pressing interests underground.[6] Those interests will not remain buried and may emerge later in the process to destroy an otherwise robust and elegant solution.

How Do We Excavate Interests from Positions?

Once the interests of parties to a negotiation are dug up, do they necessarily overlap, creating a zone of agreement? Not always. When we dig beneath inconsistent positions, the interests that emerge may be commonly held, compatible, or conflicting.

It would be wonderful if the challenging task of identifying the interests that support a stated position could be finalized during the pre-negotiation planning stage. However, the interests identified early on represent only half of the story. Effective negotiation requires continuously listening for information that indicates the emergence of new interests or needs. A particular interest may not develop until the negotiation takes a specific direction—in other words, not all interests necessarily exist at the outset of a negotiation.

Often, it is these latent interests, if not fully recognized, that come to present the greatest impediments to a negotiated agreement. Understanding, therefore, that identifying interests is an ongoing process throughout the stages of negotiation, what approaches can we utilize

---

5   This can be even more complicated in the case of a negotiation assisted by a third-party mediator, as that mediator brings to the process another potentially conflicting series of interests. See C. Hanycz, "Through the Looking Glass: Mediator Conceptions of Philosophy, Process and Power" (2005) 42 Alta. L. Rev. 819.

6   See *e.g.* C. Provis, "Interests vs. Positions: A Critique of the Distinction" (1996) 12 Negotiation Journal 305, who warns that focusing exclusively on interests encourages negotiators to conceal a conflict's true characteristics and dynamics.

Thinking Inside the Box ...

Martha has worked for All Canadian Holidays (ACH) for 11 years and recently applied for a promotion to the position of regional vice-president for eastern Canada, which she read about in an internal posting in the company newsletter. Martha's current manager is very impressed with her work and her employment reviews, which have been overwhelmingly positive to date and have led Martha to receive several promotions during her time at ACH. Martha participates in the staged interview process for this position, which culminates in a three-person interview panel. Three days later, her manager breaks the news that Martha will not be receiving the promotion. Martha is devastated and leaves her job.

Fast-forward eight months to a meeting between Martha and her manager (both represented by lawyers), negotiating in an attempt to avoid going to trial over Martha's constructive dismissal action.

Martha has taken the position that she was constructively dismissed from her job when she was passed over for the promotion and is suing for $300,000. ACH is taking the position that Martha voluntarily quit her job and is entitled to nothing.

Imagine that the following interests were revealed through excavation of the positions, working in an integrative bargaining framework. Keep in mind that many of these interests, in the context of dispute resolution negotiation, may be intentionally hidden so as to avoid the vulnerability associated with their being revealed:

1. **Common or Shared Interests**
   - Both want Martha to continue her career with ACH, although this interest is denied by Martha.
   - Both ACH and Martha wish for Martha to be fairly compensated by ACH.
   - Neither Martha nor ACH wish to engage in litigation and would both prefer to settle this matter.
   - Both Martha and ACH want this matter and its resolution to be confidential.

2. **Compatible Interests**
   - ACH recognizes Martha's high profile in the travel industry and does not want Martha harming the reputation of ACH through negative comments to others in the industry. Martha does not want to appear personally unprofessional by making disparaging comments about her former employer, especially if there is a way for Martha to return to ACH with a promotion commensurate with her record.
   - Martha wants to be elected to an industry-wide advisory board and cannot hold such a position unless she is currently employed in the industry.
   - With its quarterly shareholder's report soon due, ACH does not want to be in the position of having to reveal ongoing employment litigation to its shareholders as it fears this will negatively impact its share price.
   - In the ethnic community to which Martha belongs, there is a general sense that litigation is not a valuable process in which to engage, spurring Martha's interest to settle this matter outside of court.

3. **Conflicting Interests**
  - As the strongest candidate for the job, Martha needed her merit to be recognized through a promotion. ACH did not want to promote Martha because it was very concerned about finding an appropriate replacement for the challenging position she held. ACH had a deep business interest in not destabilizing Martha's department, which it felt it would have done by promoting her.

Can you think of other possible interests for each category?

in an integrative framework to identify both existing and emerging interests? Although many scholars have suggested ways to identify interests in this process, the following excerpt from Fisher and Ury surely says it best.

Roger Fisher and William Ury
Getting to Yes: Negotiating Agreement Without Giving In, 2d ed.
(New York: Penguin Books, 1991) at 44-50

How do you identify interests?
The benefit of looking behind positions for interests is clear. How to go about it is less clear. A position is likely to be concrete and explicit; the interests underlying it may well be unexpressed, intangible, and perhaps inconsistent. How do you go about understanding the interests involved in a negotiation, remembering that figuring out *their* interests will be at least as important as figuring out *yours*?

Ask "Why?" One basic technique is to put yourself in their shoes. Examine each position they take, and then ask yourself "Why?" Why, for instance, does your landlord prefer to fix the rent—in a five-year lease—year by year? The answer you may come up with, to be protected against increasing costs, is probably one of his interests. You can also ask the landlord himself why he takes a particular position. If you do, make clear that you are asking not for justification of this position, but for an understanding of the needs, hopes, fears, or desires that it serves. "What's your basic concern, Mr. Jones, in wanting the lease to run for no more than three years?"

Ask "Why not?" Think about their choice. One of the most useful ways to uncover interests is first to identify the basic decision that those of the other side probably see you asking them for, and then to ask yourself why they have not made that decision. What interests of theirs stand in the way? If you are trying to change their minds, the starting point is to figure out where their minds are now.

Consider for example, the negotiations between the United States and Iran in 1980 over the release of 52 U.S. diplomats and embassy personnel held hostage in Tehran by student militants. While there were a host of serious obstacles to a resolution of this dispute, the problem is illuminated simply by looking at the choice of the typical student leader. The demand of the United States was clear: "Release the hostages." During much of 1980, each student leader's choice must have looked something like that illustrated by the balance sheet below.

As of: Spring 1980
Currently Perceived Choice of: An Iranian student leader
Question Faced: "Shall I press for immediate release of the American hostages?"

If I say yes ...
- − I sell out the Revolution.
- − I will be criticized as pro-American.
- − The others will probably agree with me; if they do and we release the hostages, then:
  - − Iran looks weak.
  - − We back down to the U.S.
  - − We get nothing (no Shah, no $).

  - − We don't know what the U.S. will do.

But ...
- + There is a chance that economic sanctions might end.
- + Our relations with other nations, especially in Europe, may improve.

If I say no ...
- + I uphold the Revolution.
- + I will be praised for defending Islam.
- + We will probably all stick together.
- + We will get fantastic TV coverage to tell the world about our grievances.
- + Iran looks strong.
- + We stand up to the U.S.
- + We have a chance of getting something (at least our money back).
- + The hostages provide some protection against U.S. intervention.

But ...
- − Economic sanctions will no doubt continue.
- − Our relations with other nations, especially in Europe, will suffer.
- − Inflation and economic problems will continue.
- − There is a risk that the U.S. might take military action (but a martyr's death is the most glorious).

However ...
- + The U.S. may make further commitments about our money, nonintervention, ending sanctions, etc.
- + We can always release the hostages later.

If a typical student leader's choice did look even approximately like this, it is understandable why the militant students held the hostages for so long: As outrageous and illegal as the original seizure was, once the hostages had been seized it was not irrational for the students to *keep* holding them from one day to the next, waiting for a more promising time to release them.

In constructing the other side's currently perceived choice, the first question to ask is "Whose decision do I want to affect?" The second question is what decision people on the other side now see you asking them to make. If *you* have no idea what they think they are being called on to do, *they* may not either. That alone may explain why they are not deciding as you would like.

Now analyze the consequences, as the other side would probably see them, of agreeing to or refusing to make the decision you are asking for. You may find a checklist of consequences such as the following helpful in this task:

Impact on my interests
- Will I lose or gain political support?
- Will colleagues criticize or praise me?

Impact on the group's interests
- What will be the short-term consequences? The long-term consequences?
- What will be the economic (political, legal, psychological, military, etc.) consequences?
- What will be the effect on outside supporters and public opinion?
- Will the precedent be good or bad?
- Will making this decision prevent doing something better?
- Is the action consistent with our principles? Is it "right"?
- Can I do it later if I want?

In this entire process it would be a mistake to try for great precision. Only rarely will you deal with a decision-maker who writes down and weighs the pros and cons. You are trying to understand a very human choice, not making a mathematical calculation.

Realize that each side has multiple interests. In almost every negotiation each side will have many interests, not just one. As a tenant negotiating a lease, for example, you may want to obtain a favorable rental agreement, to reach it quickly with little effort, and to maintain a good working relationship with your landlord. You will not only have a strong interest in *affecting* any agreement you reach, but also one in *effecting* an agreement. You will be simultaneously pursuing both your independent and your shared interests.

A common error in diagnosing a negotiation situation is to assume that each person on the other side has the same interests. This is almost never the case...

Thinking of negotiation as a two-person, two-sided affair can be illuminating, but it should not blind you to the usual presence of other persons, other sides, and other influences. In one baseball salary negotiation, the general manager kept insisting that $500,000 was simply too much for a particular player, although other teams were paying at least that much to similarly talented players. In fact the manager felt his position was unjustifiable, but he had strict instructions from the club's owners to hold firm without explaining why, because they were in financial difficulties that they did not want the public to hear about.

Whether it is his employer, his client, his employees, his colleagues, his family, or his wife, every negotiator has a constituency to whose interests he is sensitive. To understand that negotiator's interests means to understand the variety of somewhat differing interests that he needs to take into account.

The most powerful interests are basic human needs. In searching for the basic interests behind a declared position, look particularly for those bedrock concerns which motivate all people. If you can take care of such basic needs, you increase the chance both of reaching agreement and, if an agreement is reached, of the other side's keeping to it. Basic human needs include: security, economic well-being, a sense of belonging, recognition, and control over one's life.

As fundamental as they are, basic human needs are easy to overlook. In many negotiations, we tend to think that the only interest involved is money. Yet, even in a negotiation over a monetary figure, such as the amount of alimony to be specified in a separation agreement, much more can be involved. What does a wife really want in asking for $500 a week in alimony? Certainly she is interested in her economic well-being, but what else? Possibly she wants money in order to feel psychologically secure. She may also want it for recognition: to feel that she is treated fairly and as an equal. Perhaps the husband can not afford to pay $500 a week, and perhaps the wife does not need that much, yet she will likely accept less only if her needs for security and recognition are met in other ways …

Make a list. To sort out the various interests of each side, it helps to write them down as they occur to you. This will not only help you remember them; it will also enable you to improve the quality of your assessment as you learn new information and to place interests in their estimated order of importance. Furthermore, it may stimulate ideas for how to meet those interests.

Fisher and Ury's list of ways to identify interests is certainly not exhaustive. Often, underlying interests can be uncovered through careful pre-negotiation research into, for example, the history of the situation, the current and former parties and their relationships, historical data concerning past deals, or terms of agreement that might be affecting the present situation. Similarly, careful consideration of the cultures to which the opposing party and negotiator belong may serve to reveal certain collective interests that may be at play.[7] So, interests are dug up not only through effective questioning and reflective speculation but also by moving outside of the current negotiation situation to consider external information that might be fuelling parties' positions.

Perhaps with tongue in cheek, Lax and Sebenius have the following to say about probing interests:

> In the end, interests are bound up with psychology and culture. Some settings breed rivalry; others esteem the group. Some people are altruists; others sociopaths. To some, ego looms large; to others, substance is all. Airport bookstore wisdom names Jungle Fighters, Appeasers, Win-Winners

---

7   For a discussion of intercultural competence in conflict resolution, see M. Lebaron, "Windows on Diversity: Lawyers, Culture and Mediation Practice" (2003) 20 Conflict Res. Q. 463.

and Win-Losers. Professionals diagnose personality Types A and B and victims of cathected libido. Others have developed such classes, sometimes wisely, but for now we stress that *perceived* interests matter, that perceptions are subjective. Thus, to assess interests is to probe psyches.[8]

How Do Interests Impact Options in an Integrative Framework?

Once we feel confident that we have created a list of the underlying interests of all parties and representatives in a negotiation that is as complete as possible, the next step is to consider the connection between those interests and the new value or "options" that they can generate in an integrative framework. Be reminded that this process is not so much a linear progression as it is a cyclical one: as we advance through the step of generating options that may serve to satisfy emerging interests, new interests may be revealed that we will need to address. This process requires a flexibility that a negotiator can find extremely challenging as she strategizes toward the ultimate objectives of the negotiation. It also requires patience and maturity to recognize that forcing the negotiation forward on the basis of "new information" will at best lead to inelegant, fleeting agreements that do not possess the sound foundation to withstand time and shifting relationships. Rather, a negotiator is advised to pause when a new interest is revealed—or even suggested—and return to a fuller consideration of that and any related interests before generating new options.

Simply stated, a full and accurate set of interests serves to *inform* an expanded value climate by providing a basis upon which new value and options might be built. When the negotiation is focused (or refocused) away from positions on interests, the actual needs of the parties can be better addressed and compensated, leading to richer and more enduring agreements. In chapter 4, we take a closer look at strategies for generating options and creating new value to meet the interests of all parties in an integrative framework. Before moving to that discussion, we consider the other major framework that analyzes negotiation in relation to its value climate—distributive bargaining.

Distributive Bargaining: Dividing the Pie

A distributive bargaining perspective assumes that a fixed (and often insufficient) amount of resources is available to address the existing interests in a negotiation or in a stage of a negotiation. A negotiator who adopts a distributive approach recognizes that all available value to meet the revealed interests has been identified and is now "on the table," with no additional options left to be generated. Once a negotiator assumes a distributive stance, she no longer focuses on identifying interests or generating new value to meet those interests; instead, she focuses solely on collecting—or "claiming"—the best portion of the available resources in order to satisfy her client's objectives.

---

8   D. Lax & J. Sebenius, "Interests: The Measure of Negotiation" (1986) 2 Negotiation Journal 76 at 89.

Another way of understanding the distributive approach is through a "zero-sum game" explanation. A zero-sum or "win–lose" approach to negotiation assumes that for every amount of value gained by one party, an equal amount of value is lost by the other party. Again, the idea here is that the value pool has a finite number of units that will be distributed in some ratio among the negotiators present. For each unit that you gain, I must necessarily lose one. In direct relation to any growth in the size of your slice of pie, the size of my slice of pie shrinks.

Strategies for Operating Within a Distributive Framework

Roy Lewicki, Bruce Barry, and David Saunders propose four strategies that are fundamental to operating within a distributive framework.[9] Keeping in mind the goal of dividing the available value or options for settlement in a way that is most favourable to one's client, they suggest the following strategies:

1. **Push for a settlement close to your opponent's (usually unknown) resistance point (RP).**[10] By shifting the settlement very close to your opponent's "bottom line," you are able to claim the largest portion of the zone of settlement for your client. If, for example, a buyer is willing to pay up to $500 for a ruby necklace and you are willing to sell that necklace for as little as $200, then the zone of settlement is between $200 and $500. Even if you don't know the buyer's bottom line, a distributive framework would encourage pushing for a settlement as close to the buyer's RP as possible.

   Depending on the tactics employed, you will be able to sense from the negotiation dynamics when you are approaching (or when you have gone beyond) the buyer's RP. If, for example, the buyer agrees to purchase the necklace for $450, then you have successfully captured a huge portion of the available value (that is, the value in the settlement range between $200 and $500) for your client, recalling that a distributive framework accepts that all available value has been identified and focuses on its division.

2. **Convince your opponent to alter her RP by influencing her beliefs about the strength of her position.** Using a variety of methods, you may be able to convince

---

9   Slightly modified from R. Lewicki, B. Barry & D. Saunders, *Essentials of Negotiation*, 4th ed. (New York: McGraw-Hill Irwin, 2007) at 33.

10   More is said in chapter 8 about "resistance price" (also known as *resistance point*). It refers essentially to the least favourable offer that the other side will accept, below which they will walk away from the negotiation. Among other things, RP is often affected by a party's alternatives to a negotiated agreement: if you are selling a car for $10,000 and you have received an offer for $7,000, subsequent negotiations with another potential buyer will only remain viable, all other things being equal, provided that the amount offered by the potential buyer does not dip below $7,000. In that scenario, the seller's RP would likely be $7,000.

your opponent to modify her RP. The most common way to undermine an opponent's confidence in her position is to use objective criteria that suggest her position is not supportable. For example, if the buyer above says that she is convinced she can purchase a ruby necklace like the one you are selling for $400, you might present her with a series of advertisements from other jewellery stores offering comparable ruby necklaces that range in price from $600 to $900.

Unless the buyer can counter that "objective criteria" of the market value of ruby necklaces with something that supports her claim that she can buy a ruby necklace for $400, her confidence in that position will be undermined. This may result in her elevating her RP at least to $600 to match the objective criteria that you have provided.

Depending on what your RP is, the elevation of your opponent's RP has either created a range of settlement where none existed before (for example, if your RP was to sell the necklace for a minimum of $500) or expanded an existing one (if your RP was to sell the necklace for a minimum of $350). Again, the objective in a distributive framework is to divide the available value in a way that optimizes your client's interests and, presumably, results in a final agreement.

3. **If no settlement range exists, convince your opponent to lower his RP in order to create a settlement range or raise your own RP in order to create a zone of agreement.** The explanation here is similar to the one for the strategy presented above, except that we have added the possibility of you lowering your RP in order to create a range of settlement that includes both RPs. Imagine, for example, that the roles are reversed and you have stated the firm position that you will not accept anything less than $600 for the sale of your ruby necklace. At that point, the interested buyer shows you several advertisements of your competitors that indicate comparable ruby necklaces being sold in the price range of $350 to $500. In the face of objective criteria that serve to erode your position, one strategy of distributive bargaining is to adjust your own RP in order to create a range of settlement if it is clear that none exists.

Of course, this example is oversimplified. A proper integrative phase to this negotiation might well have revealed any number of other interests that each party to this potential sale has, be they shared, complementary, or conflicting. These other interests too could serve to adjust your RP. For example, if you are heading into your store's financial year-end and you wish to minimize your inventory, that could encourage a shift in your RP so that it no longer corresponds with your perceived value of the ruby necklace. Alternatively, the buyer may have a history of purchasing jewellery from your store and be very reluctant to risk buying from another dealer that might be disreputable. All of these interests can impact positions and RPs. It is important to recognize, within a distributive framework, the flexibility of RPs in order to create a range of settlement, if that is desired.

4. **Convince your opponent to believe that the proposed agreement is the "best possible" (not that it is all she can get or that you are besting her outcome).** Here, we return to some of those most basic human needs that may influence negotiation outcomes. It is commonly accepted that a party to a negotiation will be more apt to enter into an agreement if he is convinced that he is getting the best possible deal that he can get, given the unique circumstances of that negotiation. If a party feels he was "bested," even if that proposed agreement is more favourable than his RP, he is unlikely to settle as his ego needs will outweigh those interests that favour a deal.

Conversely, you can surely think of a situation where you agreed to a settlement that fell outside of your RP, simply because you believed it was the best possible deal that you could get. Who among us has paid more than our RP for a house or a car or an outfit on the basis of a conviction that we got the best possible deal for that item?

Satisfying human needs around recognition, ego, and self-esteem will not only encourage the attainment of a negotiated agreement, but will ensure the longevity and endurance of that agreement. If we wake up the day after a negotiation only to hear that our opponent has been bragging about how significantly he bested us in the negotiation, we will quickly search for ways to unravel the deal in an attempt to satisfy these pressing psychological needs. As Carrie Menkel-Meadow notes,

> the underlying needs produced by some injuries may not be susceptible to full and/or monetary satisfaction. The need to be regarded as totally normal or completely honorable can probably never be met, but the party in a negotiation will be motivated by the desire to satisfy as fully as possible these underlying human needs. Some parties may have a need to get "as much X as possible," such as in demands for money for pain and suffering. This demand may simply represent the best proxy available for satisfying the unsatisfiable desire to be made truly whole— this is to be put back in the position of no accident at all. It may represent a desire to save for a rainy day or to maximize power, fame or love.[11]

Triggers for Adopting a Distributive Framework

We have suggested above that a negotiator should rarely begin a negotiation with a distributive approach and should only realign her framework when other options prove untenable. The problem with a distributive negotiation, improperly utilized, is that it seeks to divide the value pool of the negotiation before that pool has been maximized and all options for expanded resources have been exhausted. As a result, we talk of value being "left on the table" following a round of distributive bargaining that was either engaged in incorrectly or prematurely.

That said, in keeping with the maxim that "all roads lead to Rome," all negotiations eventually move to a distributive framework. It is only a matter of *when* that approach is best adopted, given its limitations related to maximizing the value that becomes the bedrock of an enduring agreement.

There are a number of what we think of as "triggers" that could lead a negotiator to adopt a distributive framework either at the outset of a negotiation or at some point during its development. The following list of triggers is by no means exhaustive, but provides a sense of the context in which a distributive framework is in the best interests of the client.

1. **Additional value is absent.** Recalling our contention that an effective negotiation strategy can be achieved by a negotiator orienting herself to the given value climate of a situation, it is important to recognize the flexibility and adaptability that is required by sometimes sudden, unanticipated, or dramatic shifts in that climate.

---

11   C. Menkel-Meadow, "Toward Another View of Legal Negotiation: The Structure of Problem Solving" (1984) 31 UCLA L. Rev. 754 at 795.

Whether sudden or gradual, there comes a time in the life of a negotiation when the parties and their representatives have explored and used up all opportunities to create additional value to satisfy the various interests of those at—and not at—the table. When the capacities of the integrative framework have been thoroughly exhausted, a party is best served when her negotiator shifts to a distributive framework.

Ordinarily, the decisive moment to change frameworks occurs following one or several rounds of robust integrative bargaining when positions are bracketed in favour of a broad and deep excavation of their underlying interests. However, periodically, this situation exists *ab initio*, when assessing the value climate in advance of a negotiation simply does not suggest an opportunity to plumb interests and generate options in response. Even when such an extreme situation is revealed through advance planning and analysis, there is no harm in engaging in even a brief inquiry at the very outset of the negotiation to check your own analysis and ensure that you have not somehow missed a rich opportunity for an integrative approach.

When the moment arrives where no additional value can be generated and all options for agreement are on the table, a negotiator acting in the best interests of his client must think seriously about shifting to a distributive framework. Not only is there nothing to be gained by remaining in integrative mode in the absence of opportunities for creating new value, but a negotiator increases his vulnerability if the opposing negotiator moves into a distributive framework first, a mismatch that will be explored next.

2. **Your opponent rigidly adheres to a distributive framework.** A red flag should go up when an opponent, even in the face of additional potential value, refuses to adopt an interest-based approach. In such a scenario, a negotiator should then move to a distributive framework. If your opponent adheres to a distributive framework and claims all available value, your client's interests will clearly be exploited by your continued attempt to generate additional options and value.

   While Ury, as noted earlier, advocates "negotiation ju-jitsu" to convert the intransigent bargainer to an interest-based approach, this strategy is not without its limitations. Certainly, there is a possibility of success and, ultimately, a much improved negotiation and agreement. However, there is also the worry that while you are attempting to shift your opponent to an appreciation of the potential for added value and generating mutual gains, he may be busily scooping up—often through the use of highly competitive tactics—all of the new value that you are creating. A potentially safer route in the face of stubborn resistance to implementing an integrative framework is limiting your client's exposure to loss of value by moving your approach to a distributive framework.

3. **Negotiators are unprepared.** In a perfect world, all negotiators would spend a significant amount of creative effort preparing for a negotiation; they would study positions in order to reveal underlying interests and think about additions to the value climate that would favour the satisfaction of these interests. The key notion here is that of spending time and energy in preparing for a negotiation so that such opportunities can be investigated and harnessed during the negotiation itself. If, however, the situation at hand does not allow for an expansive pre-negotiation planning phase, adopting a distributive framework is recommended to avoid

exploitation of your client. Moving to a distributive stance can be especially important if your opponent *has* had a more fulsome opportunity to prepare and you have come to the negotiation in the eleventh hour.

The problem with starting a negotiation without having had the opportunity to prepare fully is that a lack of familiarity with the driving interests behind your opponent's position especially may lead to a vulnerability that is best avoided. Imagine a situation where you are handed a negotiation brief at the last moment, or where other matters have intervened to prevent you from carefully preparing your approach. It is likely, in such circumstances, that your opponent has fully canvassed the opportunities and will commence the negotiation in a distributive framework with an eye on claiming all of the available value. If you are less aware of all of the interests at play in the negotiation and of a meaningful array of options available to establish a lasting agreement, chances are that your opponent will take advantage of your information gap and move to a distributive stance.

All of this emphasizes the critical importance of a full pre-negotiation planning stage in every negotiation. By not allowing yourself the opportunity to study the value climate and plan your approach accordingly, you may end up in such a deficit position that you may have to adopt a defensive distributive framework to avoid exploitation.

4. **Attractive "alternatives" to a negotiated agreement are present.** Another trigger to shift to a distributive framework may be the realization that your client's alternative to a negotiated agreement is relatively stronger than the opposing party's. If you are operating from a position of strength, a distributive framework may be best, simply due to an absence of meaningful motivation or inclination to engage in a full work-up of potential options and value. If you happen to have a particularly strong alternative, or if one evolves through the negotiation, the inclination would be to adopt a distributive framework to optimize your client's interests by claiming the available value. Given the positive alternative to this negotiation, there may simply not be the pressing need to explore interests and opportunities for additional gain.

The Prisoner's Dilemma

One of the most common examples used to illustrate the tension between the integrative and distributive frameworks is one borrowed from game theory: the prisoner's dilemma. Although there are many variations on the fine details, essentially the story goes that two alleged criminals (prisoners A and B) are arrested and held in separate cells, away from each other. The police have information that could convict them of a small crime, but there is insufficient evidence to support the conviction of the larger crime in which the police are convinced they jointly participated.

In an attempt to elicit this additional information, the police offer each of the prisoners an "information-for-lenience" deal in the hopes that at least one of them will provide the necessary evidence to convict the other of the larger crime. The outcomes of this offer are as follows:

1. If neither "talks" by providing additional evidence to convict the other, each will serve four years in prison for the lesser crime.

2. If one talks, providing evidence, and the other does not, the one who provides evidence will serve a reduced sentence of one year, while the other will serve a 20-year sentence for the larger crime.
3. If both talk, their evidence will be used to convict each other and they will both serve 10 years in prison (20 years for the larger crime, reduced by 50 percent for providing evidence).

It is here that we see the tensions of integrative and distributive bargaining frameworks revealed most acutely. Both prisoners have an incentive to provide evidence to better their individual positions:

1. If one prisoner provides evidence and the other does not, the one who provides evidence reduces his sentence from four years to one year.
2. If both prisoners provide evidence, they avoid a 20-year sentence and settle for a 10-year sentence for cooperating with the police.

Thus, the prisoners appear doomed to serving 10-year sentences and not maximizing their joint gains unless they can overcome this dilemma. Each prisoner is likely to conclude that to provide evidence is the optimal strategy. This puts them in the upper left quadrant of the matrix (below) and the position known as the "Nash equilibrium." Thus they both provide evidence, incriminate each other, and each get a 10-year sentence. The optimal position from their joint perspective is not chosen.

		Prisoner A	
		Does Provide Evidence	**Doesn't Provide Evidence**
Prisoner B	**Does Provide Evidence**	A: 10 years in prison B: 10 years in prison	A: 20 years in prison B: 1 year in prison
	Doesn't Provide Evidence	A: 1 year in prison B: 20 years in prison	A: 4 years in prison B: 4 years in prison

The prisoner's dilemma highlights the attractiveness of using an integrative framework. It also, however, highlights the vulnerability that can be avoided by adopting a distributive framework in certain contexts. Seeking to create joint gains—the scenario where no one talks—only works if all parties adopt the same approach. But, as negotiation often includes a certain amount of distrust of the motives and behaviours of your opponent, the more common scenario, the Nash equilibrium, provides a less favourable outcome but reduces vulnerability.

A Word About Tactics

The framework chosen for a negotiation does not necessarily dictate the tactics to be utilized during bargaining. For example, while commonly used in tandem, it is important to understand that a distributive approach to negotiation is not synonymous with a competitive approach. Often, the literature uses these concepts interchangeably, but it is more accurate to think of a distributive framework as one that considers the resources available in the negotiation as scarce.

Competitive or cooperative/collaborative tactics are specialized techniques or interpersonal behaviours that you might adopt in order to achieve outcomes within a particular framework. Once it has been determined that the value climate of a particular stage in a negotiation requires either an integrative or distributive framework, a negotiator must choose, contextually, the tactics that will optimize the outcomes within that framework.

Although scholars have suggested different typologies of negotiation tactics and techniques, arguably the two categories of tactics that are most widely adopted are *competitive* and *cooperative/collaborative*.[12] Chapter 4 discusses these tactics further. For our purposes here, it is sufficient to recognize that these behaviours are not dictated by the overall framework—integrative or distributive—in which they operate.

A number of negotiation scholars have thought about the factors that go into making the strategic choice between competitive and cooperative behaviours in a negotiation. Among them, Donald Gifford proposes a contextual approach that is perhaps the most persuasive. Gifford suggests that a negotiator should consider several factors when choosing a negotiation strategy, including the following:

- the opponent's negotiation strategy
- relative bargaining power
- future dealings with the opponent
- the attitude of the negotiator's client
- pressure to reach agreement
- the stage of the negotiation
- the negotiator's personality
- negotiation norms[13]

As part of the pre-negotiation planning process, not only will you select your opening framework for approaching the available value in your negotiation, but also you will likely focus on how best to achieve the goals of that framework (that is, the generation or the distribution of value) through the selection of behavioural tactics. Many factors will influence the latter, as noted above, and you may end up utilizing a combination of tactics in a contextual, customized strategy that is responsive to your relative strengths and weaknesses, your own personal comfort zone, expected "rules of the game" in your given situation, the positions and approaches of your opponent, and other key drivers.

Keep in mind that there are a number of misconceptions related to tactics. Although competitive tactics are commonly associated with a distributive bargaining approach to claiming value, that need not be the case. Further, negotiators who use competitive tactics

---

12   It should be noted that, depending on the writer, the concepts of *cooperative* and *collaborative* techniques are presented as either distinct or interchangeable. There appears to be a pervasive inconsistency in the literature that resists clarification.

13   D. Gifford, "A Context-Based Theory of Strategy Selection in Legal Negotiation" (1985) 46 Ohio St. L.J. 41 at 58-71.

are almost always characterized as aggressive, hostile, and overbearing. Conversely, negotiators who use cooperative/collaborative tactics are almost always characterized as flexible, friendly, and polite. These portrayals are misleading. One of the most effective approaches to a distributive framework, wherein a negotiator focuses on claiming value for his client, is to adopt a friendly, outgoing, and agreeable persona. Doing this is so counterintuitive to the "hard bargainer" commonly cast in distributive scenarios that it can serve to disarm an opponent and provide a certain complacency in response. It is critical, therefore, to be clear about terminology and to maintain appropriate conceptual distinctions among these levels of abstraction.

Final Considerations

We propose a theory of strategic negotiation that urges the reflective negotiator to plan her approach to a given negotiation based primarily on an assessment of its value climate. According to this model, the negotiator's approach depends on whether opportunities exist to create value in addition to those obvious and visible resources available to satisfy the parties' needs.

It is important to note that, for ease of understanding, we have intentionally dichotomized the distinction between value climates that trigger the use of an integrative framework and those that trigger the use of a distributive framework. While many negotiations we engage in will fall easily into one category or the other, it must be stressed that many negotiations will not. For example, it is very common to face a negotiation where some issues are situated in a value climate that is rich with opportunities to generate additional resources through an integrative approach. In that same negotiation, other issues (or aspects of issues) may be situated in a value climate that is severely limited and defined by its incapacity to provide sufficient resources to satisfy all parties' needs.

A skilled negotiator is able to move fluidly between these two frameworks, using an integrative framework to create value for one issue and then switching to a distributive framework when a limited value climate surrounds the next issue. Such moves are made strategically, so that value is both optimized and maximized before it is ultimately claimed.

The following chapter presents a step-by-step approach to negotiation that views the value climate as the primary predictor of a negotiation strategy.

Notes and Questions

1. Do you agree that value climate is the key factor for a reflective negotiator to consider when planning how to approach a given negotiation? Explain.
2. The value climate typically considered in a negotiation is the *client's* value climate. What if the negotiation climate of a negotiator also engages the values of a third party (potentially a public-interest party) who is not at the table? Should those values form part of the negotiation's value climate? For more information on the professional obligations of the negotiator, see chapter 2.

Selected Further Reading

R. Axelrod, "Effective Choice in the Prisoner's Dilemma" (1980) 24 J. Conflict Resolution 3.

R. Axelrod, "More Effective Choice in the Prisoner's Dilemma" (1980) 24 J. Conflict Resolution 379.

T. Barton, "Creative Problem Solving: Purpose, Meaning and Values" (1998) 34 Cal. W.L. Rev. 273.

J. Bendor *et al.*, "When in Doubt: Cooperation in a Noisy Prisoner's Dilemma" (1991) 35 J. Conflict Resolution 691.

J. Cohen, "When People Are the Means: Negotiating with Respect" (2001) 14 Geo. J. Legal Ethics 739.

R. Condlin, "Cases on Both Sides: Patterns of Argument in Legal Dispute Negotiation" (1985) 44 Md. L. Rev. 65.

R. Friedman, "Missing Ingredients in Mutual Gains Bargaining: Are They Mutually Exclusive?" (1994) 10 Negotiation Journal 243.

H. Gardner, *Changing Minds: The Art and Science of Changing Our Own and Other Peoples' Minds* (Cambridge, MA: Harvard Business School Press, 2004).

D. Gifford, "The Synthesis of Legal Counselling and Negotiation Models: Preserving Client-Centered Advocacy in the Negotiation Context" (1987) 34 UCLA L. Rev. 811.

G. Goodpaster, "Rational Decision-Making in Problem Solving Negotiation: Compromise, Interest-Valuation and Cognitive Error" (1993) 8 Ohio St. J. Disp. Resol. 299.

R. Mnookin, "Why Negotiations Fail: An Exploration of Barriers to the Resolution of Conflict" (1993) 8 Ohio St. J. Disp. Resol. 235.

L. Morton, "Teaching Creative Problem Solving: A Paradigmatic Approach" (1997) 34 Cal. W.L. Rev. 375.

S. Salent & T. Sims, "Game Theory and the Law: Ready for Prime Time?" (1996) 94 Mich. L. Rev. 1839.

CHAPTER 4

Strategic Negotiation: Moving Through the Stages

Colleen M. Hanycz

Introduction

In this chapter, we continue our consideration of strategic negotiation with a model that outlines the key phases in a typical process. Certainly the order, timing, and nature of the phases in a negotiation depend upon the facts of the situation, the negotiators, professional and ethical considerations, and a variety of other factors. Nonetheless, it is valuable to understand how a negotiation is likely to evolve and to consider the different strategic choices that can be made in order to optimize a client's outcomes.

A staged model of strategic negotiation might imply that the process unfolds in a straight line, through a series of phases until, it is hoped, a satisfy-

ing agreement is reached. However, such linearity is simply not accurate when speaking about most negotiations. Rather, negotiation at its best is far more complex and responsive to shifting internal and external contexts. It would be more accurate, in fact, to say that many negotiations proceed like a hermit crab—they take a bold step forward, followed by a slight shuffle to the side or even a slide backwards before another step forward. Often, it is best to allow a negotiation to steep—to reveal itself—gently, providing plenty of opportunities to respond effectively to new information as it emerges, even if a response requires temporarily halting the forward motion in order to return to an earlier stage in the process.

How can we explain the tendency of a negotiation trajectory to evolve in this way: stepping forward, then back? In the pages that follow, we will return to this phenomenon and ultimately underline that strategic negotiation requires a near-constant review of emerging information to shift between integrative and distributive frameworks when necessary to optimize outcomes. For example, a negotiator who adopts a distributive framework based upon her initial diagnosis of a scarcity of resources must be willing to pause in claiming value should new information arise that suggests additional resources may be generated in the negotiation. Instead of pushing forward, that negotiator should cycle back to a phase in the process that would permit a robust investigation of these emergent resources, and the options they reveal, before returning to claiming value. It is the ability to revisit earlier stages in a negotiation as needed that distinguishes the most effective negotiators. Only by doing so can value truly be maximized and claimed in a way that best serves a client's objectives.

Overview: A Model of Strategic Negotiation

Notwithstanding the comments above, negotiations often develop in patterns that reveal specific and distinct phases (or stages).[1] In terms of how these phases are defined and articulated, a number of scholars have suggested different frameworks. Roy Lewicki, Bruce Barry, and David Saunders, for example, propose the following staged model of negotiation, based on Leonard Greenhalgh's work on integrative negotiation:

Preparation: deciding what is important, defining goals, thinking ahead how to work together with the other party.

Relationship Building: getting to know the other party, understanding how you and the other are similar and different, and building commitment toward achieving a mutually beneficial set of outcomes. Greenhalgh argues that this stage is extremely critical to satisfactorily moving the other stages forward.

Information Gathering: learning what you need to know about the issues, about the other party and their needs, about the feasibility of possible settlements, and about what might happen if you fail to reach agreement with the other side.

Information Using: at this stage, negotiators assemble the case they want to make for their preferred outcomes and settlement, one that will maximize the negotiator's own needs. The presentation is often used to "sell" the negotiator's preferred outcome to the other.

Bidding: the process of making moves from one's initial, ideal position to the actual outcome. Bidding is the process by which each party states their "opening offer" and then makes moves in that offer toward a middle ground.

Closing the Deal: the objective of this stage is to build commitment to the agreement achieved in the previous phase. Both the negotiator and the other party have to assure themselves that they reached a deal they can be happy with, or at least accept.

Implementing the Agreement: determining who needs to do what once the agreement is reached. It is not uncommon for parties to discover that the agreement is flawed, that key points were

---

1   D. Lax & J. Sebenius, *The Manager as Negotiator: Bargaining for Cooperation and Competitive Gain* (New York: Free Press, 1986) [Lax & Sebenius, *The Manager as Negotiator*].

missed, or that the situation has changed and new questions exist. Flaws in moving through the earlier phases arise here, and the deal may have to be re-opened or issues settled by mediators, arbitrators or the courts.[2]

It is important to recognize that there are a variety of negotiation models proposed in the literature, and each of these models aligns with a unique theoretical approach to strategic negotiation. The staged model of strategic negotiation we propose here flows from the resource-based approach to negotiation outlined in chapter 3. It suggests a general path that can be adopted in order to move through the negotiation. Keep in mind, however, that in every phase of a negotiation, negotiators must be flexible and adapt to environmental and relational changes that may lead them back to earlier phases.

Phase I: Pre-negotiation Planning

If you are entering a three-day negotiation scheduled to begin on Tuesday, which day is the most important? Some would say that the opening day, Tuesday, is critical as you establish yourself in the eyes of the negotiator on the other side of the table. Some would say Wednesday, day two, is perhaps more important as you will be, by then, into the heavy lifting of the negotiation, moving back and forth between issues in an effort to seek resolution. I have often urged my students to consider the possibility that Monday and, to a lesser extent, Friday may actually be the two most important days of your Tuesday to Thursday negotiation.

When we think of pre-planning as a staple of effective negotiation, it is easy to see how strategic practice extends far beyond the confines of the time actually spent "at the table." Rather, the activities that occur before and after the negotiation often lay the groundwork for maximizing your client's objectives in a representative negotiation. And, to be sure, it is only through the effective planning and implementation of your negotiation goals that they can be fully realized.

Reservation Points and the Zone of Agreement

How does the pre-negotiation planning phase inform a negotiator's strategy going into a negotiation? We have already considered the importance of accurately diagnosing the "value climate" of a particular negotiation (see chapter 3); that is, determining whether the situation is characterized by scarce or adequate resources to meet the needs of the respective negotiating parties. Throughout each phase of a negotiation, identifying an opportunity to generate (or to *reveal*) additional value should persuade the negotiator to adopt the appropriate strategic approach. But that is not the only factor that impacts strategy.

---

2   R. Lewicki, B. Barry & D. Saunders, *Essentials of Negotiation*, 4th ed. (New York: McGraw-Hill Irwin, 2007) at 93-94. For a different approach, see the steps suggested in B. Patton, "Negotiation" in M. Moffitt & R. Bordone, eds., *The Handbook of Dispute Resolution* (San Francisco: Jossey Bass, 2005) at 287.

Reservation Points and Target Points

In addition to the value climate of a given negotiation, the representative negotiator must also develop with her client an initial *reservation point* (also called *resistance point, reservation price, minimum disposition,* or *RP*) prior to negotiation. Your client's RP is arguably the most important strategic decision to emerge from pre-negotiation planning. If your client's "blue sky" estimation of the best outcome of negotiation can be called the *target point,* then the reservation point is thought of as the walkaway package, or the least favourable agreement that your client could accept before abandoning the negotiation in favour of a better alternative. For a vendor, the RP is the lowest price that he will take for an item. For a buyer, it is the highest price she will pay. One penny less than the RP will not be acceptable to a vendor and the buyer will not pay one penny over her RP.

Certainly, all negotiators aim for results that are better than their RPs, but it is crucial to be aware of your client's minimum disposition when framing a strategic approach. According to Donald Gifford, among other strategic benefits, determining an RP prior to the negotiation helps prevent both the negotiator and her client "from being swept away during the negotiation process," noting that "without an explicit minimum disposition, a lawyer occasionally accepts a bad deal for her client because she becomes anxious or is persuaded by the other party's assertions during bargaining."[3]

Thinking Inside the Box …

The relative independence of reservation points in a negotiation varies. RPs can be either completely inflexible, existing independently of any other factors, or, alternatively, RPs can be reactive and responsive, shifting in accordance with changing environmental forces in the negotiation.

Imagine a situation where your Ottawa client is trying to sell her house for which she paid $400,000 two years ago. As you attempt to set her reservation point before a bargaining round with a prospective buyer, you consider a number of factors in arriving at the absolute lowest price she would take for her house. Your research into market value (objective criteria) tells you that the house is roughly worth $440,000 at this time. Your client informs you that she has tried unsuccessfully to sell the house three times over the past year and that she is moving "home" to St. John's to be with her ailing mother at the end of the month. She also reveals that she has had some issues with her roof and furnace, both of which will need to be replaced (at a cost of $30,000) before next winter.

Weighing all of these and other factors, you might recommend an initial RP of $400,000 at the outset, subject to modification as new information emerges during the negotiation. Your client tells you that while she would like to get as much money from the house sale as possible, she will be able to buy a comparable property in St. John's

---

3   D. Gifford, *Legal Negotiation: Theory and Application* (St. Paul, MN: Thomson West, 1989) at 50.

for $275,000, so she would accept $400,000 at this point in order to have a sale in hand before she leaves Ottawa. Again, depending on new information that might be revealed by the prospective buyer, this number could change.

Compare this situation with a scenario where the same client is trying to sell the same house and has two prospective buyers. Buyer #1 has offered $480,000 to purchase the house, and you are now planning a meeting with Buyer #2 to hear his offer. In this case, your client's reservation point is generally much easier to fix. Even if all of the available information is the same as described above, the fact that you have an open offer of $480,000 "in your pocket" will have a direct influence on the RP. Unless there are other significant intangibles affecting the RP such as your client strongly preferring Buyer #2 for other reasons, etc., then the RP in this scenario would likely be set, firmly, at $480,000.01. Anything "less" than that would not result in an agreement as your client already has another firm offer to accept.

Of course, these are simplified examples as there are often other variables, even in the most straightforward real estate deal, that will impact the attractiveness of different offers. Anything from proposed closing dates to the ownership of various fixtures in the house to whether or not the sale has any prerequisite conditions that must be fulfilled will all affect the ultimate value of the offered purchase price to a prospective vendor. That said, when there is a firm offer, even if it fails to correspond with available objective criteria such as market value indicators, it will usually have a significant effect upon fixing the reservation point.

Representative negotiators must appreciate that the RP should reflect more than simply what a client *desires* or what he *believes* to be the value of the item that he is selling. While one of the most difficult tasks is convincing a client that his view of his item's worth is not realistic, it is crucial to engage in that task before approaching the negotiation table. As we will discuss below, if a client's RP going into a negotiation is to be considered "strategic," then it must be principled in that it must be informed by the consideration of a variety of factors other than what that client wants to achieve. That said, there are times when a client will simply say to you, "I'm willing to sell my house *if I can get $300,000 for it*. Otherwise, I won't sell." This RP may be disconnected from any rational standards but is nevertheless your client's walkaway price.

Why do we need to fix a client's RP prior to commencing a negotiation? Once you have diagnosed your client's RP and the initial value climate of the negotiation, you can then start to build a strategic approach that will lead to the maximization of your client's objectives. As always, being flexible and willing to revisit these assessments in the face of new or better information is key to implementing this strategy effectively.

Zone of Agreement

A negotiator must consider all of the factors that influence his client's and the opposing party's strategies in a negotiation. As such, a negotiator must consider the RP of his client *and the RP of the opposing party in the negotiation.* What do you think is the absolute most money that the prospective buyer will pay for your client's house? As any real estate agent will tell you, this number may or may not be aligned with available objective criteria, as purchasing a new home is often an exercise involving equal parts rationality and emotion. You might try to determine if the prospective buyer has made offers on other similar properties in the neighbourhood and in what amount. You might try to determine the available funds of that buyer to be spent on a home. If the prospective buyer is listing his current home for sale, you might glean some information from determining the listed price for that property. All of these facts might provide insight into his target and RPs.

Why is it crucial for a negotiator to identify the respective RPs of both her client *and* the other parties in the negotiation? Simply put, the crucial calculation is the way in which these RPs combine to establish the parameters of a *zone of agreement* for the negotiation. When you plot the respective RPs along a continuum, the existence or absence of an overlapped area—a zone of agreement—is central to negotiation strategy. If you have accurately assessed the RPs of both parties and they do not overlap, then the likelihood of agreement is minimal. For example, let's say your client is unable to accept anything less than $400,000 for the sale of her house and the prospective buyer cannot spend one penny more than $380,000. There is no zone of agreement here and, in the absence of any potential expansion of the pie to create or reveal additional value, agreement is very unlikely.

But, if those RPs are reversed, then the zone of agreement as the distance between the vendor's absolute lowest price ($380,000) and the buyer's absolute highest price (in this reversed RP scenario, $400,000), is equal to the $20,000. As you will learn through experience, the zone of agreement for a negotiation is constantly under construction, as party representatives spend much of the negotiation itself attempting to identify, revise, and confirm its shifting parameters. Ideally, a negotiator will achieve an agreement that is as close to the other side's RP as possible, while recognizing that the opposing negotiator is seeking the same result.

Below we suggest a variety of pieces in the planning puzzle that should be considered in establishing an acceptable RP with your client. Did you notice that we didn't say a *terrific* RP or an RP that makes your client *very happy*? Generally speaking, achieving your client's RP in a negotiation tends to fall outside of the range of outcomes that will leave you with a "happy" client, but it always falls within those outcomes that your client can live with.

Although a good representative negotiator never aims for the RP as a strategy, he knows what the RP is so that his strategy can be continually informed by it as the negotiation evolves. In the case of a lawyer negotiator, as with certain other representatives (especially in an extended negotiation) a representative should repeatedly review the emerging information with the client in order to arrive at a revised RP that remains acceptable to the client.

Connecting the Zone of Agreement to the Value Climate

Before thinking about the various factors that should influence your initial assessment of the RPs of both your client and the opposing party, let us consider how the zone of agreement—the overlap between the opposing RPs—impacts strategy. If, as in the first example, there appears to be no zone of agreement, does that mean that negotiating is a waste of time, in the absence of any settlement potential? No. Rather, the impact of the zone of agreement that you have evaluated will depend upon your assessment of the current value climate. Let's look a little more closely at that connection.

If you have determined that the value climate is without opportunities to generate or uncover additional value, then clearly this non-existent zone of agreement is quite limiting. Moreover, if this is simply a one-off negotiation focused on one resource (usually money), then it is very unlikely that a reasonable potential for agreement exists if a zone of agreement is absent. A negotiation with a value climate characterized by scarcity demands a distributive framework.

If, however, you have determined that the value climate does have opportunities to create additional value—and if this negotiation is not *purely* about price—then an apparent lack of a zone of agreement is not, in itself, fatal. Imagine a situation where the vendor cannot or will not accept less than $400,000 for the sale of her home and the buyer cannot or will not pay more than $380,000 for the purchase of her home, *but* there appears to be other non-price value that might be added to create a zone of agreement. Perhaps it is very valuable to the vendor that the buyer is willing to purchase some of the furniture in the home in addition to the home itself. Perhaps the buyer would be willing to take possession of the home immediately, something that would reduce the vendor's financing costs, freeing up more monetary resources to lower her RP. Perhaps the vendor, through her business, is willing to enter into a lucrative contract with the buyer's advertising firm, ancillary to the house deal. Suddenly, as a direct result of your assessment of the value climate, you have created additional value that, when added to the mix, serves to generate a zone of agreement.

Even in the most discouraging situations where there appears to be a huge chasm between the respective RPs of two negotiation parties, there may be additional value that, when generated or identified, will serve to bridge that gap and create a zone of agreement where none existed before. This is the way in which your assessment of the value climate of a given negotiation can dramatically impact the various elements that, together, form your strategy. It further illustrates how an effective negotiator often moves from *identifying* an unfavourable opposing RP into *manipulating* that party toward shifting the RP into something that favours a zone of agreement.

As noted at the outset, flexibility is key to the strategic negotiation process. Whether you are considering the value climate of your negotiation or assessing factors such as RPs, it is best to assume a responsive stance and continually integrate new information into your evolving strategy. Roger Fisher and William Ury speak, for example, of avoiding setting a "bottom line" before entering a negotiation for several reasons: (a) it limits your ability to benefit from what you learn during the negotiation; (b) its rigidity "inhibits imagination" by reducing the incentive to invent a creative, interest-based solution; and (c) it is likely to be set too favourably, as it is subjective and, often, arbitrary.[4]

While the risks proposed by Fisher and Ury are accurate, they can be countered by being flexible and carefully gathering all available information before determining the initial RP. So, for example, your assessment of a client's negotiation RP, evaluated in the pre-negotiation phase, may be very different from the assessment of her RP closer to or during the negotiation

---

4   R. Fisher & W. Ury, *Getting to Yes: Negotiating Agreement Without Giving In,* 2d ed. (New York: Penguin Books, 1991) at 98-99.

itself if new information is revealed. Rather than see our client's RP as something immovable and, therefore, potentially limiting as indicated by Fisher and Ury, we must instead develop an ability to integrate new information into our analysis of it and reformulate it and, hence, our strategic approach to the negotiation. This integration and reformulation often occurs throughout the pre-negotiation and negotiation stages, as the process evolves and new information emerges.

We review the factors that critically influence a negotiator's assessment of reservation points below.

Gathering Information and Drafting the Issues

One of the first steps in negotiation planning is to begin to frame your client's negotiation "story." What information do you have and, within that bundle of information, how much of it could be labelled as "facts"? What issues arise from this story and what, exactly, are your client's positions and interests pertaining to those issues? If your client seems to have assumed an unsupported position surrounding, for example, the value of her property, what other factors—besides market value—are prompting her to set its value so high? If your client is trying to sell the family farm that her grandparents and parents were raised in, she may be importing into her assessment of its value a variety of subjective factors that may not be supportable. Similarly, if your client has outstanding debts in excess of $450,000 that she needs to cover through the sale of her home, again her RP of $450,000 may not be viable if the market value for her property is $200,000.

The process of gathering facts and information and identifying any existing information gaps can be extremely challenging in that it may require some difficult "reality checking" with your client as you move toward establishing a reasonable RP. Certainly, the complexity of this process multiplies as you attempt to sketch the story of the opposing party in the negotiation. How does the prospective buyer of your client's property see this situation? Why does he want to buy this property? Is there some sort of subjective connection to this property that may serve to leverage his initial RP to some level beyond that which might be established by objective criteria? What are his needs and aspirations going into the negotiation? What are his target points for the negotiation?

Gathering facts and information respecting your client and the opposing party often results in a map that includes some small pieces of information separated by huge gaps of missing information. However, identifying those gaps is equally important to collecting the available information as information and non-information will have a significant impact upon both establishing a tentative RP for the opposing party and shaping your own strategy. It is not sufficient, however, simply to acknowledge that you don't have "all the facts"; rather, you must identify the exact facts that you are missing as you move toward the bargaining round of the negotiation process. As we will see shortly, the opening information gathering phase of a negotiation is among the most crucial stages of this process in that it has the greatest potential either to confirm or to dramatically modify your initial strategic analyses.

What do you do with the issues that emerge from the information gathered? Sometimes a negotiation may be framed around a single issue such as the acceptable selling price for a specific item. As noted by Lewicki, Barry, and Saunders, single-issue negotiations often dictate a distributive framework "because the only real negotiation issue is the price or 'distribution' of that issue."[5] By contrast, multi-issue negotiations may allow for creatively "packaged" solutions in an integrative framework that benefit all parties. In even the most unambiguous case of a single-issue negotiation, effective negotiators attempt to create additional value, often even in the absence of issues that might be satisfied by such value.

When someone offers to buy a residential property, in addition to the amount of money to be paid, that offer may also include added "value" to address other potential issues such as a willingness to be flexible around the closing date, the availability of different forms of financing, or the agreement to purchase various pieces of furniture that might be cumbersome to move. Sometimes anticipating—and addressing—potential issues that the opposing party might have in what appears to be a single-issue negotiation can move parties some distance toward reaching an agreement.

Whatever your initial information tells you about existing issues, the pre-negotiation planning process should include generating a well-developed list of your client's issues as well as a tentative list of what you think to be her opponent's issues. In negotiations that are centred on the resolution of an existing dispute especially, these lists may be easy to compose, relying upon the already framed issues of the dispute. Other times, these lists will be quite sketchy at this stage of the process, subject to plenty of modification once some of the information gaps have been filled.

Once the lists are completed, the issues should be prioritized in an early attempt to think about packaged solutions. There is a strong connection between this exercise and the formulation of a strategic negotiation plan.

Objective Criteria

Objective criteria represent one of the key factors that should inform the initial RP. Objective criteria are pieces of evidence that are external to and independent of the negotiation at hand, separate from the respective desires and beliefs of the negotiating parties. These pieces of evidence serve to bolster the position assumed by a party (and her negotiator) in a way that is perceived by the opposing party as being non-partisan and credible. Surely the most common objective criteria in transactional negotiations are market value indicators surrounding the item being negotiated. If you approach your client's real estate negotiation armed with information that an identically designed house beside hers sold for $400,000 six months ago, and the same type of house one street over sold for $410,000 last year, chances are your argument that your client's house is worth $400,000 will be perceived as more credible by the opposing party. In theory, the objective criteria supporting a value claim are notionally "indisputable." Nonetheless, but perhaps not surprisingly, representative negotiators often devote an unseemly amount of time and energy debating the validity—the objectivity—of objective criteria used by their opponents. As part of the pre-negotiation planning process intended to identify the RPs of the respective participants and, consequently, to reveal the zone of agreement of the negotiation, finding truly objective criteria to support your client's position (and RP) can be invaluable.

---

5   Lewicki, Barry & Saunders, *supra* note 2 at 96.

Thinking Inside the Box ...

Throughout *Getting to Yes*, Fisher and Ury emphasize the central importance of using objective criteria to support your approach in a principled negotiation. By consistently locating your arguments within the context of objective criteria—and by insisting that your negotiating opponent do the same—the more likely you are to achieve an agreement that reflects the values, interests, and entitlements of all parties and that promises to endure during the post-negotiation implementation phase.

If we look at objective criteria as a foundation for negotiating principled agreements that exist *independent of* the desires of the negotiating parties, think of scenarios in which each of the following could be identified as "independent standards"—objective criteria that might form the basis of a lasting agreement:

- market value
- legal precedent
- family traditions
- professional standards
- industry practices
- religious rules of observance
- medical opinion
- estimated cost of replacement
- laboratory report
- shared moral standards

Now think of ways in which each of the objective criteria listed above could be "challenged" by an opposing negotiator who wished to avoid the result or outcome dictated by the criterion. For example, in trying to negotiate your client's purchase of a vintage motorcycle for a price below $50,000, the vendor's lawyer presents you with three indicators of market value (the original bill of sale for the bike, newspaper listings for similar bikes, and the standard "blue book" value of the bike) that suggest the motorcycle to be worth roughly $75,000. How might you avoid or distinguish these objective criteria being used to dictate the vendor's reservation point and move that RP back into range with the objectives of your client (that is, encourage the vendor to sell the bike for $50,000 despite this evidence of market value)?

At this stage of the pre-negotiation planning process, what value is there in considering the objective criteria of the opposing party? If you are able to discover the objective criteria the opposing party and negotiator will rely on to support their position, you have one piece of information that may help you estimate your opponent's RP. After all, often one of the goals of negotiation is to achieve an agreement that is located as close as possible to the opposing RP without forcing a collapse of the negotiation by going beyond that point. If you are aware of objective criteria (case law, market value indicators, other offers the opposing party is holding, etc.), not only can you consider ways to distinguish and disarm the impact of this criteria, but you will be able to move toward an appreciation of your opponent's RP. Gradually, a zone of agreement will begin to take shape in your strategy.

GENERAL AND SPECIFIC OBJECTIVE CRITERIA

Objective criteria are regarded as either *general* or *specific*. *General objective criteria* are pieces of evidence that are widely available and indirectly support a party's position on one or more of the matters at issue in the negotiation. For example, we might be able to uncover legal precedent dealing with similar facts or market value indicators for items or property similar to the items or property under negotiation. The main advantage of general objective criteria is that they are more widely available and accessible when we are planning our negotiation strategy. That said, while this type of evidence can be helpful in bolstering our position, it is often vulnerable to attack by our opponent on the basis of its unspecific applicability to the matters at issue in our negotiation. In other words, the general nature of this type of objective criteria opens it up to attempts by an opponent to challenge its use, arguably making it less "objective."

Lawyers who engage in dispute resolution regularly rely upon judicial precedent to argue in support of a client's position, although a good advocate is equally adept at deflecting and distinguishing the same precedent if its application would result in an unfavourable outcome for his client. The downside of general objective criteria is that it may generate such diverse arguments surrounding its utility and applicability as to virtually remove its ability to stand as objective. If you think a specific objective criterion that you hope to use will be challenged, it might be better to abandon it in search of something better armed against claims of *un*objectivity or inapplicability.

Specific objective criteria include evidence that directly supports a party's position in a negotiation. For example, if you enter into a negotiation trying to sell your home and you have already received one open offer for its purchase, this offer may be used as a specific objective criterion supporting your claim of the property's value (assuming that the claim aligns with the terms of the offer). Or, if a certified appraiser conducted a value appraisal of your home, assuming that the appraiser's independence was not called into question, the resulting appraisal would be a specific criterion supporting your claims around value. While specific objective criteria may be more difficult to obtain, they tend to be more immune to being discredited by the other party in a negotiation typically because no argument can be made about their inapplicability to the matters directly at issue. The fact is that these pieces of evidence are based explicitly on the matters at issue, so the only question becomes whether or not the target points and RPs that they support serve to create a zone of agreement for the negotiation.

Identifying objective criteria for the parties in a negotiation at the planning stage is only the first step in using this important information. Once the negotiation begins, framing the issues and their potential solutions in terms of mutually acceptable standards—or, objective criteria—leads parties to a solution that is principled and enduring. It may be helpful to think of objective criteria as solid guideposts in the otherwise shifting sands of a negotiation. Effective negotiators certainly use their skills to enhance the impact of favourable criteria, while attempting to diminish the effects of objective criteria that are unfavourable to their client's position. The more a piece of evidence can withstand these competing tugs, the more it approaches the status of a truly objective criterion.

Alternatives

While sometimes painstaking, every moment spent at the task of pre-negotiation planning will further ensure enhanced outcomes for your client during the bargaining round. Before being able to assess a client's RP or that of the opposing party, a negotiator must have considered her client's alternatives to a negotiated agreement. Knowing what will happen if you don't reach an agreement will have a profound impact on establishing an RP that is both viable and as close to the target points as possible.

Imagine a situation where a client's inability to sell his house in the next 30 days will trigger the bank's foreclosing on his mortgage. While that fact does not directly impact available objective criteria that would suggest a market value for the property and thereby inform the RP, it should nonetheless direct your strategic approach to the negotiation. Assuming that losing the house to foreclosure would be an undesirable alternative to a negotiated agreement for your client, the initial RP that you set might be less favourable than if there was no risk of foreclosure. Conversely, if your client has already received one favourable offer for his property from someone else, that offer serves to frame his "alternative" to reaching an agreement in the upcoming negotiation and will directly affect his initial reservation point, notwithstanding objective criteria that suggest a lower price.

One of the common terms of art used by negotiators when looking at alternatives is "BATNA," or best alternative to a negotiated agreement. Fisher and Ury refer to BATNA as "the measure for agreements that will protect you against both accepting an agreement that you should reject and rejecting an agreement that you should accept."[6] The entire objective of entering into a given negotiation is to achieve a set of outcomes that is *better* than those that you would achieve without the negotiation. As such, establishing your initial RP and planning your resulting negotiation strategy must always include a consideration of what you could achieve if you didn't enter this negotiation.

Fisher and Ury identify BATNA as a better strategic measure for a negotiation than RP, simply due to the relative flexibility of BATNA and its responsiveness to new information. Perhaps this assessment stems from a view of RP as fixed and rigid. Clearly it would be better to look at RP—the key indicator in a negotiation—as something with an ongoing capacity to integrate all available information (alternatives, objective criteria, etc.) and the ability to respond to emergent information as the negotiation unfolds. Only in this way can your ultimate strategic assessment of the value climate of your negotiation be responsive and effective in optimizing your client's results.

Equally important to considering your own alternatives to a negotiation is considering the alternatives held by your opponent. If your client is a major league sports franchise embarking on a contract negotiation with a potential player and you are aware that the potential player has already been offered a position by another team, this will assist you in speculating his BATNA and, therefore, his RP going into your negotiation. Again, you must be aware that there are usually gaps—often significant—in your information about the other side's position, and filling in those gaps is an ongoing task.

That said, knowing that the potential new player has an open contract offer with another franchise carries you some distance to speculating about his initial position, and his target

---

6   Fisher & Ury, *supra* note 4 at 99.

and reservation points. What you may not know, in trying to formulate his BATNA, is that he does not want to play for that team, because he is reluctant to move his young family so far away from extended family *and* he has heard poor things about the management of that franchise. Or, he grew up in your client's city and has had a dream since boyhood about playing for that team. All of these may serve to impact his assessment of his own alternatives, and his RP, in ways unknown to you until you begin to ask questions in the actual negotiation.

Something else to be aware of when evaluating your alternatives is the inherent tendency of negotiators to inflate the attractiveness of their alternatives. David Lax and James Sebenius recount the following experiment, conducted at Harvard (and replicated broadly):

> [P]layers were given detailed information about the history of an out-of-court negotiation over insurance claims arising from a personal injury case. They were not told whether the negotiators settled or if the case went to court. Each player was assigned to the role of either the plaintiff or the insurance company defendant. After reading the case file, the players were privately asked to give their true probability estimates that the plaintiff would win the case and, given the win, the expected amount of the ultimate judgment. Systematically, those assigned to the role of the plaintiff estimated the chances and the expected amount of winning as much higher than those assigned to the role of the insurance company defendant. Players who were not assigned a role prior to reading the case gave private estimates that generally fell between those of the advocates for each position.[7]

The process of evaluating alternatives should be characterized by realistic, non-adversarial objectivity, to the extent that such an approach is ever possible. One possible result of coupling an overestimation of one's alternatives with an underestimation of an opponent's alternatives is the *apparent* absence of a zone of agreement. This is especially unfortunate in those situations where a healthy zone of agreement exists and would have been uncovered if an accurate assessment of respective alternatives and resulting RPs had been made.

A significant measure of uncertainty is involved in determining alternatives, both your own and, to a larger degree, those of your opponent. It is also possible that evaluating the alternatives of the parties to a negotiation will lead to the conclusion that the potential outcomes of a particular negotiation are likely certainly inferior to the available alternatives. If this conclusion withstands the addition of other factors that might not be currently under consideration—such as the impact on the relationship between the parties—then it remains to a representative negotiator to recommend the alternatives over the process at hand.

Opportunities to Create Value?

Throughout the pre-negotiation planning process, the representative negotiator should be alert to emerging opportunities to create value. Again, we think of value as existing or potential resources that could serve to meet the interests and needs of one or more parties to a negotiation. Of particular interest in the negotiation planning process is identifying

---

7 D. Lax & J. Sebenius, "The Power of Alternatives of the Limits to Negotiation" (1985) 1 Negotiation Journal 163 at 169.

value that might enhance your client's outcomes. Paradoxically, this is often achieved by finding value that appears to favour the interests of your opponent, at least at first glance. If you can identify some item of value to the opposing party that either didn't exist previously or was somehow hidden, that item may become the centrepiece that moves the opponent's RP either into the zone of agreement, a position within the zone of agreement that is more favourable than your client's RP, or right to your client's target point.

One of the most important tasks at each stage of a negotiation is to review and reconsider opportunities to create value. In doing so, you may find that your perception of the value climate of the negotiation has shifted from one of scarce resources to one of more abundant resources that will allow all parties to achieve their interests and positions. That shift often follows the identification of new value that is critical in informing your strategy. As noted in chapter 3, your perception of the value climate of your negotiation will determine whether you adopt an integrative or distributive framework, a choice that will structure almost every aspect of your strategic approach to the negotiation. Being aware of the necessity to continually revisit the suitability of the adopted framework and the possibility of moving from one framework to another is critical to maximizing your client's outcomes in a negotiation.

The first step in seeking opportunities to create value at the pre-negotiation planning stage is to develop some understanding of both the *positions* and the *interests* underlying those positions for the opposing party. If you think of a party's positions as *what* that party wants, and his interests as *why* he has adopted those positions, you are in the best possible place to identify additional value that could be implemented to meet those underlying interests with or without addressing the positions built upon them. By accurately identifying the interests that lie beneath a party's position, you can often find a corresponding value that satisfies those interests that might not otherwise have been proposed because it does not directly address the stated position.

Students of negotiation will be familiar with the Ugli Orange story used to illustrate the value of excavating interests from positions. In that scenario, told in various ways, we see two sisters bickering over one orange and asking their mother to intervene to settle their property dispute. The first child argues that the orange is rightfully hers because she is the oldest. The second child counters that the orange is actually hers because she asked for it first. If the mother charged with resolving this conflict does not excavate below these claims to reveal each child's *interests* in having the orange, she might analyze this as a value climate of scarce resources requiring a distributive framework. The likely outcome of compromise would be to divide, somehow, the orange between the children, giving each child somewhat less than what she originally asked for.

But, as the story goes, the clever mother who asks each child *why* she wants the orange—in other words, what her *interests* are in the orange—might learn that one child needs the orange peel for a school project, while the other wants only the juice to drink. That mother would then be in a situation to *create value* as she resolves the dispute by giving one child the entire peel and one child the entire juice of the orange. In this case, when working at the level of interests, we have revealed a value climate of abundant resources sufficient to satisfy all of the parties' respective interests.

By thinking of positions and interests in advance of the negotiation, often a negotiator can begin to identify possible avenues of "new" value to be explored during the negotiation to expand the pie to such a degree that her own client will be able to reach a level equal to or greater than her most favourable objectives. Sometimes the pie can be expanded by simply creating or revealing additional value that satisfies the opposing party's interests rather than taking away from your client's portion of the pie. Granted, much of this opportunity to create value will occur at the negotiation table rather than in advance, but it is certainly good practice to identify additional resources—perhaps to be used later as a concession that costs your client little or nothing—through careful planning.

At this point in your pre-negotiation planning, your strategy should begin to take shape. Depending on the information available to you, you may be able to pinpoint your client's initial reservation point and perhaps the RP of the opposing party as well. If you cannot set the RPs exactly, you could consider a range of tentative opposing RPs, each one contingent upon the way in which specific information gaps would fill during the negotiation.

Phase II: Opening the Bargaining Round

The better the pre-negotiation planning, the more smoothly this next phase is likely to unfold. Assuming that you have had advance access to a reasonable amount of information respecting both sides of the negotiation, you may well enter the actual negotiation with clear positions, targets, and even RPs in mind. On the other hand, you may be missing significant portions of the information necessary to accurately estimate the positions, interests, alternatives, and RPs of the other parties. In this case, you commence the bargaining round with the need to fill in some information gaps before the rest of your strategic evaluation can follow. Regardless, the energy expended planning your time "at the table" will make you less susceptible to surprise and, probably, more able to integrate new information into your strategy as it emerges.

Structural Protocol

We have focused extensively on negotiation planning as it pertains to the *substance* of the negotiation, but until now we have spent little time thinking about structural protocol—the *process* and *relational* aspects of negotiation. Often, the way in which a negotiation unfolds, procedurally, is a highly strategic matter that requires careful planning because it has a significant impact on the overall process and outcome of that negotiation.

A variety of concerns affect structural protocol. Further on in this book, you will read about cross-cultural considerations and the importance of being alert to the different cultural cues that we and the other parties give at the beginning of a negotiation (chapter 6). You will also read about the impact of power (chapter 7), gender (chapter 8), emotion (chapter 9), and communication (chapter 10) on negotiation processes and outcomes.

At this point, turn your mind to the idea of how you plan to open your negotiation. Will you greet the other parties and negotiators and spend some time in unrelated chit-chat at the beginning? Or will you enter the room abruptly, diving immediately into the substance of the negotiation? While these stances may appear automatic, your demeanour and personal approach is as much a matter for strategic planning and implementation as any other.

You should also consider the effect of the physical environment on the negotiation. Where will you conduct the negotiation? Is there an advantage to be gained—or lost—by negotiating on your "turf" or that of your opponent? Is there a time of day that would be strategically better for your client's interests in this negotiation, or do you want to use time in a different strategic manner, perhaps using artificial deadlines to increase pressure to settle? Where will everyone sit in the room—will all parties be at one table, or will there be a main table and a secondary table? Who will sit where? These physical aspects of the negotiation that seem so peripheral may have a significant effect once the bargaining is under way.[8]

There are no clear "best practices" regarding negotiation protocols. In some instances, structural protocol is dictated by the personality and other individual characteristics of the negotiators. In others, it is dictated by "rules of the game" that come from the context in which the negotiation is located. For example, it is widely known that certain Eastern cultures prefer to conduct business negotiations that include a very long introductory phase, often with extended social interaction between the negotiators, before the true substance of the negotiation can be raised. Knowing the structural protocol of your negotiation will help you plan your critical first impression "at the table."

Issue Agenda

Parties will often spend time establishing individual issues at the pre-negotiation planning stage and then revisit them collectively at the outset of the negotiation. Generally speaking, each negotiator arrives at the negotiation with his or her own set of issues, prioritized and often connected to specific options that resolve these issues and satisfy the positions and interests that underlie them. What remains to be done is to create a joint statement—or agenda—of issues to be considered during the negotiation.

There are many strategic aspects of the issue agenda that need to be considered. As a starting point, how many issues are too many issues to raise at the outset of the negotiation? Should you simply present your own issues as the agenda and expect the other side to follow along, or is it wiser to offer a joint issue agenda that strategically privileges your issues through the ordering of the agenda items? If you expect to move through the issues as ordered, is it better to handle the bigger issues first—the ones that threaten to scuttle the entire negotiation? Or, should you build momentum by achieving agreement on a series of smaller and less important issues? Clearly, making a list of issues is not the neutral "housekeeping" task that it might appear to be at first glance.

I often advise students that thorough and effective pre-negotiation planning may give them a slight advantage at the issue agenda stage. If you have gathered your information well and feel you are able to estimate the targets, alternatives, and RP of your opponent with some accuracy, then a good suggestion is to seize control of the negotiation from the start by presenting an issue agenda to the group to guide the negotiation. As Gary Goodpaster notes on this point,

> While this is often a useful technique to advance negotiations, it is also a powerful tactic because a document tends almost irresistibly to set the agenda and focus the parties, not only on particular issues, but also on a prescribed resolution for those issues. It is really a way to take the

---

8   Professional interests and obligations regarding negotiation tactics—discussed further in chapters 2 and 5—must always be kept in mind and must inform these planning considerations.

initiative in negotiations. The other party's choices include either working with the document, ignoring it, offering a counter-document, or using enormous self-discipline in dealing with the document for selective advantage.[9]

Supplying the issue agenda in a negotiation achieves two strategic advantages. First, it creates a road map that parties can use to frame the negotiation as it unfolds. We have observed countless negotiations that are not framed by an issue agenda get sidetracked or drift along without a sense of forward propulsion toward agreement. Second, it makes your issues and their order the "default." By using your issue agenda, you frame the negotiation in the way that suits your strategic objectives, and any movement away from this framing is unlikely. Rather, the other negotiators in the room may try to recast the issues in a way that favours their aspirations, but it is unlikely that they will be able to move the entire group away from this initial framework.

Keep in mind that if you have failed to adequately prepare for the negotiation and your suggested issue agenda does not fully reflect the issues of the negotiation, it will be discarded immediately as irrelevant. That is the worst-case scenario, so never try to grab control of the negotiation process unless you are adequately prepared and able to count on a high degree of support for your framing of the collective issues.

Filling in Information Gaps to Inform Strategy

It is likely that your pre-negotiation planning revealed a number of gaps in your information. As part of pre-negotiation planning, you will likely have identified all of the missing information on your side of the negotiation; that is, information that forms the basis of your opponent's strategy. Depending on the situation, you may also have been able to identify, at least speculatively, a good portion of the information that your opponent will *not* have about your case and will likely be looking for in the early moments of the bargaining round.

Some negotiators enter the room and dive into questions following a brief greeting. One of the suggestions that we stress when doing negotiation training is, instead, to start off with the issue agenda. Then, you can move into questions to fill in any gaps in your information. If you happen to be negotiating with an opponent who takes a similar tack, the "question period" may seem rather disjointed as each player tries to fill in the missing pieces of her own particular puzzle.

A lot of discussion in negotiation literature focuses on the benefits of using open-ended versus closed-ended questions in this stage of a negotiation. Choosing the most appropriate type of questions has always seemed rather intuitive; most likely, you will naturally gravitate toward the type of questions that will best fill in the information picture for you. Sometimes, open-ended questions—beginning with "Why," "What," "How," or "Explain"—are best, while other times more closed-ended questions are called for if you are seeking a very particular factual detail, such as, "The phone call on April 10th came at 7:00 pm?"

---

9   G. Goodpaster, "A Primer on Competitive Bargaining" (1996) J. Disp. Resol. 325 at 361.

If this stage of the bargaining round was simply about filling in information gaps, it would be rather straightforward. It has, however, a far more strategic function. As the facts in the negotiation are revealed, you must think about how each of them serves to shape the strategy that you have developed. If you have just learned, through questioning, that the vendor has already received another offer for her car in the amount of $12,000 and all of your pre-negotiation planning led you to develop an RP for your client of $10,000 in her attempt to

---

Thinking Inside the Box ...

One of the best outcomes of effective questioning early in the negotiation is discovering, or confirming, the interests underlying your opponent's positions on the various issues being negotiated. Sometimes these interests may be obvious and other times they may be hidden and take some extensive "excavation" to uncover.

John Lande suggests a set of questions that might help you reveal the interests that lie buried beneath an opponent's positions:

1. What do you want?
2. Why do you want that? (Be careful about your tone.)
3. How would [what you are asking for] help you? If you got that, how would you feel? (Use the identified feeling as the next level of interest and perhaps repeatedly probe for additional levels of interest below that.)
4. Why doesn't what [your client] is suggesting work for you?
5. In a dispute, people often don't get all that they want. What do you really need to be satisfied?
6. What do you need to get so that you can leave today feeling good (or okay) about the settlement or that you can at least live with?
7. It sounds as if what you are really most interested in is _____. Is that right?
8. Some people in your situation might be concerned about _____. Is that a concern for you?
9. What do you think are [your client's] underlying interests in this situation? Which of these interests do you share, if any? Is there a way you can think of that you can achieve your interests and also allow him/her to achieve his/hers?[10]

Negotiation literature refers interchangeably to the "interests" and "needs" of a party in a negotiation. Recognizing that a party has *needs* he wishes to satisfy may help to explain the way in which those needs serve to drive not only the positions that party adopts in a transaction or dispute, but also the various strategic approaches that are followed. Often, an understanding of the true bedrock needs is the first step in achieving a mutually satisfactory resolution or deal.

---

10   John Lande, "Questions to Help Identify Negotiators' Interests," online: University of Missouri School of Law <http://www.law.missouri.edu/lande/negotiatorsinterests.htm>.

purchase the car, this new fact necessarily impacts your strategy. If nothing else, you will need to seek better instructions from your client as to how she wishes to proceed—or not—in negotiating the purchase of the car.

If your bundle of missing information consists of details that will help you speculate on your opponent's strategic markers, there is another bundle of missing information you should seek during this stage of the bargaining. Perhaps more important to the overall strategic framework that you assume for the balance of this negotiation is whether you are able to confirm the existence, absence, and potential for additional value to satisfy the interests of all parties in the negotiation. As we discussed in chapter 3, one of the early accomplishments in an actual negotiation is to find out if there are additional resources with which to expand the pie. As with the first bundle of missing information, you fill in gaps regarding the value climate of the negotiation with effective questions and answers.

Let's revisit our house sale scenario. Your client wishes to sell her home in Ottawa in order to move back to St. John's and purchase a comparable home, something that will cost her roughly $275,000. You have considered a number of factors including her alternatives, objective criteria, and interests, all of which lead your client to assume an RP of $400,000 for her home. Now, fast forward to the bargaining round when the potential buyer reveals that he owns a vacation property in St. John's that he would be willing to loan to her, rent-free, for up to six months while she is able to find a home in that city and move in after closing the deal. Suddenly, there is some extra value on the table that may affect your client's RP in a way that would expand the zone of agreement for this negotiation. By asking questions early in the process, you can identify some additional value in a climate that may well include enough value to satisfy everyone's needs. As detailed in chapter 3, recognizing the value climate as one that permits an integrative bargaining approach will dramatically affect the way in which you approach your opponent.

As you are busy filling in information gaps and adjusting your overall strategy accordingly, remember that your opponent will likely be doing the same thing. Pay attention to the questions that are asked of you and the way in which those answers might impact your opponent's strategic approach. Again, new avenues for creating value may be revealed in the answers to questions that may prove critical in guiding your next steps in this phase.

Controlling the Agenda: Pitching or Catching?

As the fact-gathering stage comes to an end, you may find yourself feeling that it is time for the first offer of the negotiation to be put into play. This first offer most often occurs in a negotiation value climate that favours a distributive approach to bargaining, characterized by an absence of additional value and a single-issue negotiation most commonly around price. By now, you may be formulating an idea as to where a good starting offer might be located on the continuum running between your client's reservation and target points.

One of the key strategic decisions to make about an offer is whether to make the first offer of the bargaining round or to wait for the other side to do so. Usually, this decision is dictated by the extent to which you feel confident that you have managed to fill in the gaps in your information and, therefore, confirmed your strategy. If you have achieved a position characterized by complete or near-complete information, there is a strategic gain to be realized by making the first offer.

Anchoring

Anchoring describes a phenomenon whereby the opening offer in a negotiation largely dictates the final deal. Assuming that the opening offer is not totally outside the scope of reality (for example, offering to pay $50,000 for a house appraised at $500,000), making the first offer establishes a benchmark (an anchor) around which all subsequent negotiation activity will closely revolve.

On various occasions, I have tested the claims of this phenomenon among my students. Taking a very straightforward purchase and sale transaction with a wide zone of agreement between $80,000 and $180,000, I asked 10 pairs of students who separately conducted the negotiation to reveal (a) the amount of the first offer and (b) the amount of the final price, if a deal was reached. Almost without exception, the negotiations that began with an offer of $100,000 ended up settling, eventually, for a sale price between $85,000 and $110,000, whereas those negotiations for the same property that began with an offer of $150,000 ended up settling for a sale price between $140,000 and $165,000.

When you are able to anchor a negotiation with the first offer, certain assumptions are made about the information that you have. As noted by Lewicki, Barry, and Saunders,

> Cognitive biases in anchoring and adjustment are related to the effect of the standard (or anchor) against which subsequent adjustments are made during negotiation. The choice of an anchor (e.g., an initial offer or an intended goal) might well be based on faulty or incomplete information and thus be misleading in and of itself. However, once the anchor is defined, parties tend to treat it as a real, valid benchmark by which to adjust other judgments.[11]

So, if anchoring a negotiation with the first offer serves to privilege that offer for the rest of the bargaining, why am I not suggesting that you *always* anchor your negotiation with the first offer? Quite simply, unless you have all of the necessary information, anchoring may not be in your client's best interests because you may make a first offer that is far too generous. Again, take the house sale scenario for your client moving to St. John's. If you have not done all of your homework well and you anchor by making a first offer to sell the house for $425,000 (based on your client's RP), you may have missed the opportunity to sell the house for $500,000, if only you had known more about the buyer's interests, alternatives, objective criteria, and reservation points.

In a situation where, for whatever reason, you do not have a comfortable level of information, your best strategy may well be to wait for that first offer. Although you lose your opportunity to anchor, you gain information on your opponent's strategy and underlying position and interests.

Phase III: Generating Value and Options

In the event that the early fact-gathering exercises of the negotiation do not identify your value climate as single-issued and under-resourced, you may face a valuable opportunity for integrative bargaining. Certainly, the best way to identify new value is by conducting a

---

11   Lewicki, Barry & Saunders, *supra* note 2 at 123.

thorough review of the interests that underlie the respective positions occupied by your client and the other parties in the negotiation. Much of this work will have begun in the pre-negotiation planning phase. Yet, with the additional information gathered through the probing questions asked in the opening of the bargaining round, you may find yourself far better informed at this point in the process as to the aspirations, needs, and goals of all parties at the table.

As noted in the Ugli Orange story, there is a far greater likelihood of finding overlap between differing interests than between opposing positions. By excavating interests from beneath the positions they support, new value—new opportunities for agreement—are often revealed.

Of course, spending a great deal of time in understanding the interests underlying each party's positions may not be particularly fruitful in a single-issue negotiation around, for example, the rate of pay to be set for members of a union employed as park rangers in a provincial park. At first glance, this negotiation situation would seem to have a value climate of scarce resources, prompting negotiators to assume a distributive framework in order to divide that limited value in the way most favourable to their respective clients.

However, even in a situation like this, it is beneficial to investigate whether there might be, in fact, a number of interests held in common by both sides, such as assuring a positive collective image in the media portrayal of the bargaining so that the taxpaying public might be favourably disposed to funding a generous budget. Reaching an agreement with a minimum of acrimony might be of significant value to both sides. Identifying common interests and the corresponding values they support is clearly helpful to all parties.

Options for Agreement

One of the best ways to create or reveal additional value in this phase of the negotiation is to review the issue agenda, along with the respective positions taken by each party on each issue, in an effort to search for common interests. Once a list of interests—be they common, conflicting, or complementary—has been tabulated, negotiators may move toward brainstorming, one of the key ways of generating options for agreement.

An integrative framework is one that seeks to maximize the resources available to satisfy competing interests, rather than one that urges compromise around a scarce resource in order to achieve agreement. There are a number of options for agreement that are unique to an integrative framework and have the capacity to carry parties closer to an enduring resolution.

LOGROLLING

In a negotiation characterized by multiple issues that are prioritized differently by the parties to the negotiation, there is often an opportunity to achieve an acceptable agreement through logrolling. Logrolling is a way of "packaging" a resolution whereby each party concedes on the issues that are of a lower priority in exchange for concessions made by opponents on issues of greater priority (but of lower priority to those making the concessions).

In our house sale scenario, imagine that your client, the vendor, is somewhat flexible on the price that she gets as she has other sources of income to finance her move to St. John's.

What is of major importance, however, is that she close the house deal and move to St. John's by July 1 so that she can march in a Canada Day parade there. In an integrative framework that recognizes the added value generated by these interests, we might conceive of a situation where the potential buyer who has limited funds but is very flexible on timing might make an offer that is somewhat lower than what the buyer could expect for her property but that includes a provision offering to close the deal very quickly. This "packaging" of options results in all parties making concessions and being compensated for those concessions through the concessions of others.

Bridging

In bridging, none of the negotiating parties satisfy their original *positions*, but a closer consideration of underlying interests leads to new solutions that accommodate all interests. Obviously, this approach requires significant mutual candour among parties respecting the nature and scope of their respective interests, as well as some ordering and prioritization of those interests.

A great example of bridging comes from Dean Pruitt in a hypothetical scenario of a couple attempting to agree on where to vacation. The wife wants to go to the seashore and the husband to the mountains. As Pruitt notes,

> In bridging, neither party achieves its initial demands but a new option is devised that satisfies the most important interests underlying those demands. For example, suppose that the husband in our example is mainly interested in fishing and hunting and the wife in swimming and sunbathing. Their interests might be bridged by finding an inland resort with a lake and a beach that is close to woods and streams …
>
> Bridging typically involves a reformulation of the issues based on an analysis of the underlying interests on both sides. For example, a critical turning point in our vacation example is likely to come when the initial formulation "Shall we go to the mountains or the seashore?" is replaced by "Where can we find hunting, fishing, swimming and sunbathing?"[12]

Bridging is closely tied to the respective interests of the negotiating parties and sometimes requires that all parties forego achieving lower priority interests in favour of higher priority ones. If the wife in Pruitt's example also wanted to do some antique shopping, it might be the case that this lesser desire would have to be discarded in order to find a solution that would address at least the key interests of both spouses.

Integrative Bargaining: Maximizing Resources

Although the integrative or "problem solving" approach affords enhanced opportunities to address all of the parties' underlying interests and needs in a solution, it is not without its critics. While a strong proponent of the problem-solving approach to negotiation, Bruce Patton does a solid job of summarizing its main critiques:

---

12 D.G. Pruitt, "Achieving Integrative Agreements" in M. Bazerman & R. Lewicki, eds., *Negotiating in Organizations* (Beverly Hills, CA: Sage Publications, 1983) at 41-42.

It Glosses Over the Hard Facts of Distributive Life
The earliest critique was that the guidelines for problem solving are useful for finding creative, value-enhancing options but ultimately offer little help in coping with the reality of distributive conflict in which interests are opposed. Or, put another way using a traditional dichotomy (inspired by labor negotiations) that divides negotiation into integrative and distributive contexts, problem solving is helpful with the former but not with the latter …

It Takes Two to Tango
A second common critique of the problem-solving approach is that it only works if both sides are committed to it. Of course, to a large extent, this is true of any approach to negotiation, so it is not on its own a reason to stick with the status quo.

Sometimes the Person Is the Problem and Can't Be Separated
This persistent critique questions the ability of the negotiator to take a collaborative, "side by side" stance when the other negotiator's behavior and role in the relationship is itself the issue. The response given in *Getting to Yes* is that you can separate the behavior from the person's character and address the behavior side-by-side, which has the advantage of assuming in a potentially self-fulfilling way that others are capable of changing their behavior.

It Sounds Simpler Than It Is
The last critique of the problem-solving approach is that it is presented as much easier to pull off and much safer to try than it really is. This critique has at least some validity. First of all, a masterful effort can require a great deal of skill, subtlety and technical expertise simply on the substantive level, before we get to the interpersonal. Even the concept of "interests" is much more slippery than it first appears …[13]

Despite the criticisms surrounding integrative bargaining, each of which Patton proceeds to rebut in his article, there is a solid cadre of support for this approach to negotiation. Among other benefits, integrative agreements generally are more enduring due to an absence of unsatisfactory compromising and more supportive of the relationships among the parties. Certain advocates of integrative bargaining might suggest it as a panacea for negotiation difficulties, leading as it often does to creative and satisfying outcomes that address underlying interests rather than positional demands.

While we are not blind to these benefits, we see the chief value of the integrative approach as its ability to maximize value—to get onto the table as many resources as available for division among the parties. By assessing the value climate of a negotiation as one with the potential for additional resources, we are able to adopt an integrative framework and use its tools and techniques to generate as much of those resources as possible.

That said, it is clear that all negotiations eventually reach a point when the accumulated and generated value must be claimed; that is, a point when our role as a representative negotiator shifts to taking as much of the expanded pie for our client as we can get. When we recognize that there is no further value to be found or created, we shift to a distributive framework in order to divide that value in a way that favours the interests and positions of our client.

---

13   Patton, *supra* note 2 at 295-99.

Phase IV: Claiming Value

In many ways, distributive bargaining is the misunderstood child of negotiation theory and practice, often equated, wrongly, with underhanded and aggressive tactics, and the general absence of progressive thinking. While integrative bargaining may lead to enhanced relationships, both among negotiators and within the wider community, distributive bargaining is often maligned for destroying relationships among its victims and leaving parties worse off than they were before the negotiation.

The fact remains that value, once maximized, must be distributed. If you happen to be a lawyer negotiating on behalf of your client, you are bound by certain professional obligations, often labelled broadly as "zealous advocacy," that require you professionally to do the very best you can to achieve your client's objectives. For other representative negotiators not specifically bound by such professional obligations, surely there remains a similar drive to achieve the best possible outcome for their principal, driven by any number of personal and/or professional interests.

Distributive bargaining is so named because negotiators working within this framework divide—or distribute—a specific resource, often money. As discussed earlier, a distributive framework necessarily flows from the diagnosis of a value climate characterized by a scarcity of resources available to satisfy the various demands of the parties involved in a negotiation. This diagnosis may take place at the outset of the negotiation planning process or it may evolve after a vigorous round of value creation using an integrative framework. Either way, all negotiations eventually arrive at the point where the remaining step in the negotiation is to distribute the value pool.

As Lax and Sebenius write regarding the value creating and value claiming approaches,

> Both of these images of negotiation are incomplete and inadequate. Value creating and value claiming are linked parts of negotiation. Both processes are present. No matter how much creative problem solving enlarges the pie, it must still be divided; value that has been created must be claimed. And, if the pie is not enlarged, there will be less to divide; there is more value to be claimed if one has helped to create it first. An essential tension in negotiation exists between cooperative moves to create value and competitive moves to claim it.[14]

A shift to a distributive framework does not necessarily mean that your client has no interest in the relational aspects of the negotiation and favours instead his substantive objectives. What it does tend to mean, however, is that the relational outcomes of the negotiation are either less important than or else closely aligned with the substantive objectives. A distributive framework lends itself more to achieving certain negotiation outcomes than it does to achieving relational outcomes. In the event that the relational outcomes of a negotiation are a priority, there will be less focus on one's own substantive achievements inherent in a distributive framework and greater focus on the mutual achievements inherent in an integrative framework that seeks to maximize value for all parties.

---

14   Lax & Sebenius, *The Manager as Negotiator, supra* note 1 at 34.

Competitive and Cooperative Tactics

Recent negotiation literature often casts distributive bargaining in a negative light and mistakenly equates it with the worst tactics of competitive bargaining.[15] Recognizing that the value available to satisfy all parties' interests in a negotiation has been maximized and that the point has arrived to focus on the favourable distribution of value does not necessarily mean that parties will adopt immediately—or at all—an aggressive, competitive approach to distributing that value. In fact, it may be strategically beneficial to continue the negotiation in a cooperative style, building on the goodwill established through a robust phase of integrative value generation.

Generally speaking, a competitive approach is characterized by a negotiator's emphasis on his client's interests and substance in the negotiation. This approach excludes an acknowledgement of the opposing interests or positions, finding them to be insufficiently important to warrant a shift in approach. Unfortunately, certain stereotypical behaviour is linked to this approach. For example, a competitive approach can be defined as one that prioritizes one's own interests (or those of one's client) above the interests of others. Although a competitive approach is often equated with aggressive, borderline ethical behaviour, this is not a necessary connection. Perhaps the most effective negotiators working in a competitive style are those who are able to avoid the stereotypical behaviours associated with this approach while still firmly asserting the interests of the client above those of the other party in the negotiation.

"Remember, in this negotiation you're the 'Paula Abdul.'"

Figure 4.1   *Source*: cartoonresource.com.

A cooperative (or collaborative) approach to bargaining is perhaps best defined as one in which the negotiator acknowledges the importance of the opposing party's interests in achieving an optimal distribution of the available value in the negotiation. The cooperative approach is not to be confused with integrative bargaining, which is an approach that follows a diagnosis of a value climate with some potential for the generation of new value or the identification of existing but hidden value. An integrative bargaining approach is one that attempts to reveal and generate value until there is no more to be created.

By contrast, a cooperative approach remains closely fixed on dividing value within a distributive framework, but one that recognizes the importance not only of your own client's interests, but of the interests of the other party who will need to agree ultimately on the terms of the final transaction or dispute resolution. Often the cooperative approach is one that is defined as "relational" in that it focuses not only on the substance of the negotiation but on the effect that the process may have on the relationship among the participants. Remember that the focus is still on distributing the value of the negotiation in a way that optimizes your client's objectives.

---

15   See *e.g.* Goodpaster, *supra* note 9 at 349-63.

Both competitive and cooperative strategies, when used effectively, should form part of a principled negotiation. A principled negotiation is characterized as reasoned and rational in that it justifies both positions and requested or offered concessions using objective criteria. Each time you present an offer and encourage your opponent to accept it, you do so by referring to objective criteria of the correctness of your offer. When you concede a point, you reason as to the way in which that concession is linked to your overall approach to the negotiation and the way in which it should be matched with a concession of equal value. When all the positions and moves made during a bargaining round are principled, there is far greater likelihood that any agreements achieved will be long-lasting.

Thinking Inside the Box ...

The following list is a sampling of the common tactics employed by negotiators working within a distributive framework. The objective of each of these tactics is a favourable division of value. Some can be characterized as *competitive*, in that they focus primarily on maximizing personal outcomes, while others can be characterized as *cooperative*, in that they attempt to reverse the potentially negative relational impacts that result from claiming scarce resources. Think about scenarios in which these tactics could enhance or impede the negotiation objectives of your client:

- **Bogey.** Using this tactic, a negotiator pretends that a relatively unimportant issue is very important so that it can be offered up as a major concession at some point in the negotiation. This tactic allows a negotiator to seek an equally significant concession in exchange.
- **Difference splitting.** Often, when the rounds of back and forth concessions appear to be nearing an end, yet negotiators remain some distance apart in their offer positions, someone will suggest splitting the difference between them to achieve agreement through one, final, *joint* concession. Where concessions up to this point are generally tied to principled reasons, this final concession is usually made only in the name of achieving agreement.
- **Avalanche or snow job.** This tactic is used when a negotiator seeks to bury the opposing party in an overload of information in order to try to make it impossible for that party to separate the important from the unimportant in developing an effective strategy. As essential as information is to planning and implementing a negotiation strategy, having too much—especially when it contains red herrings—is arguably as detrimental as not having enough.
- **False final offer.** Just as it sounds, a false final offer means a negotiator asserts, strategically, that she has reached her "bottom line," with no further room to make concessions or reconsider a subsequent offer. While some final offer statements are accurate if the negotiator truly has reached the end of her instructions from her client, this tactic is commonly used to halt the back and forth concessions dance of negotiation. Using this tactic can be extremely risky; it may bring about the end of a negotiation where there was actually additional room to bargain.

- **Take it or leave it.** Similar to the false final offer, the take it or leave it tactic is usually used immediately following the opening of the bargaining round. This tactic is widely known as *Boulewarism* after a VP of General Electric, Lemuel Bouleware, who was famous for opening his negotiations with a single, firm offer of terms of an agreement and for not allowing any further discussion or counter-offers. As with the false final offer tactic, genuine Boulewarism often signals that a negotiator has no remaining room to bargain. It is, however, used far more commonly as a tactic to generate an inaccurate perception.
- *Ad hominem.* The *ad hominem* occurs when one negotiator attacks not only the positions and ideas of the opposing negotiator, but also his personal traits. By implying or stating that the opposing negotiator is stupid, ruthless, incompetent, or unethical, a negotiator seeks to discredit the opposition's argument and achieve certain gains. A similar tactic is at play when one negotiator attempts to flatter the other, often with personal comments about aspects of the opposing negotiator's personality, character, intelligence, or appearance.
- **Trojan Horse.** Using the Trojan Horse tactic, the negotiator begins a negotiation with an abundance of friendly, interactive, and engaging comments and actions, establishing a strong, positive rapport with her opponent. Alternatively, this friendly approach may be suddenly adopted in the middle of a negotiation, marking a move away from a more typically aggressive or even hostile approach. In both cases, the Trojan Horse tactic is an attempt to achieve certain gains by creating a positive personal impression with the opposing negotiator.

Can you think of any other competitive or cooperative tactics that might serve your client's objectives in the distributive phase of bargaining? Regardless of the procedural or substantive gains that potentially flow from employing these tactics, it is critical to remember that professional and ethical considerations may—and often must—inform your decision about their availability and use in a given negotiation. For example, while "false trial offers" can potentially positively affect a negotiation outcome in favour of your client, they typically also amount to lies.

Closing and Confirming: Agreements and Commitments

All good negotiations must come to an end, and one of several events will trigger the conclusion of the bargaining round. You may reach a final agreement with acceptable terms for the transaction or dispute being negotiated. Conversely, you may identify the absence of a zone of agreement or you may face an insurmountable impasse on one of the key issues under negotiation. These last two possibilities result in either a complete breakdown of the negotiation or, depending on the circumstances, in a pause in the bargaining round while objectives and alternatives are reconsidered by the parties. Negotiation in these cases may recommence at a later date, if the parties believe it to be within their respective best interests, with or without the assistance of a third-party neutral.

Negotiation literature emphasizes the importance of achieving *commitments* rather than simply *agreements*, as illustrated by the following passage by Richard Shell:

> The goal of all negotiations is to secure commitment, not merely agreement. You want a deal that sticks under which the other side will reliably perform. Sometimes a mere handshake will be enough to secure performance, particularly if the parties have a long-standing relationship and trust each other. Other times, more elaborate commitment devices such as contracts, public ceremonies and explicit penalties are required.
>
> A student of mine once told a story in class that illustrates the difference between agreements and commitments better than most academic discussions that I have heard. Her story also shows how knowledge of negotiation dynamics can help you improve others' lives as well as your own.
>
> My student—let's call her Theresa—was helping to run a volunteer organization that took inner city kids out to the country on Saturdays for recreational activities. She and others in her group chartered buses, got athletic equipment, arranged for adult volunteers to chaperone, brought food enough for all, and gave the kids a day away from the stress and hardship of life on the streets.
>
> Everything was working fine except the adult volunteers. These well-meaning people were easy enough to persuade when she and others in the organization solicited their help. But many failed to appear on their assigned Saturday. Worse still, they were usually too embarrassed to call and let Theresa know that they would not be there. This left the buses short on chaperones and the games short on supervisors.
>
> Theresa faced a commitment problem that was threatening the whole program. How could she get volunteers to show up on their assigned day? Then she and her organization hit on an idea. When she called the volunteers to clear their schedule and assign them a day, she gave them each an important additional assignment: to bring an essential item from the day's lunch— hamburger meat, rolls, salad, charcoal for the fire, and so on. With this simple additional promise, the number of volunteers who showed up skyrocketed. Why? People who previously had failed to show had apparently comforted themselves with the thought that one less volunteer would not matter on the trip. But now that they had a concrete image of what their participation meant (hamburgers are useless without charcoal, and vice versa), each person knew that his or her contribution mattered. Each was part of the team. A failure by one would mean a loss for all. The volunteer's self-esteem and sense of responsibility, which had led him or her to volunteer in the first place, now prompted actual performance.[16]

As Shell proceeds to explain, the key distinction between agreements and genuine commitments is the "risk of loss" faced by parties for non-performance. An agreement to do something holds little risk for the person making it. However, a commitment goes beyond a mere signal of willingness to perform because "costs" are involved should the person who makes the commitment back out of the promise made.

If negotiators are unable to reach an agreement, or to move from agreement to commitment, for whatever reason, they should think of their final task as leaving the situation no

---

16   R. Shell, *Bargaining for Advantage: Negotiation Strategies for Reasonable People* (New York: Penguin Books, 1999) at 196-97.

worse off than when they began. As such, a negotiation that ends in a deadlock might be rectified by the addition of a third-party neutral—such as a mediator, conciliator, or arbitrator—a possibility that negotiators should canvass their clients on at this point. Even better, negotiators should address how to deal with the possibility of impasse at the outset of the negotiation, before it arrives and emotions run high.

Assuming that you are able to achieve an agreement among the negotiators and clients, how do you proceed to memorialize that agreement and confirm its terms? While recording the details of the agreement might seem to be a rather neutral and mechanical task, it is exactly the opposite. Similar to our earlier discussion about the cognitive impact of anchoring, drafting the agreement serves to create a benchmark around which only minor revisions will be made.

In addition, as the drafter, you will often assume in the eyes of the other negotiator a somewhat heightened role as the memory keeper of the negotiation so that any revisions of the initial draft are seen naturally to require your consent or adjustment. While in many negotiations, this subtle shift is not substantively meaningful, in complex, multi-issue negotiations it may make a huge difference to the way in which your client's interests are highlighted in the final agreement.

What should be in the final agreement? While the contents of a "good agreement" will vary widely depending on the circumstances of the negotiation, there are several basic components and characteristics that every agreement should include:

- Each issue originally identified in the issue agenda should be reflected in the agreement; otherwise, parties whose issues seem to have dropped off the table are less likely to be satisfied with the agreement.
- The terms of the agreement should be clear and manageable in order to avoid difficulties at the implementation stage of the agreement.
- The agreement should include terms that speak to resolving any conflicts that emerge from its implementation. If there is a specific jurisdiction whose laws are to govern the agreement, that should be stated, as should any views shared by parties about resorting to the courts or to court alternatives in order to settle any arising disputes.
- Ideally, the final agreement should include specific commitments that are meant to improve the likelihood of implementation. For example, if parties agree to the publication of the agreement (for example, through media releases or other public postings), they are less likely to defect from the agreement as new accountability pressures are brought to bear and other party's interests—such as reputation protection—are triggered. In these circumstances, it is often a good idea to include the actual text of the media release. However, keep in mind that leaving in ambiguities for further work can be a recipe for disaster.

The most important moments in a negotiation are those that precede the bargaining round and those that follow it. Once you have had an opportunity to come away from the negotiation and compare your outcomes with your client's targets and RPs, only then can the true substantive success of your negotiation be measured. Then, if the balance of outcomes achieved is truly a good one, the agreement will endure as all parties feel confident that it was the best agreement they could have reached in that particular situation.

Final Considerations

This chapter proposes a staged approach to the strategic negotiation process. The unique features of this particular approach include the way in which value climate is used to shape and re-shape the planning and bargaining phases of negotiation. In the event that resources are abundant, or at least sufficient to satisfy the various and often competing interests of the parties, then negotiators are able to achieve tremendous benefit through an integrative framework. That said, there comes a time in every negotiation, either at its outset or following the maximization of available value, when there are simply no further resources to be generated. At this time, the effective negotiator shifts into a distributive framework, claiming the value necessary to satisfy her own client's objectives. Finally, once the resolution options have been assessed and evaluated and agreement has been achieved, parties in this model focus carefully on structuring that agreement to include commitments that will guarantee its endurance and the mutual satisfaction of all parties involved.

Notes and Questions

1. In this and the preceding chapter, we have looked at various factors that impact the way in which a negotiator approaches, plans, executes, and implements an effective negotiation strategy. In the chapters that follow, we will consider other factors that influence the process and outcomes of strategic negotiation. How might all of these factors influence your decision to move from value creating to value claiming, the way you make those decisions, your preparation for the negotiation, and the way in which you record agreements?

2. This chapter and the others in this book raise professional and ethical issues. In so doing, we are signalling our view that effective negotiation is only possible if it is also done professionally and ethically. As you read through each chapter, think about how your own ethical views affect your choices, approaches, and tactics. What about professional obligations and standards? What would you do if you discover that your counterpart in the negotiation is acting unethically? What would you do if your client—as part of his or her approach to creating value—asks you to overstate some of his or her interests?

Selected Further Reading

K. Allred, "Distinguishing Best and Strategic Practices: A Framework for Managing the Dilemma Between Claiming and Creating Value" (2000) 16 Negotiation Journal 387.

B. Downie, "When Negotiations Fail: Causes of Breakdown and Tactics for Breaking the Stalemate" (1991) 7 Negotiation Journal 175.

D. Gifford, "A Context-Based Theory of Strategy Selection in Legal Negotiation" (1985) 46 Ohio St. L.J. 41.

R. Korobkin, "Bargaining Power as Threat of Impasse" (2004) 87 Marq. L. Rev. 867.

H. Kristensen & T. Garling, "The Effects of Anchor Points and Reference Points on Negotiation Process and Outcome" (1997) 71 Organizational Behaviour and Human Decision Processes 85.

D. Lax & J. Sebenius, "Dealcrafting: the Substance of Three-Dimensional Negotiation" (2002) 18 Negotiation Journal 5.

D. Lax & J. Sebenius, *The Manager as Negotiator: Bargaining for Cooperation and Competitive Gain* (New York: Free Press, 1986).

D. Lax & J. Sebenius, "The Power of Alternatives or the Limits to Negotiation" (1985) 1 Negotiation Journal 163.

R. Lewicki & J. Hiam, *The Fast-Forward MBA in Negotiation and Dealmaking* (New York: John Wiley & Sons, 1999).

R. Lewicki & N. Stark, "What's Ethically Appropriate in Negotiations: An Empirical Examination of Bargaining Tactics" (1995) 9 Social Justice Research 69.

L. Thompson, E. Peterson & S. Brodt, "Team Negotiation: An Examination of Integrative and Distributive Bargaining" (1996) 70 J. Personality & Social Psych. 66.

S.B. White & M.A. Neale, "Reservation Price, Resistance Point and BATNAs: Determining the Parameters of Acceptable Negotiated Outcomes" (1991) 7 Negotiation Journal 379.

PART IV

Ethics

CHAPTER 5

Representative Negotiators of Integrity

Frederick H. Zemans

"Negotiation is a moral and ethical process, worthy of deep philosophical, political, legal and human respect."

Carrie Menkel-Meadow[1]

The Ethical Representative Negotiator

There is virtually no negotiation—personal, professional, or in the workplace—where ethical and moral issues do not arise. This chapter explores whether there are or should be accepted ethical and moral expectations and standards for representative negotiators.

Kevin Gibson describes negotiation as a "value-based enterprise," and argues that negotiation necessarily involves questioning the nature of our personal values. In each negotiation, negotiators must make conscious decisions about the process they will use and the posture they will adopt. These decisions reflect personal values with respect to moral issues such as fairness, rights, and justice.[2] We would argue that such decisions become even more complex in the context of representative negotiation.

---

1 C. Menkel-Meadow, "The Ethics of Compromise" in A.K. Schneider & C. Honeyman, eds., *The Negotiator's Fieldbook* (Washington, DC: ABA Press, 2006) 155 at 156.

2 K. Gibson, "Ethics and Morality in Negotiation" in A.K. Schneider & C. Honeyman, eds., *The Negotiator's Fieldbook* (Washington, DC: ABA Press, 2006) 175.

The terms *morality* and *ethics* are often used interchangeably in the discussion of integrity in negotiation. However, *morality* refers to personal values, learned at home, at school, and in religious, cultural, and social communities; these values pertain specifically to what Gibson describes as the "quality of being virtuous."[3] Moral conduct is behaviour that has "virtue"—conformity to the ideals of right human conduct based on principles of right and wrong.[4] *Ethics* refers to "a set of moral principles: a theory or system of moral values … moral issues or aspects (such as rightness) or a consciousness of moral importance."[5] Ethical conduct is behaviour that is honourable and reflects moral principles. In the context of the workplace or a profession, ethical conduct is generally referred to as "practical ethics" or "applied ethics." A number of private and public sector organizations have developed codes of ethical conduct that set standards for dealing with matters such as sexual harassment, confidentiality, and fraud. These organizations include the provincial and national bar associations, provincial law societies, local real estate boards, municipalities, and major employers. We discuss codes of ethics and their role in answering moral and ethical dilemmas later in this chapter.

Scenarios Involving Moral and Ethical Issues

Consider the following scenarios. How would you address the moral and ethical issues they raise?

1. You are graduating from university and have decided to sell your five-year-old Vespa. (Your grandparents have offered you their car to allow you to explore Central America and to celebrate your graduation with honours in History.) You placed an ad on a local website and Leslie responds by email that she is interested. You listed the Vespa at $5,500. Leslie comes to see and test drives the Vespa and offers you $4,000 cash. You have been told that the Vespa is worth about $2,500 on a trade-in and needs some work done on the brakes. You are inclined to accept Leslie's offer and not mention the brakes, particularly since Leslie is moving out of the province to undertake graduate work.

    Is this a proper commercial negotiation? Would it make any difference if Leslie is a good friend?

2. You are looking for a summer job in northern Canada, after second-year law school. You have always had an interest in working on Aboriginal law issues and are hoping that you might be able to get a position in either the public or private sector. You are concerned about some of your grades in first-year law school. You found the

---

3   *Ibid.*

4   *Webster's II, New Riverside Dictionary, s.v.* "morality."

5   *Merriam-Webster Online Dictionary, s.v.* "ethics."

adjustment to law school very difficult and were particularly stressed out for personal reasons during the final Christmas exams of first year. (Christmas final exams in first year are being abolished at many Canadian law schools because some faculties believe that Christmas is too early for law students to receive grades that will appear on their transcripts.) You were disappointed to receive a C in Contracts and a B in Criminal Law, which were two of your favourite courses. One of your professors told you that she regretted that the law school grade profile did not provide for pluses, as she would have given you a B+ in Criminal Law, if such a grade was available. You have prepared a resumé to send out to lawyers and law departments in Yellowknife and have changed your Contracts grade to C+ and your Criminal Law grade to B+.

Is this an ethical or moral course of action? Can this change be excused as mere exaggeration? What are your concerns? Do you think the change in grades is changing a material fact? What are the potential legal and personal implications? Would you change the grades in this situation?

3. You are visiting Barcelona for the first time with your new significant other and he admires a beautiful old pocket watch and chain in the street market in the square in front of your hotel. The antique dealer is an elderly woman who tells you that she is the widow of the dealer who operated the stand since the Second World War. She insists that the watch and chain are valuable and that the weight of the gold makes them worth at least US$500. You don't believe the watch is that valuable but desperately want to impress upon your new significant other that he is very import-ant to you. You talk to the antique dealer for some time and she indicates that 20 percent is the most that she can take off the price. You walk away and look at other watches in the market but don't find anything that you like as much. You return and tell the dealer that US$200 in cash is all that you are prepared to offer. Your special friend indicates that he is prepared to kick in another US$100 to get the watch, but you decline and start shouting at the dealer that she is being highly unreasonable and unresponsive to young Canadians. The dealer doesn't understand all of your English but becomes very flushed and embarrassed with your behaviour in the public market and finally agrees to sell the watch and chain for US$275.

Is your behaviour appropriate? Have you negotiated ethically? How did the vendor feel about you after the sale? Would such behaviour be appropriate in attempting to negotiate the return of a pair of shoes to a local Canadian shoe store, in face of their well-known no return policy?

These scenarios are hypothetical, but they present moral and ethical issues that we com-monly encounter in both our personal and professional lives. Consider these problems and reflect on potential issues that you may confront in your own negotiations while represent-ing a friend, a colleague, or a stranger. Do moral and ethical issues become more complex when you are a representative negotiator and not merely representing yourself? Do the terms or basis of your retainer or representation change how you would and should behave in a negotiation? Is there a moral or ethical standard of behaviour that can guide your actions? Do the facts, circumstances, or relationships determine your approach and analysis of these issues?

Competing Impulses in Negotiation

Ethics, morality, and integrity are critical aspects of all negotiations. We begin our discussion of these aspects by considering how they are influenced by four fundamental, distinct, and competing impulses in negotiation.

Peter Adler believes that the diverse approaches to negotiation devolve into four basic schools of thinking about how humans behave in the face of real or imagined conflict:[6]

> One presupposes that all of us are fundamentally competitive. A second assumes we are, at core, cooperative. A third takes for granted that all of us will seek to do what is morally correct. A fourth assumes we are rational and pragmatic.
>
> These four impulses—pursuing your own fair share, uniting with others to achieve a common end, insisting on doing what is right, and using logic and reason to solve practical problems— seem to have evolutionary roots that date back to our origins on the African savannah.

In most negotiations, we can find the presence of and dynamic interaction among the competitive, cooperative, moral, and pragmatic impulses (see figure 5.1).

Each impulse carries different assumptions about human nature and lends itself to a particular negotiation strategy. In many chapters in this book, we explore the relationship between competitive and cooperative negotiation strategies, and when these strategies are generally exercised or should be exercised by negotiators. We also discuss the influence of culture, power, and gender on our inclination to be more or less competitive and cooperative in representative negotiations.

In this chapter, we examine the relationship and tensions between moral and pragmatic impulses in negotiation as well as the relationship between an ethical negotiating philosophy and competitive and cooperative negotiation strategies. Are cooperative or competitive negotiators more likely to act ethically or pragmatically in negotiation? How can negotiators determine what is ethical or moral in the context of a particular negotiation? Many negotiations begin with one side or the other saying, "It's the principle of it!" That principle may be legal, ethical, religious, cultural, or based on the negotiator's personal moral code. What room does this position leave for negotiation?

The pragmatic impulse, which is situated directly across from the moral impulse in figure 5.1, is based on rational problem-solving. This impulse tends to underlie approaches to interest-based negotiation. According to Adler, a great deal of the literature on interest-based negotiation

> assumes that people know and understand their needs, that interests can be rationally and dispassionately analyzed, and that elegant if not super-optimum solutions can be found. Fisher and Ury's famous dictums of separating the people from the problem, focusing on interests, generating possibilities, and insisting on objective criteria are an attempt to create a rational, if not quasi-scientific critical inquiry process that leads to a more easily negotiated result.[7]

---

6   P.S. Adler, "Protean Negotiation" in A. Kupfer Schneider & C. Honeyman, eds., *The Negotiator's Fieldbook* (Washington, DC: ABA Press, 2006) 17 at 18. The discussion in this section and the next is based on Adler.

7   *Ibid.* at 21.

However, Gerald Wetlaufer, among others, is skeptical about the integrative approach that Fisher and Ury developed in their book *Getting to Yes*:

> We have, in certain respects, allowed ourselves to be dazzled and seduced by the possibilities of integrative or 'win-win' bargaining. That, in turn, has led to a certain amount of overclaiming. The reason, I think, is that if we hold these possibilities in a certain light and squint our eyes just hard enough, they look for the entire world like the holy grail of negotiations. They seem to offer that which we have wanted most to find. What they seem to offer—though in the end it is only an illusion—is the long-sought proof that cooperation, honesty and good behavior will carry the day not because they are virtuous, not because they will benefit society as a whole, but because they are in everyone's individual and pecuniary self-interest. But however much we may want "honesty" to be "the best policy" in this strong sense, the discovery of integrative bargaining has not, at least, so far, provided that long-sought proof.[8]

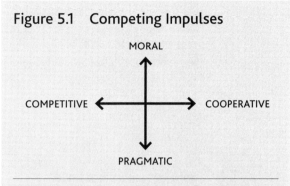

Figure 5.1   Competing Impulses

Source: P.S. Adler, "Protean Negotiation" in A. Kupfer Schneider & C. Honeyman, eds., *The Negotiator's Fieldbook* (Washington, DC: ABA Press, 2006) 17 at 19.

Let us return to Adler's discussion of the four impulses in the negotiation paradigm. Just as a creative tension exists between the competitive and cooperative approaches, so too a polarity exists between the moral and pragmatic aspects of negotiation.[9] We recommend an approach to negotiation that integrates competitive and cooperative negotiation strategies. As well, we urge wise negotiators to recognize that they must consider, utilize, and integrate an appropriate ethical and pragmatic approach in their negotiation planning and strategies. Next, we consider how negotiators can effectively integrate the tensions among the various negotiation impulses.

The Protean Negotiator

An "effective negotiator," says Robert Benjamin, "requires a thinking frame that is adaptive, dynamic, fluid, and shifting and a model of negotiation that can house a variety of negotiation rituals."[10] Adler concurs and calls this type of negotiator a *Protean negotiator* after Proteus, the sea god who was able to change form at will. Protean negotiators should be

---

8   R. Fisher & W. Ury, *Getting to Yes: Negotiating Agreement Without Giving In*, 2d ed. (New York: Penguin Books, 1991); see G.B. Wetlaufer, "The Limits of Integrative Bargaining" in Menkel-Meadow & M. Wheeler, eds., *What's Fair: Ethics for Negotiators* (San Francisco: Jossey-Bass, 2004) at 49.

9   D.A. Lax & J.K. Sebenius, *The Manager as Negotiator: Bargaining for Cooperation and Competitive Gain* (New York: Free Press, 1986). Lax and Sebenius describe the tension between creating and claiming in their discussion of these issues.

10   R. Benjamin, *The Protean Sensibility: Recommending Approaches to Leadership and Negotiation* (2004) [unpublished].

able to read and change their strategy according to the context. They should be able to "dance the competitor's jitterbug, the collaborator's tango, the moralist's waltz, and the pragmatist's four step. One dance may be more comfortable than the others, and the dances can be sequenced, but they are all in the repertoire."[11] Protean negotiators are creative and responsive to the negotiation situation, as well as the personalities, gender, culture, and values of those involved.[12]

We urge that the Protean become the Canadian negotiation dance of the 21st century. Negotiators and certainly representative negotiators must learn to effectively combine collaborative and competitive dances, always remembering the importance of morality. Ultimately, despite their remarkable routine, they and their new or old partners must conclude with an effective pragmatic foxtrot. We encourage negotiators to keep dancing and to develop their negotiation routines. They should respond to the music and the rhythm, and to the routines of their various partners—and be ethical, creative, and strategic.

Discussions of ethics for lawyers or other representative negotiators often confuse what is ethical (as determined by a particular corporate standard or according to a professional code of conduct) with what is prudent or wise. This is the choice between dancing the slow moralist's waltz and the often faster pragmatist's foxtrot.

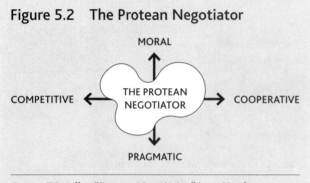

Figure 5.2   The Protean Negotiator

MORAL

COMPETITIVE ← THE PROTEAN NEGOTIATOR → COOPERATIVE

PRAGMATIC

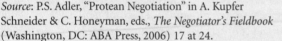

Source: P.S. Adler, "Protean Negotiation" in A. Kupfer Schneider & C. Honeyman, eds., *The Negotiator's Fieldbook* (Washington, DC: ABA Press, 2006) 17 at 24.

Let's look briefly at four approaches to ethical reasoning: *end-result ethics, duty ethics, social contract ethics*, and *personalistic ethics* (see figure 5.3). These approaches can help negotiators not only reflect on their own ethical approach to negotiations but also consider how their approach might be developed further. Which approach or approaches to ethical reasoning do you, as a representative negotiator, deem appropriate?

We encourage negotiators to reflect on their moral and ethical foundations, and, at the same time, to acknowledge their own attraction and commitment to a specific set of personal morals. (An analytical process for the resolution of moral problems appears in figure 5.4.)

Rather than attempt to determine what is moral or ethical based on ends, duties, or the social norms of the community, 20th-century philosopher Martin Buber and his followers assert that people should simply consult their own conscience. In *Ethics and Leadership: Putting Theory into Practice*, William Hitt develops an ethical problem that contrasts the philosophies based on ends, duties, and the social norms of a community with Buber's personalistic, or conscience-based, approach to ethics:

---

11   Adler, *supra* note 6 at 24.

12   Adler, *supra* note 6 at 23.

Figure 5.3   Four Approaches to Ethical Reasoning

Ethical System	Definition	Major Proponent	Central Tenets	Major Concerns
End-result ethics	Rightness of an action is determined by considering consequences.	Jeremy Bentham (1748–1832) John Stuart Mill (1806–1873)	• One must consider all likely consequences. • Actions are more right if they promote more happiness, more wrong as they produce unhappiness. • Happiness is defined as the presence of pleasure and absence of pain. • Promotion of happiness is generally the ultimate aim. • Collective happiness of all concerned is the goal.	• How does one define happiness, pleasure, or utility? • How does one measure happiness, pleasure, or utility? • How does one trade off between short-term vs. long-term happiness? • If actions create happiness for 90% of the world and misery for the other 10%, are they still ethical?
Duty ethics	Rightness of an action is determined by considering obligations to apply universal standards and principles.	Immanuel Kant (1724–1804)	• Human conduct should be guided by primary moral principles, or "oughts." • Individuals should stand on their principles and restrain themselves by rules. • The ultimate good is a life of virtue (acting on principles) rather than pleasure. • We should not adjust moral law to fit our actions, but adjust our actions to fit moral law.	• By what authority do we accept particular rules or the "goodness" of those rules? • What rule do we follow when rules conflict? • How do we adapt general rules to fit specific situations? • How do rules change as circumstances change? • What happens when good rules produce bad consequences? • Are there rules without any exceptions?

Continued on the next page.

Figure 5.3   Continued

Ethical System	Definition	Major Proponent	Central Tenets	Major Concerns
Social contract ethics	Rightness of an action is determined by the customs and norms of a community.	Jean-Jacques Rousseau (1712–1778)	• People must function in a social, community context to survive. • Communities become "moral bodies" for determining ground rules. • Duty and obligation bind the community and the individual to each other. • What is best for the common good determines the ultimate standard. • Laws are important, but morality determines the laws and standards for right and wrong.	• How do we determine the general will? • What is meant by the "common good"? • What do we do with independent thinkers who challenge the morality of the existing social order (e.g., Jefferson, Gandhi, Martin Luther King)? • Can a state be corrupt and its people still be "moral" (e.g., Nazi Germany)?
Personalistic ethics	Rightness of an action is determined by one's conscience.	Martin Buber (1878–1965)	• Locus of truth is found in human existence. • Conscience within each person calls them to fulfill their humanness and to decide between right and wrong. • Personal decision rules are the ultimate standards. • Pursuing a noble goal by ignoble means leads to an ignoble end. There are no absolute formulas for living. • One should follow one's group but also stick up for what one individually believes.	• How could we justify ethics other than by saying, "it felt like the right thing to do"? • How could we achieve a collective definition of what is ethical if individuals disagreed? • How could we achieve cohesiveness and consensus in a team that only fosters personal perspectives? • How could an organization assure some uniformity in ethics?

Source: Derived from W. Hitt, Ethics and Leadership: Putting Theory into Practice (Columbus, OH: Battelle Press, 1990).

Figure 5.4   Analytical Process for the Resolution of Moral Problems

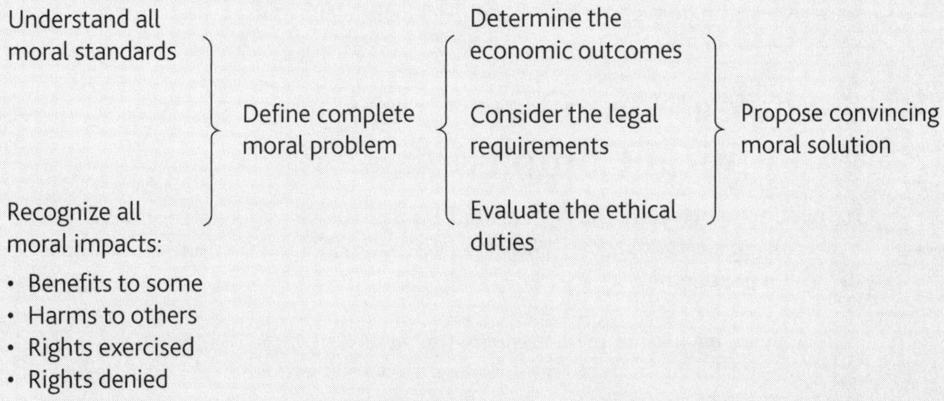

Understand all
moral standards

Define complete
moral problem

Determine the
economic outcomes

Consider the legal
requirements

Evaluate the ethical
duties

Propose convincing
moral solution

Recognize all
moral impacts:

- Benefits to some
- Harms to others
- Rights exercised
- Rights denied

Source: L.T. Homer, *The Ethics of Management*, 4th ed. (New York: McGraw-Hill/Irwin, 2003).

The setting is an outdoor hotel swimming pool on a warm July morning. At this particular time of day, there are only two persons present—a father who is fully clothed, sitting in a lounge chair beside the pool and reading the newspaper, and his five-year-old daughter, who is wading in the pool. While the father is engrossed in reading the sports page, he hears his daughter scream for help. She has waded into the deep end of the pool and is struggling to keep her head above water. At this moment, what is the right thing for the father to do? And what system of ethics will he use? If he chooses end-result ethics, he will compare the utilities associated with ruining his clothes, watch and billfold with those associated with saving his daughter's life. If he chooses rule ethics, he might first check to see if the hotel has posted any rules that prohibit a fully clothed person from entering the pool. And if he chooses social contract ethics, he might reflect on the social contract that he has with his family members. Obviously, he will choose none of these. He will jump into the pool immediately to rescue his daughter.[13]

Hitt argues that the motivation to action is clearly the father's conscience telling him, "Act now!" The nature of human existence provides us with opportunities to develop our own set of values—known as our conscience. Contemporary literature and movie scripts are filled with questions such as, how can this woman go to sleep at night, or how can this man look at himself in the mirror? Personalistic ethics posit that moral decisions and judgments must be made by individuals; they are not absolute. People must determine what is right and appropriate to do, individually; they should not impose their standards on others. Individual moral codes may be, but are not necessarily, informed by a belief in the moral imperatives of Judeo-Christian, Islamic, or other religious beliefs. We will discuss later the

---

13   W. Hitt, *Ethics and Leadership: Putting Theory into Practice* (Columbus, OH: Battelle Press, 1990) at 121-22. See discussion in R. Lewicki *et al.*, *Negotiation*, 5th ed. (New York: McGraw-Hill Irwin, 2006) at 244-45.

extent to which codes of professional conduct effectively create and set out ethical standards that build on those of the great philosophers and whether these codes are helpful to representative negotiators confronting ethical issues.

A Look at Our Own Moral and Ethical Compass

In the short article that follows, Howard Raiffa considers social dilemmas and how we react to them.[14] In another article, "Negotiation Analysis,"[15] Raiffa discusses a similar scenario to the following dilemma.[16]

> One miserably hot summer afternoon, you are driving from Toronto to Lake Muskoka on a holiday week-end. Traffic is crawling along a stretch of two-lane one way highway that usually presents no problem. Finally after an interminable delay, you discover the trouble: a mattress on the road; cars have to squeeze to one side to pass it. Should you stop your car and move the mattress? There will be at least some inconvenience to you and possibly a bit of danger involved if you stop. "Why should I be the fall guy? Let someone else be the good guy. Anyway, I'm already late, because of the delay for my appointment."

What would you do? Would you stop and move the mattress? Do you think there would be a difference in response between genders? Between different cultural groups?

How much are we individually willing to sacrifice for the good of others when we get no immediate tangible reward other than the self-satisfaction of doing good? In "Ethical and Moral Issues," Raiffa looks at the social dilemma of having to choose between acting nobly and selfishly. If you act nobly, you will help others at your expense; if you act selfishly, you will help yourself at the expense of others. Others have to make similar decisions. To highlight the tension between helping yourself and helping others, the social dilemma suggests that if all participants act nobly, all do well and society flourishes. But regardless of how others act, you can always do better for yourself, as measured in tangible rewards (profits), if you act selfishly—though doing so is at the expense of others. (The best tangible reward accrues to you in this game if you act selfishly and all others act nobly. But if everyone acts selfishly, all suffer greatly.) Think about how you would likely act in both the "game" scenarios.

---

14   These social dilemmas were developed by Thomas Schelling, a leading negotiation scholar.

15   This text was co-written with John Richardson and David Metcalfe.

16   H. Raiffa, with J. Richardson & D. Metcalfe, "Negotiation Analysis" in H. Raiffa, J. Richardson, & D. Metcalfe, *Negotiation Analysis: The Science and Art of Collaborative Decision Making* (Cambridge, MA: Belknap Press of Harvard University Press, 2002). The model for this scenario was developed by Thomas Schelling.

Howard Raiffa
"Ethical and Moral Issues"

in H. Raiffa, *The Art and Science of Negotiation* (Cambridge, MA:
Belknap Press of Harvard University Press, 1982), footnotes omitted

It's often said that dishonesty in the short run is poor policy because a tarnished reputation hurts in the long run. The moral question is: Should you be open and honest in the short run because it is right to act that way, even though it might hurt you in the long run?

The hundreds of responses I have obtained to a questionnaire on ethical values are instructive. The distributions of the responses from students of business administration, government, and law are reasonable. But the students do not overwhelmingly say, "That sort of behavior may be borderline in my opinion for others, but is unacceptable to me." Most say, "If I were in that situation, I also probably would act in that borderline way"; and a few say, "I think that that behavior is unethical, but I probably would do the same." That's disturbing to me.

One student defended herself—even though the questionnaires were anonymous—by stating that most businesspeople in their ordinary activities are not subjected to those moral dilemmas. …

Let's abstract and simplify by looking at a simple laboratory exercise concerning an ethical choice. Imagine that you have to choose whether to act nobly or selfishly. If you act nobly, you will be helping others at your own expense; if you act selfishly, you will be helping yourself at others' expense. Similarly, those others have similar choices. In order to highlight the tension between helping yourself and helping others, let's specify that if all participants act nobly, all do well and the society flourishes; but regardless of how others act, you can always do better for yourself, as measured in tangible rewards (say, profits), if you act selfishly—but at the expense of others. Leaving morality aside for the moment, the best tangible reward accrues to you in this asocial game if you act selfishly and all others act nobly. But if all behave that way, all suffer greatly.

To be more concrete, suppose that you are one player in a group of 101, so that there are 100 "others." You have two choices: act nobly or act selfishly. Your payoff depends on your choice and on the proportion of the "others" who choose to act nobly (see figure 1). If, for example, 0.7 of the others act nobly, your payoff is $40 when you act nobly and $140 when you act selfishly. Notice that regardless of what the others do, if you were to switch from noble to selfish behavior, you would receive $100 more; but because of your switch, each of the others would be penalized by $2 and the total penalty to others would be $200—more than what you personally gain. The harm you cause to others, however, is shared: you impose a small harm on each of many.

If the others can see that you are acting selfishly, then acting unselfishly may be your prudent action from a cold, calculating, long-term-benefit point of view. Your good reputation may be a proxy for future tangible rewards. But what if the others (because of the rules of the game) cannot see how you, in particular, behave? Suppose that all anyone learns is how many of the others chose the selfish opinion?

I learned about this game from Thomas Schelling, who dubbed it the "*N*-Person Prisoner's Dilemma Game," a direct generalization of that famous two-person game. In the literature, these games are called "social dilemmas" or "social traps," and are sometimes discussed under the heading of "the problem of the commons" or "the free-rider problem." Whenever anyone uses "the commons," there is a little less for everyone else. The "commons" could be a town green, common grazing land, a common river, the ocean, or the atmosphere. Overpopulating our common planet is a prime manifestation of this problem. Whenever we enjoy a public benefit without paying our due share, we are a "free rider." One variation of the free-rider problem is the noble-volunteer problem: Will a hero please step forward—and risk his or her life for the good of the many?

Figure 1   Payoffs for the Social Dilemma Game

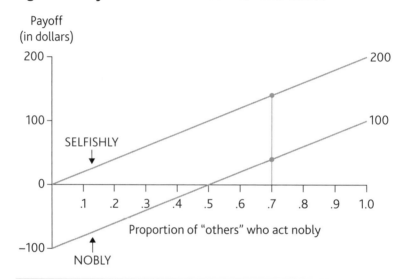

Source: H. Raiffa, "Ethical and Moral Issues" in H. Raiffa, *The Art and Science of Negotiation* (Cambridge, MA: Belknap Press of Harvard University Press, 1982) 15 at 16.

Subjects were asked to play this social dilemma game not for monetary payoffs, but as if there would be monetary payoffs. There might, therefore, be some distortion in the results—probably not much, but in any case the experimental results are not comforting. Roughly 85 percent of the subjects acted non-cooperatively—acted to protect their own interests. Most subjects believed that only a small minority of the others would choose the cooperative (noble) act, and they saw no reason why they should be penalized; so they chose not to act cooperatively. They felt that it was not their behavior that was wrong, but the situation they were participating in. Unfortunately, many real-world games have these characteristics. A few subjects acted cooperatively because they were simply confused; but others—the really noble ones—knew exactly what was going on and chose to sacrifice their own tangible rewards for the good of the others, even though the others did not know who was acting for their benefit. If the rules of the game were changed to make "goodness" more visible, then more subjects would opt for the noble action—some, perhaps, for long-range selfish reasons. This suggests a positive action program: we should try to identify asocial games (social dilemmas) and modify the rules, if possible (which is easier said than done).

Now let's suppose that you are in a position to influence the one hundred others to act nobly by publicly appealing to their consciences. Do you need to influence all to follow your lead? No. You will get a higher monetary return for yourself by converting fifty selfish souls to the noble cause than by joining the ranks of the selfish. But balancing tangible and intangible rewards, you might still prefer to act nobly if you could get, say, forty conversions; with fewer conversions, you might be sacrificing too much. Suppose that you are wildly successful: seventy-five others join your coalition. Say that seventeen of these would have acted nobly anyway; three are despicable poseurs who join the nobles but who will defect secretly; and fifty-five have actually been swayed by your moral pleadings. Now you not only have benefited financially, but you feel morally righteous as well. Unfortunately, your actions have also made it more profitable for the remaining twenty-five who have not joined your coalition. Each conversion adds $2 to the payoff of each of the others, including the selfish holdouts—they've been helped by your successful proselytizing. This may really bother some of the converted ones; it's unfair, they may argue, that the selfish, undeserving ones should profit from the noble actions of the majority. (A real-world analogue is the case where most of the nations of the world might agree not to catch blue whales, and because of this pact, it becomes easier for one noncooperating whaling country to find its prey.) Some of your converts may be so bothered to see that the undeserving are doing better than themselves that they may decide to defect. They may argue that the coalition is not working, when in absolute terms it may be working for them; but it may not be working in comparative terms. It rankles them that they are helping someone who is taking advantage of their noble behavior. So a few defect, and as a result, the coalition can easily come apart.

Integrity in Negotiation

According to Roger Fisher, "Most ethical problems facing lawyers in a negotiation stem from a conflict of interest between the lawyer's obligation to the client (presumably to get the best deal) and two of the lawyer's other interests: behaving honourably toward others involved in the negotiation and self-interest in preserving reputation and self-esteem."[17]

It is often asserted that a lawyer or other representative negotiator is obliged to bluff and deceive those on the other side to the extent that it is ethically possible to do so. James White writes, "In one sense the negotiator's role is at least passively to mislead his opponent … while at the same time to engage in ethical behaviour." And, "Anyone who would maximize his potential as a negotiator must occasionally do things that would cause others to classify him as a 'trickster,' whether he so classifies himself or not."[18]

Here we discuss the principal ethical issues confronting a representative negotiator and specifically the dilemma between behaving honourably and the expectation that a third-party representative, and particularly a lawyer, should be zealously asserting the claims or

---

17   R. Fisher, "A Code of Negotiation Practices for Lawyers" (1985) 1:2 Negotiation Journal 105. This article is excerpted below on pages 130-34.

18   J.J. White, "The Pros and Cons of Getting to Yes" (1984) 34 J. Legal Educ. 115 at 118-19.

concerns of her clients. How far should a representative go on behalf of an unethical and deceptive client? At what point are the representative's actions in asserting claims on behalf of a client immoral and potentially illegal? Richard Shell confronts these issues, and he proposes that although negotiators should "aim high" in their ethical conduct, a minimum of ethical standards are required in any negotiation (see the excerpt from Shell's "Bargaining with the Devil Without Losing Your Soul: Ethics in Negotiation," on pages 116–27). Though Shell discusses these issues in the American context, he maintains that the basic principles of fairness and prudence in bargaining conduct are global.[19]

Three Schools of Bargaining Ethics

In order to help negotiators aim high with respect to ethics in negotiation, Shell goes beyond minimum ethical standards to focus on common schools of bargaining ethics. Shell does not suggest that a single approach to ethics in negotiating is clearly superior (whether morally or pragmatically) to the others. Rather, he outlines three schools of bargaining ethics, allowing negotiators to decide which approach best defines their approach to ethical practice: (1) the "It's a game" Poker School, (2) the "Do the right thing even if it hurts" Idealist School, and (3) the "What goes around, comes around" Pragmatist School.[20]

The "It's a game" Poker School, originally conceptualized by Albert Carr,[21] was discussed and analyzed in a seminal article by James White. Carr claims "the ethics of business are game ethics, different from the ethics of religion."[22] Thus, business ethics are distinguished from personal morality or ethics in which "the golden rule" would normally apply. Advocates of this approach claim that, in the context of commercial negotiations, deception and bluffing are exonerated because experienced negotiators expect such strategies as part of the "rules" of negotiating and consequentially place no reliance in them. People who adhere to the Poker School readily admit that bargaining and poker are not exactly the same. However, they point out, deception is essential to play effectively in both arenas. White writes:

> a negotiator hopes that his opponent will overestimate the value of his hand. Like the poker player, in a variety of ways he must facilitate his opponent's inaccurate assessment. … I submit that a careful examination of the behavior of even the most forthright, honest, and trustworthy negotiators will show them actively engaged in misleading their opponents about their true position. … To conceal one's true position, to mislead an opponent about one's true settling point, is the essence of negotiation.[23]

---

19 G.R. Shell, "Bargaining with the Devil Without Losing Your Soul: Ethics in Negotiation" in C. Menkel-Meadow & M. Wheeler, eds., *What's Fair: Ethics for Negotiators* (San Francisco: Jossey-Bass, 2004) 57. This article is reproduced below.

20 *Ibid.* at 65.

21 A.Z. Carr, "Is Business Bluffing Ethical?" (1968) 46 Harvard Business Review 143; A.Z. Carr, *Business as a Game* (New York: New American Library, 1968).

22 Carr, "Is Business Bluffing Ethical?" *ibid.* at 143.

23 J.J. White, "Machiavelli and the Bar: Ethical Limitations on Lying in Negotiation" (1980) American Bar Foundation Resolution Journal 926 at 928.

Skilled players, in both poker and bargaining, are likely to exhibit a robust and realistic distrust of the other negotiator(s). This school nevertheless recognizes that both "games" have strict rules. (In poker, for instance, hiding cards is not permitted.) Proponents of the Poker School approach do not believe that members should be precluded from playing because outsiders disagree with the School's central assumptions. Idealists and pragmatists disagree with the Poker School approach, arguing that there are *no* strict rules in negotiation. Though "the game" depends on the presumption that the rules are known by all negotiators, laws and codes of conduct vary in different circumstances and communities and may not be known by the novice or visiting negotiator.

David Lax and James Sebenius address the ethical issue of power (without challenging the game metaphor) by asking, "are the 'rules' known and accepted by all sides?" Further, they ask, "how can any 'rules' of the game meet the mutual 'awareness and acceptance of the rules' test?"[24] They suggest that all parties must not only understand the rules of the game but also be equally free to enter and leave the situation.[25] The question is not just a matter of the ethics of honesty in negotiation, but the ethics of power exercised in negotiation relationships.

The "Do the right thing even if it hurts" Idealist School, derived from Kant and the concept of duty ethics, holds that behaviour that is considered unethical in daily life must also be unethical in the commercial and business context. The Idealist School of negotiation ethics says, "bargaining is an aspect of social life, not a special activity with its own set of rules. The same ethics that apply in the home should carry directly into the realm of negotiation."[26] If it is wrong to lie or mislead in a social context, it is wrong to do so in a negotiation. Idealists argue that lying in a negotiation is a selfish act designed to achieve personal gain, and, therefore, unethical. Idealists generally prefer to be candid, even if it means surrendering some strategic advantage. Idealists do not rule out deceptions altogether; "harmless" ones are permissible. A major shortcoming of this position is that idealists may be open to exploitation by canny parties. "Idealists think that the members of the Poker School are predatory and selfish. For its part, the Poker School thinks that idealists are naïve and even a little silly."[27] Shell, himself, expresses a personal preference for the Idealist approach, proposing that negotiators should at least aim for this standard, even if they occasionally fall short of it in their personal or professional life.

The "What goes around, comes around" Pragmatist School recognizes the game aspects of the Poker School approach but eschews the idea of "necessary" deceptions. Lying is wrong not because it is unethical but because it is impractical. Erosion of trust will lead to long-term losses that more than offset short-term gains. Shell's analysis is perhaps weakest here; he identifies the main difference between the pragmatists and the idealists as the fact that the former will lie a bit more often than the latter.

---

24   D.A. Lax & J.K. Sebenius, "Three Ethical Issues in Negotiation" (1986) 2:4 Negotiation Journal 363.

25   *Ibid.* at 365, citing S. Bok, *Lying: Moral Choices in Public and Private Life* (New York: Pantheon Books, 1978).

26   Shell, *supra* note 19 at 67.

27   *Ibid.*

Shell provides examples of how each of these schools would respond during a negotiation to a buyer's direct question: "Do you have another offer?" in the section titled "The Ethical Schools in Action," toward the end of the excerpt that follows.

Minimum Ethical Standards

Shell asserts in his article below that negotiators are not bound by a general "good faith" duty in the negotiation of commercial contracts. Thus, he suggests, the best bright-line standard for judging whether a negotiation has been conducted ethically is the law of fraud. Shell explains how the elements of fraud analysis can help evaluate ethical conduct. According to the six key elements of fraud analysis, "[a] bargaining move is fraudulent when a speaker makes a (1) knowing (2) misrepresentation of a (3) material (4) fact (5) on which the victim reasonably relies (6) causing damages."[28]

G. Richard Shell
"Bargaining with the Devil Without
Losing Your Soul: Ethics in Negotiation"

in C. Menkel-Meadow & M. Wheeler, eds., *What's Fair: Ethics for Negotiators* (San Francisco: Jossey-Bass, 2004) 57

Ethics Come First, Not Last

Your attitudes about ethical conduct are preliminary to every bargaining move you make. Your ethics are a vital part of your identity as a person, and, try as you may, you will never be able to successfully separate the way you act in negotiations from the person you are in other parts of your life. That is "you" at the bargaining table as well as "you" in the mirror every morning.

Your personal beliefs about ethics also come with a price tag. The stricter your ethical standards, the higher the cost you must be willing to pay to uphold them in any given transaction. The lower your ethical standards, the higher the price may be in terms of your reputation. And the lower the standards of those with whom you deal, the more time, energy, and prudence are required to defend yourself and your interests.

I'll give you my bias on this subject right up front: I think you should aim high where ethics are concerned. Personal integrity is one of the four most important effectiveness factors for the skilled negotiator. Negotiators who value "personal integrity" can be counted on to negotiate consistently, using a thoughtful set of personal values that they could, if necessary, explain to others. This definition puts the burden on you as an individual—not me as judge—to construct your own ethical framework. I learned long ago that the best way to teach others about values is to raise tough questions, give people tools to think about them, then get out of the way.

---

28   *Ibid.* at 58.

Reasonable people will differ on ethical questions, but you will have personal integrity in my estimation if you can pass my "explain and defend" test after making a considered, ethical choice. After we have examined some ways of thinking about your own duties, we will look at how you can defend yourself when others use ethically questionable tactics against you.

The Minimum Standard: Obey the Law

Regardless of how you feel about ethics, everyone has a duty to obey the laws that regulate the negotiation process. Of course, bargaining laws differ between countries and cultures, but the normative concerns underlying these different legal regimes share important characteristics. I will look briefly at the American approach to the legal regulations of deception as an example of the way law works in negotiations, but basic principles of fairness and prudence in the bargaining conduct are global, not national.

American law disclaims any general duty of "good faith" in the negotiation of commercial agreements. As an American judge once wrote, "In a business transaction both sides presumably try to get the best deal. … The proper recourse [for outrageous conduct] is to walk away from the bargaining table, not sue for 'bad faith' in negotiations." This general rule assumes, however, that no one has committed fraud. As we shall see, the law of fraud reaches deep into the complexities of negotiation behavior.

There are six major elements of a fraud case. A bargaining move is fraudulent when a speaker makes a (1) knowing (2) misrepresentation of a (3) material (4) fact (5) on which the victim reasonably relies (6) causing damages.

A car dealer commits fraud when he resets a car odometer and sells one of his company cars as if it were brand new. The dealer knows the car is not new; he misrepresents its condition to the buyer; the condition of the car is a fact rather than a mere opinion, and it is a fact that is important ("material") to the transaction; the buyer is acting reasonably in relying on the mileage as recorded on the odometer when she buys the car; and damages result. Similarly, a person selling her business commits fraud when she lies about the number and kind of debts owed by the business.

Lies about important facts that go to the core of a deal are not unknown in business negotiations. But most negotiators don't need a lawyer or an ethicist to tell them that such misrepresentations ought to be avoided. These are cases of fraud, pure and simple. People who try to cheat you are crooks.

More interesting questions about lying arise on the margins of the law of fraud. What if the dealer says you had better buy the car today because he has another buyer ready to snatch the car away tomorrow? That may be a statement of fact, but is it material? It looks like Sifford's little lie about his catalogue price. [Earlier in the chapter, the author relates a story in which the late Darrell Sifford, a Philadelphia newspaper columnist, is able to get a remarkable deal on a globe by lying to the store clerk, saying that he had seen the same globe in a catalogue for a lower price.] Assuming Sifford is innocent of legal fraud in the globe case, should we hold a professional car dealer to a different legal standard? Is the car dealer's lie about the other buyer fraudulent or just a form of creative motivation?

Suppose the seller does not state a fact but instead gives an artfully phrased opinion? Perhaps the person selling her business says that a large account debt "could probably be renegotiated" after you buy the firm. Could this opinion be deemed so misleading as to be fraudulent if the seller knows for a fact that the creditor would never consider renegotiation?

Let's look briefly at each element in the law of fraud and test where the legal limits lie. Surprisingly, though we would all prefer to see clear black and white rules outlining our legal duties, staying on the right side of the law often requires a prudent respect for the many gray areas that inevitably color an activity as widespread and multifaceted as negotiation. Knowing what the law is helps you stay within its boundaries, but this knowledge does not eliminate the need for a strong sense of right and wrong.

Element 1: Knowing

To commit fraud, a negotiator must have a particular state of mind with respect to the fact he or she misrepresents. The misstatement must be made "knowingly." One way of getting around fraud, therefore, might be for the speaker to avoid direct contact with information that would lead to a "knowing" state of mind.

For example, a company president might suspect that his company is in poor financial health, but he does not yet "know" it because he has not seen the latest quarterly reports. When his advisers ask to set up a meeting to discuss these reports, he tells them to hold off. He is about to go into negotiation with an important supplier and would like to be able to say, honestly, that so far as he knows the company is paying its bills. Does this get him off the hook? Perhaps. But many courts have stretched the definition of "knowing" to include statements that are, like the executive's in this case, made with a conscious and reckless disregard for their truth.

Nor is reckless disregard for truth the limit of the law. Victims of misstatements that were made negligently or even innocently may obtain relief in certain circumstances. These kinds of misstatements are not deemed fraudulent, however. Rather, they are a way of recognizing that a deal was based on a mistake.

Element 2: Misrepresentation

In general, the law requires a negotiator to make a positive misstatement before a statement is judged fraudulent. A basic legal rule for commercial negotiators is, "Be silent and be safe."

As a practical matter, of course, silence is difficult to maintain if one's bargaining opponent is an astute questioner. In the face of inconvenient questions, negotiators are often forced to resort to verbal feints and dodges such as, "I don't know about that" or, when pressed, "This is not a subject I am at liberty to discuss." When you choose to lie in response to a pointed question probing the strength of your bargaining position, you immediately raise the risk of legal liability. As we shall see below, however, some lies are not material, and the other party may be charged with a duty to discount the truth of what you tell them.

Surprisingly, there are circumstances when it may be fraudulent to keep your peace about an issue even if the other side does not ask about it. When does a negotiator have a duty to voluntarily disclose matters that may hurt his bargaining position? American law imposes affirmative disclosure duties in the following four circumstances:

1. *When the negotiator makes a partial disclosure that is or becomes misleading in light of all the facts.* If you say your company is profitable, you may be under a duty to disclose whether you used questionable accounting techniques to arrive at that statement. You should also update your prior statement if you show a loss in the next quarter and negotiations are continuing.

2. *When the parties stand in a fiduciary relationship to each other.* In negotiation actions between trustees and beneficiaries, partners in a partnership, shareholders in a small corporation, or members of a family business, parties may have a duty of complete candor and cannot rely on the "be silent and be safe" approach.

3. *When the nondisclosing party has vital information about the transaction not accessible to the other side.* A recent case applying this exception held that an employer owed a duty of disclosure to a prospective employee to disclose contingency plans for shutting down the project for which the employee was hired. In general, sellers have a greater duty to disclose hidden defects about their property than buyers do to disclose "hidden treasure" that may be buried there. Thus, a home seller must disclose termite infestation in her home, but an oil company need not voluntarily disclose that there is oil on a farmer's land when negotiating to purchase it. This is a slippery exception; the best test is one of conscience and fairness.

4. *When special codified disclosure duties [exist], such as those regarding contracts of insurance or public offerings of securities.* Legislatures sometimes impose special disclosure duties for particular kinds of transactions. In the United States, for example, many states now require home sellers to disclose all known problems with their houses.

If none of these four exceptions applies, neither side is likely to be found liable for fraud based on nondisclosure. Each party can remain silent, passively letting the other proceed under its own assumptions.

Element 3: Material

Many people lie or deliberately mislead others about something during negotiations. Often they seek to deceive by making initial demands that far exceed their true needs or desires. Sometimes they lie about their bottom line. Perhaps, like Sifford, they embellish their story about why they are entitled to a particular price or concession.

Of course, initial demands and bottom lines may not be "facts" in the ordinary sense of the word. One may have only a vague idea of what one really wants or is willing to pay for something. Hence, a statement that an asking price is "too high" may not be a misrepresentation as much as a statement of opinion or preference.

Suppose, however, that an art gallery owner has been given authority by an artist to sell one of the artist's paintings for any price greater than $10,000. Is it fraud for the gallery owner, as part of a negotiation with a collector, to say, "I can't take less than $12,000"? In fact, she does have authority to sell the painting for anything above $10,000, so there has been a knowing misrepresentation of fact. Suppose the buyer says, "My budget for this purpose is $9,000," when she is really willing to spend $11,000? Same thing. The legal question in both cases is whether these facts are "material."

They are not. In fact, lies about demands and bottom-line prices are so prevalent in the bargaining that many professional negotiators do not consider such misstatements to be lies, preferring the term "bluffs."

Why? Such statements allow the parties to assert the legitimacy of their preferences and set the boundaries of the bargaining range without incurring a risk of loss. Misleading statements about bottom-line prices and demands also enable parties to test the limits of the other side's commitment to their expressed preferences.

The American legal profession has gone so far as to enshrine this practice approvingly in its Model Rules of Professional Conduct. These rules provide that "estimates of price or value placed on the subject of a transaction and a party's intention as to an acceptable settlement of a claim" are not "material" facts for the purposes of the ethical rule prohibiting lawyers from making false statements to a third person.

There are thus no legal problems with lying about how much you might be willing to pay or which of several issues in a negotiation you value more highly. Demands and bottom lines are not, as a matter of law, "material" to a deal.

As one moves from bluffs about how much one wants to spend or charge toward more assertive, specific lies about why one price or another is required, the fraud meter goes up. One common way to back up a price demand, for example, is Sifford's "I can get it cheaper elsewhere" argument, used by consumers the world over. Negotiators often lie about their available alternatives. Is this fraudulent?

When a shopper lies to a storekeeper that she can get an item cheaper across town, the statement is not "material." After all, the seller presumably knows (or should know) at least as much about the value of what he is selling as the buyer does. If the seller wants to sell it for less than the asking price, who knows better than the seller what the right price is?

But suppose we switch roles. Suppose the seller lies about having another offer that the buyer has to beat? For example, take the following older, but still important legal case from Massachusetts.

A commercial landlord bought a building and negotiated a new lease with a toy shop tenant when the tenant's lease expired. The proprietor of the toy shop bargained hard and refused to pay the landlord's demand for a $10,000 increase in rent. The landlord then told the shop owner that he had another tenant willing to pay the $10,000 amount and threatened the current tenant with immediate eviction if he did not promptly agree to the new rate. The tenant paid but learned later that the threat had been a bluff; there had been no other tenant. The tenant successfully sued for fraud.

In another case, ... a real estate agent was held liable for fraud, including punitive damages, when she pressured a buyer into closing on a home with a story that a rival buyer (the contractor who built the house) was willing to pay the asking price and would do so later that same day.

What makes these lies different in a legal sense from the "I can't take less than $12,000" statement by the art gallery owner or the "I can get it cheaper elsewhere" comment by a shopper? I think the difference has to do with the fact that the victims in these cases were "little people"—small business and customers—who were being pressured unfairly by professionals. The made-up offers were "material" facts from the buyers' point of view. They were specific, factual, coupled with ultimatums, and impossible to investigate.

But I do not think a court would have reached the same result if both parties had been consumers or both sophisticated professionals. Nor would I expect to see results like this outside a wealthy, consumer-oriented country such as the United States. Still, it is worth noting that such cases exist. They counsel a degree of prudence on the part of professional sellers or buyers when dealing with the public.

Element 4: Fact

On the surface, it appears that only misstatements of objective facts are occasions for legal sanctions. Businessmen seeking to walk close to the legal line are therefore careful to couch their sales talk in negotiation as opinions, predictions, and statements of intention, not statements of fact. Moreover, a good deal of exaggeration or puffing about product attributes and likely performance is viewed as a normal aspect of the selling process. Buyers and sellers cannot take everything said to them at face value.

The surface of the law can be misleading, however. Courts have found occasion to punish statements of intention and opinion as fraudulent when faced with particularly egregious cases. The touchstone of the law of fraud is not whether the statement at issue was one of pure fact but rather whether the statement succeeded in concealing a set of facts the negotiator preferred to keep out of sight.

Suppose you are borrowing money from a bank and tell the bank as part of your application that you plan to spend the loan on new capital equipment. In fact, you are really going to pay off an old debt. Fraud? Possibly.

In the memorable words of a famous English judge, "The state of a man's mind is as much a fact as the state of his digestion." Lies regarding intention even have a special name in the law: promissory fraud. The key element in a promissory fraud case is proof that the speaker knew he could not live up to his promise *at the time the promise was made*. In other words, he made the promise with his fingers crossed behind his back. If you are the victim, you must also show that the other side's intention going into the deal went to its very heart—that is, that the statement of the intention was "material."

What about statements of opinion? Self-serving statements about the value of your goods or the qualifications of your product or company are the standard (legal) fare of the negotiating table. However, when negotiators offer statements of opinion that are flatly contradicted by facts known to them about the subject of the transaction, they may be liable for fraud. In one New York case, for example, the seller of a machine shop business opined to a prospective buyer that the buyer would have "no trouble" securing work from his largest customer. In fact, the seller was in debt to his customer, intended to pay off this debt from the proceeds of the sale to the buyer, and had virtually no work there due to his reputation for poor workmanship. The buyer successfully proved that the sale had been induced by the seller's fraudulent statement of opinion and collected damages.

What seems to matter in these cases is unfairness. If a statement of intention or opinion so conceals the true nature of the negotiation proposal that a bargaining opponent cannot accurately assess an appropriate range of values or risks on which to base the price, then it may be fraudulent.

Element 5: Reliance

Negotiators who lie sometimes defend themselves by saying, in effect, "Only a fool could have believed what I said. The other party had no business relying on me to tell him the truth—he should have investigated for himself."

As we saw in our discussion of lies about other offers, this defense works pretty well when both sides are on roughly the same footing. But when one side has a decided advantage, as does a professional buyer or seller against a consumer or small business, American courts are more sympathetic to the idea that the victim reasonably relied on the lie.

In addition, courts are sympathetic to those who, in good faith, rely on others to treat them fairly in the negotiation process and who have that trust violated by more powerful firms trying to steal their trade secrets and other information. There have been a number of cases, for example, allowing recoveries to independent inventors and others who disclosed trade secrets in the course of negotiations to sell their discoveries. The prospective buyers in these cases are typically big companies that attempted to use the negotiation process as a way of getting something for nothing. The prudent negotiator, however, always secures an express confidentiality agreement if secret information or business plans must be disclosed in the course of the information exchange process.

One trick that manipulative negotiators use to avoid liability after they have misstated important facts or improperly motivated a transaction is to write the true terms and conditions into the final written agreement. If the victim signs off on the deal without reading this contract, he will have a hard time claiming reasonable reliance on the earlier misstatements in a fraud case later on.

For example, suppose you negotiate the sale of your company's principal asset, an electronic medical device, to a big medical products firm. During the negotiations, the company assures you that it will aggressively market the device so you can earn royalties. The contract, however, specifically assigns it the legal right to shelve your product if it wishes. After the sale, it decides to stop marketing your product and you later learn the company never really intended to sell it; it was just trying to get your product off the market because it competed with several of its own.

In a case like this, a court held that the plaintiffs were stuck with the terms of the final written contract. The lesson here is clear: *Read* contracts carefully before you sign them, and question assurances that contract language changing the nature of the deal is just a technicality or was required by the lawyers.

Element 6: Causation and Damages

You cannot make a legal claim for fraud if you have no damages caused by the fraudulent statement or omission. People sometimes get confused about this. The other negotiator lies in some outrageous and unethical way, so they assume the liar's conduct is illegal. It may be, but only if that conduct leads directly to some quantifiable economic loss for the victim of the fraud. If there is no such loss, the right move is to walk away from the deal (if you can), not sue.

Beyond the Law: A Look at Ethics

As you may have noticed, the legal rules that govern bargaining are suffused with a number of ethical norms. For example, professionals with a big bargaining advantage are sometimes held to a higher standard when negotiating with amateurs and consumers than they are when they approach others as equals. Parties that stand in special relationships to each other, such as trustees or partners, have heightened legal disclosure duties. Lies protecting important factual information about the subject of the transaction are treated differently from lies about such things as your alternatives or your bottom line. Silence is unacceptable if an important fact is inaccessible to the other side unless you speak up.

I want to challenge you to identify what *your* beliefs are. To help you decide how you feel about ethics, I will briefly describe the three most common approaches to bargaining ethics I have heard expressed in conversations with literally hundreds of students and executives. See which shoe fits—or take a bit from each approach and construct your own.

As we explore this territory, remember that nearly everyone is sincerely convinced that they are acting ethically most of the time, whereas they often think others are acting either naively or unethically, depending on their ethical perspective and the situation. Thus, a word of warning is in order. Your ethics are mainly your own business. They will help you increase your level of confidence and comfort at the bargaining table. But do not expect others to share your ethics in every detail. Prudence pays …

The Ethical Schools in Action

As a test of ethical thinking, let's take a simple example. Assume you are negotiating to sell a commercial building, and the other party asks you whether you have another offer. In fact, you do not have any such offers. What would the three schools recommend you do?

A Poker School adherent might suggest a lie. Both parties are sophisticated business-people in this deal, so a lie about alternatives is probably legally "immaterial." But a member of the Poker School would want to know the answers to two questions before making his move.

First, could the lie be easily found out? If so, it would be a bad play because it wouldn't work and might put the other side on guard with respect to other lies he might want to tell. Second, is a lie about alternatives the best way to leverage the buyer into making a bid? Perhaps a lie about something else—a deadline, for example—might be a better choice.

Assuming the lie is undetectable and will work, how might the conversation sound?

Buyer: Do you have another offer?

Poker School Seller: Yes. A Saudi Arabian firm presented us with an offer for $_____ this morning, and we have only forty-eight hours to get back to it with an answer. Confidentiality forbids us from showing you the Saudi offer, but rest assured that it is real. What would you like to do?

How would an idealist handle this situation? There are several idealist responses, but none would involve a lie. One response would be the following:

Buyer: Do you have another offer?
Idealist Seller 1: An interesting question—and one I refuse to answer.

Of course, that refusal speaks volumes to the buyer. Another approach would be to adopt a policy on "other buyer" questions:

Buyer: Do you have another offer?

Idealist Seller 2: An interesting question, and one I receive quite often. Let me answer you this way. The property's value to you is something for you to decide based on your needs and your own sense of the market. However, I treat all offers with the greatest confidence. I will not discuss any offer you make to me with another buyer, and I would not discuss any offer I received from someone else with you. Will you be bidding?

Of course, this will work for an idealist only if he or she really and truly has such a policy—a costly one when there is another attractive offer he or she would like to reveal.

A final idealist approach would be to offer an honest, straightforward answer. An idealist cannot lie or deliberately mislead, but he is allowed to put the best face he can on the situation that is consistent with the plain truth:

Buyer: Do you have another offer?

Idealist Seller 3: To be honest, we have no offers at this time. However, we are hopeful that we will receive others soon. It might be in your interest to bid now and take the property before competition drives the price up.

How about the pragmatists? They would suggest using somewhat more sophisticated, perhaps deceptive blocking techniques. These techniques would protect their leverage in ways that were consistent with maintaining work relationships. Once again, assume that the buyer has asked the "other offer" question and there are no other offers. Here are five ways a pragmatist might suggest you block this question to avoid an out-and-out factual lie about other offers while minimizing the damage to your leverage. Some of these blocking techniques would work for idealists too:

- *Declare the question out of bounds*: "Company policy forbids any discussion of other offers in a situation like this." Note that, if untrue, this is a lie, but it is one that carries less risk to your reputation because it is hard to confirm. If there really is such a company policy, an idealist could also use this move to block the question.
- *Answer a different question*: "We will not be keeping the property on the market much longer because the market is moving and our plans are changing." Again, if untrue, this statement is a mere lie about a rationale that troubles pragmatists less than idealists.
- *Dodge the question*: "The more important question is whether we are going to get an offer from you—and when."
- *Ask a question of your own*: "What alternatives are you examining at this time?"
- *Change the subject*: "We are late for our next meeting already. Are you bidding today or not?"

Blocking techniques of this sort serve a utilitarian purpose. They preserve some leverage (though not as much as the Poker School) while reducing the risk of acquiring a reputation for deception. Relationships and reputations matter. If there is even a remote chance of a lie coming back to haunt you in a future negotiation with either the person you lie to or someone he may interact with, the pragmatists argue that you should not do it.

So—which school do you belong to? Or do you belong to the school of your own, such as "pragmatic idealism"? To repeat, my advice is to aim high. The pressure of real bargaining often makes ethical compromisers of us all. When you fall below the standard of the Poker School, you are at serious risk of legal and even criminal liability.

Bargaining with the Devil: The Art of Self-Defense

Regardless of which school of bargaining ethics you adopt, you are going to face unscrupulous tactics from others on occasion. Even members of the Poker School sometimes face off against crooks. Are there any reliable means of self-defense to protect yourself and minimize the dangers? This section will give you some pointers on how to engage in effective self-defense against unethical tactics at the bargaining able.

Maintain Your Own Standards—Don't Sink to Theirs

It is tempting to engage in tit for tat when the other side uses unethical tactics. We get angry. We lose perspective and start down the unethical path ourselves.

Avoid this trap. First, no matter what school of bargaining ethics you adhere to, you need to keep your record clean both to maintain your self-respect and to avoid gaining a reputation for slippery dealing. Second, as soon as you begin acting unethically, you lose the right to protest other people's conduct. Their behavior may give you a legitimate claim to extract concessions, or it may form the basis for a legal case. Once you join them in the gutter, you forfeit your moral and legal advantage.

Table 1 is a tool to keep yourself out of trouble with deception. You'll have to decide for yourself whether the advice passes muster under your personal ethical standards. So far as I know, all of the alternatives are legal, so Poker School adherents who find themselves in a tight spot in which a lie will not work should feel free to use them. Pragmatists usually prefer to avoid lies if relationships matter, so these will be helpful to them too. Idealists can use any of these that involve telling the truth in a way that does not mislead or deflecting a question with an obvious, transparent blocking maneuver.

Remember, there is no commandment in negotiation that says, "Thou shalt answer every question that is asked." And as an aspiring idealist, I have found it useful to follow this rule: *Whenever you are tempted to lie about something, stop, think for a moment, and then find something—anything—to tell the truth about.* If the other side asks you about your alternatives or your bottom line, deflect that question and then tell the truth about your goals, expectations, and interests.

A Rogue's Gallery of Tactics

As my final offering on this topic, here is a list of the more common manipulative tactics you will encounter at the bargaining table:

- Decide which school of bargaining ethics you belong to.
- Determine whether you can use your relationships to offset the dangers of unethical conduct by others involved in the transaction.
- Probe, probe, probe. Do not take what you hear at face value.
- Pause. Remember that you do not have to answer every question.
- Do not lie. Instead, find a way to use the truth to your advantage.

We have seen some of these before, but I will summarize them again for ease of reference. Note that only some of them involve overt deception.

I do not label these unethical because most of them are well within the boundaries of the Poker School, and some can work even for pragmatists when there is no relationship problem in view.

Table 1 Alternatives to Lying

Instead of Lying About	Try This
Bottom line	Blocking maneuvers.
	Ask about their bottom line.
	Say, "It's not your business."
	Say, "I'm not free to disclose that."
	Tell the truth about your goal.
	Focus on your problems or needs.
Lack of authority	Obtain only limited authority in the first place.
	Require ratification by your group.
Availability of alternatives	Initiate efforts to improve alternatives.
	Stress opportunities and uncertainties.
	Be satisfied with the status quo.
Commitment to positions	Commit to general goals.
	Commit to standards.
	Commit to addressing the other side's interests.
Phony issues	Inject new issues with real value or make a true wish list.
Threats	Use cooling-off periods.
	Suggest third-party help.
	Discuss use of a formula.
Intentions	Make only promises you can and will keep.
Facts	Focus on uncertainty regarding the facts.
	Use language carefully.
	Express your opinion.

Summary

Ethical dilemmas are at the center of many bargaining encounters. There is no escaping the fact that deception is part of negotiation. And there is no escaping the importance people place on personal integrity in their dealings with others at the bargaining table. One ethical slip, and your credibility is lost, not just for one but for many deals. Effective negotiations take the issue of personal integrity very seriously. Ineffective negotiators do not.

How do you balance these two contradictory factors? I have presented three frameworks for thinking about ethical issues: the Poker School, the Idealist School, and the Pragmatist School. I personally think you are better off sticking to the truth as much as possible. I sometimes lose leverage as the price of this scruple, but I gain a greater measure of ease and self-respect as compensation.

Where you come out on bargaining ethics, of course, is a matter for you to decide. My only injunction to you is this: negotiators who value personal integrity can be counted on to behave consistently, using a thoughtful set of personal values that they could, if necessary, explain and defend to others.

Can Answers Be Found in Codes of Conduct?

What about the nature of the ethical relationship between a lawyer and client or another representative negotiator and his client? Do codes of conduct help answer the moral and ethical dilemmas that have been discussed in this chapter? The Canadian Bar Association's *Code of Professional Conduct* calls upon lawyers to undertake duties with "integrity,"[29] "honest[y] and candour,"[30] and to observe a "standard of conduct that reflects credit on the legal profession and the administration of justice generally and inspires the confidence and trust of both clients and the community."[31] Is this "standard of conduct" set by the Canadian Bar Association helpful in determining how a lawyer should behave in the situations discussed in this chapter? Should we set our standards solely on the basis of "complying"? Julian Webb writes:

> Virtue also conveys, more generally, a commitment to fairness, and an idea of 'wholeness' that we have become perhaps less accustomed to apply to people than things. Yet it is 'wholeness' that … is critical, particularly as a counterbalance to the morally deadening consequences of too close an adhesion to a narrowly defined role morality. There is no virtue in blind adherence to a role or a rule. By 'wholeness' I am thus trying to convey a sense of being true to oneself, not as a metaphysical being, but as an embodied self in constant interaction with others."[32]

In 2002, lawyers in the American Bar Association (ABA) engaged in a debate pertaining to a proposed "duty of fair dealing"[33] in settlement negotiations and an existing duty not to make "false statements of material fact or law."[34] The latter, however, does not include "statements of opinion or those that merely reflect the speaker's state of mind."[35] As ABA Model Rule 4.1, comment 2, states:

---

29 Canadian Bar Association, *Code of Professional Conduct* (Ottawa: Canadian Bar Association, 2006) c. I.

30 *Ibid.* c. II (Advising Clients)

31 *Ibid.* c. XVI (Avoiding Questionable Conduct, Commentary 10).

32 J. Webb, "Ethics for Lawyers or Ethics for Citizens? New Directions for Legal Education" (1998) 25 Journal of Law and Society 134-50 at 143.

33 American Bar Association, Section on Litigation, *Ethical Guidelines for Settlement Negotiations* (Chicago: American Bar Association, 2002) s. 2.3.

34 *Ibid.*, s. 4.1.1.

35 *Ibid.*

Under generally accepted conventions in negotiation, certain types of statements ordinarily are not taken as statements of material fact. Estimates of price or value placed on the subject of a transaction and a party's intentions as to an acceptable settlement of a claim are ordinarily in this category ...[36]

Commenting on negotiations of counsel in mediation, the ABA Ethics Committee concluded that "statements regarding a party's negotiating goals or its willingness to compromise, as well as statements that can fairly be characterized as negotiation 'puffing,' ordinarily are not considered 'false statements of material fact' within the meaning of the Model Rules."[37]

Dispute resolution scholar Kimberlee Kovach denounces the opinion of the ABA Ethics Committee, saying that it allows deceit "under the characterization of 'puffery' in negotiation," and also allows "attorneys to make misrepresentations to the mediator as well as one another." Kovach finds this particularly troubling, given the ABA's endorsement of a mediator's duty to "promote honesty and candor between and among all participants."[38] Her response focuses on the ethical and moral tensions between the moral imperative "do not lie" and commonly accepted practices of deception within the field of representative negotiation.

According to Robert Piercey, some moral philosophers derive ethics from deeper moral norms that must trump more contingently situated ethics.[39] Thus, "do not lie" trumps any suggestion of any type of deception in negotiation, including puffery or misleading about one's client's bottom line. Others claim the contrary—that morality is derived from localized and particularized ethical discourse. For the ABA, puffery and misleading about the bottom line are seen as ethically acceptable, since both are customarily part of the rules of the negotiation game that all players should know.

Webb believes that social virtues, expressed in such terms as friendship, care, beneficence, sympathy, and solidarity, are more important than the minimal standards set by the legal profession and should assist us in exploring the nature and limits of social and professional responsibility.[40]

---

36   *Ibid.*

37   American Bar Association Standing Committee on Ethics and Professional Responsibility, *Lawyer's Obligation of Truthfulness When Representing a Client in Negotiation: Application to Caucused Mediation,* Formal Opinion 06-439 (Chicago: American Bar Association, 2006), online: BNA <http://www.bna.com/bnabooks/ababna/annual/2006/42.pdf>.

38   K. Kovach, "Ethics Opinion a Step Back in Time, Complicates Responsibility of Mediators" (2006), online: American Bar Association Committee on Ethics <http://www.abanet.org/dch/committee.cfm?com=DR018000> citing Standard VI, 4 of the Model Standards of Conduct for Mediators approved by the American Bar Association, the American Arbitration Association, and the Association for Conflict Resolution in August 2005, which can be found at <http://www.abanet.org/dispute/news/ModelStandardsofConductforMediatorsfinal05.pdf>.

39   R. Piercey, "Not Choosing Between Morality and Ethics" (2001) 32 The Philosophical Forum 53 at 54.

40   Webb, *supra* note 32 at 144.

Julie Macfarlane argues that the ethical dilemmas mediators encounter are much too multi-dimensional to be summarized in a generic code such as the Canadian Bar Association—Ontario ADR Section Model Code of Conduct for Mediators.[41] She also suggests that these types of codes are too general to be useful and that practitioners must develop "internal norms," rather than rely on external ones. "The current approach—largely limited to the development of voluntary codes of conduct for mediators—consistently underestimates and oversimplifies the complexities of what it means to mediate ethically."[42] Macfarlane argues that "codes of conduct … are neither conceptually nor structurally able to address the complex and unique moral dilemmas of practice," and that the "norms and practices for a case must be generated from the actual interaction between the parties and the mediator."[43]

Mediation is negotiation with impartial and neutral third-party facilitators. Does Macfarlane's concern about the utility of codes of conduct for mediators extend to codes of conduct for third-party negotiators? Who should write such codes—the legal profession, unions, the real estate industry, or experts on professional or business ethics? Are codes of conduct helpful in negotiations? Are they used? And whom do the codes protect—the public or the negotiator, the individual mediator or the mediation's professional work group? How effectively are codes enforced? In the last 100 years we have seen the proliferation of codes of professional conduct. Accountants, lawyers, and brokers are all subject to mandatory ethics courses that attempt to raise the "ethical consciousness" in business and the professions. Many of these codes are after-the-fact attempts to convince the public, shareholders, and regulators that corporations and their representatives are taking their monopolies seriously and monitoring and policing their professional ethics.

In 2000, Wilkinson, Walker, and Mercer conducted a study focusing on whether lawyers in Ontario consulted their code of professional conduct, and specifically whether the Professional Conduct Handbook ("the Handbook") was considered a useful tool. The authors reported that "the Handbook actually inhibited the ethical deliberations of those lawyers who referred to it for assistance in solving their specific problems."[44] They concluded that "the net effect of these results is that the lawyers who did not consult the Handbook arguably behaved more ethically more often than those who did refer to the Handbook."[45] On the basis of their findings, the authors observed that ethical rules can actually serve to impede moral development. If lawyers can simply turn to a specific rule when facing an ethical

---

41   Canadian Bar Association—Ontario ADR Section Model Code of Conduct for Mediators, online: Ontario Ministry of the Attorney General <http://www.attorneygeneral.jus.gov.on.ca/ english/courts/manmed/codeofconduct.asp>. The code was drafted for lawyer and non-lawyer mediators and has been adopted as the code of mediator conduct for the Mandatory Mediation Program in the Ontario Superior Court in Ottawa, Toronto, and Windsor. Ontario Rules of Civil Procedure, R.R.O. 1990, Reg. 194 R.24.1 Mandatory Mediation.

42   J. Macfarlane, "Mediating Ethically: The Limits of Codes of Conduct and the Potential of a Reflective Practice Model" (2002) 40 Osgoode Hall L.J. 49 at 51.

43   *Ibid.*

44   M.A. Wilkinson, C. Walker & P. Mercer, "Do Codes of Ethics Actually Shape Legal Practice?" (2000) 45 McGill L.J. 645 at 647.

45   *Ibid.* at 680.

dilemma, "they will be dissuaded from rational deliberation and from accepting personal responsibility for their actions."[46]

As we have discussed, representative negotiators, and lawyers specifically, are often torn between an obligation to achieve a successful outcome for their client and a desire to negotiate with integrity. In "A Code of Negotiation Practices for Lawyers" below, Fisher outlines a solution to this ethical and moral dilemma. The code Fisher presents was drafted by lawyers and negotiation experts for the Harvard Negotiation Project.[47] Do you think that the code is helpful for negotiators? Is the code a useful guide for non-lawyers who are representative negotiators? Do you find the "model of just behavior" section of the code (see page 132) helpful in dealing with the issues discussed in this chapter? Does the code that Fisher and others developed address some of the competing interests of representative negotiators that we discussed in chapter 2?

Roger Fisher
"A Code of Negotiation Practices for Lawyers"
(1985) 1:2 Negotiation Journal 105-10

Most ethical problems facing lawyers in a negotiation stem from a conflict of interest between the lawyer's obligation to the client (presumably to get the best deal) and two of the lawyer's other interests: behaving honorably toward others involved in the negotiation and self-interest in preserving reputation and self-esteem.

It is often asserted that a lawyer is obliged to bluff and deceive those on the other side to the extent that it is ethically possible to do so. Professor James White of Michigan has written, "In one sense the negotiator's role is at least passively to mislead his opponent … while at the same time to engage in ethical behavior." And, "Anyone who would maximize his potential as a negotiator must occasionally do things that would cause others to classify him as a 'trickster,' whether he so classifies himself or not" (White, 1984, pp. 118-119).

It may be possible to limit these ethical problems by conducting a preliminary negotiation between lawyer and client, clarifying the basis on which the lawyer is conducting the negotiation. The following two drafts are intended to stimulate discussion of this possibility. The first is in the form of a memorandum that a lawyer might give to a new client, and the second an attached draft code of negotiating behavior.

Memorandum to a New Client: How I Propose to Negotiate

Attached to this memorandum is a Code of Negotiation Practices for Lawyers. It has been prepared by lawyers and other professional experts in the negotiation process and is based on a draft first produced by the Harvard Negotiation Project at Harvard Law School.

I would like to obtain your approval for my accepting this code as providing the general guidelines for any negotiations I may conduct on your behalf. I would also like you to know that I will follow these guidelines in any negotiations that you and I may have with each other, for example over the question of fees. Finally, I commend the code to you because I think it provides useful guidance on

---

46   *Ibid.* at 650.

47   Fisher, *supra* note 17.

how you, yourself, might wish to conduct negotiations with others, even though you are not a lawyer.

The reason I would like your approval of my following this code in my negotiations as your lawyer is to avoid any future misunderstanding. In addition, I would like to put to rest the canard that because I am a lawyer, I have a "professional" duty to you as my client to engage in sharp or deceptive practices on your behalf—practices that I would not use on my own behalf and ones that might damage my credibility or my reputation for integrity. Let me explain.

The Code of Professional Responsibility approved by the American Bar Association provides that a lawyer should advance a client's interest zealously. The Code of Professional Responsibility does little to clarify this standard, and the Bar Association has failed to adopt proposed changes that would more explicitly permit a lawyer to balance the duty to be a partisan on behalf of a client with the duty to adhere to ethical standards of candor and honesty.

The result is that in the absence of client approval to do otherwise, it can be (and has been) argued that a lawyer should conceal information, bluff, and otherwise mislead people on behalf of a client even (1) where the lawyer would be unwilling for ethical reasons to do so on his or her own behalf; and (2) where the lawyer's best judgment is that to do so is contrary to the public interest, contrary to wise negotiation practices, and damaging to the very reputation for integrity that may have caused the client to retain the lawyer.

It is no doubt possible that in a given case a lawyer may obtain a short-term gain for a client by bluffing, threatening, actively misrepresenting the extent of the lawyer's authority, what the client is willing to do, or other facts, or by engaging in browbeating or other psychological pressure tactics. Yet many lawyers and academic experts believe that a practice of trying to settle differences by such tactics is risky for clients, bad for lawyers, and bad for society.

I believe that it is not a sound practice to negotiate in a way that rewards deception, stubbornness, dirty tricks, and taking risks. I think it wiser for our clients, ourselves, and our society to deal with differences in a way that optimizes the chance of reaching a fair outcome efficiently and amicably; that rewards those who are better prepared, more skillful and efficient, and who have the better case as measured by objective standards of fairness; and that makes each successive negotiation likely to be even better. (This does not mean that a negotiator should disclose everything or make unjustified concessions.)

The attached code is intended to accomplish those goals.

I hope you will read it and approve my trying to adhere to it. I will be happy to discuss it with you now and at any time during negotiations. Some of the ideas underlying the Code are discussed in the book *Getting to Yes: Negotiating Agreement Without Giving In* by Roger Fisher and William Ury (Houghton Mifflin, 1981). If you would like, I would be happy to provide you with a copy.

A Code of Negotiation Practices for Lawyers

I. Roles

1. Professional. You and those with whom you negotiate are members of an international profession of problem solvers. Do not look upon those on the other side as enemies but rather as partners with whom cooperation is essential and greatly in the interest of your client. You are colleagues in the difficult task of reconciling, as well as possible, interests that are sometimes shared but often conflict.

2. Advocate. You are also an advocate for your client's interests. You have a fiduciary obligation to look after the needs and concerns of your client, to make sure that they are taken into account, and to act in ways that will tend to ensure that they are well satisfied. It is not enough to seek a fair result. Among results that fall within the range of fairness, you should press with diligence and skill toward that result that best satisfies your client's interests consistent with being fair and socially acceptable.

3. Counselor. Clients, motivated by anger or short-term considerations, sometimes act, and may ask you to act, in ways that are contrary to their own best interests. Another of your roles is to help your clients take long-term considerations properly into account, come to understand their enlightened self-interest, and to pursue it.
4. Mediator. Furthermore, a negotiator often has to serve as a mediator between a client and those on the other side. Two lawyers, negotiating with each other, sometimes best function as comediators, trying to bring their clients together.
5. Model of just behavior. Finally, as a lawyer and negotiator, you should behave toward those with whom you negotiate in ways that incorporate the highest moral standards of civilization. Your conduct should be such that you regard it as a praiseworthy model for others to emulate and such that, if it became known, it would reflect credit on you and the bar. You should feel no obligation to be less candid for a client than you would be for yourself, and should not behave in ways that would justifiably damage your reputation for integrity.

II. Goals
As a negotiator, your goal is a good outcome. Such an outcome appears to depend on at least seven elements:

1. Alternatives. The outcome should be better for your client than the best available alternative that could be reached without negotiating.
2. Interests. Your client's interests should be well satisfied. The interests of other parties and the community should be sufficiently satisfied to make the outcome acceptable to them and durable.
3. Options. Among the many possible outcomes, an agreement should be the best possible—or as near to it as can reasonably be developed without incurring undue transaction costs. Possible joint gains and mutually advantageous tradeoffs should be diligently sought, explored, and put to use. The result should be an elegant solution with no waste. This means that it could not be significantly better for your client without being significantly worse for others.
4. Legitimacy. The outcome should be reasonably fair to all as measured by objective criteria such as law, precedent, community practice, and expert opinion. No one should feel "taken."
5. Communication. If negotiations are to reach a wise outcome without waste of time or other resources, there must be effective communication among the parties. Communication should not halt when one or more of the parties wants to express disagreement. Even when a given negotiation fails to produce satisfactory results, communication lines should remain open.
6. Commitments. Pledges as to what you will or won't do should be made not at the outset of a negotiation but after differences of perception, interest, and values are fully appreciated. Commitments should be mutually understood and carefully crafted to be realistic and easy to implement.
7. Relationship. Both the way each negotiation is conducted and its outcome should be such that in future negotiations, it will be easier rather than harder for the parties to reach equally good or better outcomes.

III. Some Good Practices
There is no one best way to negotiate—a way that is applicable to every issue, context, and negotiating partner. In many situations, whether haggling in a bazaar or negotiating a new union contract, customs and expectations may be so fixed that any benefit that might occur from negotiating in a different way would be outweighed by the transaction costs of trying to do so. Nevertheless, the general rules of thumb and seven-element framework for analysis that follow may help even the most seasoned negotiator to continue to learn from experience and to improve the tools at his or her disposal.

A. General Guidelines

1. Authority. You and your client should establish the extent of your authority in terms that are as clear as circumstances permit. This includes the scope of the subject over which you will be negotiating and your authority to discuss questions, develop recommendations, make procedural commitments, and make final commitments on behalf of a client. If a client approves your use of this Code, you have authority to discuss any issue raised by the other side; to seek to develop a proposal that you and the other negotiators can conscientiously recommend; and, if in your judgment the circumstances so warrant, to commit your client to those terms. In almost all circumstances, however, even though you have such extensive authority, you will find it wise to obtain your client's approval of the terms of an agreement before it is finally accepted. Likewise, it is also prudent to let those with whom you are negotiating know at an early stage that that is your intention.

2. Commitment. As negotiations proceed there is often considerable uncertainty as to the degree of the parties' commitment to points on which agreement seems to have been reached. Matters drafted and tentatively accepted cannot be reopened without some cost. Accordingly, it is useful to remind your fellow negotiators from time to time of your understanding of the present status of points on the table. (For example: "My understanding is that we are now, without any commitment from either side, seeking to develop the terms of a possible agreement—terms that we both think might be acceptable." Or: "Our acceptance of this point is on the premise that we are able to reach agreement on all the other points in a package; if other points are not resolved to our mutual satisfaction either party is free to reopen this point.")

3. Two judges. Two negotiators are like two judges in that no decision will be reached unless they agree. A lawyer's skill in dealing with a judge is thus highly relevant to the way in which he or she should treat a fellow negotiator. (A negotiation is less like a quarrel and more like an appellate argument; less "You idiot!…" and more "Your honor…") If an argument has too little merit or is too extremely partisan in your favor to be advanced before a judge, then you should not advance such an argument in the context of a negotiation. Nor should you be less honest or candid than you would be in court with a judge. And, no matter how predisposed you may be, you should be as open to reasoned argument as you would want a judge to be.

B. In Pursuit of a Good Outcome

1. Develop a best self-help alternative. You should compare all proposed terms with your client's best alternative to a negotiated agreement. This means that you should understand the best that your client can do through unilateral action, self-restraint, agreement with some other party, or litigation. In a dispute, one standard with which to compare any proposed settlement is the expected value to your client of the litigation option. You should make a thoughtful and realistic assessment of the possible outcomes of litigation, including the human and financial costs, the uncertainty of result, and the damage to relationships that is often involved. You should not let any personal interest in trying a case, vindicating a position, enhancing a reputation, or earning substantial fees bias your judgment.

2. Clarify interests. You should come to understand fully the interests of your client, not simply the stated wants, but the underlying needs, concerns, fears and hopes. Do your best to make sure that the other side appreciates them. Make sure that you fully appreciate the other side's interests. One element of being well prepared is to be able to present the other side's point of view more persuasively than they can—and to explain convincingly why you still differ.

3. Generate options. Create a wide range of options that you believe are reasonably fair and take account of the legitimate interests of all parties. Encourage joint inventing by the parties, without commitment, of possible ways to reconcile the differing interests involved. To aid the process of inventing possibilities, postpone the process of evaluating and deciding among them.

4. Maximize legitimacy. Develop your knowledge of the law, precedents, expert opinion, and other potential objective standards of fairness applicable to the matter under negotiation. Discover and arm yourself with fair standards that effectively protect your client's interests. Do extensive research on standards previously advanced or accepted by those on the other side. Persuasively present the case for criteria that are both fair and take full account of the interests of your client. Be open to persuasion, but be an effective advocate for those standards that are most favorable to your client's interests to the extent that legitimate arguments can be found for them. In a negotiation, as in a courtroom, discussing what is fair does not mean giving in to the other side's demands.

5. Communicate effectively. Listen. The more you know about the other side's thinking, the greater chance you have of being able to persuade them. Unless you know what is on their minds, you are shooting in the dark. Acknowledging good points is one way of encouraging good communication.

6. Commit carefully. Commitments should generally be made at the end of the negotiation, not at the beginning. To reduce the risk of having either side lock itself into a fixed position before it fully understands the problem, consider the desirability of preparatory discussions at which both sides take no position and advance no proposals. Both sides clarify interests and perceptions, generate options, and suggest possible standards for determining a fair outcome.

When you do make an offer, remain willing to examine any proposed change that (1) would make the proposal better for both sides; (2) would make it substantially better for either side without significantly damaging the interests of the other; or (3) would in your eyes make the proposed agreement objectively fairer. Likewise, you should be prepared and open to considering any counteroffer that meets the same standards.

7. Build relationships. Throughout a negotiation, you have two crucial relationships—with the other side and with your client. In addition, you must continue to live with yourself. A good relationship is built and maintained by adhering to some basic values:

Be honest. Your obligation to your client never requires you to be dishonest. You must, of course, keep some matters confidential. Full disclosure is not expected or required.

Keep promises. Honor commitments. The easiest way to keep all promises is to make very few. If circumstances are going to make it impossible or unreasonable to keep a commitment, be the first to let people know.

Consult. Nothing is more basic to a good working relationship than advance communication. A rule of thumb is ACBD: Always Consult Before Deciding on matters that will significantly affect others.

Be open. A policy of listening, learning, taking advice, and being flexible builds the kind of relationship that encourages joint problem solving.

After the Negotiation

We encourage negotiators to reflect upon and learn from their ethical and moral behaviour in negotiations. Engage in self-reflection and periodically seek feedback from the other parties to the negotiation to learn about how you are perceived and whether you are considered effective and ethical. Barry Stuart, former chief judge of the Territorial Court of Yukon and an advocate of using the Aboriginal tradition of peacemaking circles in restorative justice efforts, suggests that negotiators reflect upon the following after a negotiation:[48]

---

48   B.D. Stuart, *Peacemaking Circles: Principles for Introduction and Design of Peacemaking Circles* (LL.M. Thesis, Osgoode Hall Law School, 1999) [unpublished].

	What I Want to Feel About Myself While Driving Home	What I Want the Other Parties to Feel About Me While Driving Home
Honesty	"I want to feel I have been honest."	"That they have felt I have been honest."
Respect	"It is important for me to respect others, to respect their interest, their views."	"That they respect and understood me."
Listening	"If I don't listen, I won't be showing respect, but I really want to be sure I listen to hear what they say."	"That they feel I did hear them, and they know that."
Fair	"Whatever happens, fairness is important. I don't want to leave with something that is not fair for them or for me."	"That they believe I tried to be, and was, fair."
Trust	"This may be hard, but I really want to leave feeling I trusted them—you know, really trusted them."	"That they could trust me and believed that I didn't deceive them or didn't want to deceive them."
Practical	"What we do has to make sense, moves us along. My input has to help move things along to a conclusion."	"I want to be seen as working towards a result, being interested not just in winning, but interested in solving problems. I want them to think I am realistic."

Notes and Questions

1. You have recently graduated from a leading Canadian law school and are articling for a boutique litigation firm in Victoria. The senior partner asks you to meet with a long-standing corporate client who has a minor family law matter. (The firm doesn't usually handle domestic cases, but is taking on this matter as a favour to the ongoing client.) The client is in the midst of negotiating a domestic contract with his much younger companion and does not want the companion to know about his substantial off-shore assets. Basically, he wants his new companion to have a half-interest in the condo they live in and in his favourite antique sailboat, but not have any claim on his other assets in Canada and the Cayman Islands. The client has asked you to attend the negotiation meeting with his significant other and not reveal any of his assets other than his sailboat, car, condo, and the various furnishings, paintings, and antiques in the condo. Just before the negotiation, the client calls and says that his significant other would like an affidavit setting out all of his assets. He asks you to draw up the affidavit for him to swear en route to the meeting with his companion, who will be unrepresented at the negotiation.

   Do you have any problems with going ahead and preparing for this negotiation? Which assets would you list in the affidavit? What ethical issues arise from this scenario and how would you deal with them? Would you discuss your concerns with other colleagues? With the senior partner of your firm? Would you consult a code of conduct in the time available for you to reflect on this negotiation?

Selected Further Reading

J.R. Cohen, "The Ethics of Respect in Negotiation" (2002) 18 Negotiation Journal 115.

P.C. Crampton & J.G. Dees, "Promoting Honesty in Negotiation: An Exercise in Practical Ethics" (1993) 3 Business Ethics Quarterly 359.

R.A. Friedman & D.L. Shapiro, "Deception and Mutual Gains Bargaining: Are They Mutually Exclusive?" (1995) 11 Negotiation Journal 243.

K. Gibson, "Ethics and Morality in Negotiation" in A.K. Schneider & C. Honeyman, eds., *The Negotiator's Fieldbook* (Washington, DC: ABA Press, 2006) 175.

D.A. Lax & J.K. Sebenius, "Three Ethical Issues in Negotiation" (1986) 2 Negotiation Journal 363.

R.J. Lewicki & R.J. Robinson, "Ethical and Unethical Bargaining Tactics: An Empirical Study" (1998) 17 Journal of Business Ethics 665.

C. Menkel-Meadow, "Ethics, Morality and Professional Responsibility in Negotiation" in P. Bernard & B. Garth, eds., *Dispute Resolution Ethics: A Comprehensive Guide* (Washington, DC: ABA Press 2002).

R. Mnookin & L. Susskind, *Negotiating on Behalf of Others: Advice to Lawyers, Business Executive, Sports Agents, Diplomats, Politicians and Everybody Else* (Thousand Oaks, CA: Sage Publications, 1999).

E.H. Norton, "Bargaining and the Ethics of Process" (1989) 64 N.Y.U.L. Rev. 494.

S.R. Peppet, "Can Saints Negotiate? A Brief Introduction to the Problems of Perfect Ethics in Bargaining" (2002) 7 Harv. Negot. L. Rev. 83.

C. Provis, "Ethics, Deception and Labor Negotiations" (2000) 28 Journal of Business Ethics 145.

N.A. Welsh, "Perceptions of Fairness" in A.K. Schneider & C. Honeyman, eds., *The Negotiator's Fieldbook* (Washington, DC: ABA Press, 2006) 165.

G. Wetlaufer, "The Ethics of Lying in Negotiation" (1990) 75 Iowa L. Rev. 1219.

J.J. White, "Machiavelli and the Bar: Ethical Limitations on Lying in Negotiation" (1980) 4 American Bar Foundation Research Journal 926.

PART V

Perspectives, Lenses, and Issues Pertaining to Legal Negotiation

Shapeshifters and Synergy: Toward a Culturally Fluent Approach to Representative Negotiation

Michelle LeBaron

Introduction

The same joke was repeated to me three times by different people the last time I was at a conference in Pittsburgh to speak about conflict and culture. "If world destruction happens," the joke went, "the best place to be would be Pittsburgh. We won't hear about it for at least five years." Each time the joke was told, those within earshot laughed and rolled their eyes. The joke's self-deprecating humour masks a certain comfort level in being "off the radar" and the boon of being able to learn from mistakes made by others in other settings in designing and adopting conflict resolution and negotiation processes and programs.

The joke reminded me of ways that Canada has lagged behind the United States in institutionalizing community and academic programs on negotiation. Canadian law schools, mirroring this pace, have been slow to implement negotiation courses and pursue scholarship in conflict resolution. There are many such programs in Canada today at all levels, but I remember 25 years ago when the number of peer mediation programs in Canadian high schools could be counted on one hand, and academic programs in negotiation were seedlings that had just germinated.

Some argue that this delay has enabled Canadian scholars and practitioners to learn from and build on the development of the US field. Others argue that Canadian social policy is more culturally fluent than corresponding US policies, and that this has shaped Canadian scholarship and practice of negotiation to accommodate wider degrees of difference. The often-cited metaphors of the melting pot (United States) and the salad bowl (Canada) are seen as evidence for Canadian openness to cultural pluralism that has infused negotiation practice with sensitivity to cultural differences. While there are no definitive data to prove or disprove these assertions, they are widespread in Canada. All the same, interest in an ongoing inquiry into ways of increasing negotiating effectiveness does seem to characterize practice and scholarship in Canada.

In this chapter, I will build on this inquiry by examining the effect of cultural fluency on representative negotiation and by identifying ways that representative negotiators might improve their cultural fluency. I will explore the importance of cultural fluency for the relationship between the representative and client and between representative negotiators as they balance a range of interests. Drawing on negotiation scenarios, intercultural communication theories, and the use of metaphor, I will suggest ways of enhancing the negotiation process. Finally, I will suggest ways that the intersection of representative negotiation and cultural fluency can be investigated further, generating ongoing contributions to local and global scholarship and practice.

Cultural Fluency and Representative Negotiation

The term *cultural fluency* was first used in *Bridging Cultural Conflicts: A New Approach for a Changing World*,[1] and it was then elaborated on by Tatsushi Arai in *Conflicts Across Cultures: A Unique Experience of Bridging Differences.*[2] It refers to awareness of culturally bound world views—our own and others'—and the capacity to be attentive to how these world views shape what we see, interpret, and attribute in conflict. According to Trevor Farrow's negotiator-as-professional model outlined in chapter 2, a representative negotiator simultaneously keeps track of his or her own cultural lenses and expectations as well as those of the other parties in a negotiation. In addition, a representative negotiator is cognizant of the influence of collective cultural frames and values on those involved in the negotiation; these include professions, geographic associations, and a whole range of group-identity memberships ranging from political and religious affiliations to sexual orientation and race. Cultural fluency is the capacity to notice and monitor the ongoing effects of these kaleidoscopic lenses.

The negotiator-as-professional model proposed by Farrow fits well with the concept of cultural fluency. Farrow proposes that effective representative negotiators track four sets of interests: client interests, representative interests (which may include those of the representative negotiator's bargaining opposite), ethical interests, and public interests. The negotiator-as-professional model allows for the inclusion of a greater degree of cultural fluency in negotiations. Earlier approaches to representative negotiation, in contrast, took fewer interests into account, envisioning the negotiator skating as smooth and effective a course as

---

1   M. LeBaron, *Bridging Cultural Conflicts: A New Approach for a Changing World* (San Francisco: Jossey-Bass, 2003).

2   M. LeBaron & V. Pillay, eds., *Conflicts Across Cultures: A Unique Experience of Bridging Differences* (Boston: Intercultural Press, 2006).

possible in between client's and opponent's interests. By recognizing a negotiator's self-interests and the public's interests, Farrow makes room in the negotiation for two fundamental elements of cultural fluency—self-observation and attention to collective values, beliefs, and needs.

The term *fluency* is most often applied to language acquisition. It is also useful when thinking of building cultural awareness in negotiation because, like language acquisition, the process of becoming culturally fluent is incremental, uneven, and relational. The process is incremental because it takes time, patience, and practice. Negotiators must review their own cultural perceptions and become aware of how their templates and ideas about self and others shape their expectations and strategies. The process is uneven because a negotiation requires constant attention to multiple levels simultaneously. In addition, when something unexpected or unfavourable happens in a negotiation, negotiators are likely to return to cultural scripts that provide a sense of security as they focus on regaining their footing. Anyone who has tried to function in a new language knows what it's like to revert to the more familiar terrain of their first language in a time of crisis or challenge. The process is relational because it looks at the ways in which approaches, strategies, and attitudes mesh, align, or collide, depending on the culturally shaped expectations, values, and beliefs of those involved.

Cultural fluency enhances our abilities to

- *anticipate a range of possibilities for ongoing interaction* with a given individual or group;
- *remain conscious of cultural influences* embedded in our and others' meaning-making processes that lead to assumptions about "common sense";
- *express cultural assumptions* in a way that makes them accessible to others unfamiliar with our ideas of "how things are done around here"; and
- *participate mindfully in dynamic and complex cross-cultural interactions* to co-create a constructive future with others.

Like learning a language, building cultural fluency is a developmental process, never fully achieved. It is impossible to completely know the nuanced beliefs, values, and deep, behaviour-shaping grammar of a cultural group to which we do not belong, or the influence of group values on a specific individual in any given context. Cultural groups—whether religious, racial, or professional—share unspoken ideas of common sense ways to do things. These ideas are not universal in any given group; there can be more diversity within a group than between groups. Cultural values shift with time, location, generation, and major events, traumatic or triumphant. Attaining an encyclopedic understanding of cultural identities—our own and those of others—is impossible. However, negotiators can become more culturally fluent through an understanding of intercultural communication patterns and world views. Culturally fluent representative negotiators formulate functional hunches, ask useful questions, and avoid costly missteps.

Cultural fluency is relevant both to relations between representatives and clients and to relations at play in representative negotiations, including the dynamics between representatives and each side's clients, as we will see in the first negotiation scenario below. This negotiation scenario involves an exchange between a representative and a client that will be explored using intercultural communication theories.

Understanding Representative Negotiation Through Intercultural Communication Theories

Intercultural communication theorists and practitioners are concerned with improving communication across cultures by building understanding about differences in cultural patterns, relational understandings, and communication approaches. As we listen in on a representative negotiation, let's try to understand how intercultural communication theories may be helpful to culturally fluent representative negotiators. This negotiation takes place in Egypt, and involves a family law lawyer and a client who is seeking a divorce from her husband. We enter the negotiation just as the client asks her lawyer about the progress of her divorce.

The scene is tense. The lawyer has just told his client the "good news"—that he filed an alimony case on her behalf. When his client protests that she does not want support, but only a divorce, the lawyer explains that an application for alimony puts pressure on husbands to agree to a divorce. The client reluctantly accepts this strategy in the light of her lawyer's superior knowledge of the legal system, and the lawyer then moves on to ask questions about previous abuse in her marriage, which she denies.

> Counsel: So, your difficulties with your husband are so serious that you see no possibility of going back?
>
> Client: None at all.
>
> Counsel: To give me tools in the upcoming discussions with his lawyer, I'd like to ask you some questions about your relationship. (looking down) Did he, uh, perform his husbandly duties with you on a regular basis?
>
> Client (looking quizzically at her lawyer): That is not something I'm interested in discussing.
>
> Counsel (looking skeptically and indignantly at his client): Well, I just want to be able to achieve the best result possible.

As the conversation proceeds, the client tells her lawyer that she has been reading Islamic teachings and law related to divorce. She read that, according to Islam, a woman may get a divorce when she does not feel attracted to her husband without having to provide further justification. Her lawyer retorts that he is bound to work within the legal system and its rules of engagement. Likening the process to war, he suggests that each party must use maximum force to destroy the other party and guarantee victory. The negotiation ends with the client confused and upset.

This exchange is an excerpt of a longer and increasingly conflictual conversation in a film about the difficulties of a woman struggling to get a divorce in the 1980s in Cairo.[3] The client is an educated, upper-middle-class woman in her fifties who wants only closure—she

---

3   This scenario is based on the film Uridu Hlan (I Need a Resolution), referenced in the PhD dissertation of Egyptian lawyer Amr Abdalla, Inter-personal Conflict Patterns in Egypt: Themes and Solutions (PhD Thesis, Institute for Conflict Analysis and Resolution, 2001) at 2.

does not want to be on public display, nor does she want to ask for ongoing spousal support. Her lawyer, a male similar in age, sees divorce through cultural lenses as a fault-based war that can only be won through sustained escalation. Throughout the scene in the film, we see the operation of different communication starting points between two people who appear to share national, cultural, and religious affiliations.

The client in this negotiation uses a direct, specific, low-context[4] approach to communication. She knows what she wants and asks the lawyer to pursue a straight course to achieving it. Low-context communication relies on minimal contextual cues for understanding. This kind of communication is focused and linear, built on a logical chain of thought and practical messages. Direct communication involves stating desired ends as clearly as possible. It is often linked to assertiveness—approaches that advocate by naming what is desired.

Her lawyer, in contrast, uses high-context, diffuse, less direct communication to ask about his client's sexual relations with her husband. High-context communication[5] relies on shared cultural cues or contextual understandings to convey meaning. Diffuse, indirect communication tends to be abstract, avoiding naming issues directly to save face, maintain status, or avoid confrontation. The lawyer's use of war terms to describe the legal system and divorce suggests that he inhabits a different universe of understanding than his client. The client is left with the impression that the legal system is so high-context that she can do no more than go along with her lawyer's suggestions.

The lawyer's question about conjugal duties communicates his ideas about a "good" husband and the role of a husband. Throughout the conversation, different understandings and expectations of the negotiation and litigation processes and the cultural meanings of marriage and divorce increase tension between the parties.

In this negotiation, the client well understands the lawyer's question and its roots in cultural values. By her response, she asserts her view that marital relations are private and that she is entitled to get on with her life without disclosing humiliating information. She is suspicious of her lawyer's tactics and the mounting delays and costs that are unfolding along with the alimony application. As the scene continues in the film, the client becomes increasingly impatient with her lawyer, who seems not to take account of her wishes. It concludes with the client standing up from her chair, emphasizing loudly: "I *just* want a divorce, and by the most direct route possible!"

This lawyer, in conflict with his client over negotiating strategy, may have difficulty advocating effectively on her behalf. The difficulty would arise because his and her respective perceptions of the values applicable to this case are at odds. At the time this film was released, Egyptian courts drew on a mix of modern secular and conservative traditional values in adjudicating family issues. Divorce was available, but difficult for women to obtain, particularly if their husbands were uncooperative.[6] Amr Abdalla attributes these difficulties

---

4   The term low-context communication refers to direct, explicit messages that are meant to be understood literally. H.C. Triandis, *Culture and Social Behavior* (New York: McGraw Hill, 1994).

5   The term high-context communication refers to the importance of context in conveying a message. Triandis, *ibid*.

6   Abdalla, *supra* note 3 at 198.

to "misconceptions about Islam and … negative practices, especially against women, [through which] traditional values got mixed up with Islam." While the lawyer's view of divorce is infused with traditional values about roles and responsibilities in family relations, the client's view is not; she believes that her divorce would be served best by secular laws interpreted through the lens of egalitarian Islamic teachings.

Intercultural communication theories help decode the layers of this exchange. They identify the cultural patterns influencing the lawyer's and client's communication strategies, clarify each party's starting point, and generate educated speculation on the source of the misunderstanding. Once the patterns are identified, understanding the broader cultural context—in this case, shifting and contested mores in contemporary Egyptian society—helps interpret the behaviour of the client and the lawyer. Here, the client rejects the lawyer's thinly veiled paternalism in his reference to her husband's conjugal duties, and, by extension, fault-based divorce, by returning to her direct and specific request. In doing so, she counters her lawyer's perception of the legal system as incorporating traditional cultural values. She rejects the osmotic influence of these traditional cultural values in the legal system. She considers such values as irrelevant to her desired outcome. Her lawyer, a system insider, elicits information that he believes will give him power in the negotiation, even if it is not relevant in a strictly legal sense. His client's rejection of the question about conjugal duties poses a challenge for the lawyer: he will be at a disadvantage if his counterpart draws on both traditional and secular cultural values to build the husband's case. Ultimately, the differences in cultural starting points and applicable values may spawn questions about whether the lawyer can represent the client effectively.

Balancing Competing Interests and Values

Drawing on Farrow's negotiator-as-professional model, the lawyer in the first negotiation scenario is balancing four sets of interests—his client's, his own, his counterpart's, and the public's. Informing these interests are divergent values related to the role of the legal system in divorce. The exchange the lawyer has with his client brings at least three of these value sets into conflict. The first two—his and his client's—are clearly at odds. If his ideas about the involvement of traditional values in divorce are strongly or deeply held, can he effectively advocate on behalf of a client who does not share these values? Will his representation be less ardent or less effective if he acts against internally held ideas based on values that seem right and normal to him? This problem is endemic to legal practice, and lawyers have long responded to it by pointing to the right of every person to have effective representation. Being effective necessitates putting personal values aside (within the boundaries of legal and ethical behaviour, of course), and acting as the client instructs. But what is the gap between this ideal and the effectiveness of counsel who is conflicted not only over strategy, but over treasured values? Recent work in cognitive science yields questions about the extent to which setting aside personal values is even possible.

Public interests are the other problematic point to be considered. If a lawyer, as a representative negotiator, is influenced by or owes allegiance to public interests, the thorny problem of identifying what those interests are surfaces. How are varying ideas of what constitute public interests accommodated? When the essence of public interests is contested, as it is in the first negotiation scenario, whose picture of the collective will be incorporated in the lawyer's approach? Culturally fluent negotiators who find themselves in conflict with clients over collective values explore the genesis of values—their own, their client's, and those incorporated into the legal system and its practice—and work to find integrative ways to achieve the client's desired ends in ways that do not directly clash with collective expectations and norms. Even if the legal system or other applicable rules ultimately impede the achievement of fully integrative solutions, the exploration of ways to accommodate diverse values is likely to enhance procedural satisfaction for all parties.

This negotiation scenario, while based in Egypt, plays out in societies around the world every day as clients instruct their lawyers to represent them in negotiation or litigation. In the 25 years since the advent of the *Charter of Rights and Freedoms*, Canadian courts have defined a series of fundamental privileges, subject only to the limits justified in a free and democratic society. Yet we are far from a consensus on public interests as they relate to a range of social issues, from gun control to climate change. The same tensions that played out in the Egyptian negotiation scenario play out in Canadian lawyers' offices daily, winding themselves into intricate webs with interrelated tensions that can only be untangled with patience, awareness, and cultural fluency.

Metaphors in Representative Negotiation

In this section, we'll turn to a negotiation scenario that's closer to home to explore metaphor as a tool that representative negotiators can use to build cultural fluency. They arise from Mary Clark's metaphor analyses of world views.[7] Clark contrasts two world views that inform contemporary human behaviour. The first, a billiard-ball gestalt, conjures up a world where linear cause and effect inform negotiator behaviour. Strategies are formulated in logical, sequential ways that are goal-oriented and mappable. Cultural factors may be taken into account, but they tend to be marginalized through either distorting generalizations (for example, women are relational negotiators; European-Canadians are competitive) or diffuse references (for example, culture is everywhere in negotiation and should be taken into account). Viewing a negotiation on only one plane—such as a billiard table where cues send balls in particular directions—leaves representative negotiators with a sparse set of tools. They miss the multi-directional, dynamic, and intricately interdependent nature of negotiation. And they miss the deep salience of culture in negotiation.

The second gestalt proposed by Clark is Indra's Net. This image arose over 2,000 years ago from the Mahayana Buddhist tradition. The net is a metaphor for a world of interconnectedness, where interdependent entities interact, whether they be human bodies, economies or other social arrangements, ecosystems, or galaxies. Within each entity, the parts are likewise interdependent, and it is their reciprocal interactions that keep the whole universe functioning.[8]

Indra's Net has jewels at each intersection, so every jewel is connected to and reflective of all other jewels. Used as a lens for understanding representative negotiation, Indra's Net

7   M.E. Clark, *In Search of Human Nature* (London: Routledge, 2002).

8   *Ibid.* at 9.

asks the negotiator to pose questions that extend beyond the linearity of the billiard table. Time, space, and multidirectional relationships come into focus. For example, questions about the impact of possible outcomes on colleagues, community members, or descendents come to mind, evoking and extending Farrow's ideas of public interests. Suppose the negotiation is about a business venture. Social, economic, and environmental impacts over time are part of the public interests that the negotiator-as-professional keeps in mind.

To learn more about the different ways that the billiard table and Indra's Net shape negotiation dynamics, we drop in on Nelly's office, the location of the second negotiation scenario. Once again, we examine the relationship between counsel and client as the foundation of representative negotiation.

A newly minted lawyer in a prairie city has just completed a series of negotiation courses offered through a local institute. The program drew, as many have for decades, on game theory to inform negotiation strategy. Game theory rests on the assumptions developed by John Nash that negotiators are rational, can accurately compare their desires for various things, are equal in bargaining skill, and have knowledge of the tastes and preferences of the other. While these ideals are never fully reached, game theory has been widely used in scenarios such as prisoner's dilemma to show negotiators how reciprocal trust, information sharing, and communication can operate to maximize mutual gains.[9]

David Sally and Gregory Jones identify two archetypes used in negotiation training that arise from recent work on game theory and negotiation. In the first archetype, the negotiator has a low level of strategic sophistication and focuses on some combination of the client's and his or her own interests and desired outcomes without inquiry into the counterpart's interests. This model invites negotiators to optimize outcomes by withholding information, masking intentions, and disclosing little about their best or worst alternatives to a negotiated agreement. In the second archetype, the negotiator has a higher level of strategic sophistication involving awareness of the potential for improved outcomes arising from collaboration and information-sharing. This model surfaces in interest-based negotiation training that seeks to demonstrate to negotiators that taking their counterparts' interests into account can achieve better outcomes, not only in material gains but also in relational terms.[10]

Nelly is confused. The courses she took were more aligned with Sally and Jones's second archetype, but she finds the strategies she learned are not as widely applicable as she had hoped. Let's listen in as Nelly discusses her relationship with a client in a child-protection matter with a colleague.

Nelly: I just don't understand her. She says she wants her little girl Chloë back, but comes late to our meeting with the social worker. When she and I went over her budget last week, I advised her to take off the extra pair of Sunday shoes for Chloë because that didn't leave enough money in the food column. Sure enough, they had been added back in—and coffee was spilled on the copy she gave to the social worker!

---

9   D.F. Sally & G.T. Jones, "Game Theory Behaves" in Andrea Kupfer Schneider & Christopher Honeyman, eds., *The Negotiator's Fieldbook: The Desk Reference for the Experienced Negotiator* (Washington, DC: American Bar Association, 2006) at 87-94.

10   R. Fisher & W. Ury, *Getting to Yes: Negotiating Agreement Without Giving In* (New York: Penguin, 1983).

Colleague: Sounds like you need to manage your relationship with your client more directively.

Nelly: She doesn't seem to understand how the system works, or how to work the system.

Colleague (shrugging her shoulders): Yeah, sounds like she just doesn't get it.

In this glimpse into Nelly's perceptions of her relationship with her client, we see that Nelly has tried to give her client strategic advice. Coming on time, dressing well, and producing a budget that covers necessities are part of meeting the social worker's perceived interests. Nelly's negotiation training has taught her that anticipating the social worker's interests would spawn openings for her client's interests to be advanced. But it did not work out that way.

Nelly's training in interest negotiation arose primarily from a billiard-ball gestalt. She was taught that attending to material issues of both her client and her counterpart would yield results. Communication and process-structuring skills were also a focus of her program, and she had done well at learning to ask clarifying, consequential, and probing questions. She had practised identifying issues and underlying interests, and sequencing negotiations to resist leaping to solutions. Informing these skills and approaches were a set of cultural values that was never articulated. These values included individualism, autonomy, atomism, and instrumentalism. Within these values, the following cultural assumptions are embedded:

- Each person is an independent agent who will act to maximize his or her own interests.
- Action plans can be reliably formulated to move sequentially from one point to another.
- Cultural values are more or less consistent among people, and if they are not, they can be expressed as interests and accommodated.
- Issues can be divided into categories from simpler to more complex and pursued strategically.

Nelly's approach included incremental steps to show the social worker that her client was capable of basic life skills, steps that she hoped would build credibility and trust between her client and the social worker. She explained the steps patiently to her client, and heard no opposition. Yet her client acted contrary to the steps that had been planned. The only predictable element of the whole situation seemed to be the social worker's continued distrust of her client, and the ongoing placement of Chloë in foster care.

Nelly wondered why her client was acting contrary to her self-interests. If Nelly were in a similar situation, she was quite sure she would follow her lawyer's instructions to the letter. Then Nelly remembered an experience she had years before. She had been raised in an English family that had to stretch every dollar to make ends meet. Her mother was a practical woman who had higher ambitions for her children than herself, culminating in Nelly's acceptance to an exclusive private high school. Though the tuition was far beyond the family's means, Nelly was offered a scholarship that covered it entirely. It was a hardship for the family to purchase the prescribed school uniform, but they had managed. All except for the socks. Nelly's mother took one look at the socks and their price tag, and flatly refused to buy them from the prescribed supplier. She substituted generic black socks from the corner haberdasher.

Nelly's first day of school was accompanied by a stern reprimand over the inappropriate socks. For two weeks afterwards, every day included embarrassing confrontations and repeated corporal punishment. Yet Nelly never breathed a word of her humiliation to her mother. She saved her meagre spending money, forgoing lunch, and bought a pair of regulation socks in secret two weeks later.

Her mother never knew about the socks, and Nelly never told her. Though her grades were fine, Nelly hated that school with an intensity no one in her family could understand. Nelly wondered whether there were things that her client had experienced that might explain her choices just as the imperative of the right socks explained her own. In asking these questions, Nelly was moving out of a billiard-ball gestalt, and beginning to glimpse her client from an Indra's Net world view.

Indra's Net, with its interconnections and complexity, sees each person as part of a whole. The individual is not considered a distinct unit, but part of an interdependent collective. Actions are viewed without consideration for how well they may maximize individual gains, but with awareness of their many unpredictable effects and culturally bound meaning. Negotiation strategy informed by the net metaphor does not see the client or social worker as disconnected, and it does not see strategy as a series of steps leading to a specific goal. Rather, it considers that all parties, including the lawyer, are involved in a system that contains and connects them, shaping their perceptions, choices, and agency. Emphasis falls away from "objectively reasonable" strategies and lands instead on understanding the context from which strategies arise.

Suddenly, Nelly saw the reintroduction of the Sunday shoes to the budget in a different light. Without knowing a great deal about her client's religious or family upbringing, she guessed that Sunday shoes for Chloë had a great deal of meaning. She realized that she had gone without food for two weeks to save money for a particular brand of socks —something that made no sense unless someone knew the context in which the behaviour took place.

When Nelly next met with her client, her approach changed. Rather than prescribe a set of actions to build relations with the social worker, she asked her client to tell her some stories from her childhood. After she heard the stories with their themes of disenfranchisement and exclusion, Nelly understood her client's lack of trust in the system more clearly. When Nelly asked about the Sunday shoes, her client replied that "every decent child has Sunday shoes." Despite her array of questioning techniques, Nelly never found out why Sunday shoes were linked to decency, but she understood they were important beyond their material value. And this understanding led her to improved communication with her client. Together, they worked on a plan to present to the social worker that would provide a decent life for mother and daughter. The plan included Sunday shoes.

This scenario may seem trivial, as though Indra's Net is merely a blanket of empathy draped over a billiard table. However, to understand the shift from Nelly's original client communications to her more productive later ones, we need to look at qualitative factors. Nelly's awareness of her interconnection with her client led her to a more compassionate understanding, one that recognizes the primary values of belonging and self-respect. Nelly became a more effective representative negotiator because she had inquired into context— her own, her client's, and the social dynamics enveloping them—and came away with a deeper understanding of how the context related to the interests of all involved.

Effective representative negotiators consider how metaphors shape their ideas about negotiation, effectiveness, and an acceptable range of strategies and outcomes. Perhaps, if representative negotiators see themselves through the metaphor of a *shapeshifter*, they might be more readily encouraged to act in ways that take complexity and context into account. Shapeshifters, or tricksters, are mythical figures in many cultures around the world.[11] They frequently get into trouble with the gods or people because they are clever, opinionated, and sometimes reckless. Their genius extends to questioning established orders and ways of doing things. Fortunately for them, they also take on new forms in order to escape capture or confinement. In the end, tricksters are welcomed back from exile even after disturbing the order of things because their questions are valued, and are even essential to healthy societies.

Metaphors as Resources for Exploring Commonalities

Metaphors are useful not only for thinking about our roles as representative negotiators, but also for examining the dynamics of negotiation processes. Let's listen in on a negotiation between two representatives and pay particular attention to metaphors that indicate world views and resources that have integrative potential. The context is a multi-party negotiation related to logging and other activities in a west-coast watershed. The conservation representative at the table has worked over the course of the negotiation to advocate outcomes that minimize environmental damage and protect wilderness values. The logging industry representative has maintained that selective logging can satisfy a wide range of values including employment, economic prosperity, sustainability, and recreation. On this day, the representatives are discussing the effects of logging on wildlife—in particular, on the mottled muskrat. The scientific data concerning mottled muskrats varies. Some scientists say these muskrats are seriously endangered because of loss of habitat. Others say they are thriving, and point to the rapid increase in their population after being introduced into Western Europe (where they are widely considered pests because of damage from their avid burrowing).

> Conservation representative: Our field studies from this watershed show a precipitous decline in the mottled muskrat population over the past four years. Stream flows are significantly down from three years ago. As an indicator species, the muskrat alerts us that wildlife in this area is already severely compromised. Unless amelioration is undertaken and a moratorium put on further land development and exploitation, the pot will run dry and everything in it will be ruined.

> Logging industry representative: Our studies show a steady increase in the mottled muskrat population. This is surely a back-burner issue that can simmer for a while without derailing progress in these negotiations.

Both representatives use metaphors to emphasize their points. In this case, both metaphors arise from a cooking context, which evokes commonality and positive associations. The metaphors are vibrant with physical referents including smells, textures, and the comfort of good food. But the representatives are not comforted. The logging industry representative

---

11   L. Hyde, *Trickster Makes This World: Mischief, Myth and Art* (New York: North Point Press, 1998).

sees the conservation representative's focus on the mottled muskrat as an unnecessary diversion, and one with little substance. Meanwhile, the conservation representative sees the state of the mottled muskrat as pivotal because it points to an ecological system in crisis. As the discussion continues over whether and how to address the mottled muskrat issue, the representatives become less productive. They come to an impasse over the contested importance of the issue, and each walks away from the table with mounting questions about the other's good faith.

Anyone who has tried to negotiate with another representative who has divergent values that are informed by a clashing world view can see themselves in this situation. Let's assume that both representatives are acting in good faith: they sincerely believe what they've said about mottled muskrats. They both want a fair process in which their values are given credence, the facts as they see them are accommodated, and their needs for acknowledgment and recognition are accommodated. At the same time, they both want an outcome that will reflect as many of their constituents' values as possible. Somewhere in the background is the elusive idea of public interests, and each representative claims to speak on its behalf.

Overnight, the representatives reflect on the negotiations of the previous day. Attentive to metaphors, they realize that each has drawn on cooking metaphors to discuss the issue. The next day at the table, they draw consciously on food and cooking metaphors in their search for progress. Even though the food and cooking metaphors had been used the previous day to point to different approaches, the negotiators realized that the metaphors might prove fertile as a frame for ongoing exploration.

> Logging industry representative: Let's return to the mottled muskrat issue for a few minutes. I was struck last night by the way we each took our discussion into the kitchen. And I got to thinking—good cooks make sure they use good ingredients. While I am confident in our team of scientists, the substantial differences between our data and yours makes me wonder if we shouldn't ask a new consultant—someone we can both agree on—to take another look at the mottled muskrat population.

> Conservation representative: Sure, that makes sense to me. I suggest that whoever we choose makes sure to take a careful look at longitudinal data and projections. Good cooks care about the ongoing health and well-being of those they are serving, not only about the current meal.

The impasse between the negotiators was broken by a discussion based on a common metaphor. The ambiguity of the metaphor gave both representatives a way to communicate that avoided escalating confrontation or personalizing blame. Each representative was able to emphasize his values through the metaphor in a way that the other could accept as legitimate. The metaphor helped the logging industry representative think of a creative way through the impasse, and its overarching commonality likely made it easier for the conservation representative to accede.

Of course, tapping into common metaphors is not always this easy. Many times, people involved in negotiations draw on metaphors from quite different realms. For example, logging industry representatives may refer to the forest in farming terms such as *harvesting*, *managing*, and *replanting*, while conservation representatives may refer to the forest in spiritual terms such as *temple* and *sanctuary*. When power and resources are attached to unmarked metaphors, those who use alternative metaphors for the same thing may find themselves marginalized. The use of different metaphors in a discussion, whether implied or explicitly named, often points to divergent world views.

Parties who use similar metaphors do not necessarily have similar world views. In the exchange above, the conservation and logging industry representatives may have quite different approaches to and associations with cooking. Still, the metaphor provides a space in which they can explore commonalities rather than focus on the very different ideas they may have about food sources and preparation.

Coming back for a moment to the metaphor of war used by the Egyptian lawyer in the first negotiation scenario, we can see that a metaphor communicates a whole set of values and understandings in a tightly wrapped, dense bundle. The war metaphor associates particular ideas with the negotiation process: attacking, defending, demolishing arguments of the other side; winning, shooting, being wiped out.[12] The Egyptian lawyer's client resisted this metaphor, evoking instead images of closure through her insistence on a "direct route" to her divorce. War may involve strategies and the use of surprise, stealth, and unpredictable tactics. Travelling by a direct route invokes none of these things, and instead turns attention to expediency, efficiency, and safe arrival at a destination. In the film, the divorce snaked its way through several years before it was obtained; the client's preferred metaphor did not govern, and she described herself as lost in a labyrinthine process that seemed to have no end.

If the lawyer in this matter had "tried on" his client's metaphor, talking with her about the route and possible pitfalls along it, she might have felt acknowledged and empowered to have had more meaningful input into the process. While a lawyer is an expert on the terrain and routes of the legal system, even a first-time traveller in this area will want to make choices about where to stop, how fast he or she is comfortable moving, and whether to take the most direct or a subsidiary road.

If the client had realized that her frustration stemmed, at least in part, from her adverse reaction to the lawyer's war references, she might have been able to step away from arguments about relevance and strategy and initiate a deeper conversation about both parties' approaches and ways of thinking about the divorce process. This conversation might have brought the differences in their view of divorce and appropriate ways of pursuing it to the forefront, and given the client more choices about how to engage and whether to continue with this lawyer.

Metaphors, Intercultural Communication, and Cultural Fluency

So far, we have used two sets of resources to deepen cultural fluency: metaphors and intercultural communication tools. As metaphors are windows into world views, they allow negotiation counterparts to understand a great deal of information about the other in context without having to ask directly. Metaphors give clues about how situations and the people in them are perceived—by themselves and others. They also provide insight into agency, power, manoeuvrability, acceptable strategies, fruitful or offensive lines of inquiry,

---

12 G. Lakoff & M. Johnson, *Metaphors We Live By* (Chicago: University of Chicago Press, 1980) at 4.

the primacy of certain values identified by intercultural communication scholars (for example, individualism vs. communitarianism; particularism vs. universalism),[13] acceptable outcomes, and many other things. As we have seen, metaphors can provide meaning structures through which people can talk about difficult or contentious issues. Listening closely to metaphors used in a negotiation yields a lot of information about the cultural lenses being employed by self and others.

Culturally fluent negotiators attend to and use metaphors in ways that address the whole range of substantive interests at stake as well as the relational interests of clients, counterparts, self, and the public. Because metaphors are high-context, they communicate more meaning than can be said explicitly. Culturally fluent negotiators use metaphors to convey empathy, understanding, and respect as well as to work toward accurate and common understandings.

Cultural fluency is essential for negotiators who interact with culturally diverse negotiating parties and representatives. Culturally fluent negotiators are attuned to a range of starting points to relate to others of different cultures. They have access to a wide range of metaphors that animate and inform their actions. They can be still and open; engaged and strong. But they are always curious, comfortable with ambiguity, and respectful in negotiations. Metaphors help sustain curiosity in a negotiation. They are inherently ambiguous, and invite clarification through questions and observations to uncover how they are being used and what series of associations they are intended to invoke. Metaphors help save face; they soften the edges of confrontation by offering a space removed from the substance of an issue that facilitates indirectness and tact. Negotiators who are attentive to metaphors and intercultural communication starting points will find they can move more fluidly and effectively through a negotiation.

Representative Negotiation, Cultural Fluency, and Ethics

Even the most seasoned representative negotiators will run into challenges, including problems that do not easily fit a collaborative approach. In some situations, problems may seem stubbornly distributive, so shifting conversations to an integrative framework may be challenging and ultimately counterproductive. Cultural dimensions are relevant to how a problem is seen and understood since cultural patterns shape thinking related to conflict as holistic or atomized; hopeful or critical; dissectable or indivisible. As Colleen Hanycz writes in chapter 3, recognizing when an integrative or distributive framework best fits a negotiation is an important part of strategic assessment and negotiation planning. Another essential element of culturally fluent representative negotiation is attention to ethical considerations. This

---

13   C. Hampden-Turner & F. Trompenaars, *Building Cross Cultural Competence* (New Haven, CT: Yale University Press, 2000). Individualism is a focus on the individual as the centre of relating and decision making; communitarianism is the group as primary reference point. Particularism is the exclusive adherence to specific values that fit a distinct context; universalism emphasizes broad, overarching values that are meant to apply across contexts.

exploration takes us back to the elusive question of what constitutes public or collective interests and how cultural fluency relates to ethical practice.

In their seminal article, James Laue and Gerald Cormick write about the ethics of third-party intervention in community disputes.[14] They suggest that third-party mediators and facilitators have a duty to advocate for the inclusion and active engagement of a wide range of people in the negotiation process, including those who are disadvantaged or powerless in society. Laue and Cormick suggest, for example, that people who live downstream from a proposed hydroelectric project should be considered as potential parties to a negotiation even if the main stakeholders believe that these people live far enough away that they can be disregarded. Another example arises from a group of people who live just over the hill from a leaking tank farm, including transient workers and others who are not organized enough to demand a place at the table. Laue and Cormick conclude that it is the third party's duty to advocate for the inclusion and meaningful participation of those whose interests may be affected by the negotiation process, even when the question is unpopular. Meaningful participation may include building capacity through training, developing coalitions, or engaging advocates. It may also mean considering funding (including transportation, daycare, and per diems) for those parties who can least afford to participate in a process with others funded by employers or well-resourced sources.

Applying Laue and Cormick's work to representative negotiation, we formulate some questions. In the negotiation between the representatives of the conservation group and the logging industry, we ask, Whose voices are not being heard? How about wildlife? The perspectives of those who advocate on behalf of wildlife values might broaden or deepen the conversation, or take it in a completely different direction. How about people who have lived on the land in question? Perhaps Aboriginal peoples, who have a historical understanding of the habits and population fluctuations of the mottled muskrat could contribute to the negotiation. Increasingly, Aboriginal knowledge is being considered alongside Western science to deepen understandings of resources and the environment.

While representative negotiators cannot and should not take it upon themselves to define public interests, they should engage parties and their counterparts in inquiry. They should ask who else, beyond the main stakeholders, ought to be represented at the negotiation—which may include people who are less able to self-finance or articulate their concerns. In response, negotiators may need to broaden the scope of issues, consider the issues from a wider time or spatial perspective, or ensure that divergent ways of seeing an issue are not sidelined because they do not fit with a dominant metaphor or image shared by a majority of representatives or parties. They may also need to take a look at the context surrounding a negotiation and how that context shapes conversations.

Culturally fluent negotiators assume neither the universality of values nor the absence of complementary possibilities. They are committed to working across diversity, even when doing so is challenging and requires more work to get on the same page. They trust the wisdom of communities and the capacity of groups to find constructive ways through dif-

---

14   J. Laue & G. Cormick, "The Ethics of Intervention in Community Disputes" in G. Bermant, H. Kelman & D. Warwick, eds., *The Ethics of Social Intervention* (Washington, DC: Hemisphere Publishing, 1978) 205.

ficult problems. Even as they advocate making room for divergent views, they recognize and respect the need for closure and effectiveness. And so they attend to public interests, not as defined personally by any one party or representative, but as they emerge from the process.

Representative negotiators are encouraged to ask questions such as those that follow when they plan their negotiation strategy:

- Who else could or should be a part of this negotiation process?
- Whose views might help us see a different perspective on these issues?
- If we imagine those involved in the negotiations as members of a club, who is not a member? How can we create different categories of membership or mechanisms for involvement to welcome a wide range of voices into this process?
- Does the negotiation process being used give some participants better access to voice or power than others? If so, how can the process expand to welcome diverse perspectives?
- Does the negotiation process being used resonate with certain cultural values and not with others? If so, how can the process be expanded or shifted to welcome diverse values?
- Where does the wisdom about these issues live? How can we bring it to the table?
- What kinds of wisdom are welcome here? What kinds of wisdom are we less likely to seek out, and how might unnamed or unsought wisdom help?
- Which metaphors are we using to talk about the issues, and how would the issues look if we tried on different metaphorical glasses?
- Which metaphors are used by some people in the negotiation that may inadvertently exclude others because they communicate specialized expertise or abstract notions that are not widely shared (for example, lawyers using technical legal terminology in ways that distance clients or others involved in the process)?[15]
- Whose views, including those of people at the table, might be marginalized because some people involved in the process share specific ways of seeing an issue or aspect of the negotiation?
- How is the outcome of this negotiation likely to affect future generations—children and grandchildren, flora and fauna?
- What unforeseen consequences may flow from our negotiation, and how can we be cognizant of our social responsibility given these consequences?

Representative negotiators who ask these types of questions emulate culturally fluent behaviour and show an appreciation for negotiation principles that take public interests into account. Their outcomes are more likely, therefore, to be durable, wise, and satisfying to a wide range of interested parties.

---

15   M. LeBaron & Z.D. Zumeta, "Windows on Diversity: Lawyers, Culture and Mediation Practice" (2003) 20:3 Conflict Resolution Quarterly 463.

Process and System Design Implications

We began this chapter with a discussion of Canadian contributions to the study and practice of representative negotiation. I suggested that we see ourselves as valuing and employing cultural fluency, perhaps because of the ubiquitous salad bowl metaphor that evokes Canadian multiculturalism. It is beyond the scope of this work to draw conclusions about the verity of that image, or its robustness in a world seemingly more bent than ever on divisions over identity and world views. Perhaps a useful contribution to the ongoing conversation about Canada's potential offerings to this field is to set out possibilities and questions, which may crystallize to form new perspectives and answers.

Canadian scholars and reflective practitioners can articulate a culturally fluent approach to representative negotiation that is informed by (among other things)

- official federal and provincial policies of multiculturalism
- awareness of the contributions to social and economic prosperity and Canadian identity by new immigrants to Canada
- input from Aboriginal peoples on their views of land, resources, and cultural identity
- the *Canadian Charter of Rights and Freedoms* as it espouses values of inclusion, respect for difference, and human dignity
- positive accounts of negotiated solutions that take diverse perspectives into account.

From this articulation, Canadian practitioners and scholars can continue to develop processes, systems, and capacities to inform and support effective negotiation and representative negotiation across wide ranges of differences, even differences that are divisive or threatening. This book is a step in that direction, moving away as it does from assumptions and orthodoxies that would prescribe particular negotiation approaches or processes in universal ways.

Multiculturalism asks us to find a balance between holding precious identities related to places and times outside Canada and identifying ourselves as part of the nation in which we currently live. Perhaps Canadian contributions to negotiation theory and practice can follow the same approach: balancing specific cultural ways of doing things with public interests, seeing the latter as relevant even in matters typically seen as bi-party, commercial negotiations. Chapter 2 in this book takes us in that direction.

As negotiation scholarship and practice continue to develop in Canada, we may not only produce a variety of culturally fluent negotiation approaches and processes, but also design systems for dispute resolution that honour diversity. Canadians can show leadership in questioning orthodoxies and habits of practice in negotiation, designing systems for dispute resolution that include negotiation as a legitimate first step. Are there ways that negotiation can be encouraged and fostered before conciliation or mediation is used in administrative tribunals, for example? Are there ways that cultural preferences related to setting, timing, privacy, face-saving, authority, party-identification, and third-party assistance can be accommodated in the context of representative negotiations that take place in the shadow of the law, whether in the context of litigation or administrative processes? Across the country, more and more applications of alternative dispute resolution are being explored and implemented. Those involved in negotiating these programs within agencies, organizations, and systems can advocate a culturally fluent design that makes room for a wide range of system users and avenues to resolution.

While Canadians have a positive image of themselves regarding diversity, we cannot pretend to have a uniformly positive record of celebrating or even accommodating difference. Blemishes in our history that include mistreatment of Aboriginal peoples and the internment of Japanese citizens during World War II spawn important questions about current relations and strained intercultural dynamics. There is a huge need to develop effective public processes for negotiating contentious social issues that include dialogue and respectful interaction, and, possibly, healing. There is also a need to question traditions and assumptions held by those in ethnocultural majority groups of "how things are done around here." Making multiculturalism part of negotiation practice means including a wide range of people in negotiation process design.

Toward Culturally Fluent Practice

As we come together in conversations across disciplines, class lines, and cultural contexts to evolve approaches to negotiation, we must remind ourselves that we are all interdependent. Effective representative negotiators realize that they inhabit a web of relations. They respect differences and recognize that control over complex issues and processes is impossible. Prediction, after all, is only an educated guess more likely to be accurate when based on principles of cultural fluency. Informed by recent work on cognitive science, they understand the importance of seeing their clients and counterparts as having kaleidoscopic, dynamic world views. They seek to recognize cultural factors, including those that cannot be measured in material terms, such as Sunday shoes. They foster positive momentum, drawing on sound knowledge of negotiation strategies and theories while recognizing always that human relationships are the foundation of effective negotiations. Awareness of their own cultural lenses and those of clients and counterparts informs their behaviour, as does a concern for the broader implications of negotiation outcomes. When their cultural lenses show them something quite different from what their clients or counterparts see, they use dialogue to increase understanding and find connections amidst the differences.

Effective representative negotiators take risks, sharing information that supports better problem solving even while voices from the billiard-ball gestalt whisper to withhold. They shapeshift, changing modes when a particular approach is not working. They recognize the importance of metaphors, listening closely to the metaphors used by clients and counterparts as windows into their world views. They ask questions using these metaphors to deepen their understanding of parties' perceptions, values, and tensions. And they search for integrative metaphors—mirrors in which all parties can see themselves—to create synergy across the differences.

Notes and Questions

1. From your experience, identify a negotiation where one or more people acted with cultural fluency. What effects did the culturally fluent behaviour have on others? How did cultural fluency affect peoples' procedural satisfaction or the outcome of the negotiation?

2. What metaphors come to mind related to your participation in negotiations? Are different metaphors useful at different stages or for different kinds of issues? What understandings do the metaphors frame as "logical"? What blindspots might be associated with a particular metaphor?

3. What is the role of cultural informants—those not involved in a negotiation but whose advice may be sought about the relevant patterns or behaviours that can be expected from negotiation participants of a given ethnocultural or other group? When cultural informants are used to help build cultural fluency, how can negotiators remain mindful of the possibility that parties in their negotiation may or may not act in accordance with cultural patterns?

4. Given that every participant in a negotiation will be influenced by multiple cultural patterns, which cultural identities will be most salient or important to recognize and acknowledge?

5. Are there times when cultural identity may preclude effectiveness (for example, if the parties are unwilling to negotiate with a woman, or someone from a particular community or profession)? In such times, how should negotiation participants respond?

6. Given the importance of ethical considerations in representative negotiation and their interconnectedness to power and cultural fluency, how can negotiators engage in ways that acknowledge entrenched power dynamics? What are the limits on negotiators' capacities to challenge such dynamics? When should a negotiator cease participating in a process that involves a significant power imbalance?

Selected Further Reading

Beyond Intractability, <http://www.beyondintractability.org>.

E.M. Clark, *In Search of Human Nature* (London: Routledge, 2002).

A. Kupfer Schneider & C. Honeyman, eds., *The Negotiator's Fieldbook* (Washington, DC: American Bar Association, 2006), especially the following articles:

    P. Adler, "Protean Negotiation," 17.

    M.C. Campbell & J.S. Docherty, "What's in a Frame?" 37.

    H. Gadlin, A. Kupfer Schneider & C. Honeyman, "The Road to Hell Is Paved with Metaphors," 29.

    K. Gibson, "Ethics and Morality in Negotiation," 175.

    C. Honeyman & A. Kupfer Schneider, "Introduction: A 'Canon of Negotiation' Begins to Emerge," 1.

Power and Negotiation

Michael Coyle

Introduction

"[T]he fundamental concept in social science is Power, in the same sense in which Energy is the fundamental concept in physics."

Bertrand Russell[1]

The student of negotiation has at least three cogent reasons to focus on the effects of power in the bargaining context. First, each negotiator wishes to know how much scope exists for their own tactics and strategy to affect the bargaining outcome and, correspondingly, how much of the field of possible outcomes in a particular case is predetermined by the extrinsic power relations between the parties. We might label this an *instrumental concern* about power: to what extent are external power dynamics likely to determine the outcome? Second, the negotiator has a *tactical concern*: to understand which moves, if any, either at or away from the table, might be effective to transform an existing power dynamic to the negotiator's advantage. Third, for those involved in efforts to resolve legal disputes, power raises a *justice concern*: namely, whether the use of out-of-court settlement negotiation permits resource differentials to trump legal values in the resolution of rights disputes.

---

1   B. Russell, *Power: A New Social Analysis* (New York: Routledge, 1938) at 4.

Thinking Inside the Box ...

Does Might Make Right? How Not to Use Power

In 416 BC, at the height of the Peloponnesian War with Sparta and its allies, after years of attempting to convince the island state of Melos to join the Athenian alliance, Athens threatened to invade the island. With a fearsome show of naval and military power, the Athenians forced the islanders to the bargaining table. Their message was clear: surrender or be destroyed. As recounted by Thucydides, the ensuing discussions were a textbook example of power dominating negotiations. Relying on their upper hand militarily and economically, the Athenian negotiators refused to discuss the fairness of their position. In the end, unable to obtain the Melians' agreement, the Athenians overpowered the island, slaughtered the men of Melos, and sold the women and children into slavery. The outcome was a catastrophe for the inhabitants and economy of Melos. Athens ultimately lost the war and historians have long wondered whether its actions at Melos significantly damaged its reputation with its own allies and eroded its own raison d'être.

This story begs the question: would interest-focused negotiations have rewritten history? Armed with an understanding of the psychological effects of power disparity in negotiation, might each side have employed tactics that could have avoided this tragic outcome?

Source: Thucydides, *History of the Peloponnesian War*, Book V. For an interesting power analysis of the confrontation, see H. Waelchli & D. Shah, "Crisis Negotiations Between Unequals: Lessons from a Classic Dialogue" (1994) 10:2 Negotiation Journal 129.

In approaching the first two of these concerns we might take note that *negotiation* may be described as a process whereby one party seeks to influence another to accede to a state of affairs desired by the first party.[2] As such, by its very nature, negotiation seems intimately related to the concept of power—commonly defined as the ability to exert influence over one's neighbours and one's surroundings.[3] We might be tempted, then, to surmise that the task of the negotiator is nothing more or less than to try to exercise power effectively, albeit in a relatively civilized manner. Is this a reasonable conclusion: that negotiation is nothing more than an extension of power dynamics that exist external to the table? If we accept that each negotiator comes to the table with different resources, socio-economic circumstances,

---

2   See *e.g.* J.Z. Rubin & B.R. Brown, *The Social Psychology of Bargaining and Negotiation* (New York: Academic Press, 1975) at 260; R. Fisher, "Negotiation Power: Getting and Using Influence" (1983) 27:2 American Behavioral Scientist 149 at 149-50 (*negotiation* is defined as "including all cases in which two or more parties are communicating each for the purpose of influencing the other's decision").

3   See D.A. Lax & J.K. Sebenius, *The Manager as Negotiator: Bargaining for Cooperation and Competitive Gain* (New York: Free Press, 1986) 250; Fisher, *ibid.* at 150; R. Lewicki *et al.*, *Negotiation*, 5th ed. (New York: McGraw-Hill Irwin, 2006) at 183.

and personal strengths, does each negotiator have the same opportunity to negotiate effectively?

The third concern, about the appropriateness of using negotiation processes to settle disputes about legal rights, was forcefully articulated more than 20 years ago by Owen Fiss. In "Against Settlement,"[4] Fiss argued that imbalances in the parties' financial resources, combined with the absence of neutral judicial direction, mean that too often the disputant with fewer resources settles for a result that unjustly fails to measure up to their legal entitlement. Of course, disparities in the parties' resources may also affect their access to justice through the courts. Nevertheless, the concern that power imbalances might make negotiation inappropriate for settling legal disputes continues to fuel academic debate.

This chapter will examine the role and significance of power at the negotiation table, whether the negotiations are aimed at creating new arrangements between the parties ("transactional negotiations") or at settling a dispute over the parties' legal entitlements ("rights negotiations"). It is divided into four parts:

1. the sources of bargaining power;
2. the effects of power at the table;
3. understanding power-related negotiation tactics; and
4. the legitimacy of using negotiation to settle rights disputes.

The Sources of Bargaining Power

> *"A power I have, but of what strength and nature*
> *I am not yet instructed."*
>
> William Shakespeare[5]

Common Misconceptions: Attributes and Power

Negotiators typically focus on whether there are *external* factors that will limit or assist their ability to persuade the other side to come to a desired agreement.[6] Negotiators wish to know, in other words, whether there is "a level playing field" in which they can employ the negotiation strategies and tactics presented elsewhere in this textbook. In focusing on this question, negotiators frequently look to the external attributes of the other side—attributes that may appear to give the other side an advantage from the outset of the negotiation. However, it is a mistake to assume that those who have attributes ordinarily associated with power in society at large will necessarily enjoy an advantage in negotiation.

---

4   O.M. Fiss, "Against Settlement" (1984) 93 Yale L.J. 1073 at 1075.

5   W. Shakespeare, *Measure for Measure*, act 1, sc. 1, lines 79-80.

6   For law students, in particular, this will be a familiar premise. For centuries the judicial approach to inequality of bargaining power in the context of contract law (in the areas of undue influence and unconscionability, for example) has focused on the external attributes of the parties. Cases

ECONOMIC RESOURCES

Power in the marketplace does not necessarily translate into a bargaining advantage. Consider the case of a company that currently dominates a market dependent on new technologies. When negotiating with a small start-up company that has secured a patent which would greatly benefit the large company, does the latter necessarily enjoy an advantage? In reality it is just as likely, depending on the importance of the patent and the technical needs of the large company, that the start-up company will come to the negotiation with every reason to be confident of a good outcome. In fact, in certain cases wealth and resources may amount to a significant vulnerability in negotiation. It has been noted, for example, that the wealth of the parents of a kidnapping victim is of little assistance in negotiating the ransom demand.[7] Indeed, it is precisely because of their wealth that they are vulnerable. The same holds true for a company that has just completed a year of record profits: it may then be more vulnerable, not less, to union demands for a wage increase in collective bargaining.

Thinking Inside the Box ...

Not for Sale ... Yet

In January 2005, when Viacom offered Mark Zuckerberg, founder of Facebook, $750 million for the social networking website, he rejected the offer, and left the negotiating table. At that time, Zuckerberg was 22 years old, living in what the *New York Times* referred to as a "barren" apartment. What, then, was the source of Zuckerberg's bargaining power? Zuckerberg seemed to have a clear understanding of the strength of his alternatives. Since its creation three years earlier, Zuckerberg's Facebook website had attracted an exploding number of the younger demographic that fuels the on-line industry. In 2006, several major Internet companies were vying for that market share in an attempt to regain their industry leadership. Was Zuckerberg right about his BATNA (best alternative to a negotiated agreement)? In September 2006, Yahoo offered Zuckerberg $900 million for Facebook, a sum that Zuckerberg also turned down.

Source: Saul Hansell, "Yahoo Woos a Social Networking Site" *New York Times* online edition, September 22, 2006.

---

such as the English *Lloyd's Bank v. Bundy*, [1974] 3 All E.R. 757 (C.A.) and the Canadian *Morrison v. Coast Finance Ltd.* (1965), 54 W.W.R. 257 (B.C.C.A.) emphasize the external attributes of the parties, questioning, e.g. whether the plaintiff was elderly, blind, uneducated, or unsophisticated in comparison to the party with whom they are contracting. See G.H.L. Fridman, *The Law of Contracts*, 5th ed. (Toronto: Carswell, 2006) 314-23. For a general review of the application of negotiation theory to the jurisprudence, see D. Barnhizer, "Power, Inequality and the Bargain: The Role of Bargaining Power in the Law of Contract—Symposium Introduction" (2006) Michigan State Law Review 841.

7   Lax & Sebenius, *supra* note 3 at 249.

This is not to say that access to economic resources can never offer an advantage in negotiations; obviously it can. Thus, a union with a considerable strike fund may be able to hold out for longer and make higher demands in negotiations that could lead to a strike, than a union with an impoverished strike fund or no strike fund at all. The point is, it would be a strategic error to assume that in every negotiation, the party with greater economic resources has a bargaining advantage.

COERCIVE POWER

Physical strength is another attribute commonly associated with power. Again, however, depending on the bargaining context, this quality frequently does not translate into a negotiation advantage. For a prospective house buyer or a Canadian government representative seeking to renegotiate free-trade arrangements with the United States, brawn is unlikely to influence the outcome. Even in marriage breakdown negotiations where there is a history of abuse by one spouse, there is evidence to suggest that a physical power advantage does not translate into better negotiation outcomes.[8]

AUTHORITY

Negotiators often assume that representatives endowed with superior organizational authority will wield more influence at the bargaining table. After all, a negotiator with a broad mandate from his client is less constrained in the options he is free to propose. In fact, however, sometimes having a limited mandate can be an advantage. Thus, some negotiators will deliberately seek a limited authority to settle, knowing that having a restricted mandate may work in their favour by limiting the perceived bargaining range. Once again, bargaining power does not necessarily correlate with authority as established away from the table.

OTHER ATTRIBUTES

The same point can be made about virtually all other physical or external attributes that the parties bring to the negotiation table: whether they be strength of personality, status, social connections, or political or spiritual influence. All of these attributes might translate into influence in some settings, but they are not necessarily indicators of strength at the bargaining table. This is not simply a theoretical point. Negotiators who lower their aspirations solely based on a counterpart's apparent external qualities make a serious strategic error.[9]

---

8   See D. Ellis & N. Stuckless, *Mediating and Negotiating Marital Conflicts* (Thousand Oaks, CA: Sage Publications, 1996) at 80. The authors' studies focused on mediation clients participating in a divorce mediation process with an effective screening protocol and consistent monitoring of abusive behaviour. In these circumstances, imbalances in marital power were found to be unrelated to imbalances in the outcomes of mediation.

9   Barnhizer, *supra* note 6; D. Barnhizer, "Inequality of Bargaining Power" (2005) 76 U. Colo. L. Rev. 139 at 199-223 (examining judicial attempts to assess and assign legal consequences to adversarial parties with power disparities); R.S. Adler & E.M. Silverstein, "When David Meets

One of the main reasons that the "attribute" approach to power fails to explain negotiation dynamics is that it treats power as a quality possessed by one party. In fact, however, negotiation dynamics depend upon the relationship and the actions of at least two parties, as well as their situations, needs, and preferences. Negotiation is an *interdependent* process where each party seeks to influence another toward a desired outcome. What matters, therefore, is the relationship between the negotiating parties rather than the attributes of one party or the other.

Locating the True Sources of Bargaining Power

If analyzing each party's attributes in isolation cannot offer an adequate explanation of bargaining power, what are the operative sources of power at the negotiation table? Our analysis sheds some light on the requirements of an accurate explanation of bargaining power. Any such explanation must recognize that bargaining power is relational and situation-dependent.[10] Perhaps the most common, and useful, definitions of bargaining power describe power in terms of the relative ability of each party to influence the other toward the desired outcomes. Thus, the "bargaining power" of party A means the ability of party A to move party B toward a range of outcomes desired by A.[11] Note the focus on *relative* power: what the parties care about is their ability to influence *each other*.[12]

If bargaining power is the ability to influence outcome, it might be said that every negotiation tactic amounts to an effort to create or use bargaining power. Concerns about bargaining

---

Goliath: Dealing with Power Differentials in Negotiations" (2000) 5 Harv. Negot. L. Rev. 1 at 48 ("How concerned should a negotiator be—especially one with superior bargaining power—that pursuing an advantage in a contract will result in a court finding that the agreement is unconscionable? Our best answer: some but not much").

10   M. Foucault, *The History of Sexuality Vol. I: An Introduction*, trans. by Robert Hurley (New York: Pantheon, 1978) pt. 4, c. 2 at 92-102 ("Power is not an institution, and not a structure; neither is it a certain strength we are endowed with; it is the name that one attributes to a complex strategical situation in a particular society").

11   J.Z. Rubin & Brown, *supra* note 2 at 2; Lax & Sebenius, *supra* note 3 at 250. See also Adler & Silverstein, *supra* note 9 at 13-20 (analyzing sources of bargaining power and techniques for increasing bargaining power); B.J. Flick, "Negotiation Theory and the Law of Collective Bargaining" (1989-1990) 38 U. Kan. L. Rev. 81 at 86-99 (evaluating negotiation tactics and strategy in context of obligation to bargain in good faith); R.H. Lawton, "Negotiating from Strength: Advantage Derived from the Process and Strategy of Preparing for Competitive Negotiation" (1986-1987) 14 Pepp. L. Rev. 839 at 851-60 (surveying strategies and tactics for achieving superior results in law student mock negotiations); E.J. Lawler, "Power Processes in Bargaining" (1992) 33 Sociological Quarterly 17 at 21; D. Willer, M. J. Lovaglia & B. Markovsky, "Power and Influence: A Theoretical Bridge" (1997) 76 Social Forces 571 at 573.

12   It is also possible that the combined, total power of the parties at the table tends to affect the process and outcome. Thus, the greater the *mutual* dependence the more likely the parties are to negotiate cooperatively, particularly if the mutual dependence is part of a long-term relationship. See Lawler, *ibid.* at 23. See also the discussion under "Dependence Theory: The Power of Preferences" below.

power, however, typically focus on whether there are factors that might limit the parties' freedom to seek an outcome that is based solely on the parties' interaction at the table. We will see later that the concept of bargaining power cannot be clinically separated from the parties' dealings at the table. Nevertheless, it is necessary to have a starting point, and it is logical to begin with an understanding of the factors that determine the power dynamics *at the moment a negotiation commences*. In other words, we will begin by asking: what determines the potential influence of each party when they come to the bargaining table?[13]

What circumstances external to the table may be said to tilt the probable outcome toward the interests of one side? Here, two main theories have been developed by negotiation researchers. The first defines negotiation power in terms of mutual dependence; the second focuses on the parties' alternatives to a negotiated agreement.

DEPENDENCE THEORY: THE POWER OF PREFERENCES

The proponents of dependence theory suggest that A's power over B arises from A's control over resources that B desires and the value that B places on those resources.[14] Thus, dependence theory suggests that the nature and intensity of the parties' preferences will affect the outcome of their bargain.[15] Again, recall that negotiation is a mutually dependent process. Therefore, the relative power of the negotiating parties is a function not only of B's desire for A's resources, but also of A's desire for what B can bring to the table. In fact, even this is clearly a simplification. One party's desire for what the other might trade will only be relevant to the negotiation outcome to the extent that the other party is prepared to trade what the first desires. In other words, it is not only desires to acquire resources that will influence a negotiation outcome, but also relative willingness to part with those resources.

For a simple example of how dependence theory suggests that preferences will affect negotiation outcomes, consider a proposed car purchase. Assume that A owns an antique Rolls-Royce once owned by John Lennon. B is interested in buying the car. Whether the two parties will in fact reach agreement and the terms of that agreement will largely depend on A's willingness to part with what may be a treasured possession, A's desire for ready cash, B's level of interest in the car (perhaps he is an avid Beatles fan), and the marginal value B places on his money. Note that all of these preference factors are largely determined prior to the parties' meeting to negotiate. In that sense, all of these preferences may fairly be said to contribute to the relative bargaining power that each party brings to the table.

---

13 Willer, Lovaglia & Markovsky, *supra* note 11 (defining power as "the structurally determined potential for obtaining favoured payoffs in relations where interests are opposed").

14 R.M. Emerson, "Exchange Theory, Part 11: Exchange Relations, Exchange Networks, and Groups as Exchange Systems" in J. Berger, M. Zelditch Jr. & B. Anderson, eds., *Sociological Theories in Progress*, vol. 2 (Boston: Houghton Mifflin, 1972) 58 at 62-72; L. Greenhalgh, S.A. Neslin & R.W. Gilkey, "The Effects of Negotiator Preferences, Situational Power, and Negotiator Personality on Outcomes of Business Negotiations" (1985) 28:1 Academy of Management Journal 9 at 29; Adler & Silverstein, *supra* note 9 at 8.

15 D.A. Lax & J.K. Sebenius, "The Power of Alternatives of the Limits to Negotiation" (1985) 1:2 Negotiation Journal 163 at 172-73.

Thinking Inside the Box ...

First Nations Land Claims Negotiations

Aboriginal protests about land rights have recently become a familiar sight to Canadians. The occupation of land near Caledonia, Ontario by members of the Six Nations of the Grand River, which began in February 2006, attracted considerable attention from the local public, national media, the courts, and the police. It was followed by railway blockades near Tyendinaga, Ontario in the spring of 2006 and in 2007, and further rail and highway interruptions on the "Aboriginal National Day of Action" in June 2007. The federal government has a policy to deal with the negotiation of First Nations land claims that allege the government has violated their legal rights. Frustrated by what they see as inadequate progress on those claims, First Nations are increasingly turning to public protests. Can you explain in terms of power and negotiation theory what First Nations may be trying to achieve?

As of March 31, 2007, 865 of the specific land claims filed with the federal government for negotiation remained unresolved. The average land claim in negotiation in Ontario had been in the system for almost 16 years without an outcome. Despite a steadily increasing backlog, the federal government had not made significant changes to its negotiation process in 15 years. In terms of negotiation theory, how might you explain the government's decision not to change its approach to negotiating land claims? What is the BATNA of the government in a land claim negotiation? In your view, is a blockade likely to improve a First Nation's negotiated outcome? Are there other options the First Nations might pursue to increase their power at the table? Reconsider these questions after reading the Fiss article excerpted later in the chapter. What barriers, if any, might First Nations face in taking a land claim to court?

Source: Land claims data are available online at <http://www.ainc-inac.gc.ca/ps/clm/nms_e.pdf >.

Occupation at Caledonia, Ontario by members of the Six Nations of the Grand River

The recognition that preferences affect bargaining outcomes[16] has significant implications for the negotiator. First, a party entering negotiations may benefit by gaining as much information as possible about the preferences of their counterpart. Second, a party may be able to improve its negotiation outcomes by taking actions to alter its counterpart's preferences. Thus, the manufacturer of an MP3 player may be able to increase its sale price if it undertakes an advertising campaign to convince the public that the player is socially desirable. Such efforts to influence perceptions in the marketplace, if effective, will increase both the number of agreements to buy the product and its selling price. Third, a negotiator may increase her effective bargaining power by reviewing her client's preferences prior to the negotiation. Preferences are, after all, a function of the human mind. It follows that each party generally has the ability to change the value he or she places on various negotiation outcomes.

Consider a real estate transaction in which a negotiator is acting on behalf of a commercial developer. The negotiator discovers that there is a large electronic billboard on the property. If, instead of insisting that the billboard be removed, the negotiator consults the client to reassess its preferences, she may learn that the client prefers to permit the billboard to stay during the development phase—in exchange for the client's use of one of the panels to advertise the development. What has occurred? By revisiting her client's preferences, the negotiator made possible a better outcome for her client than would have otherwise been available.

As the preceding analysis makes clear, the parties' preferences can be expected to influence negotiation outcomes independently of the tactics and strategies deployed at the bargaining table. Preferences cannot tell the whole story, however. A full understanding of the parties' relative power at the outset of negotiation requires more than an analysis of the parties' respective preferences; it must also include an analysis of the availability of desirable alternatives to each of the parties.

ALTERNATIVES THEORY: THE POWER OF BATNAS

Every student of negotiation understands the importance of the parties' alternatives. The rational negotiator will identify his client's best alternative to a negotiated agreement (BATNA) and will use that reference point to define the range of acceptable negotiated outcomes. Accordingly, in every negotiation between rational actors, the range of possible bargaining outcomes will in theory be established by the distance between the parties' BATNAs.[17] Of course, in most cases, outside of free markets where negotiating parties have

---

16   See *e.g.* Lax & Sebenius, *ibid.* at 172. The effect of preferences on bargaining outcomes remains a controversial issue. Some studies indicate that relative BATNAs are more significant (though of course the notion of one's BATNA incorporates a judgment as to preferences in relation to the subject matter of the negotiation). In other words, BATNA and preferences are clearly linked. T.C. Schelling suggests that tactical decisions by one party to make irrevocable commitments to a position are more relevant to the bargaining outcome than the parties' initial preferences: *The Strategy of Conflict* (Cambridge, MA: Harvard University Press, 1960) at 122.

17   R. Fisher & W. Ury, *Getting to Yes: Negotiating Agreement Without Giving In*, 2d ed. (New York: Penguin Books, 1991) 100; Lax & Sebenius, *supra* note 15 at 165-66; Lewicki, *supra* note 3 at 36-38.

perfect information, neither party can be absolutely certain of the alternatives available to the other side, or of the subjective desirability of those alternatives from the other side's perspective. This means that the possible bargaining range as identified by the parties themselves will depend in part upon each party's *perception* of the other's situation.

Many writers identify the parties' relative BATNAs as the primary determinant of the parties' relative bargaining power.[18] Reflecting on first principles lends support to this conclusion. After all, regardless of the intensity of A's desire for what B brings to the table, A should never agree to an outcome that costs A more than the price available to A elsewhere. Thus, the power that B derives from A's preferences is directly affected by the range of equally acceptable alternatives available to A. All other things being equal,[19] a plaintiff in out-of-court settlement discussions should never accept a compensation offer that is significantly less than the likely value of a court award.

In practice, the calculation of one's BATNA can be a complicated and subjective process. Many experiments on negotiation power manipulate their subjects' perceived BATNAs simply by providing the subject with instructions that assign a financial value to their best alternative.[20] In the real world, however, possible negotiation outcomes may consist of multifaceted trades on different issues—an aggregation that may not be available (and therefore has no ready equivalent) away from the bargaining table. In such cases, a party's BATNA is not capable of objective determination. For the negotiator who represents a client, the task of calculating approximately equivalent alternatives will require careful discussion with the client about her preferences and priorities as between different alternatives.

Consider the challenge of calculating BATNAs in a litigation setting. The client's alternative to settlement is a court judgment. In many cases it will not be possible to predict with certainty whether the judgment will favour the client or if so what the amount of the court's award will be. A good negotiator will make an educated guess as to the potential value of a favourable judgment, and discount that value by the probability of loss. Next, the negotiator should discuss the client's subjective evaluation of the costs associated with pursuing a court verdict. The financial costs will include not only lawyers' and experts' fees and expenses, but also the value of the client's time invested in the litigation, and the subjective time value to the client of deferring receipt of any compensation. Other aspects of the client's BATNA calculation are clearly subjective, including the client's tolerance for risk, the emotional burden, if any, felt by the client in pursuing an adversarial process, and, in cases where there is a relationship at risk, the potential long-term costs of damage to that relationship. All of these factors must be considered in calculating the clients' BATNA (that is, the net value to the client of pursuing litigation). Finally, after assessing the client's BATNA, the negotiator and client should engage in a similar process aimed at estimating the *other* side's likely perception of the value and cost of the litigation alternative.

---

18   Lax & Sebenius, *ibid.*; Fisher & Ury, *ibid.* at 179; R.J. Wolfe & K.L. McGinn, "Perceived Relative Power and Its Influence on Negotiations" (2005) 14 Group Decision and Negotiation 3 at 6. The conclusion that the parties' initial BATNAs are a key factor in determining negotiation outcome is supported by considerable empirical evidence. See *infra* note 35.

19   That is, taking into account all of the costs of pursuing the case. See the discussion on tangible and intangible costs below.

20   Lax & Sebenius, *supra* note 15 at 170.

It is essential to keep in mind that relative bargaining power depends upon both parties' BATNAs. It is a mistake for A to assume, because his own alternatives to agreement seem poor, that he should reduce his expectations, for the probability of A obtaining a particular outcome in the negotiation depends equally on B's available alternatives. If B has no attractive alternatives either, A may be in a position to insist on a more favourable outcome than he would otherwise have thought possible. The foregoing analysis should make clear that the relative power of the parties may be affected by events that alter either party's alternatives, and also by actions that are effective in altering either party's *perception* of those alternatives. This in turn suggests three approaches that should be considered by a party who seeks to alter the power balance in a negotiation.

First, it has long been recognized that it is in the interest of a negotiating party to fully investigate its own alternatives prior to the negotiations, and, if possible, to create new or improved options for meeting its interests away from the table. Improving A's BATNA directly increases the value of A's possible negotiation outcomes. Either B must propose outcomes that exceed the value of the improved alternative, or A will reject B's proposals in favour of its (now improved) alternatives. A common example of proactive BATNA improvement is the case of a manufacturing company that chooses to increase its product inventories in anticipation of collective bargaining negotiations. The desired impact: to insulate the company from the threat of a breakdown in the negotiations.

Second, it may be possible to render the other party's alternatives less desirable. This will also shift the power dynamic and therefore the perceived bargaining range. The Maltese military base negotiations described in "Thinking Inside the Box …" on page 170 represents a classic example of this strategy in action. In multi-party negotiations, a desire to weaken the other side's BATNA frequently leads to the formation of coalitions at the table on some or all of the issues. The purpose of forging such alliances is often to increase the negative consequences for the stronger party should they fail to reach agreement with each of the other parties.[21] The same desire to create favourable power dynamics is also at the root of class action claims. The pooling of the plaintiffs' legal and financial resources gives them access to a level of court pressure that would not otherwise be available to any of them individually. If the case has merit, that pressure may effectively weaken the BATNA of the defendant and thereby encourage a negotiated outcome that meets the plaintiffs' interests.[22]

Third, recall that what actually motivates negotiating parties is their *perceptions* of both parties' alternatives.[23] These perceptions are not necessarily well-founded. First, in the case of complex relationships, it may not be easy or even possible for either party to project with

---

21   On the dynamics of coalition building and their link to power dynamics in negotiation, see Rubin & Brown, *supra* note 2 at 71-73; Lewicki *et al.*, *supra* note 3 at 342-43; S.B. Bacharach & E.J. Lawler, *Power and Politics in Organizations: The Social Psychology of Conflict, Coalitions, and Bargaining* (San Francisco: Jossey-Bass, 1980) at 58-59. Note that potential coalition members may be found not only at the bargaining table itself but also among outsiders who exercise influence on one or more of the parties.

22   So, too, laws permitting employees to negotiate collectively through unions reflect an express legislative effort to ensure a balance of power at the collective bargaining table.

23   Wolfe & McGinn, *supra* note 18 at 17; *Lawler*, supra note 11 at 27; Lewicki *et al.*, *supra* note 3 at 187.

Thinking Inside the Box …

Raising the Stakes

In 1971, Britain entered into negotiations with Malta over renewing British rights to lease a Maltese naval base. Due to advances in technology, the rights to the naval base had become strategically less important to Britain than they had been in the past. As a result, at the outset of the discussions Britain was not prepared to offer generous terms for the lease renewal. Malta's response made clear that it was asking the Soviet Union, Libya, and other Arab states to consider the possibility of renting the base. In the end, Malta was able to quadruple the annual rent it charged Britain for the naval base, largely because Britain did not want another country to control it.

Source: D.A. Lax & J.K. Sebenius, *Manager as Negotiator* (New York: Free Press, 1986) 56-57, citing W. Wriggens, "Up for Auction: Malta Bargains with Great Britain, 1971" in I.W. Zartman, ed., *The 50% Solution* (New York: Anchor-Doubleday, 1976).

---

precision the ultimate costs of non-agreement. Further, psychological biases may distort the parties' perceptions of their likelihood of success without agreement. Experimental studies have repeatedly shown, for example, that lawyers who represent plaintiffs tend to overestimate their chances of success in court and the likely size of a court award. Defendants' counsel experience a similar but reverse effect, biasing their BATNA estimates in favour of their client.[24] Such cognitive biases frequently interfere when staking out adversarial positions leads the parties unwittingly to over-emphasize information that appears to corroborate their position and to undervalue information that appears to contradict their bias.[25]

Accordingly, just as improving the alternatives at play will alter the bargaining range, so too can changing the other side's perception of one's alternatives. Consequently, in many cases, an effective negotiator will need to take steps to clearly bring home to his counterpart the probable costs of non-agreement.[26] In the negotiation of a legal dispute, a plaintiff may strengthen its position in this way by filing a court action prior to the negotiations. It is for the same reason that a union will take care to set a strike date prior to the commencement of collective bargaining negotiations.

THE INTERACTION OF PREFERENCES AND BATNAS

No single theory is capable of explaining all the possible influences on human interaction; likewise, the outcome of a particular negotiation can depend upon an almost infinite number of variables. Still, focusing on the parties' relative alternatives and preferences offers a robust way of understanding the scope for bargaining at the table. It is true that the capacity and

---

24   Lax & Sebenius, *supra* note 15 at 166-70.

25   Lawler, *supra* note 11 at 28.

26   For a useful discussion of this point, see W. Ury, *Getting Past No: Negotiating Your Way from Confrontation to Cooperation* (New York: Bantam Books, 1993) at 138-42.

willingness of one side to punish or to impose costs on the other may influence the outcome in a particular case,[27] but properly understood this is merely another variable that influences the other side's BATNA. It is also true that in some cases, a party's resistance point (and, accordingly, the bargaining range) may not be strictly based on its BATNA (its walk-away point having been decided for emotional or arbitrary reasons). However, a rational negotiator knows that her client's resistance point should be equivalent to the client's BATNA, and a good negotiator will suggest to her counterpart that this approach is also in her counterpart's best interest. Finally, it is undoubtedly the case that sometimes a party's desire to preserve an important relationship may seem more important to that party than its strict financial or practical alternatives to negotiation. Even here, however, the range of settlements acceptable to that party can be explained from the perspective of preferences and BATNAs.[28]

Note that the nature of the parties' preferences and their BATNAs are intimately related: the value that A places on what B brings to the table influences the extent to which A will be equally satisfied with outcomes that can be achieved away from the table. In other words, the parties' relative power depends not just on the resources that each party controls but also on each of the party's preferences in relation to those resources—and the resources that can be obtained elsewhere.[29]

Figures 7.1 and 7.2 help us visualize the influence of BATNAs and preferences on the range of rational bargaining outcomes. Figure 7.1 focuses on BATNAs; the parties' actual estimated BATNAs are represented by points X and Y. The distance between X (the value of A's BATNA) and Y (the value of B's BATNA) defines the range of possible outcomes that would in fact be at least minimally acceptable to each side. In a world of perfect information, X to Y is the actual bargaining range. In this world, the value of the parties' known alternatives at the outset of negotiations predetermines the scope for bargaining at the table.

In the real world, A frequently does not know with certainty the value that B places on her best alternative to agreement. In such a case, A cannot accurately identify the actual bargaining range in advance; A's best estimate of the range might be from X to Z. This estimate will be A's *perception* of the bargaining range, and for A (unless A's perception changes) this range will in fact define A's initial understanding of the scope for bargaining at the table. (Of course, if B does not know the value A places on its own BATNA, B will perceive yet another range of "possible" outcomes, perhaps Y to W.) As we have seen, if B can succeed in altering in B's favour A's perception of A's own BATNA, or of B's BATNA (or both), then B will succeed in altering the range of possible outcomes in her favour.[30]

---

27 For an example of power analyzed as the ability to impose costs, see R. Emerson, "Power-Dependence Relations" (1962) 27:1 American Sociological Review 31.

28 After all, each party's "best" alternative to settlement must be interpreted in the context of *all* of that party's preferences, including the desire to maintain good relations.

29 P.H. Kim, R.L. Pinkley & A.R. Fragale, "Power Dynamics in Negotiation" (2005) 30:4 Academy of Management Review 799 at 803-4; Greenhalgh, Neslin & Gilkey, *supra* note 14 at 12, 29; Lawler, *supra* note 11 at 26-28.

30 Note that B will not necessarily obtain an outcome outside A's original perception of the bargaining range, but the *average* value of the possible bargaining outcomes will have improved in B's favour. For an interesting discussion on how alternatives limit the bargaining range, see Lax & Sebenius, *supra* note 3 at 48-49.

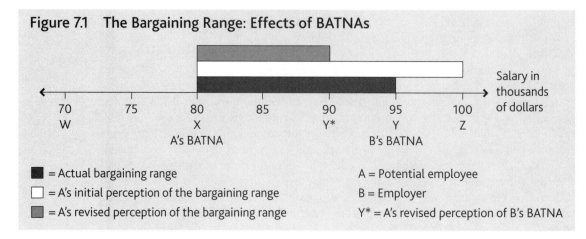

Figure 7.1   The Bargaining Range: Effects of BATNAs

■ = Actual bargaining range

□ = A's initial perception of the bargaining range

▨ = A's revised perception of the bargaining range

A = Potential employee

B = Employer

Y* = A's revised perception of B's BATNA

Note that in each of the above situations (perfect assessment by both parties of the parties' best alternatives, or imperfect assessment) the possibility of a rational agreement will ordinarily be described by a *range* of potential outcomes.[31] Thus, the relative strength of the parties' BATNAs does not determine a particular outcome; that will depend on the parties' preferences and their interaction at the table.

Next, consider a negotiation where there is more than one issue. Now there arises the possibility of additional "trades" by the parties which, if the parties have different preferences on the additional issues, could increase the total value to both of any negotiated outcome. Discussion of the parties' respective preferences may result in a new range of "integrative" outcomes. Here, the role of differences in preferences is to open up the possibility of a new range of bargaining outcomes. In figure 7.2, this range is represented by the shaded area below the curve. Note that in this situation too the combination of alternatives and preferences does not determine a particular outcome, only the range of rational outcomes.[32] Again, the parties' actual outcome will depend on their interaction at the bargaining table.

The Effects of Power at the Table: From Theory to Practice

Complexity: Thus far, we have assumed that the range of potential bargaining outcomes is established *at the outset of negotiations* by the interrelationship of the parties' initial BATNAs, perceived BATNAs, and their preferences. The real world is more complex. Outside events can change the parties' alternatives while the negotiations unfold. One party may reconsider

---

31   Unless, of course, there is no overlap between the outcomes both parties would consider acceptable. In such a case, not only is there no range of acceptable agreements, there is in fact no possibility of agreement.

32   For a more detailed explanation of the Pareto frontier that appears in figure 7.2, see Lax & Sebenius, *supra* note 3 at 42-45.

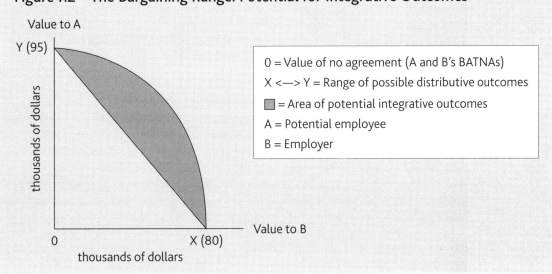

Figure 7.2   The Bargaining Range: Potential for Integrative Outcomes

his preferences in response to the other party's moves at the table. The negotiation may involve several issues, and for each of these issues the relative strength of each party's alternatives may differ. We know that the initial power balance determines only a range of outcomes, within which the parties' interaction will determine the actual negotiation outcome. Finally, empirical evidence suggests that the focus of the parties' interaction during a negotiation will change, from power to interests to positions, back to power, and so on.[33]

It has been said of disputes that they are subjective, unstable, reactive, complicated, and incomplete.[34] The same can be said of the role of power in actual negotiations: it is situational, variable, relational, and reactive. By definition, it is difficult to reproduce the subtleties of real-world power effects through experiments, whether they involve test subjects in short, simulated one-issue exchange negotiations, prisoner dilemma exercises, or any other exercise where the subject is asked to derive his preferences and perceived alternatives from a set of instructions. Nonetheless, experimental studies in this area have produced results that shed light on the possible impacts of power on outcomes and on the parties' behaviour during the negotiation process.

Power and outcomes: A large body of experimental evidence confirms that negotiators' initial BATNAs are a dominant factor in determining a range of negotiated outcomes. Subjects in simulated negotiations who are assigned objectively higher BATNAs tend to achieve

---

33   A.L. Lytle, J.M. Brett & D.L. Shapiro, "The Strategic Use of Interests, Rights, and Power to Resolve Disputes" (1999) 15 Negotiation Journal 31.

34   L. Felstiner, R. Abel & A. Sarat, "The Emergence and Transformation of Disputes: Naming, Blaming and Claiming …" (1980) 5 Law and Soc'y Rev. 631 at 637.

better negotiation outcomes than parties with lower BATNAs.[35] This is unsurprising: as we have seen, negotiators who come to the table with more attractive BATNAs have a higher threshold for accepting agreements. However, BATNAs do not determine a specific outcome, except in cases where the parties' respective BATNAs indicate that no agreement is possible. There is also experimental evidence to support the proposition that the parties' preferences play a key role in influencing the outcome.[36]

Interestingly, there is a significant body of experimental evidence which suggests that the more equal the parties' apparent bargaining power, the more they tend to reach integrative agreements.[37] Simulated negotiations between parties who begin with significant differences in the value of their alternatives and their degree of mutual dependence suggest that power imbalance results in fewer agreements overall and, where agreements are reached, they tend to be more distributive.[38] In other words, situations of perceived power imbalance seem to lead to agreements that miss opportunities for productive trades between the parties. To understand why this might be the case, we need to consider how perceived power disparities might affect the parties' behaviour.

Power and process effects: A number of negotiation studies suggest that a significant imbalance in bargaining power at the outset of a negotiation can impair the effectiveness of the parties' communication and reduce the chances that they will explore integrative options. There is evidence that a party who enjoys a perceived power advantage over her counterpart will be less likely to seek information about the other side's preferences, more likely to use hostile tactics, and more likely to push for distributive outcomes.[39] It appears, then, that where a party has stronger alternatives and a weaker preference for what the other has to

---

35   Lax & Sebenius, *supra* note 15 at 171-72; Wolfe & McGinn, *supra* note 18; P.H. Kim & A.R. Fragale, "Choosing the Path to Bargaining Power: An Empirical Comparison of BATNAs and Contributions in Negotiation" (2005) 90:2 Journal of Applied Psychology 373 at 374.

36   See Greenhalgh, Neslin & Gilkey, *supra* note 14 at 23, where the authors conclude that party preferences have the strongest direct influence on outcomes. It should be noted that some researchers have suggested that other variables, such as negotiator personality and aspirations, also have a significant correlation to outcome.

37   L. McAlister, M.H. Bazerman & P. Fader, "Power and Goal Setting in Channel Negotiations" (1986) 23 Journal of Marketing Research 228 at 235-36; Rubin & Brown, *supra* note 2 at 214-21; Lawler, *supra* note 11 at 27, 30; E.J. Lawler & S.B. Bacharach, "Comparison of Dependence and Punitive Forms of Power" (1987) 66:2 Social Forces 446 at 459; Wolfe & McGinn, *supra* note 18 at 6. Not all of the experimental research supports the conclusion that power disparities are associated with more distributive outcomes. See J.-S. Rioux, "Crisis Negotiation Outcomes Among Equals and Unequals, Democracies and Non-democracies" (1999) 36:1 International Politics 25 at 38 (arguing that Rubin & Brown's work should be retested).

38   Rubin & Brown, *supra* note 2 at 221-23; McAlister, Bazerman & Fader, *supra* note 37; Wolfe & McGinn, *supra* note 18. Compare J.-S. Rioux, *supra* note 37.

39   Lawler, *supra* note 11 at 30; Kim, Pinkley & Fragale, *supra* note 29 at 813-14; Rubin & Brown, *supra* note 2 at 213-33, 278.

offer, it will be less likely to invest in joint problem-solving. Interestingly, the evidence also suggests that in situations of power imbalance, the weaker party will not necessarily be induced to adopt more cooperative tactics,[40] either because they believe they need to counter the power imbalance or because they resist agreeing to an outcome motivated by power alone. This is the so-called power paradox: attempts to rely on power in a negotiation may lead to greater, not less, "face-saving" resistance from the other side.[41]

The apparent tendency for power imbalances to negatively influence the effectiveness of negotiations is a phenomenon that both parties in such situations should anticipate and plan to address. The "stronger" party may need to adjust its tactics, both to counter "the power paradox" and to avoid missing opportunities for value creation. For its part, the party that perceives itself to be at a significant power disadvantage may wish to explore tactics that alter the relative power dynamic, and tactics that promote value creation.

Power-Related Strategies and Tactics

*"Power may be at the end of a gun, but sometimes it's also
at the end of the shadow or the image of a gun."*

Jean Genet[42]

We have seen that the parties' perceived BATNAs and relative preferences are extrinsic factors that may be said to define the range of possible outcomes in a negotiation. BATNAs, for example, define the bargaining range; and preferences for particular outcomes, where there are a number of issues, will not inexorably determine a solitary outcome. Further, as we have seen, the parties will not have perfect information regarding their counterpart's BATNA and preferences. Finally, not all negotiators behave rationally, relying on their client's BATNA to define their resistance point. For all these reasons, it follows that the negotiator's tactics at the table will also affect each party's ability to maximize their interests. It is logical here to focus on two types of power-related tactics: tactics aimed at altering the power dynamic and tactics aimed at avoiding the negative effects associated with power imbalance.

---

40   C.K.W. De Dreu & G.A. Van Kleef, "The Influence of Power on the Information Search, Impression Formation, and Demands in Negotiation" (2004) 40 Journal of Experimental Social Psychology 303 at 305-6; C.T. Christen, "Predicting Willingness to Negotiate: The Effects of Perceived Power and Trustworthiness in a Model of Strategic Public Relations" (2004) 16:3 Journal of Public Relations Research 243 at 249; Lawler, *supra* note 11 at 26-28; McAlister, Bazerman & Fader, *supra* note 37 at 235. Some writers, however, suggest that in situations of power imbalance, the weaker party is more likely to act submissively, seeking to understand and satisfy the other's interests: Rubin & Brown, *supra* note 2 at 221-22.

41   For a discussion of this paradox and practical advice on tactics designed to avoid such resistance, see Ury, *supra* note 26 at 130-56.

42   Jean Genet, *Prisoner of Love*, trans. by Barbara Bray (London: Pan Books, 1989) 84.

Tactics Aimed at Altering the Power Dynamic

The following are common tactics aimed at changing the power dynamic between the parties in negotiation.

1. **Understand and rely on your own BATNA as a source of power.** A frequent mistake is to be intimidated by the status, resources, or reputation of the other side. Having carefully explored your own alternatives to agreement, relying on your knowledge of those alternatives and communicating to the other side that you have such alternatives leaves you invulnerable to any outcome that will actually worsen your situation. Be prepared to end the negotiations if the other side seems unwilling or unable to explore agreements that will advance your interests more than your BATNA.

2. **If possible, take action to improve your BATNA or to weaken theirs.** Power dynamics need not be static. Even after the negotiations begin, if it is feasible, continue to explore other options to address your interests away from the table. Methods of achieving this are as diverse as the subject matters of negotiation. Can you take further steps in a lawsuit? Can you find alternative suppliers? Obtain other job offers? While remaining sensitive to whether your behaviour might be perceived as a violation of trust at the bargaining table, remain vigilant as to whether there are other opportunities that could strengthen your BATNA. Equally, depending on the situation, it may be possible to enlist the support of the public or other allies to reduce the other side's attraction to non-agreement outcomes.

3. **Reality-check the other side's perception of their BATNA.** Many negotiators come to the table with unrealistic aspirations. In such cases, diplomatic questioning about their perceived alternatives may bring them to focus more clearly on the reality of their BATNA. We have seen that parties involved in disputes frequently overestimate their chances of success. Here, a number of tools may help to bring them to their senses. Independent market studies or other objectively generated information, neutral fact-finders, mediators, and non-binding arbitration are all effective ways of avoiding reactive devaluation and helping your counterpart come to a more realistic assessment of their likely non-agreement outcome.

4. **Many negotiators use a variety of distributive tactics to *disguise or exaggerate their BATNA.*** Such tactics can range from subtle techniques aimed at creating a false impression that they are close to their resistance point, to explicit deception. The student will already be familiar with tactics that involve creating misleading perceptions of the bargaining range by manipulating the pattern of offers and concessions. Opening with an extreme position or with a publicly stated precondition before negotiations can begin, offering progressively smaller concessions, even expressing frustration or anger with the other side's positions—all are examples of tactics aimed at disguising one's true resistance point. A famous military example of explicit deception is Chief Tecumseh's tactic at Fort Detroit in the War of 1812. By repeatedly parading the same soldiers in front of the fort, Tecumseh was able to convince the American general that he had a much larger force than was actually at his disposal, leading the general to surrender without a fight. For a more modern

example, consider the tactics used by Canadian union leader Bob White in the 1984 contract negotiations between the United Auto Workers and General Motors. After those negotiations, White commented that he had advised GM that his union had access to a sizable strike fund, although no such fund existed. White's bluff was clearly intended to deceive GM about the union's alternatives and, thus, to increase the pressure on GM to improve its offer to the union.[43]

Misrepresenting one's BATNA can be a risky tactic, however. If the deception is uncovered, it can cause long-lasting damage to your reputation and tarnish relationships. In addition, any tactic aimed at disguising your BATNA will be ineffective if the other side has acquired accurate information about your alternatives. Finally, all such tactics tend to eliminate from the perceived bargaining range agreements that would, in fact, be beneficial to the bluffing party—agreements that might, depending on the other side's BATNA, have been the only agreements that could have been acceptable to both sides.

Common and effective responses to pattern-of-offer type tactics include the other side refusing to accept any pattern of offers, demands, or concessions as relevant to the underlying values at stake in the negotiation, and insisting that objective criteria determine the range of acceptable agreements. The same responses will offer some protection against explicit deception about the other party's BATNA. Vigilance, due diligence, and effective information-gathering are the main defences against misrepresentation at the bargaining table.

5. **Address their preferences.** Because both parties' preferences condition the range of acceptable outcomes, a good negotiator will question the other side to better understand their interests and preferences. As Roger Fisher and William Ury have pointed out,[44] finding out what the other side really wants and generating creative options to address both sides' interests can be a powerful tool for shifting the bargaining range. Because the list of possible outcomes is not necessarily known or discoverable by either side at the outset of negotiations, it is essential to explore whether opportunities exist for adding value to the overall agreement. In other words, the negotiator should explore whether an apparently distributive situation can be turned into an opportunity for integrative trades.

6. **Some negotiators will *misrepresent their preferences*, making a false demand that they later intend to "give up" in return for a concession from the other side.** This attempt to manipulate the other party's perception of the preferences at play is known as the "bogey." Because statements of preference are more difficult for the other side to verify than statements of fact, this kind of deception is harder to uncover. This tactic, however, is fraught with risk: if the other side takes the representation on its face and offers to satisfy the stated preference, the party issuing the false demand may then be pressed to offer value in return!

---

43   For a fascinating overview of the negotiations, see *Final Offer: A National Film Board of Canada Release*, directed by R. Collison & S. Gunnarsson, produced by R. Collison, S. Gunnarsson, J. Kramer & J. Spotton (Canada: National Film Board of Canada, 1985).

44   Fisher & Ury, *supra* note 17 at 181-83.

> ## Thinking Inside the Box ...
>
> ### *What If They Won't Come to the Table?*
>
> It goes without saying that in order to reach an agreement, back-and-forth communication is required. (The old saying "it takes two to tango" certainly applies to negotiation.) What do you do, then, if the other side refuses to bargain? In *Getting Past No: Negotiating Your Way from Confrontation to Cooperation*, William Ury suggests that fear and distrust may lie behind the other party's rigid position. He suggests the following tactics to break through the impasse:
>
> 1. Suspend your natural reaction and regain your mental balance.
> 2. Overcome the other side's defensiveness. Do not be an adversary; step to their side.
> 3. Ask and accept: understand the reasons for their position and their BATNA.
> 4. Build them a "golden bridge": a face-saving route for them that will meet your interests.
> 5. Know your BATNA. Use the power of your BATNA to educate the other side and bring them to the table. Use the minimum power necessary to avoid provoking a negative reaction.
>
> *Source*: W. Ury, *Getting Past No: Negotiating Your Way from Confrontation to Cooperation* (New York: Bantam Books, 1993).

7. **Tailor your strategy to avoid the "power paradox."** We have seen that where there is a perceived power imbalance, there is potential for ineffective bargaining. Fisher and Ury recommend a number of related tactics aimed at redirecting the parties' focus from an ineffective battle of wills toward criteria for settlement that both sides can see as legitimate. This is the so-called strategy of "negotiation ju-jitsu": avoiding the cycle of escalation and retaliation by refocusing the parties' attention to interests and objective criteria.[45]

For a party that enters the bargaining process with an attractive BATNA, it may be tempting to devote less attention to opportunities that might be available through the negotiation. Indeed, it may be possible for such a negotiator to present his demands and obtain satisfaction without great difficulty, particularly where the other side's preferences and BATNA make it vulnerable. The danger of this approach is that it may leave value on the table. Worse, failing to heed the other party's concerns may damage relationships or fail to secure any agreement at all because of the other side's desire not to be seen as submitting to illegitimate tactics. Thus, even the party perceived to enjoy greater power at the table can benefit from diplomatically exploring the other side's interests and considering opportunities for integrative gain.

---

45 *Ibid.* at 107-28.

Changing the Process: Mediation

Mediation is an avenue frequently put forward as offering potential to moderate the effects of power imbalances in negotiation.[46] Mediation involves the assistance of a third-party neutral who has no power to impose an outcome on the parties. Generally, mediation is possible only where both parties agree to the process. The beneficial aspects of a mediator's role in cases of power imbalance can include fostering open communications and directing the parties' focus toward interests, preferences, and opportunities for joint gain. A mediator may also play a useful role in "reality-checking" both parties' perceptions of the strength of their BATNAs and in focusing the parties on the possible use of objective criteria to assess settlement options. Where appropriate in light of the parties' expectations, the mediator can also help the parties to avoid impasse by presenting options to the parties which it would be awkward (for reasons of saving face or otherwise) for either party to table directly. All of these functions are commonly accepted aspects of the mediator's role in assisting parties to negotiate effectively.

In the language of power tactics, a mediator cannot normally influence either party's BATNA or their underlying preferences, but may be able to influence the parties to adjust their perceptions of their BATNAs, to avoid communication traps, and to consider integrative options. To what extent is it appropriate for a mediator, hired by both negotiating parties, to intervene more directly to address power differences between the parties? Can the mediator be said to have a duty, based on the trust reposed by the parties in the mediator, to ensure that neither side is unfairly subjected to power pressures at the table? To what degree could a mediator, who lacks any binding authority, be effective in playing such a role? These questions are among those addressed in the article excerpted below.

Michael Coyle
"Defending the Weak and Fighting Unfairness:
Can Mediators Respond to the Challenge?"
(1998) 36 Osgoode Hall L.J. 625 at 628-52, footnotes omitted

Analyses to date of the role of power and power imbalances in mediation suffer from … limitations. They generally recognize that power imbalance between the parties is a factor to which the mediator should be sensitive, and note that the mediation process offers certain tools that may reduce the impact of such an imbalance. However, there has been little published analysis, outside the context of family mediation, of the dilemma faced by the mediator where a powerful party engages in apparently unfair behaviour that the ordinary tools of mediation have not remedied, and where termination of the mediation appears to the mediator to leave the weaker party in a worse position than if the mediation had not occurred …

There is evidence that many practising mediators care deeply about issues relating to procedural and substantive fairness in the negotiations they chair … What, for example,

---

46   See *e.g.* Lax & Sebenius, *supra* note 3 at 172-76; Ury, *supra* note 26 at 146-47.

should the mediator do in a situation where one party appears to be using a gross inequality of power to extract consent to an outcome that is not consistent with the mediator's view of the likely judgment of a court? (The presence of counsel on both sides may not alter this power dynamic, particularly if the weaker party has little in the way of financial resources to pursue the issue in court.) If one party does not have the resources to support a court action and the stronger party reveals to the mediator that it has deceived the other in relation to a material fact, and if the stronger party cannot be persuaded to rectify the deception, are the ethical mediator's only available options to remain silent or terminate the process? These are important questions both for practising mediators and potential participants in mediation ...

The mediator's distance from the dispute (and from the benefits or trades that form the basis of an ultimate agreement) is what permits the mediator to bring a new and useful perspective to the dispute. A mediator who is perceived by either party as being too close to one party's interests will be viewed as merely another advocate at the table. In short, the mediator will not be effective ...

Prima facie, insofar as mediation is a voluntary process in which, by definition, the mediator has no power to impose a particular settlement, it is problematic to expect that mediation can assure an outcome that meets any standard of fairness independent from what the parties are ultimately able to agree upon. On the other hand, it is well recognized that mediators have the right to withdraw from the mediation process at any time. However, this prerogative does not equip mediators with the power to determine the parties' settlement for them. Apart from the power to withdraw, the only other power that mediators' functions would permit them to exercise directly in relation to fairness of substantive outcome appears to be the power to question the parties about the standards of fairness implicit in their positions or in a proposed settlement ...

Proponents of mediation have argued that one of mediation's virtues lies in its potential both for empowering the parties and assisting them in recognizing the authenticity of the interests of other disputants. As regards the potential for mediation to foster such a transformation of the parties, Lon Fuller has argued that the central quality of mediation is "its capacity to reorient the parties toward each other, not by imposing rules on them, but by helping them to achieve a new and shared perception of their relationship, a perception that will redirect their attitudes and dispositions toward one another." Others, like David Luban, have described the possibilities mediation opens up for fostering discussion undistorted by power, social class, and ideology, and for empowering disputants in their ability to cope with other conflicts and with social structures generally ...

Some commentators have pointed to empirical evidence that negotiation parties that enjoy a significant power imbalance appear more prone to non-cooperative, manipulative, or exploitative behaviour. In light of this concern, many mediation practitioners advocate efforts by the mediator to counter such behaviour and empower the weaker party. They note that the mediator's role also brings a degree of power in the sense of ability to influence the outcome of negotiations. The mediator's own power derives from a number of factors, including the mediator's personal credibility, and the mediator's various abilities to influence the ground rules of the process; to direct the parties' exchange of views; to view the parties as equally worthy of respect and to encourage the parties to act in a manner consistent with such respect; to assist the parties to articulate and explore their interests and options for settlement in a principled way; to assist the parties in accessing financial support for the negotiations; and to recommend and direct the parties towards relevant professional advice where appropriate.

What does a functional analysis of mediation suggest about the role of the mediator in relation to power? First, it is clear that power relationships among all three participants may to some degree influence the course and outcome of the process. Second, many of the standard tools of the mediator that focus on improving communications, fostering interest-based negotiations, and promoting a constructive, respectful atmosphere among the parties, may have some positive influence on the power relations at the table. The use of such tools appears to fit squarely within the functions of mediator objectivity, promotion of party autonomy, and enhancement of party communications. It is unrealistic, however, to expect that the use of these tools in a conventional way can fully eliminate the potential impact of significant differences in resources or, more importantly, of substantial variations in the strength of the alternatives to a negotiated agreement open to each party.

Further interventions by the mediator to address particular consequences of power imbalance on the negotiations will have to be reconciled with the mediator's duty of impartiality. If the stronger party engages in behaviour that appears to violate procedural or substantive fairness, the mediator appears to be returned to the basic task of reviewing the goals of the particular mediation and balancing the demands of duties that appear to conflict. It is worth keeping in mind, however, that although a significant power imbalance between the parties may render one party particularly vulnerable to exploitative behaviour by the other, this vulnerability may never be exploited by the stronger party through resort to deceptive or unfair conduct. As such, the existence of a significant power imbalance between the parties would seem to be an important, but in the end, only a contextual factor to which the mediator should be sensitive when assessing the need to respond to fairness concerns …

One way of approaching the issue of mediator duty, from both a philosophical and legal perspective, is to consider duties that may arise from promises, either express or implied. Professional mediation typically occurs in the context of a contract for services between the mediator and the parties. Such a contract will include a statement of the parties' understandings in relation to the process …

The mediation contract and the ground rules agreed to by the parties at the outset of the mediation can and should reflect the expectations of the parties with respect to fairness and the mediator's role in ensuring that these expectations prevail. The parties' expectations regarding fairness will inevitably be shaped by the factual, legal, and social background of the dispute. A review of this context at the outset of the mediation should assist the mediator in anticipating the types of process concerns that the parties may wish to discuss. The expectations of the parties in relation to disclosure might well be higher in a negotiation involving third parties, such as children, or in a mediation involving a public agency aimed at reaching a fair resolution of social justice issues, than in a mediation between represented parties who have undergone court disclosure.

The opening of the mediation process is an ideal time to discuss these expectations and to make them explicit. Although parties unfamiliar with negotiation or mediation may not be aware of the particular types of conduct of which they should be wary, the experienced mediator should be able to raise the types of issues that could arise (regarding disclosure, for example) and seek the parties' views on how they wish to address those concerns. Clarifying such issues at the outset will typically have two advantages. First, it is often easier to reach such understandings at the outset of the process, on the basis of mutual commitments, than during the heat of negotiations where the "rules" are unclear and tense bargaining is in process. Second, addressing procedural concerns at the outset will draw the parties' attention to concerns about the process that may not have previously been considered. A clear understanding of the kinds of fairness assurances that will be incorporated in the mediation process will better enable the parties, even in the absence of process agreements, to anticipate concerns and protect themselves against exploitative behaviour.

Notes and Questions

1. What do you think of the suggestion that a mediator might bring their own ethical judgments into a dialogue between two independent parties? Would the professional obligations of the mediator to protect party confidentiality and respect the parties' autonomy prevent any such interventions?
2. The author suggests that the parties and the mediator should carefully delineate at the outset of the mediation their ethical obligations to each other and the precise role to be played by the mediator in moderating the parties' dialogue. Do you think this is a realistic and helpful proposal where there is a significant power imbalance between the parties?

Power and Rights Negotiations

"Necessity never made a good bargain."

Benjamin Franklin[47]

We have seen many examples in this chapter of effective responses to power dilemmas in negotiation. It remains the case, as the above excerpt points out, that it is not always possible to avoid the dictates of bargaining power. Where the parties' relative BATNAs and initial preferences strongly tilt the outcome toward one side, the options of the other party may be quite limited.

In transactional negotiations (the purchase of a cellphone, for example), one might respond that this is simply the "way of the world." Prices and terms are determined by the parties' initial preferences and by the availability of alternatives to both the buyer and seller. However, in negotiations aimed at settling an allegation that someone's legal rights have been infringed, it can be argued that the parties' relative power should not unduly influence the outcome. Justice, it may be said, is a public good, and access to legal remedies should

---

47 *Poor Richard's Almanack*, April 1735, reprinted in *The Complete Poor Richard's Almanacks* (Barre, MA: Imprint Society, 1970).

not be tainted by the accident of resources. In Plato's *The Republic*, Thrasymachus argued that justice is nothing more than the power of the strong over the weak.[48] Societies like Canada's that purport to be governed by the rule of law can ill-afford to treat matters of justice so dismissively.

The concern that out-of-court negotiations might not be an appropriate substitute for the adjudication of legal disputes is addressed in the article excerpted below.

Owen M. Fiss
"Against Settlement"
(1984) 93 Yale L.J. 1073 at 1075-78, footnotes omitted

… [T]he case for settlement rest[s] on questionable premises. I do not believe that settlement as a generic practice is preferable to judgment or should be institutionalized on a wholesale and indiscriminate basis. It should be treated instead as a highly problematic technique for streamlining dockets. Settlement is for me the civil analogue of plea bargaining: Consent is often coerced; the bargain may be struck by someone without authority; the absence of a trial and judgment renders subsequent judicial involvement troublesome; and although dockets are trimmed, justice may not be done. Like plea bargaining, settlement is a capitulation to the conditions of mass society and should be neither encouraged nor praised.

The Imbalance of Power

By viewing the lawsuit as a quarrel between two neighbors, the dispute-resolution story that underlies ADR implicitly asks us to assume a rough equality between the contending parties. It treats settlement as the anticipation of the outcome of trial and assumes that the terms of settlement are simply a product of the parties' predictions of that outcome. In truth, however, settlement is also a function of the resources available to each party to finance the litigation, and those resources are frequently distributed unequally. Many lawsuits do not involve a property dispute between two neighbors, or between AT&T and the government (to update the story), but rather concern a struggle between a member of a racial minority and a municipal police department over alleged brutality, or a claim by a worker against a large corporation over work-related injuries. In these cases, the distribution of financial resources, or the ability of one party to pass along its costs, will invariably infect the bargaining process, and the settlement will be at odds with a conception of justice that seeks to make the wealth of the parties irrelevant.

The disparities in resources between the parties can influence the settlement in three ways. First, the poorer party may be less able to amass and analyze the information needed to predict the outcome of the litigation, and thus be disadvantaged in the bargaining process. Second, he may need the damages he seeks immediately and thus be induced to settle as a way of accelerating payment, even though he realizes he would get less now than he might if he awaited judgment. All plaintiffs want their damages immediately, but

---

48   Plato, *The Republic*, trans. by G.M.A. Grube & Rev. C.D.C. Reeve (Indianapolis: Hackett, 1992) at 338, c. 1-2.

an indigent plaintiff may be exploited by a rich defendant because his need is so great that the defendant can force him to accept a sum that is less than the ordinary present value of the judgment. Third, the poorer party might be forced to settle because he does not have the resources to finance the litigation, to cover either his own projected expenses, such as his lawyer's time, or the expenses his opponent can impose through the manipulation of procedural mechanisms such as discovery. It might seem that settlement benefits the plaintiff by allowing him to avoid the costs of litigation, but this is not so. The defendant can anticipate the plaintiff's costs if the case were to be tried fully and decrease his offer by that amount. The indigent plaintiff is a victim of the costs of litigation even if he settles.

There are exceptions. Seemingly rich defendants may sometimes be subject to financial pressures that make them as anxious to settle as indigent plaintiffs. But I doubt that these circumstances occur with any great frequency. I also doubt that institutional arrangements such as contingent fees or the provision of legal services to the poor will in fact equalize resources between contending parties: The contingent fee does not equalize resources; it only makes an indigent plaintiff vulnerable to the willingness of the private bar to invest in his case. In effect, the ability to exploit the plaintiff's lack of resources has been transferred from rich defendants to lawyers who insist upon a hefty slice of the plaintiff's recovery as their fee. These lawyers, moreover, will only work for contingent fees in certain kinds of cases, such as personal-injury suits. And the contingent fee is of no avail when the defendant is the disadvantaged party. Governmental subsidies for legal services have a broader potential, but in the civil domain the battle for these subsidies was hard-fought, and they are in fact extremely limited, especially when it comes to cases that seek systemic reform of government practices.

Of course, imbalances of power can distort judgment as well: Resources influence the quality of presentation, which in turn has an important bearing on who wins and the terms of victory. We count, however, on the guiding presence of the judge, who can employ a number of measures to lessen the impact of distributional inequalities. He can, for example, supplement the parties' presentations by asking questions, calling his own witnesses, and inviting other persons and institutions to participate as amici. These measures are likely to make only a small contribution toward moderating the influence of distributional inequalities, but should not be ignored for that reason. Not even these small steps are possible with settlement. There is, moreover, a critical difference between a process like settlement, which is based on bargaining and accepts inequalities of wealth as an integral and legitimate component of the process, and a process like judgment, which knowingly struggles against those inequalities. Judgment aspires to an autonomy from distributional inequalities, and it gathers much of its appeal from this aspiration.

Notes and Questions

1. Later in the article, Fiss points out that public adjudication can serve an important purpose by bringing to the court's attention widespread conflicts that may require changes to the existing law, so that a wider group of citizens will benefit from resolution of the disputes. What do you think of Fiss's concerns? Are there certain kinds of cases, questions of constitutional or human rights, for example, that should not be settled through private negotiation? What about compensation claims against

corporations that have negligently injured a large class of victims? Does allowing individual plaintiffs to settle these out of court and in secrecy weaken the chances of the class as a whole obtaining justice?

2. Can it be said that court processes are blind to resource disparities between the parties to a legal dispute? Do you agree that court processes necessarily offer more protection for the poor than efforts to address their rights through negotiation?

3. Is it possible that Fiss's analysis, by focusing exclusively on financial resource disparities, fails to accurately capture the complexities of the power dynamics at play in many settlement negotiations?

Some might respond to the concerns that Fiss raises by noting that a party is only likely to agree to a negotiated settlement of its legal claim where its assessment of the likely court outcome, net of the financial and emotional costs of proceeding to judgment, is equivalent to what is on offer at the negotiating table. In such a case, if a party is tempted to accept significantly less than what the law would dictate is the extent and value of their legal rights, one might reasonably conclude that the fault lies in the barriers, financial and otherwise, that our court system has placed in the way of giving effect to one's legal rights. Viewed from this perspective, it can be argued that the appropriate response to such concerns is to address the cost and accessibility of the justice system rather than limit the ability of legal disputants to reach timely settlements that meet their needs.

One way in which settlement negotiations may, in fact, better address the parties' interests than adjudication is that the negotiation process permits the parties to tailor creative and sophisticated agreements to protect their interests in the future. Contrast this with the outcomes available through the courts, with their limited array of available remedies (declarations, injunctions, damages, specific performance) and their reluctance to issue orders too complex for them to effectively supervise.

Conclusion

The potential effects of power will always be an issue in negotiations. In this chapter alone we have looked at examples illustrating the importance of bargaining power over a period stretching more than 2,400 years. The views expressed by Owen Fiss about settlement negotiations reflect a concern shared by many negotiators and academics: namely, that external power dynamics may exert significant and undue influence on the bargaining outcome. As we have seen, power dynamics do affect the probable outcome of every negotiation, whether transactional or rights-based. Sources of influence do not, after all, disintegrate at the bargaining door.

Effective power to influence bargaining outcomes, as defined at the outset of the negotiation, derives mainly from two factors: the parties' relative BATNAs and their preferences in relation to the issues under negotiation. We have seen that the effects of these two factors are mediated by each party's available information, individual perceptions, and cognitive biases. We have also seen that where there is scope for an agreement that advances both sides' interests, the interaction of BATNAs and preferences will rarely predetermine a particular outcome. Instead they serve to delineate the landscape on which the parties' interactions (including their respective negotiation strategies and tactics) will finally determine the outcome.

In this chapter we have focused on moves frequently adopted by negotiators to enhance the scope of their bargaining influence and shift the probable range of outcomes to better advance their interests. Generally, such moves involve attempts to alter the perceived bargaining range, to avoid resistance behaviours associated with the "power paradox" or, by addressing preferences creatively, to add to the projected cumulative value of the deal for both parties. Effective negotiators will be sensitive to the potential impacts of power at the table, and ensure that their inventory of bargaining tactics includes measures aimed at addressing those impacts. Finally, in all cases, and particularly in negotiations about legal rights or public interests, effective negotiators will consider whether another process, like mediation or adjudication, would better serve their clients and the public interest.

Selected Further Reading

R.S. Adler & E.M. Silverstein, "When David Meets Goliath: Dealing with Power Differentials in Negotiations" (2000) 5 Harv. Negot. L. Rev. 1.

S.B. Bacharach & E.J. Lawler, "Power Dependence and Power Paradoxes in Bargaining" (1986) 2 Negotiation Journal 167.

D. Barnhizer, "Inequality of Bargaining Power" (2005) 76 U. Colo. L. Rev. 139.

N. Burkardt, B.L. Lamb & J.G. Taylor, "Power Distribution in Complex Environmental Negotiations: Does Balance Matter?" (1997) 7:2 Journal of Public Administration Research and Theory 247.

M. Coyle, "Defending the Weak and Fighting Unfairness: Can Mediators Respond to the Challenge?" (1998) 36 Osgoode Hall L.J. 625.

R. Fisher, "Negotiation Power: Getting and Using Influence" (1983) 27:2 American Behavioral Scientist 149.

O.M. Fiss, "Against Settlement" (1984) 93 Yale L.J. 1073.

L. Greenhalgh., S.A. Neslin & R.W. Gilkey, "The Effects of Negotiator Preferences, Situational Power, and Negotiator Personality on Outcomes of Business Negotiations" (1985) 28 Academy of Management Journal 9.

T. Grillo, "The Mediation Alternative: Process Dangers for Women" (1991) 100 Yale L.J. 1545.

P.H. Kim, R.L. Pinkley & A.R. Fragale, "Power Dynamics in Negotiation" (2005) 30 Academy of Management Review 799.

R. Korobkin, "Bargaining Power as Threat of Impasse" (2004) 87 Marq. L. Rev. 867.

E.J. Lawler, "Power Processes in Bargaining" (1992) 33 Sociological Quarterly 17.

E.J. Lawler & J. Yoon, "Power and the Emergence of Commitment Behavior in Negotiated Exchange" (1993) 58 American Sociological Review 465.

R.H. Lawton, "Negotiating from Strength: Advantage Derived from the Process and Strategy of Preparing for Competitive Negotiation" (1986-87) 14 Pepp. L. Rev. 839.

D.A. Lax & J.K. Sebenius, *The Manager as Negotiator: Bargaining for Cooperation and Competitive Gain* (New York: Free Press, 1986).

D.A. Lax & J.K. Sebenius, "The Power of Alternatives or the Limits to Negotiation" (1985) 1 Negotiation Journal 163.

D. Luban, "The Quality of Justice" (1989) 66 Denv. U.L. Rev. 381.

J.-S. Rioux, "Crisis Negotiation Outcomes Among Equals and Unequals, Democracies and Non-democracies" (1999) 36 International Politics 25.

J.Z. Rubin & B.R. Brown, *The Social Psychology of Bargaining and Negotiation* (New York: Academic, 1975).

G. Schneider, "Capacity and Concessions: An Essay on Bargaining Power in Multilateral Negotiations" (2005) 33:3 Millennium 665.

W. Ury, *Getting Past No: Negotiating Your Way from Confrontation to Cooperation* (New York: Bantam Books, 1993).

M. Watkins & S. Rosegrant, "Sources of Power in Coalition Building" (1996) 12 Negotiation Journal 47.

C. Watson, "Gender Versus Power as a Predictor of Negotiation Behaviour and Outcomes" (1994) 10 Negotiation Journal 117.

S.L. Winter, "The 'Power' Thing" (1996) 82 Va. L. Rev. 721.

R.J. Wolfe & K.L. McGinn, "Perceived Relative Power and Its Influence on Negotiations" (2005) 14 Group Decision and Negotiation 3.

Gender and Negotiation

Delee Fromm

Introduction

Many factors inform and influence how we negotiate and how we approach a negotiation—factors such as training, personality, emotional intelligence, culture, and experience. Should gender also be included in this list of factors? Some academic authors who have reviewed the research before 2000

have asserted that the evidence regarding gender differences in negotiation is not consistent or conclusive.[1] Much of the research and many of the case studies on gender differences in negotiation involving both law students and lawyers have shown little or no differences between males and females.[2]

Over the past seven years, however, there has been growing evidence of specific gender differences in negotiation when business professionals, university students, and academics have been studied. The significance and the economic ramifications of these recent findings are quite startling.

There is evidence that men are four times more likely to initiate negotiations than women.[3] An astonishing 20 percent of females state that they never negotiate at all.[4] As

---

1 See *e.g.* C. Menkel-Meadow, "Teaching About Gender and Negotiation: Sex, Truths, and Videotape" (2000) 16 Negotiation Journal 357.

2 *Ibid.*; C.B. Craver, "Gender and Negotiation Performance" (2002) 4 Sociological Practice 183; L. Burton, L. Farmer, E. Gee, L. Johnson & G. Williams, "Feminist Theory, Professional Ethics, and Gender-Related Distinctions in Attorney Negotiating Styles" (1991) 1991:2 J. Disp. Resol. 199.

3 L. Babcock & S. Laschever, *Women Don't Ask: Negotiation and the Gender Divide* (Princeton, NJ: Princeton University Press, 2003) at 3.

4 *Ibid.* at 113.

compared with men, women consider fewer situations involve negotiation and accept what is offered to them, which is highlighted by the finding that 57 percent of men negotiate their first employment package versus only 7 percent of women.[5] This gender difference has a huge economic impact on women and has been proposed as a reason for the large gender gap in wages. A small salary difference at the beginning of a career today accumulated over a lifetime can end up costing the non-negotiator at retirement in excess of $1,600,000.[6] In contrast, women excel and do better than men when they negotiate on behalf of others—obtaining a whopping 18 percent increase in compensation.[7] Researchers call situations that trigger gender differences in negotiation *situational triggers*. These findings, as well as other situational triggers, are discussed in more detail in the readings included in this chapter.

A number of reasons are put forward for these gender differences, including the following: women experience increased anxiety when negotiating in conflict situations; a tougher stance is taken in negotiations against women; men are more competitive and outcome-oriented while women value relationships over outcomes. Most authors agree that the origin of these gender differences derives from societal expectations and conditioning during childhood,[8] although recent publications on gender differences in neuroanatomy suggest that the origin may be a combination of both nature and nurture.[9]

This chapter presents findings from both law and business studies to highlight where and when gender differences tend to arise and not arise. It is important for individuals representing clients to be aware of situational triggers that may impede a female client's ability to negotiate for a particular outcome, or even her inclination to negotiate. Understanding and recognizing situational triggers may greatly enhance a woman's ability to negotiate for herself, particularly for greater remuneration, greater benefits, better assignments, and greater recognition of achievements.

The first reading looks at law students and lawyers. In an important and still relevant article entitled "Teaching About Gender and Negotiation: Sex, Truths, and Videotape," Carrie Menkel-Meadow asserts that based on her experience teaching negotiation to law students, there are no consistent gender differences. Yet, she suggests, everyone still needs to be aware of the societal perception of gender differences as this perception creates stereotypes and expectations about how men and women should behave. For example, research has shown

---

5 *Ibid.* at 1.

6 For details of this calculation, see L. Babcock & S. Laschever, "First You Have to Ask" Harvard Negotiation Newsletter (January 2004) 3 at 3.

7 D.W. Pradel, H.R Bowles & K.L. McGinn, "When Does Gender Matter in Negotiation?" Harvard Negotiation Newsletter (November 2005) 3 at 4.

8 See *e.g.* P. Heim & S. Golant, *Hardball for Women: Winning at the Game of Business*, rev. ed. (New York: Penguin Group, 2005) and D. Tannen, *You Just Don't Understand: Women and Men in Conversation* (New York: HarperCollins, 1990).

9 L. Brizendine, *The Female Brain* (New York: Morgan Road Books, 2006) at 5. Brain studies reveal that females have more neurons in the brain centres for language, hearing, emotion, and memory. Males, in contrast, have two-and-a-half times the brain space devoted to sex drive as well as larger brain centres for action and aggression.

that women who are competitive are likely to be viewed much more harshly than their male counterparts.[10] Women who act in a way that goes against societal expectations may get more push back or backlash as a result. Menkel-Meadow argues that due to the complex and dynamic nature of negotiation, it is important to explore and teach when gender matters and how it varies across different groups and issues. The research included in this chapter, which was conducted and published since 2000, does just that.

Aspasia Tsaoussis's article, "Female Lawyers as Pragmatic Problem-Solvers: Negotiation and Gender Roles in Greek Legal Practice," examines both the self-reported and actual negotiation behaviour of Greek lawyers and business students. Tsaoussis's research contradicts other findings that suggest that women tend to be weaker negotiators relative to men. She reports that a stronger determinant of successful outcomes in negotiations by lawyers is the individual's characteristics, including personality, negotiating style, persuasion, and social and emotional intelligence. Another interesting finding from this study is the real divide between what lawyers report their negotiating style to be (hard versus soft) and what style they display in negotiation simulations. Up to half of the self-proclaimed "soft" negotiators actually used abrasive bargaining tactics. When asked about behaviour during games in childhood, the largest percentage of both male and female lawyers indicated that they were "rather competitive" (75 percent and 57 percent, respectively). At the same time, female lawyers as a group were found to be tougher negotiators than business students, bank employees, and insurance company employees of both sexes.

All effective negotiators have the characteristics of a "pragmatic problem-solver." These characteristics include a heightened level of rationality, a highly developed ability to inquire effectively and to listen actively, greater flexibility and ability to empathize, greater commitment to professional integrity, and openness to adopt an integrative bargaining approach. In Tsaoussis's study, the overwhelming majority of pragmatic problem-solvers were women.

Although the ability to connect with others has often been linked to a softer feminine approach, Tsaoussis suggests that this is a misperception. She finds that this ability is a personality trait that greatly increases the chance of a successful outcome for negotiators of both sexes. This finding is consistent with the literature on joint gains and emotional intelligence (see chapter 9 for a detailed discussion). Based on her research data, Tsaoussis concludes that, for lawyers, personality plays a far greater role than gender in determining negotiation behaviour and approaches.

The lack of gender differences displayed by lawyers who negotiate for clients may also be related to one of the situational triggers discussed in "When Does Gender Matter in Negotiation?" by Dina W. Pradel, Hannah R. Bowles, and Kathleen L. McGinn. Based on their study of university students and business professionals in the workplace, the authors conclude that some situational triggers result in better outcomes for female negotiators, while others result in better outcomes for male negotiators. The situational trigger that creates an advantage for women is negotiating on behalf of others. In contrast, negotiations that involve high competition allow men to outperform women, not because women stumble

---

10   Babcock & Laschever, *supra* note 3 at 88.

in such situations but because men step up their performance. Pat Heim suggests that competition for males is the "spice" that makes the game so much more interesting.[11]

In "First You Have to Ask," Linda Babcock and Sara Laschever also examine gender differences in the workplace. They find that men are much more likely to negotiate than women. They also find that men negotiate to promote their own self-interests far more often than women do. Other research suggests that a disadvantage in negotiating for oneself may not only be a significant factor in the gender difference in wages but may also explain the under-representation of women in corporate executive positions and in professional firm management positions.[12]

In summary, it is clear that there is now cogent evidence for the importance of gender as a factor in negotiation. The most powerful findings in this area are situational triggers and how negotiated outcomes for men and women are affected differently by them. The results of studies involving law students and lawyers highlight the importance of not making assumptions about a person's negotiating ability, proclivity to negotiate, or preferred approach based solely on gender. Due to the complex and dynamic nature of negotiation, other factors, such as personality, culture, and training, can and do come into play. Awareness of how gender may influence your own negotiation behaviour and that of others will greatly enhance your ability to negotiate using a broader range of responses. In short, such awareness will make you a better and more effective negotiator when negotiating for yourself and others.

Carrie Menkel-Meadow

"Teaching About Gender and Negotiation: Sex, Truths, and Videotape"

(2000) 16 Negotiation Journal 357 at 357-64, footnotes omitted

The continuing inconclusive debate about whether there are gender differences in negotiation goals and behavior offer a great opportunity for teaching about gender issues in negotiation theory and practice. Because both theory and empirical research thus far provide conflicting claims and widely disparate results—such as the most recent studies' conclusions that "men negotiate significantly better outcomes than women" (Stuhlmacher and Walters 1999); "women behave more cooperatively than men" (Walters, Stuhlmacher and Meyer 1998); "women may obtain lower joint outcomes in integrative bargaining because of a higher level of concern for the other" (Calhoun and Smith 1999); but also that "there are no statistically significant differences in negotiation outcomes and performance between men and women" (Craver and Barnes 1999)—both teachers and students of negotiation can explore their perspectives on these claims without fear that there is a simple dispositive answer to this timeless question. This presents an opportunity for exploring the issues in many different ways in negotiation pedagogy and in negotiation practice. For anyone

---

11   Heim & Golant, *supra* note 8 at 32.

12   I. Bohnet & F. Greig, "Gender Matters in Workplace Decisions" Harvard Negotiation Newsletter (April 2007) at 3.

to baldly assert that there are clear sex-based differences in negotiation behavior is simply a lie these days (research findings and practice are too complex to assert anything), and I can use a videotape to demonstrate!

Why Do We Care?

When the question of gendered behavior comes up, it is always useful to ask why we care so much about whether there are gender differences in negotiation performance. Does it matter that women negotiate differently than blue-eyed negotiators or tall people (if they do at all)? Whether women and men conceptualize negotiation differently or whether the two genders behave differently in negotiation, there clearly is a perception that they might. These perceptions create stereotypes, expectations, and behaviors that themselves flow from these assumptions. Thus, we seek to understand which of our default, preconceived, or learned assumptions are actually correct and which are not. So, researchers continue to seek answers to questions about gender difference (unfortunately, mostly in artificial laboratory settings in social psychology departments) and practitioners continue to amass data through experience and anecdote in order to create descriptions from which we might derive prescriptions.

For some looking at the gender question, there is the hope of taking advantage of whatever gender-based attribute is thought to exist: Men can be naturally "tough" in distributive bargaining problems while women will more collaboratively solve problems. Others seek to "improve" their performances by learning to change behaviors, away from stereotypic notions of how they are expected to behave. So some women will seek to be more cautious about cooperatively sharing information when they don't know how it will be used, and some men will work harder at listening better.

For most of us with any sophistication about gender and negotiation, we know that as the conditions and situations of negotiated problems vary, so too will the salience and the expression of gender. Thus, the most effective pedagogy about gender and negotiation is to explore both when gender is or might be salient in a negotiation and when and how the significance of gender (in the demographics of the negotiators and the content of negotiated issues) might and does vary.

We are hopefully past the days of the simplest gender stereotyping—men are competitive, women are cooperative; men talk and interrupt more, women use tentative language and seek to please the other; men threaten and assert; women seek to please and concede too much, although as the recent research cited above suggests, there may be some truth in some of the stereotypes, at least *under certain conditions.* If we have learned anything from the hundreds of studies conducted on gender and negotiation (studies before 1975 are summarized in Rubin and Brown [1975]; more recent studies are discussed in Watson [1994]), it is that in negotiation gender (though a constant for the individual negotiator) is dynamic and interactive—that is, its significance and expression varies under different conditions and in different situations.

From a pedagogical perspective, it is important to teach about gender and negotiation in a nuanced, and not superficial, way which accounts for the contestedness and complexity of the issues. In thinking about teaching about gender we should ask ourselves several key questions: Why do we care about gender (in this particular context, setting, situation)? What are the underlying theories or assumptions that inform our questions about gender?

What, if anything, do we know empirically, about the operation of gender in this particular negotiation setting? And what questions should we be asking or analyzing in studying and teaching about gender in any particular negotiation? This essay reviews some of the issues implicated in teaching about gender and negotiation and suggests a variety of different ways of exploring these issues in negotiation classes and workshops.

Gender Theory in Negotiation

First, it is useful to stop and ask what is gendered in our own negotiation theory and practices (Gray 1994). Whether teaching traditional competitive, distributive bargaining models or the more likely canon of readers of this journal, integrative, problem-solving or principled negotiation, where do our concepts come from? As others have noted with respect to cultural assumptions about our negotiation goals (Avruch 2000), even *Getting to Yes* may be riddled with assumed universalisms like seeking "objective" criteria, "separating the people from the problem" and exploring "interests." If those "principles," developed by expert male negotiators in particular contexts (international, consumer, legal, and commercial disputes) were elaborated by women or in other negotiation contexts, they might look different. For example, when would "subjective" criteria be the more appropriate choice—if it makes you *feel* better, let's do it that way (especially if the other side of a negotiation is a loved one, a repeat customer, or a former enemy you are trying to make peace with)? Why do we look for those self-regarding, Hobbesian "interests" behind the positions, rather than the basic human "needs" or wants, going beyond what a negotiation principal might articulate and examine what might actually be his, her, or its (an institution's) real "needs"?

This distinction between interests and needs or concerns may seem only semantic. I prefer to see them as additive; however, interests and needs actually represent, in shorthand, a feminist critique of the very goals of negotiation activity. There may be very different content to what is "needed" or what one's "interests" are. Even if defined as instrumental "joint gain" (an improvement over individual maximization), the goals of a negotiation that seeks to maximize joint interests does not necessarily consider whether the primary or basic social needs of the parties have been met, whether justice has been done, or whether there are benefits or harms to those standing outside of the negotiation.

Thus, at least one gendered critique of negotiation theory is that the very goals of a negotiation may be situationally differentiated (social welfare vs. Pareto-optimality for the parties) and gender itself might construct different goals in different situations (relationship, family, international, environmental) which clearly might affect how those goals might be pursued (differentiated behaviors). Are we to meet, share, satisfy, satisfice, fulfill, or maximize needs or interests? All negotiation concepts might have gendered valences. And, as Robert Fisher and his various colleagues have now recognized, not all genders would necessarily "separate the people from the problem." Even if it makes analytic sense to focus on the substance of the problem, the people may be the problem to be solved. To the extent that feminist theory has controversially focused on women's particular concerns about the relationship aspect of negotiations, then once again the theories and canons of our practice may need to be reexamined in light of how both genders would define and describe their negotiation goals, purposes, and implementations. A good teacher, then, begins by questioning whether the concepts she is teaching are themselves gendered, and reflects on what might be elaborated and expanded upon by being viewed from other perspectives.

This sensitivity to the "gendered" nature of negotiation theory has its counterweight in the contested nature of gender itself and thus requires the negotiation teacher to be somewhat conversant in the controversies of gender theory (Menkel-Meadow and Diamond 1991). In both law and the constituent social science disciplines which inform negotiation research and practice (game theory, economics, psychology, communications, anthropology, sociology, political science and international relations), feminists and gender theorists have queried the assumed universalisms of their fields when the knowledge creators have mostly been men. Thus, gender theory in each field initially sought to understand whether including "the second sex" (de Beauvoir 1949) as not just another "variable" but as a different viewpoint, might transform the very concepts of the field. Consider whether two female prisoners would both "rationally defect." Might it not depend on such relational possibilities as one being the mother of the other or the two being sisters? Such an outpouring of feminist "difference" scholarship, reinventing categories, suggesting new ones and developing new theories as occurred in a variety of disciplines and subfields has not really prospered in negotiation theory. (Perhaps because the male canon of "integrative" bargaining or "joint gain" seemed so female-friendly [in theory, if not in practice]?)

This first wave of scholarship spawned a second wave of critique that feared a new essentialism, and called greater attention to assumed universal gender differences (in theories and in behaviors) than both equality feminists (Epstein 1988) and diversity feminists (Harris 1990) were willing to tolerate. For equality feminists, the genders were "on average" more alike than different, and differences in the tails of distribution of behaviors by gender were made too much of. For such "sameness" theorists, men and women are more alike than different, and human variation includes as much difference within gender categories as between them. So, for example, we might find both female and male attorneys in the categories of competitive or cooperative or effective or ineffective negotiators (Williams 1979). Diversity feminists focused instead on the differences among women, by race, ethnicity, class, and other dimensions, casting doubt on whether there was such a viable concept or testable variable as "a" woman's way of being, or negotiating.

This, in turn, raised the question of why the "gender" problem in negotiation (or any other field of human activity) has so often been conceptualized as "the woman" problem—Why are women less effective in negotiation, less competitive, achieving lower monetary or point outcomes, rather than, why are men less likely to place value on relationship preservation or less likely to process and hear information? Thus, if we focus on gender in negotiation we must note that there are two genders and that "male" negotiating behavior (if such a thing exists) is just as problematic and worth scrutinizing as "female" negotiating behavior. The deconstruction of false gender labels is often just as empowering to men (who want to be collaborative and information sharing in negotiation without the stigma of being a negotiation "sissy") as it is to women who are strong interest-maximizing competitors.

To the extent that gender is now argued to be socially constructed (by a variety of social forces, including situation), whether "gender" exists and how it is "constructed" in a particular negotiation is as interesting an aspect of negotiation analysis as any other aspect of a negotiation process that we might study or observe. The operation of gender is itself more variable. Mothers are now professionals as well as mothers; thus, individuals occupy a variety of social roles that may influence behavior, mediated through a variety of different social categories of being. And, the significance of gender might change within any interaction itself. To the extent that a woman feels she is "the same" as a man (in a negotiation context), but is treated "differently" by a man who has more conventional gendered expectations, her reactions might change (whether to deal with the gender issue explicitly, conform to gender "type," or respond with a strong "counter-gender" behavior), depending on the situation, context, and other negotiator(s).

The question of what difference a difference of gender (Eisenstein and Jardine 1985) makes certainly seems to be elusive in the aggregations of data supplied by laboratory studies, but is apparently still endlessly fascinating in the individual cases we analyze and tell stories about. Gender theory presents different explanations or sources for whatever gender differences may be thought to exist (which are replicated below in how negotiation analysts have theorized the role of gender in negotiation), including biological essentialism, socialization, power and dominance theories, and situational and interactive differences in the expression of gendered characteristics (see, for example: Deaux [1976]; Maccoby and Jacklin [1974]; Kantor [1977]; Henley [1977]; Hennig and Jardim [1977]; Fausto-Sterling [1985]; Tavris [1992]; Tannen [1993]; Thorne [1993]; and Hess and Ferree [1987]).

The effects of gender as a "variable" in negotiation practice have themselves been theorized, and students of negotiation should be aware of both the theory of and the empirical tests of those theories. Sources of presumed gender differences in negotiation are now analyzed in at least four basic categories. The most conventional and standard explanation for gender differences in negotiation behavior is *socialization*: men and women are simply socialized in different ways and to value things differently, which produces different expectations, behaviors, perceptions, outcomes, and levels of satisfaction in negotiation. So, as the standard story goes, men are more competitive, assertive, direct, have higher expectations, achieve more for themselves (and their clients in agent situations), but may also be more stubborn, less creative and problem solving and less focused on relationship while more focused on task and self. Women are accommodating, fear competition, have excessive concern for the other, but are better listeners, seek integrative and fair solutions and are most comfortable when negotiating with other women. Though the socialization theory is prevalent and basic (and actually "covers" for the even more basic—biological determinism—which no one seriously argues for in our field anymore), it actually has not been tested. If gender socialization is the crucial variable, then we should look at differences based on actual socialization practices. After a reading of portions of Carol Gilligan's *In a Different Voice* in my negotiation classes, I always ask students to reflect on and report on their own socialization experiences. What we learn is that, like most conceptions of gender as a category, gender socialization is itself a dynamic and changing process. Women have now participated in team sports, men have taken dance classes, both boys and girls have been reared by single mothers, with or without siblings, children have been reared by substitute parents when both parents are working, so that conventional and gendered patterns of socialization may be breaking down somewhat. To fully test socialization theories, negotiators would have to be sorted by different socialization practices (across genders) and then we could see if gender differences in negotiation still persisted.

A more common explanation for gender difference is that of *situational power* (or social structure or "place" as Deborah Kolb calls it [Kolb 1992]). Since women have less access to power and the powerful are more efficacious in negotiation, then power, not gender, determines negotiation outcomes. To the extent that women achieve positions of power, they too will exhibit the characteristics of powerful and efficacious negotiators (whether from a competitive or an integrative perspective). Status or power, then, is the real variable. And, since gender is merely correlated with low power or low status, findings of gender differences are artifacts of a different variable relationship.

Others argue that gender and status operate in an *additive* model that can produce more complex dynamics in assessing negotiating behavior. Women in positions of high power will exhibit different negotiating behaviors and achieve different outcomes than men in high-power settings, and women and men with little power likewise behave differently. One study, for example, found that women in lower-power settings are, in fact, the most stubborn and competitive of negotiators, particularly when confronted by negotiation partners who are high-power males (Watson 1994). Low-power males were more inclined to withdraw. To this so-called "additive" model, I would add the notion of "gender plus" (or gender minus), that is, gender as a demographic characteristic that interacts not only with power and status, but also with other demographic characteristics of the negotiators. As dimensions separate from "power" crudely defined, race, ethnicity, class, occupation, familial status, and other sociological statuses will interact differentially with gender to produce different negotiation expectations, goals, and behaviors. Ian Ayres' studies of negotiations in the car purchasing arena, for example, found that black females were the most disadvantaged in the prices demanded of them (Ayres 1991 and 1995). This *gender plus* theory, then, acknowledges that gender is a separate prism through which other demographic factors may be "refracted"—each negotiator brings an "intersectionality" (Crenshaw 1989) of a variety of personal characteristics which may affect perceptions and expectations of the other and may constrain the negotiation repertoires available for any negotiator.

Finally, a more modern theory which seeks to beg the question of essentialist or innate differences suggests that perhaps others' stereotypic *expectations* of gender-conforming behaviors will produce such behaviors or at least influence behavioral choices and outcomes. This last theory is often the most sophisticated at recognizing that negotiations are interactive, and thus different behaviors and outcomes may depend on whether the negotiation pair is same sex or mixed sex and may depend on the size and uniformity of gender composition of each negotiation team. To the extent that how one behaves in a negotiation is interdependent with the other negotiators' behavior (whether in a dyadic or multiparty negotiation), "gendered" behavior will be socially constructed from the interaction of the expectations, choices, and behaviors that each party "enacts" in relation to the perceptions, behaviors, and assumed assumptions of the others. The "gendered" quality of negotiation behavior may shift from moment to moment as participants "enact" behaviors, confront them, respond to them, ignore them, shift them, or engage in any number of infinitely complicated maneuvers around or through gender stereotyping. Thus, negotiation behaviors may be a particularly rich, albeit difficult, environment in which to test the "post-modern" and ever-changing enactments of self and other through the "constructed" and interpretive moves of "the negotiation dance."

Aspasia Tsaoussis
"Female Lawyers as Pragmatic Problem-Solvers: Negotiation and
Gender Roles in Greek Legal Practice"

(February 2007), online: SSRN <http://ssrn.com/abstract=968005>,
footnotes omitted

*The movement of women into the legal profession is one
of the great under-noticed revolutions of our time.*

Epstein (2001: 733)

*Differences in perception and in treatment based on gender
impede the educational and professional progress of women.*

Krauskopf (1994: 312)

Introduction

Over the past two decades there has been a surge of scholarly interest in alternative dispute resolution (ADR) as a viable alternative to the traditional adversarial paradigm. The delays and costs of adversary proceedings, the loaded court dockets, the revealed shortcomings and biases that plague the court system have all contributed to the impetus of ADR as a flourishing scientific field. A main strand in the now voluminous negotiation literature centers on sex-based differences, categorizing the disparate bargaining experiences of groups or individuals along the lines of gender. A sizeable body of theoretical and empirical work already exists, which demonstrates that in a variety of settings, men and women negotiate differently, because they reason differently, argue differently, and behave differently. Explaining these differences has led researchers down two divergent paths: one locates the source of all differences to be biological and innate, while the other stresses the impact of gender socialization and socially constructed gender roles.

The traditional stereotypical view of women being less confrontational than men has been used to explain pervasive prejudice in a variety of markets, from retail car sales to kidney transplantation (Ayres 2001). In the work place, women's negotiating style has been identified as a main reason accounting for their lower salaries. For example, Barron (2003) shows that when they negotiate, women are much less likely than men to use self-promoting tactics; they also make fewer offers and counteroffers. As a result, they end up with lower salaries when they compete with men for the same job. Even in simple competitive environments, as in experiments where women and men were asked to perform under competitive tournament schemes, women were found to shy away from competition, while men were drawn to it (Niederle and Vesterlund 2005: 39). According to the findings of Kaman and Hartel (1994), men get more because they ask for more, are more confident of success, and employ a more active strategy than do women. Men's greater "urge to win" has also been discussed as one of the reasons accounting for the low numbers of women in top managerial positions.

Using the classroom as a laboratory setting, we analyzed the outcomes of simulated negotiating games conducted in the context of a graduate course on Negotiation, offered to two different classes: lawyers and business students. We also collected information from questionnaires that were distributed to these two different sets of students and juxtaposed the findings with data collected from a control group population. Drawing our conclusions from the observation of negotiation behavior and the negotiators' self-assessments of their negotiating style, we found that the performance of female lawyers as negotiators is not as influenced by the widely-held societal expectations of gender-appropriate behavior as a sizeable part of the literature suggests. Rather, the most successful female negotiators in our sample displayed goal-oriented negotiating behavior that was determined primarily by individual characteristics and secondarily by the group norms that dominate the Greek legal culture, which fully embraces the traditional adversarial model.

All the lawyers in our sample, regardless of gender, were of Greek ethnic origin. This particular population was also homogeneous with respect to age, race, and socio-economic status. The average age of lawyers in our sample was 27 years old. Their common demographic background made their negotiating interactions "culturally homogeneous." In practical terms, cultural homogeneity has two implications: (a) true differences in negotiating style may be harder to discern and categorize and (b) differences in gender may be more easily identified and explained, since the ethnicity and/or culture variable has been *de facto* isolated. To put it differently, since the participants all come from similar backgrounds, one can more effectively observe and document the impact of gender and professional norms.

Our findings suggest that in simulated legal negotiations, the negotiator's personality is a stronger determinant of successful performance than his or her biological sex. We advance the thesis that a lawyer's sex is becoming less important, as the norms of the legal profession adapt to a more gender-neutral model of lawyering. The legal profession in Greece has been increasingly populated by women, with more accelerating rates in the past fifteen years. Over 60% of graduates from the country's Law Schools (which are all integrated in the public university system) are women. This makes Greece an interesting case study, because it constitutes an example of an environment that is deeply stratified along gender lines, but inversely. In recent years, a "power culture" has developed among young female law practitioners. Our work attempts to tap into this new social reality, as all indications show that young women lawyers do not appear to be disempowered by their gender.

Gender Differences in Negotiating Style: Some Findings

Sex differences in negotiation have been extensively explored over the last three decades. However, this research has continued to yield contradictory findings, with some studies suggesting little or no difference between male and female negotiators (Walters et al. 1998; Stuhlmacher and Walters 1999) and others documenting significant differences between male and female negotiators (Stamato 1992; Whitaker and Austin 2001; Miller and Miller 2002; Babcock and Laschever 2003).

The two major meta-analyses that were published in the late 1990s (Walters et al. 1998 and Stuhlmacher and Walters 1999) suggest fewer gender differences in negotiation behavior than would be expected. The first study (Walters et al. 1998) examined the results of 62 research reports on the relationship between gender and competitive behavior in dyadic bargaining interactions. The authors found that women were significantly more competitive than men when competing against an opponent who pursued a "tit-for-tat" bargaining strategy. Men were found to be more competitive than women as measured by their offers and verbal exchanges. The second study indicated that women reached less favorable negotiation outcomes compared to men, but factors such as the relative power between the negotiators and the mode of communication moderated that effect.

Although the study of gender in simulated negotiation settings is an area that has only recently attracted research attention, it has already begun to yield fruitful results suggesting that there is less of a gender split in negotiation performance than it was earlier believed. Craver and Barnes (1999) have found that while women and men may not perform identically in negotiation settings, there is no factual basis for assuming that women are weaker or less capable negotiators.

In this strand of research, we set out to capture the gender differences in the negotiating behavior of male and female lawyers in a classroom setting. Drawing from the typology of Fisher and Ury (1991) and Shell (1999), we designed a questionnaire in order to assess the impact of style on the lawyers' negotiating performance. The questionnaire was distributed during the first session of the Negotiations course to two different populations of graduate students: the first was composed exclusively of lawyers, and the second was composed of graduate business students. The questionnaires were distributed during the first class session, with the aim of capturing the instinctive or intuitive negotiating styles of both men and women respondents, before knowledge of the negotiating process "informed" their responses to specific questions.

We also observed the simulated negotiating games conducted in the context of the graduate course on "Negotiations for Lawyers" and then analyzed their outcomes. Nearly all of the games were role-play exercises, where lawyers negotiated in pairs that were selected at random, each in an assigned role. Half of the games involved single issue, zero-sum game negotiations and the other half were multi-issue negotiations, with potential for joint gains. In the single-issue negotiations, the lawyers negotiated in the role of buyer or seller, or of an employee negotiating for a raise in his or her salary. In the multi-issue games, they played the role of legal representative (e.g. acting as legal counsel for a client in a contract such as the sale of a house or the break-up of a company). To resolve disputes effectively, the lawyers in our sample were directed to systematically apply an interest-based approach (see Shell 1999, Lax and Sebenius 1986) and attempt to create value. Only one of the games was a group exercise calling upon the lawyers to claim value but to do so by working together in small groups and making strategic decisions …

Our main findings are presented in the sections that follow. We will first discuss the results which may indicate gender differences in negotiating style. Next we identify those areas where gender lines are erased and factors like individual personality traits come into play. We will attempt to explain the negotiating behavior of male and female lawyers by reference to the competitive in-group norms of the legal profession.

The Lawyers

We identified three distinct negotiating approaches: hard (or competitive); soft (or cooperative); and contextual (depending on the circumstances). More specifically, the results are as follows:

Table One   Basic Negotiating Personality (Lawyers)

	Male Lawyers	Female Lawyers
Hard negotiators	57%	35%
Soft negotiators	29%	40%
Depending on the circumstances	14%	25%

Reading Table One, we observe that a little over one-third of women lawyers described their negotiating style as hard, as opposed to close to two-thirds of men lawyers. Roughly one-third of all male lawyers described themselves as soft negotiators.

We found that the self-perceptions of female lawyers in terms of their negotiating style were initially influenced by socially-constructed expectations of appropriate gender roles. In the questionnaires that were distributed, 40 percent of all female respondents described their negotiating personality as "soft" or "cooperative." In the class discussion that followed the completion of the questionnaires, soft negotiators of both sexes were identified and explained why they adopted a cooperative negotiating personality. Because of the small class size, it was easy to observe and "keep track" of these negotiators' behaviors during the games. Observing their in-class negotiation behavior indicated yielded an interesting finding: 30% to 50% of these self-proclaimed "soft" negotiators actually used abrasive bargaining tactics in the simulated games. This suggests a real divide between self-perceptions and actual negotiator behavior. One explanation is that the self-expectations of female lawyers were initially informed by the dominant stereotypes—but during the games, their behavior was shaped by their attempted alignment with the group norms of their profession. The role-playing exercises acted as a powerful trigger that made them identify with their role-as-advocate and activated more assertive responses on their part. Investigating the interplay between gender and representation role, Bowles et al. (2005) also found that women acting as an agent for someone else intended to be more assertive in their requests than women acting on their own behalf.

There is empirical evidence to suggest that gender affects only self-expectations and not negotiation behavior. In 1994, Watson (1994) analyzed eight studies on negotiation and concluded that gender affected participants' feelings: women felt less confident when negotiating, and, even when they displayed the same negotiation behavior as men, felt less successful than the men did. The manner in which gender stereotypes are activated in the minds of negotiators has been identified as a situational variable that impacts bargaining outcomes (Kray et al. 2001).

Finally, 25 percent of women lawyers and 14 percent of male lawyers submitted a self-assessment of "neither hard nor soft" negotiator, clarifying that they feel negotiating style is highly dependent on the negotiating setting. These self-assessments cannot be properly categorized as hard or soft, since they constitute a third, distinct category that has been explored in the literature (see e.g. Savage et al. 1989, who developed a model for the selection of negotiation strategy that depends on different responses to relational and substantive concerns). There are two possible ways to interpret this finding: one is to say that the negotiators who refused to fall into the trap of the "either soft or hard" dichotomy were well on their way to becoming effective negotiators, since they had intuitively grasped that thinking in a flexible and contextual manner is key to problem-solving. In this light, women lawyers proved to be more flexible than their male colleagues. The other way to approach the result is to infer that these negotiators were less clear about their negotiating style, less assertive and self-aware than the majority of respondents—and so responded in a manner that eschewed the dichotomy out of puzzlement and not a higher degree of self-awareness.

The respondents were then called upon to clarify how they applied their basic negotiating personality in situations of professional and personal conflict. They were given four options to choose from, as can be seen from the table below:

Table Two   Negotiating Style in Situations of
Professional and Personal Conflict (Lawyers)

	Male Lawyers	Female Lawyers
Hard in professional conflict/soft in personal conflict	71%	50%
Hard in both professional and personal conflict	14%	15%
Soft in professional conflict/hard in personal conflict	15%	20%
Soft in both professional and personal conflict	0%	10%
I don't know (undecided)	0%	5%

These findings demonstrate that men are just as sensitive to the distinction between professional and personal negotiations as women. But they are also more steadfast about adopting a hard negotiating style in professional conflicts relative to women. This is a finding that has consistently come up in the empirical investigation of gender in negotiation.

The fourth question of the second part of the questionnaire checks for the impact of gender socialization. It asks respondents to think back to their childhood and provide an assessment of their behavior in group games, either in the school yard or in the neighborhood. The responses are plotted in the tables that follow:

Table Three   Behavior in Group Games during Childhood (Female Lawyers)

	Hard Negotiators	Soft Negotiators	Contextual Negotiators
Highly competitive	29%	0%	20%
Rather competitive	57%	62.5%	20%
Indifferent about winning or losing.	14%	25%	0%
Cooperative	0%	12.5%	20%
Other	0%	0%	40%

We notice that the female lawyers who had previously replied that they are either hard or soft "depending on the circumstances" are similarly undecided when it comes to identifying their behavior as children. These women, who make up a small percentage of the overall sample, are more comfortable describing rather than identifying their negotiating style.

But the most interesting finding here is the following: regardless of their self-assessment in terms of their negotiating style, the overwhelming majority of women lawyers describe themselves as "rather competitive" in group games. This finding explains their choice of profession—but it must be combined with a reading of the responses given by the male lawyers before more tenable conclusions can be reached.

Table Four   Behavior in Group Games during Childhood (Male Lawyers)

	Hard Negotiators	Soft Negotiators	Contextual Negotiators
Highly competitive	25%	0%	0%
Rather competitive	75%	50%	0%
Indifferent about winning			
or losing.	0%	0%	0%
Cooperative	0%	0%	75%
Other	0%	50%	25%

The findings from the male lawyers confirm that a self-description of "rather competitive" behavior is the most popular answer across the board. Half of all male lawyers who characterize themselves as soft negotiators were rather competitive as children. Moreover, it is quite interesting that most male lawyers who were cooperative in childhood group games grew up to become contextual negotiators, possessing greater flexibility and subtlety in their adult bargaining behavior.

The fifth question that called upon the respondents to turn in a more refined self-assessment of their negotiating style is even more revealing: 75 percent of all female lawyers who described themselves as hard negotiators specified that they were "hard in situations of professional conflict and soft in situations of personal conflict." However, it would be inaccurate to say that these tough female negotiators adopted "a masculine sex role orientation," as proposed by Greenhalgh and Gilkey (1986). First, because this characterization fails to capture the behavior of tough female negotiators in games where they were distinctly called upon to apply integrative bargaining techniques. Second, because the exact same percentage of male lawyers who described themselves as "hard negotiators" also turned in the same response. This finding clearly shows that most "tough" lawyers, regardless of sex, identify with the norms of their profession, yet are careful to draw the line between their professional and personal life.

The Business Students

The questionnaires were also distributed to the students attending the full-time Master's of Business Administration program. The class was composed predominantly of young business professionals, working in various executive positions. We distributed a total of 40 questionnaires, but received only 34 valid completed questionnaires. The male respondents outnumbered the female respondents by a narrow margin (18 males as opposed to 16 females).

It was interesting to observe that most female respondents in the MBA Program class and roughly one-third of all male respondents characterized their personal negotiating style as neither soft nor hard, but "depending on the circumstances." But the most striking finding was that close to 40% of male graduate business students gave a self-description of "soft negotiator." The results appear analytically below:

Table Five   Basic Negotiating Personality (MBA Students)

	Male MBA students	Female MBA students
Hard negotiators	28%	19%
Soft negotiators	39%	38%
Depending on the circumstances	33%	43%

If we juxtapose these results with those from the lawyers' sample, we will notice that lawyers of both sexes are significantly more competitive negotiators than MBA students of both sexes. The number of female lawyers who described themselves as hard negotiators is nearly double the number of female MBA students who turned in the same self-assessment. When asked to be more specific about their negotiating style, the responses were as follows:

Table Six   Negotiating Style in Situations of Professional
and Personal Conflict (MBA Students)

	Male MBA students	Female MBA students
Hard in professional conflict/soft in personal conflict . . .	83%	50%
Hard in both professional and personal conflict	6%	13%
Soft in professional conflict/hard in personal conflict . . .	0%	31%
Soft in both professional and personal conflict	11%	6%

Under the same lens, we conclude that lawyers who are tough negotiators report significantly higher numbers of tough bargaining behavior in both their professional and personal lives compared to the business executives. Also, the number of female business executives who report being soft negotiators in their professional conflicts is a lot higher than the relevant number of female lawyers.

Table Seven   Behavior in Group Games during Childhood
(Female MBA Students)

	Hard Negotiators	Soft Negotiators	Contextual Negotiators
Highly competitive	0%	0%	22%
Rather competitive	55%	40%	45%
Indifferent about winning or losing	15%	20%	0%
Cooperative	30%	20%	22%
Other	0%	20%	11%

Table Eight   Behavior in Group Games during Childhood
(Male MBA Students)

	Hard Negotiators	Soft Negotiators	Contextual Negotiators
Highly competitive	20%	29%	33%
Rather competitive	40%	57%	33%
Indifferent about winning or losing	20%	0%	17%
Cooperative	0%	14%	0%
Other	20%	0%	17%

We observe that most male MBA students (surprisingly, even the ones who describe themselves as soft negotiators) were rather competitive in their childhood years. The same holds true for female MBA students. What is most important for our research is that lawyers of both sexes clearly surpass the business professionals in terms of competitiveness: the percentages of female and male lawyers who were highly competitive in group games as children are quite larger than the relative percentages of the business students.

The Control Group

We tested the findings in a non-lawyer and non-MBA population, comprised mainly of bank employees and insurance company employees of different ranks. To minimize heterogeneity, we limited the sample to young adults (aged 20-30). We received 40 fully completed and valid questionnaires in total, with a near-even male to female ratio (21 female respondents and 19 male respondents).

Table Nine   Basic Negotiating Personality (Control Group)

	Males	Females
Hard negotiators	11%	33%
Soft negotiators	78%	57%
Depending on the circumstances	11%	10%

Table Ten   Negotiating Style in Situations of Professional
and Personal Conflict (Control Group)

	Males	Females
Hard in professional conflict/soft in personal conflict	22%	14%
Hard in both professional and personal conflict	17%	9%
Soft in professional conflict/hard in personal conflict	5.5%	29%
Soft in both professional and personal conflict	50%	48%
I don't know (undecided)	5.5%	0%

Women lawyers as a group are "tougher" negotiators than both the business students and the general population. Over half of the females in the control group described themselves as soft negotiators. Even more important assessments can be made by contrasting Tables Two and Ten: nearly 50% of all females in the control group assert that they are soft in handling conflicts that arise in their professional relationships, as opposed to only 10% of female lawyers. The similar percentage for the male lawyers is even more impressive: over two thirds of all male lawyers describe themselves as hard negotiators.

Do these findings confirm the obvious fact that inherently competitive people of both sexes are drawn to competitive professions? Or is it the prevailing norms of legal culture that shape inherently soft or accommodating people into fierce competitors? We aim to show that although biological inclinations undoubtedly play a role, the norms of the profession are stronger determinants of negotiation behavior.

Gender-Neutral Behavior at the Negotiating Table
Recent theoretical explanations of gender in social behavior predict that gender differences will arise only under certain circumstances and increasingly look for situational variables that may trigger these "gender effects" (see Deaux and Major 1987; Kray et al. 2001; Riley et al. 2003). Perhaps the greater number of women lawyers in the classroom (replicating the sex ratio of the actual lawyer population in Greece), combined with the negotiators' own "gender-appropriate" expectations, acted as a trigger for some of the "gender-based" differences that we observed …

Men and women seemed to be equally imbued with the values of individualism that have come to define the legal profession. In one particular group game (*Oil Pricing*), which mimics the strategic decisions made by duopolies and involves two teams in a price-bidding war under time constraints, the competitive ethics of the profession clashed with the norms of group decision-making. In this game, making the "right" strategic moves involves clarifying issues of representation and reconciling competing subjective preferences. In our lab setting, both male and female lawyers experienced a tension between empathy and assertiveness (*cf.* Mnookin et al. 1996). One characteristic outcome was that "troublemakers" were ostracized—minority voters were opinionated, "tough" negotiators in most games. Penalties included the refusal to nominate them for the role of representative and to preclude all team members from developing lengthy oral argumentation (most commonly by using the game rule of the four-minute deadline for placing bids between rounds). This was the team's way of ensuring in-group cooperation and minimizing the costs associated with allowing these troublemakers to play a leading role during negotiations.

The two most complex simulated games of the course called upon the players to resolve conflicts with high stakes in situations where an amicable future relationship is very important. In the first (*"The Bowling Ball Manufacturer"*) they had to negotiate the provisions of a long-term supply contract and in the second (*"PowerScreen"*), they had to settle a dispute over ownership rights on a particular product with the goal of continuing a long-standing business partnership. We found that when role-playing in these games, men and women were *equally* likely to exhibit the following traits:

- taking initiatives
- being assertive
- exhibiting confidence

- brainstorming different options
- resolving differences by overcoming problems of perception
- asking questions to reveal underlying interests
- setting high goals
- searching for areas of shared interest
- ability to engage in "dovetailing" (Fisher and Ury 1991: 73)
- drafting "yes-able" propositions

These characteristics were shown to be common to both sexes. Taken together, they fit the profile of the "cooperative antagonist," to use Howard Raiffa's classification (1982). Although each one of these attributes merits special attention, for the purposes of this paper we will focus on the ability to build a collaborative relationship, because it lies at the very heart of the debate concerning women's alleged proclivity to "connect." The bulk of the literature from the social sciences suggests that women are inclined to emphasize relational needs and men individual criteria in their dealings with other people (see generally Gilligan 1982). According to Kolb and Williams (2003: 174), "connection itself is often linked to a 'softer' feminine approach," something they characterize as a common misperception.

We found that the ability to connect was a personality trait that greatly increased the chances of a successful outcome for negotiators of both sexes. Observing the negotiating behavior of individual lawyers at the table and evaluating the agreements they reached, we found that both sexes were equally adept at creating value, i.e. at reaching mutually beneficial (*positive-sum game*) agreements. Of course the participants were expressly directed to be attentive to both the relationship issues and the substantive goals of the negotiation.

Furthermore, in our lab setting, the soft approach could in no way be identified with women's negotiating style. Again, behaving like an "accommodator" at the negotiating table (see e.g. Shell 1999: 10-11) manifested itself as a personality trait rather than a psychological tendency associated with either sex. Observing the outcomes of different negotiating pairs, the few men and women in our sample who were "soft" realized early on that accommodating bargainers who are willing to give in for the sake of peace get a smaller piece of the pie while role-playing in claiming-value games. Accommodation became a handicap for negotiators of both sexes, as it translated into unilateral concessions. Most negotiators in our sample eventually learned to protect themselves by using the principled method.

The Role of Personality: The Lawyer as Pragmatic Problem-Solver

Individual personality, together with economic status, political orientation, gender, family history, communication and language skills, and mood all contribute to a person's bargaining behavior (see generally Sebenius 2002). In recent years, considerable research has been conducted on the effects of personality variables in negotiation (see e.g. Gilkey and Greenhalgh 1986). Standardized personality tests like the Myers-Briggs test have been refined and their use in business settings has proliferated. However, the findings on the impact of individual differences on negotiating outcomes remain inconclusive. Some argue that the structural variables in negotiation (for example, the power imbalance between the two negotiating parties and/or the pressure exerted by constituencies) may override the effects of personality variables …

Our findings confirm the pivotal role of personality and style in negotiating perform-ance. Although all negotiating pairs in our sample were given the same set of facts and instructions, the results reached by each negotiating pair varied widely. In exercises that involved agreement on a distributive issue (e.g. deciding on a mutually satisfactory salary, as in the simulated exercise of *Sally Soprano*), the figure that the pairs agreed upon covered a wide bargaining range. This reflects the imprint of individual characteristics on nego-tiating outcomes.

What's more, the most successful negotiators in our sample all possessed a moderate to high degree of individualism. Each one brought a different mix of skills to the negotiat-ing table: for some, the prominent trait was integrity, while for others it was a confident attitude. But every one of these effective negotiators was a highly rational, goal-oriented player with advanced problem-solving skills. If we were required to group them together on the basis of a single shared characteristic, then we would characterize the successful negotiators of our sample as "pragmatic problem-solvers."

Pragmatism has distinct scientific connotations and as such is usually linked to the American intellectual tradition. Analyzing the American view of negotiation, Stempel (2002) suggests that intellectual diversity and a pragmatic approach to negotiation are American hallmarks. In our analysis, we adopt a broader view of pragmatism, in its core essence of a practical and matter-of-fact way of assessing situations or of solving problems.

Pragmatic problem-solvers are negotiators who are consistently goal-driven and results-oriented. Goal-oriented rationality in the Weberian sense is well in tune with the pragmatist doctrine of looking to an idea's observable practical consequences. Regardless of the orientation they employ, these negotiators strike a very good balance between maintaining a good relationship with the other side and aiming to cover the substantive items on their negotiating agenda. They negotiate expecting tangible rewards, but they do care about the reputational costs of harming the amiable climate of their bargaining interactions. The negotiating behavior of these pragmatic problem-solvers was in many aspects similar to what Rackham (1980 [2003]) has termed "superior" negotiating behav-ior in his widely-influential study of labor relations negotiators.

The most pronounced personality traits shared by the pragmatic problem-solvers in our sample were the following:

Figure 1   Personality Traits of Pragmatic Problem-Solvers

- a heightened level of rationality (that allowed them to maintain better control over their emotions);
- a highly developed ability to inquire effectively and to listen actively;
- greater flexibility (that allowed them to remain assertive without damaging the relationship);
- greater ability to take the other side's perspective (to empathize);
- greater commitment to professional integrity (as they perceived it in the context of the situations described in the simulated games);
- greater openness to adopting an integrative bargaining approach

All of the aforementioned personality traits constitute important variables that influence many different aspects of the negotiation. To begin with, enhanced cognitive skills have been identified by negotiation experts as a key factor associated with excellent performance in legal and business negotiations. For example, Watkins (2002) describes business negotiations in terms of four tasks: diagnosis, shaping, process management, and assessment. These tasks assume special significance during the preparation stage of negotiations, which we were not in a position to assess empirically. In-class observation was our main methodological tool, so we could only make well-reasoned estimates regarding both cognitive skills and perspective-taking ability during the planning stage. The amply-documented fact that better preparation leads to more successful negotiating was confirmed: the lawyers who had solidified their line of argumentation on the basis of objective standards were confident enough to invite the other side to explore areas of shared interests at the negotiating table.

The ability to inquire effectively and to engage in active listening was more easily manifested during face-to-face bargaining. As in other laboratory-setting studies, effective negotiators stand out by what they avoid doing rather than by what they actually do. Problem-solvers avoided engaging in tactics like defend-attack spirals and irritators. They resisted the temptation of "flaunting" their offers. They also asked more questions, especially to test understanding at all steps leading towards agreement. They used clarifying and open-ended questions to summarize the progress made in the negotiation. Finally, successful negotiators were willing to invest more time in looking for areas of common ground.

Simulated bargaining games confirm our deeply held intuitions about real-world negotiations. Personal ability is the single most important factor behind negotiating successful real-life business deals. When negotiating across national boundaries, negotiators with advanced skills are better able to overcome cultural differences. Lawyers and executives who possess sophisticated personality traits can use their personal influence in all stages of negotiating, but especially during planning and gaining commitment …

Female Lawyers as Pragmatic Problem-Solvers

An interesting finding was that the overwhelming majority of pragmatic problem-solvers in our study were women. These negotiators effectively engaged "in a dynamic kind of relationship building that is inextricably yoked to successful advocacy" (Kolb and Williams 2003: 175). They viewed their involvement in the problem-solving process as an integral part of their lawyering skills. In the laboratory setting, they were able to reach wise and efficient agreements in a favorable climate of respect for their negotiating partner (Ury 1991: 73-75).

The ability to engage more effectively in problem-solving is crucial both in the classroom and in real-life negotiations. It has also been connected to a "feminine" style of lawyering. Davis (1991: 1677) has demonstrated that the feminine style represents both attention to a broader range of client concerns and participation in problem-solving, whereas the masculine style represents a "relatively narrow interpretation of the expert's role in problem-solving" (*id.*). However, in our study, the connection of this ability to women lawyers may be in great part explained by the overrepresentation of women in the particular lawyer populations. This is the reason why we would be very hesitant to attach a gender tag to successful lawyering.

It is our understanding that the principled negotiation method appealed to women lawyers because it allowed them to turn their "feminine" attributes from handicaps to advantages. When applying the method, inherently competitive women were able to channel their drive into more constructive paths, whereas inherently cooperative women drew strength from the wide applicability of objective standards. It seems that the use of a method solves the negotiator's dilemma between adherence to the profession's competitive ideals and following one's own unique negotiating style, which is more "other-directed" than the one dictated by group norms. Women lawyers seem to be particularly troubled by this dilemma, which is two-pronged: the legal arena expects them to be tough and outspoken, but the senior partners in their law firms expect them to be deferential and courteous. Not surprisingly, a number of them experience some degree of what we could call "gender-disassociation" when applying tough bargaining tactics in their legal practice.

Observing how lawyers played the simulated games, it was obvious that the greatest obstacle in establishing cooperative relationships was the lack of trust. Although in theory all lawyers agreed that trust is the building block which forges long-lasting alliances, joint ventures and networks, in practice it was particularly difficult for them to assume the risk of "trusting first." This was hardly surprising, as an important sub-set of group norms in legal practice are rooted in "mistrust" or else, a type of "inbred conservatism" that is part innate and part "learned" when students are still in their years of basic legal studies. Here once more, the influence of occupational norms was more direct than the impact of cultural homogeneity which would be seen as inducing cooperation.

To sum up, we should keep in mind that outside a laboratory setting, a woman lawyer's decisive tone, confident attitude or assertive negotiating personality could be easily labelled as authoritative, harsh or domineering. It is easier for a man to tolerate or admire leadership qualities in a woman when these are confined to a classroom. Kolb et al. (2004: 6) point out that the image of the effective leader is still cut from masculine cloth: behavior perfectly acceptable in a male leader can seem discordant in a woman—overly harsh, too aggressive, uncaring.

In the world of business, research has consistently shown that women often lack the presumption of credibility and competence when they assume a leadership role (see esp. Rhode 2003). Despite the greater than ever numbers of women among the executive ranks, Americans—male and female—still prefer to have a male boss (Simmons 2001). Kolb and Putnam (1997) argue that most negotiations in organizations are modeled on a "masculine" paradigm, and they challenge human resource professionals to develop processes that are more inclusive, creative, and empowering.

Dina W. Pradel, Hannah R. Bowles & Kathleen L. McGinn
"When Does Gender Matter in Negotiation?"
Harvard Negotiation Newsletter (November 2005) 3

*Anticipating when gender may work to your advantage—or
disadvantage—can help you negotiate more effectively.*

The last few months have been trying for Maureen Park, the managing director of a small portfolio management firm. The firm's parent company, a large financial services concern, was performing below forecasts, and morale among Park's understaffed, overworked team of research analysts was low.

To make matters worse, Park's two best analysts both requested significant raises after their annual reviews. Both women expressed their belief that they were earning substantially less than analysts at comparable firms and probably less than lower-achieving members of their firm—including a male colleague who had been lured away from a competitor.

Park went to bat for her star performers, though management had instructed her to offer only cost-of-living raises. To her surprise, her superiors agreed to offer better incentives to both analysts. Reflecting on her triumph, Park realized with bitter irony that three of her seven direct reports would make more than she would in the coming year; she herself had accepted a small cost-of-living raise without question. If getting a raise was so easy, why hadn't she made a case for herself? Is it possible that her gender somehow influenced how Park negotiated for herself and others?

Businesspeople often ask us whether men or women are better negotiators. According to our research, gender is not a reliable predictor of negotiation performance; neither women nor men perform better or worse across all negotiations. However, certain types of negotiation can set the stage for differences in outcomes negotiated by men and by women, particularly when (1) the opportunities and limits of the negotiation are unclear; and (2) situational cues in these ambiguous situations trigger different behaviors by men and women.

These differences can create huge inequities over time. Awareness of the factors that create gender-related advantages and disadvantages can help you mitigate their consequences—and promote a more egalitarian workplace.

How ambiguity affects negotiation

At Park's firm, a high degree of uncertainty and secrecy surrounded salary negotiations. After all, analysts in the investment management industry have highly portable skills and are frequently poached by competing firms. And though all of Park's employees were performing roughly the same work, they had differing levels of experience, education, and industry reputation. These factors created a large variation in salary levels and bonus structures.

Combine these disparities with a firm in flux—where policies clashed with the need to retain key employees—and both the opportunities to negotiate and the content of what was negotiable became unclear.

When parties understand little about the limits of the bargaining range and appropriate standards for agreement, the ambiguity of a negotiation increases. In highly ambiguous negotiations, it becomes more likely that gender triggers—situational cues that prompt male-female differences in preferences, expectations, and behaviors—will influence negotiation behavior and outcomes. By contrast, in situations with low ambiguity, where negotiators understand the range of possible payoffs and agree on standards for distributing value, outcomes are less likely to reflect gender triggers. Some environments are full of triggers that encourage superior performance by women, while others are full of triggers that encourage superior performance by men. Rather than indicating innate differences between men and women, these triggers reflect stereotypes and long-standing behavioral biases.

When competition is high.

Competitive negotiations can act as gender triggers, consistent with societal expectations that men are more likely than women to be competitive and to succeed in competitive environments. Researchers Uri Gneezy of the University of Chicago, Muriel Niederle of Stanford University, and Aldo Rustichini of the University of Minnesota have shown that women and men are equally competent in "piece-rate" situations, in which individuals work to maximize their own payoff without regard for others' performance.

But men outperform women in competitive environments in which payoffs are determined by comparing relative performance. It's not that the pressure of competition causes women to stumble but, rather, that men step up their performance in competitive situations.

Consider the highly competitive job market for graduating MBAs. With Linda Babcock of Carnegie Mellon University, we analyzed differences between men's and women's starting salaries in a graduating class of MBA students at a top business school. In low-ambiguity industries (as rated by career-services experts), compensation standards were relatively clear to potential hires. These industries include investment banking, consulting, and high technology. In high-ambiguity industries, such as telecommunications, real estate, health services, and media, standards for starting salaries were less evident.

We found no difference in the salaries negotiated by male and female MBAs hired into low-ambiguity industries, which included 70% of our participants. In high-ambiguity industries, however, male MBAs negotiated salaries that were $10,000 higher, on average, than those negotiated by female MBAs. The competitive context cued negotiators to the traditionally "masculine" nature of the interaction, and the ambiguity in certain industries allowed these cues to elicit different negotiating behavior from men and women. These differences add up over time. Assuming that those 30% of MBAs who take positions in high-ambiguity industries work for 35 years and receive a 3% raise per year, the earnings gap grows to more than $600,000 over the course of a career—or $1.5 million, if those extra earnings are saved at 5% annual interest.

When negotiating for others.

One gender trigger that may favor women over men is playing the role of agent (advocating for others) as opposed to playing the role of principal (advocating for themselves). Our research suggests that, as evident in the story of Maureen Park, women perform better when negotiating on behalf of others than they do when negotiating for themselves; no such difference emerges among male negotiators.

Again with Babcock, we asked a large group of executives to negotiate compensation for an internal candidate for a new management position. Half negotiated as the candidate; the other half negotiated as the candidate's mentor. The negotiators were given no reference points or standards for agreement, creating a highly ambiguous negotiation. Female executives negotiating as the mentor secured compensation that was 18% higher than the compensation female executives negotiated when they were playing the candidate. Meanwhile, male executives performed consistently across both roles, at the level of female executives negotiating as the candidate.

It's not that our female participants felt less entitled to a good salary. Prior to the negotiation, women reported salary expectations similar to those of their male counterparts. Nor were women more or less competent at the negotiation itself. Rather, it appears that the women executives were particularly energized when they felt a sense of responsibility to represent another person's interests. Just as men excel in ambiguous, competitive environments, women are exemplary negotiators when the beneficiary is someone other than themselves.

Neutralizing gender differences in negotiation

These suggestions can help prevent gender from becoming a significant factor in negotiations:

1. Anticipate gender-related triggers.
   Some degree of ambiguity is present in all negotiations, so be aware of situations that may trigger gender stereotypes or role expectations. Work to counter gender triggers, or use them to benefit negotiation performance. In highly ambiguous, competitive environments, for example, men may be encouraged to maximize their outcomes by ramping up their competitive drive. Women, on the other hand, may be inspired by reminders that they're representing not just themselves but their colleagues, department, company, or customers.
2. Do your homework.
   Whether you're a man or a woman, learn as much as you can about what is possible or appropriate when heading into a salary negotiation or discussing a contract. Research industry norms, investigate precedent, and talk to others who are already employed at the firm or in the industry. Most important, don't be

---

Learning from Female Executives

Dozens of female CEOs and other high-level executives have told us about their experiences negotiating in traditionally masculine contexts where standards and expectations were ambiguous. Their experiences varied according to the gender triggers that were present in the negotiations.

A founder of a large grocery chain had difficulty securing loans to open her first three stores. Banking is an industry dominated by men, where norms reinforce masculine values surrounding power and money. To her detriment, the woman's loan requests triggered these masculine stereotypes. "It was only starting in store four that I was able to finally get funding from a bank," she says.

By her fourth round of negotiations, ambiguity had been reduced on both sides of the table. The entrepreneur better understood how the loan process worked, and the bank was impressed by the entrepreneur's proven track record.

In other situations, gender triggers cue superior performance in women. A leader in the advertising industry reminisced about her early days as an unknown within her firm and industry. When she began focusing on the retail business, her male colleagues asked her to take part in pitches and credited her with their success. Historically the realm of female clerks, retail offered a setting in which others expected this female executive to excel.

Many factors affect negotiation success. But even for exceptionally talented executives, when ambiguity is high, gender triggers play a critical role. As women enter historically male industries in greater numbers, gender triggers play a critical role. As women enter historically male industries in greater numbers, gender triggers cuing superior performance by men should lessen, equalizing opportunities for men and women.

afraid to ask for whatever you need to remain truly motivated and to get the job done well. You and your organization will be better off in the long run.

When negotiating her own salary, Park failed to do this basic investigative work. Her subordinates, by contrast, compared their salaries with company and industry standards, and voiced their expectations to higher-ups.

3. Create transparency surrounding compensation and benefits.

To encourage gender equity regarding compensation and career development, your company should codify and publish opportunities and benefits that it may be willing to offer. This doesn't mean standardizing benefits for all employees but clarifying the range of issues that are up for negotiation and the appropriate criteria on which decisions are based.

At Park's company, each employee had to figure out individually what was reasonable and fair, a situation that increased the likelihood that inequities would arise over time. If the company instead communicated that compensation would be based on agreed-upon performance indicators and that salaries, bonuses, and promotions could be negotiated annually, differences in compensation would be more likely to reflect real differences in performance rather than gender.

4. Articulate performance expectations.

When sending your employees into competitive bargaining situations, clearly state performance goals. Armed with transparent comparative information and a sense of acceptable targets, both men and women will achieve better outcomes. Setting high but reasonable aspirations is good for all negotiators and may be especially beneficial for women in ambiguous, competitive negotiations.

Linda Babcock & Sara Laschever
"First You Have to Ask"
Harvard Negotiation Newsletter (January 2004) 3

*When women don't negotiate for themselves, their careers
can suffer—and so can their organizations.*

Think back to the hiring process that led you to your current position. Maybe you had just received your MBA and met with a number of different companies before choosing the job you thought was right for you. Or maybe you were moving up in your company or switching to a new profession entirely. After a tough round of interviews, you were excited to be offered the job—but were you happy with the terms? Did you negotiate your salary or accept the first offer on the table? Since then, have you had any doubts about the way you did—or didn't—bargain?

Your answers to these questions probably reveal a lot about you, including one key thing: your gender. If you're a man, chances are that you haggled over your salary offer. If you're a woman, it's more likely that you agreed to the first offer on the table—and got off to a much slower financial start than most men.

In research with Michele Gelfand, Deborah Small, and Heidi Stayn, we've sought to identify unrecognized gender differences in the workplace by looking at the degree to which men and women initiate negotiations. What we found startled us. In several very different studies, the results were the same: men were significantly more likely to negotiate than women. In one study, men negotiated twice as often as women; in another, men negotiated *nine times* more frequently. Ruling out differences in age, education level, and work experience, we came to a firm conclusion: men use negotiation to promote their interests far more often than women do. This finding has serious implications not only for individuals, but for the organizations that employ them. Left unchecked, gender disparities in negotiation quickly transform into clear pay and promotion inequalities and costly employee turnover. All managers, male and female, can benefit from addressing this deep-rooted workplace problem.

The accumulation of disadvantage
Women not only initiate negotiations far less often than men, they pay an astonishingly high price as a result. In salary negotiations alone, women routinely leave hundreds of thousands of dollars on the table. Over the course of their careers, small differences between what women accept and what they could have gotten mount up dramatically.

Suppose that two 30-year-old recent MBA graduates, a man and a woman, receive job offers for $100,000 a year. By negotiating, the man raises his offer to $111,000, while the woman accepts the $100,000 without trying to get more. Even if both receive identical 3% raises for the rest of their careers, by the time they retire at 65, the difference between their annual salaries will have widened to $30,953.

The man who negotiated will also earn more than the woman during every one of the 35 years in which they both work. If he invests this "extra" yearly income in an account earning 5%, that initial $11,000—the product of a one-time negotiation—will grow to $1.6 million dollars by the time they both retire.

This is a massive return on a one-time negotiation—a conversation that may have taken no more than five minutes. It's also an extraordinary amount for a woman to *lose* by avoiding that first salary negotiation. Sociologists call this exponential transformation of small disparities into dramatic differences the *accumulation of disadvantage*.

While these numbers are staggering, they don't even account for additional wealth tied to salary, such as bonuses, stock options, and pensions. In addition, a man who negotiates his starting salary will probably negotiate better raises and more promotions throughout his career, making the financial rewards of his greater propensity to negotiate almost incalculably high.

Women sacrifice other things besides money by avoiding negotiation. Suppose that a man and a woman with similar training and skills are hired to do similar jobs. Early in his tenure, the man asks to join the team working on an important project. Joining this team raises his profile within the organization, gives him valuable leadership experience, and allows him to develop new skills. The next time his superiors need to staff a critical project, the man will have a real advantage over his more reticent female counterpart. And if he continues to ask for career-promoting opportunities more often than she does, he'll advance much faster up the organizational ladder, regardless of their respective talents and abilities.

The costs to organizations
Setting aside issues of fairness, if an organization hands out important projects, opportunities, and promotions based largely on the basis of who asks for them, that organization

will inevitably waste the skills of the most talented women on its payroll. Because men are more likely than women to ask for these opportunities and rewards, most of them will rise more quickly than their female peers—and end up filling the top spots in the organization. But some of those men will be less qualified and less able than some of the women left behind. Allowing women to get stuck in middle management simply because they don't pursue advancement as aggressively as their (sometimes less-talented) male peers can create costly inefficiencies and limit an organization's productivity. In the current economy, no company can afford to squander any of its resources, particularly one of its most important resources—its human capital.

Allowing women to accumulate disadvantages on the job by not negotiating harms employers in other ways as well. Surveys indicate that people most often leave their jobs because they feel their skills aren't being fully used or appreciated. If women see their male peers receiving better assignments and bigger raises, they may decide to leave.

Turnover is really expensive, says Steve Sanger, CEO of General Mills. "If we've invested in recruiting and developing good people, then we want them to stay."

Attrition costs American companies billions of dollars every year. On average, replacing an hourly worker costs an organization 50% of that worker's annual salary; replacing a professional worker costs 150% of her annual pay. Why so much? Add up screening and hiring costs, opportunity costs for the employees doing the hiring, and lost productivity until the replacement worker gets up to speed, and you're talking about a lot of money. Factor in the low morale of employees who have to pitch in while a replacement is found and trained, and the costs skyrocket. Our calculations show that these costs can have a huge impact on the bottom line of a typical midsize company—costing as much as 3.4% of revenues and an astounding 45% of profits.

Any initiative that reduces attrition will boost profits, in other words. Encouraging women to ask for what they want and creating a workplace environment that's receptive to women who negotiate offers businesses a genuine competitive advantage.

Why women don't ask
To enable female employees to ask for what they want, managers must first understand why most of them don't. There are two primary factors: how girls are socialized while they're growing up and how women are treated as adults.

Beginning in early childhood, girls are taught to be "communal," to make relationships a priority, and to focus on the needs of others and think less about their own needs. These lessons are conveyed by the chores they're assigned (such as looking after younger siblings), by the toys they're given (baby dolls and play kitchens), by the books they read and the television shows they watch, and by the behavior of older children and adults.

This early socialization can be so powerful that many women reach adulthood unaware that they've internalized these lessons. Focusing on the needs of others, they think less about their own needs and wants. As a result, they often fail to recognize opportunities to improve their job enjoyment and status through negotiation.

The primacy of community in women's lives also leads them to worry about the impact negotiations may have on their relationships. Many women feel that a disagreement about the substance of a negotiation—who will get and give up what—represents real conflict between the negotiators. Trained to placate rather than antagonize, to give rather than get, and to prize interpersonal peace over personal gain, women often experience more anxiety about negotiating than men do. This anxiety can deter them from asking for what they want even when they do know what that is.

Our interviews with dozens of women also confirmed that women who come across as "too aggressive" in the workplace frequently end up disliked and ostracized—and unable to get what they want anyway. All these social factors deter women from initiating negotiations.

What organizations can do

To make the most of your female workforce, the first step is to pay attention to who initiates negotiations in your organization and adjust your decision making accordingly.

Even managers who genuinely care about the advancement of women will discriminate unknowingly if they hand out assignments primarily to those who ask for them. By stopping to think whenever a man asks for an assignment whether he will do the best job or whether a woman who hasn't asked might do the job better, managers can begin to right some of the imbalances created by men's greater propensity to ask for what they want.

Managers can also employ one of the most time-honored methods of cultivating employee potential: monitoring. We've seen many women change quite rapidly after hearing the following advice from a trusted superior: Assume that everything about your working life is negotiable. Volunteer for projects that interest you. Actively pursue your professional goals.

In many cases, simply showing a woman hidden opportunities for advancement can help her view her career in a new light. Understanding that her managers can do their own jobs better when they know what she needs to meet her full potential can also relax some of the constraints holding her back.

Lastly, organizations can raise awareness among all employees about how different responses to the same behavior in men and women can deter women's progress and hurt the organization. Why do we call assertive men "go-getters" or "straight shooters" but label women who behave in similar ways "pushy" or worse? By making your organizational culture more hospitable to women who ask, you can show women that negotiating for their own advancement can be a winning strategy both for them and for your organization.

Selected Further Reading

L. Babcock, & S. Laschever, *Women Don't Ask: Negotiation and the Gender Divide* (Princeton, NJ: Princeton University Press, 2003).

L. Babcock, S. Laschever, M. Gelfand & D. Small, "Nice Girls Don't Ask" (2003) 81 Harvard Business Review 14.

I. Bohnet & F. Greig, "Gender Matters in Workplace Decisions" Harvard Negotiation Newsletter (April 2007).

L. Burton, L. Farmer, E. Gee, L. Johnson & G. Williams, "Feminist Theory, Professional Ethics, and Gender-Related Distinctions in Attorney Negotiating Styles" (1991) 1991:2 J. Disp. Resol. 199.

C.B. Craver, "Gender and Negotiation Performance" (2002) 4 Sociological Practice 183.

F.J. Flynn & D.R. Ames, "What's Good for the Goose May Not Be as Good for the Gander: The Benefits of Self-Monitoring for Men and Women in Task Groups and Dyadic Conflict" (2006) 91 Journal of Applied Psychology 272.

P. Heim & S. Golant, *Hardball for Women: Winning at the Game of Business*, rev. ed. (New York: Penguin Group, 2005).

D. Kolb, J. Williams & C. Frohlinger, *Her Place at the Table: A Woman's Guide to Negotiating Five Key Challenges to Leadership Success* (New York: Jossey-Bass, 2004).

L. Kray, A.D. Galinshky & L. Thomspon, "Reversing the Gender Gap in Negotiations: An Exploration of Stereotype Regeneration" (2002) 87 Organizational Behavior & Human Decision Processes 386.

M. Niederle & L. Vesterlund, "Do Women Shy Away from Competition? Do Men Compete Too Much?" Quarterly Journal of Economics [forthcoming].

D. Tannen, *The Argument Culture: Stopping America's War of Words* (New York: Random House, 1998).

D. Tannen, *Talking from 9 to 5: Women and Men in the Workplace: Language, Sex, and Power* (New York: Avon Books, 1994).

D. Tannen, *That's Not What I Mean!: How Conversational Style Makes or Breaks Relationships* (New York: First Ballantine Books, 1986).

D. Tannen, *You Just Don't Understand: Women and Men in Conversation* (New York: HarperCollins, 1990).

Emotion in Negotiation

Delee Fromm

Introduction

Keep a poker face. Don't get emotional. Remain cool and rational. Don't let them get to you. Good advice for negotiating? It used to be. Most researchers and academics, until fairly recently, ignored emotion completely in negotiation and focused instead on the cognitive and rational aspects of the bargaining process.[1] Formerly, emotion was considered to be an obstacle to a good negotiated outcome and a foe to an effective bargaining process. This view was encapsulated in one of the elements of principled negotiation: "separate the people from the prob-

lem."[2] Although this element allows for a constructive discussion of emotion in negotiation, as anyone who has negotiated with a very difficult counterpart can attest, the person and the feelings that the interaction creates often become the problem.

Emotion is an integral and essential part of the human experience and, thus, inherent in negotiation. Think back to a recent negotiation that you were involved in. Were you *fearful* that your counterpart in the negotiation would be better prepared or more skillful? Perhaps you were *hopeful* that the facts favoured you and that your alternatives were much better than those of your counterpart. Were you *anxious* because your career possibilities were tied

---

1   S. Kopelman, A.S. Rosette & L. Thompson, "The Three Faces of Eve: Strategic Displays of Positive, Negative and Neutral Emotions in Negotiations" (2006) 99 Organizational Behavior and Human Decision Processes 81.

2   R. Fisher & W. Ury, *Getting to Yes: Negotiating Agreement Without Giving In* (New York: Penguin Books, 1981) at 17.

to the outcome, such as a good grade? During the negotiation, were you *surprised* by some new facts you didn't know or made *angry* by the condescending attitude of the other negotiator? And at the end, were you *elated* at the outcome, or did you end up with buyer's *remorse*?

These are just a few of the emotions you may have felt during a negotiation. What about the emotions of your client or the other party? What about the emotional state you came with to the negotiation? Perhaps your mood was triggered by events unrelated to the negotiation, such as the coffee you spilled on your new, expensive suit or the speeding ticket you got on the way.[3] It is not surprising that we have been described as being in "perpetual emotion"[4] and that we often negotiate under the influence of emotion.

Recently, scientists and academics have embraced the study of emotion in negotiation, and numerous books, studies, and articles have flowed from this interest. Their research has revealed that the former view of emotion in negotiation, which considered emotion as an enemy and calm rationality as the goal, was limited in many respects. For example, evidence from the neurosciences[5] has shown that instead of being in opposition to reason, emotion is an integral part of reason and decision making. In fact, an absence of emotion has been found to have the same disruptive effect on decision making as strong negative emotion.[6] And suppressing an emotion has been found to result in impaired cognitive ability[7] and recall.[8] Also, ignored or suppressed emotions can be messy because they tend to surface and make themselves heard, usually at the most inopportune time.[9]

There are other reasons not to ignore or suppress emotion. Emotion plays many important roles: it motivates us to act; it provides us with important information about ourselves, the other party, and the negotiation; it helps organize and sharpen our cognitive processes; and it enhances the process and outcome of a negotiation when used strategically. While the emotion we experience provides us with information, the emotion we display provides information to others that can be an incentive or deterrent to their behaviour. In particular, "[n]egative emotions serve as a call for mental or behavioral adjustment whereas positive emotions serve as a cue to stay the course."[10] In a negotiation, the party who expresses a positive emotion may be signalling the importance of an interest or issue that may help in

---

3   For more about incidental emotions, see J.S. Lerner, "Negotiating Under the Influence" Harvard Negotiation Newsletter (June 2005) at 3.

4   D.L. Shapiro, "Enemies, Allies and Emotions: The Power of Positive Emotions in Negotiation" in M.L. Moffitt & R.C. Bordone, eds., *The Handbook of Dispute Resolution* (San Francisco: Jossey-Bass, 2005) 66 at 68.

5   A. Damasio, *The Feeling of What Happens: Body and Emotion in the Making of Consciousness* (San Diego: Harcourt, 1999) at 41.

6   *Ibid.*

7   M.A. Neale, "Emotional Strategy" Harvard Negotiation Newsletter (February 2005) at 3.

8   J. Gross & I. Richards, "Forget the Stiff Upper Lip" (2005) New Scientist 13.

9   D. Stone, B. Patton & S. Heen, *Difficult Conversations: How to Discuss What Matters Most* (New York: Penguin Books, 2000) at 87.

10   J.T. Cacioppo & W.L. Gardner, "Emotion" (1999) 50 Annual Review of Psychology 191.

expanding the pie and brainstorming. In contrast, the party who expresses a negative emotion may be signalling that a reservation point or limit is close. Further, a negotiator who expresses anger may be revealing the strength of his alternatives.[11]

It is becoming increasingly clear that in order to become a truly skillful negotiator, it is important not only to employ cognitive strategies and skills but also to be emotionally intelligent. Negotiating using cognitive strategies and skills alone is like building a house with tools and materials to construct the outside but no tools and materials to finish the interior. The whole tool box of emotion and cognitive skills is needed to enrich, enhance, and inform the negotiation experience. There are many advantages to being an emotionally intelligent negotiator. For example, an emotionally intelligent negotiator is able to gather more and richer information about the other side's underlying interests and reservation points; can more accurately evaluate risk, which leads to better decision making; can better perceive opportunities to use negotiation strategies and tactics that involve emotions; and can more successfully induce desired emotions in negotiation opponents.[12]

This chapter discusses various techniques and tools related to becoming a more emotionally intelligent negotiator. To a large extent, these discussions follow the broad dimensions of emotional intelligence put forward by Peter Salovey and John Mayer[13]: emotional awareness and perception (in self and others), regulation of emotion, and the use of emotion in creative and adaptive ways.

Emotional awareness—being aware of our own feelings as well as those of others—is key to becoming an emotionally intelligent negotiator, but it is elusive in many ways. Understanding the language of emotion and tuning into our body are just two methods, discussed below, that enhance emotional awareness and perception. Research shows that we are very accurate in our reading of the non-verbal emotional signals of others. And it is through such valuable non-verbal information that others reveal their interests, issues, limits, and alternatives, even when they are unaware that they are doing so. Although the focus of this chapter is on your emotions and those of the other side in a negotiation, much of the discussion also applies to the client you represent—particularly that found in the section "Perception of Emotions in Others" below.

It is important to *deal with strong negative emotions* as they arise because negotiations tend to foster such emotions. While in their grip, clear thinking is difficult. We may say and do things that we later regret. We may even give away information that we would rather keep concealed. The techniques and tools presented for dealing with strong negative emotions help keep negotiations on track in the midst of tumultuous emotional upheaval and enhance a positive environment for achieving maximum joint gains. Part of regulating strong negative emotions is learning to anticipate them by understanding and identifying the trigger points that induce them.

---

11   G.A. Van Kleef, C.K.W. De Dreu & A.S.R. Manstead, "The Interpersonal Effects of Emotions in Negotiations: A Motivated Information Processing Approach" (2004) 87 Journal of Personality and Social Psychology 510.

12   I.S. Fulmer & B. Barry, "The Smart Negotiator: Cognitive Ability and Emotional Intelligence in Negotiation" (2004) 15:3 Int'l J. Confl. Mgmt. 245.

13   P. Salovey & J.D. Mayer, "Emotional Intelligence" (1990) 9 Imagination, Cognition and Personality 185.

Becoming an emotionally intelligent negotiator involves not only being aware of and regulating emotions, but also *using emotions in creative and adaptive ways*. As such, we examine current research on the effect of positive and negative emotions and how to use such emotions strategically in negotiations. The section "Putting It All Together" below provides practical information on how to use emotion in a negotiation in a learned and principled way to achieve a desired outcome.

Emotional Awareness

Emotional awareness can be elusive for many reasons. Although we swim in a "sea of emotions"[14] and are in a state of "perpetual emotion"[15] many of us are not aware of what we are feeling, especially when we are intellectually engaged. It is usually only when we are experiencing a strong emotion or feeling that we become aware of it—particularly when it is a negative one.

> There is, however, no evidence that we are conscious of *all* of our feelings, and much to suggest that we are not. For example, we often realize quite suddenly, in a given situation, that we feel anxious or comfortable, pleased or relaxed, and it is apparent that the particular state of feeling we know then has not begun on the moment of knowing but rather sometime before.[16]

We have another significant challenge to becoming emotionally aware: we may find it hard to identify particular emotions we are feeling. Part of the difficulty with identifying emotions is that they can masquerade as other feelings. For example, anger can mask fear, shame, hurt, or self-doubt. If we want to become emotionally aware, we must become adept at unbundling and identifying feelings so that they can be acknowledged and dealt with. Douglas Stone, Bruce Patton, and Sheila Heen[17] suggest that "simply becoming familiar with the spectrum of difficult-to-find emotions may trigger a flash of recognition." Thus, understanding the spectrum of emotions and becoming fluent with the language of emotion can greatly assist in building emotional awareness.

The Language of Emotion

Although most of us struggle to put emotions into words, there are literally thousands of words in the English lexicon to describe different emotions[18] and hundreds of definitions of *emotion*.[19] Here are a few:

---

14   E. Ryan, "Building the Emotionally Learned Negotiator" (2006) Negotiation Journal 209.

15   Shapiro, *supra* note 4.

16   Damasio, *supra* note 5 at 36.

17   Stone, Patton & Heen, *supra* note 9 at 95.

18   D. Keltner & P. Ekman, "Emotion: An Overview" in A. Kazdin, ed., *Encyclopedia of Psychology* (Oxford: Oxford University Press, 2000) 162.

19   Shapiro, *supra* note 4 at 67.

[A]n emotion is a felt experience ... When someone says or does something that is personally significant to you, your emotions respond, usually along with associated thoughts, physiological changes, and a desire to *do* something.[20]

[M]ost agree in defining emotions as brief, rapid responses involving physiological, experiential, and behavioral activity that help humans respond to survival-related problems and opportunities. Emotions are briefer and have more specific causes than moods.[21]

I take emotion to refer to a feeling and its distinctive thoughts, psychological and biological states, and range of propensities to act. There are hundreds of emotions along with their blends, variations, mutations and nuances. Indeed, there are many more subtleties of emotion than we have words for.[22]

Most definitions of *emotion* refer to several components: the feeling of the emotion, thoughts arising out of or in association with the feeling, the physiological changes (for example, changes in heart rate and blood pressure), and the urge to act. These components are important because they allow us to better understand emotions and also create different tools for dealing with them. For example, understanding the thoughts associated with particular emotions allows us to cool those emotions down by applying different labels to them, changing the nature of our thoughts about them, or stopping those thoughts altogether. An understanding of the physiological changes related to emotions allows us to recognize emotions earlier through bodily awareness. There is also a behavioural component to emotion—a propensity to act or a desire to do something. Certain emotions, through physiological changes, prime us to react physically, which can have disadvantages at the negotiation table. When someone is angry, for example, blood rushes to the extremities so that there is less blood to service the higher centres of brain function. This physical reaction provides a very cogent reason for learning to recognize and deal with anger before it can affect our behaviour and cloud our thinking.

The primary emotions, of which all other emotions are blends, are *sadness, anger, fear, enjoyment, love, surprise, disgust,* and *shame.*[23] However, even these primary emotions may be difficult to identify.[24] Figure 9.1 describes a few emotions that are hard to recognize and the feelings with which they are associated. Although figure 9.1 presents only a very short list of emotions, a recent survey of emotional descriptors from thesauri produced a list thousands of words long that, when narrowed down to "discrete emotional concepts," resulted in 412 discrete emotions.[25] These findings underline how extensive and rich the human emotional experience truly is. Figure 9.2 lists a number of positive and negative emotions that negotiators should be aware of, not only in themselves, but also in the other side.

---

20 R. Fisher & D. Shapiro, *Beyond Reason: Using Emotions as You Negotiate* (New York: Penguin Group, 2005) at 4.

21 Keltner & Ekman, *supra* note 18 at 163.

22 D. Goleman, *Emotional Intelligence* (New York: Bantam Books, 1995) at 289.

23 *Ibid.* at 289.

24 Stone, Patton & Heen, *supra* note 9 at 91.

25 S. Johnson, *Mind Wide Open: Your Brain and the Neuroscience of Everyday Life* (New York: Scribner, 2004) at 41.

Figure 9.1   Hard-to-Find Feelings

Love	Affectionate, caring, close, proud, passionate
Anger	Frustrated, exasperated, enraged, indignant
Hurt	Let down, betrayed, disappointed, needy
Shame	Embarrassed, guilty, regretful, humiliated, self-loathing
Fear	Anxious, terrified, worried, obsessed, suspicious
Self-Doubt	Inadequate, unworthy, inept, unmotivated
Joy	Happy, enthusiastic, full, elated, content
Sadness	Bereft, wistful, joyless, depressed
Jealousy	Envious, selfish, covetous, anguished, yearning
Gratitude	Appreciative, thankful, relieved, admiring
Loneliness	Desolate, abandoned, empty, longing

Source: D. Stone, B. Patton & S. Heen, *Difficult Conversations* (New York: Penguin Books, 1999) at 96.

Figure 9.3 presents another categorization of emotions that is helpful in dealing with strong negative emotions: hot and cool feelings.[26] By being able to identify and label hot and cool feelings, we can start to use techniques to move away from hot feelings, which can derail a negotiation, toward cool feelings.

Emotional Self-awareness

The "main stage" or "theatre"[27] for all emotions is the body because emotions and bodily responses are so closely linked. It is in the body that the first indicators of an emotion are felt and can be recognized. When strong negative emotions are recognized early, they can be dealt with more effectively, and the reasons why they arose can be addressed more quickly. The ability to recognize emotions—especially strong negative emotions—in the body is made easier by understanding their corresponding physical signs. Figure 9.4 presents the physical signs associated with anger, rage, fury, depression, despair, despondency, anxiety, fear, and panic.

So, how do you become aware of your emotions as they arise? By tuning in to what your body is telling you. You may be thinking that with so much going on during a negotiation and with so much other information to track, tuning in to your body as well may not only

---

26   S.J. Stein & H.E. Book, *The EQ Edge: Emotional Intelligence and Your Success* (New York: Stoddart Publishing, 2000) at 44.

27   Damasio, *supra* note 5 at 39.

Figure 9.2   Emotion Words

Positive Emotions

Excited	Ecstatic	Elated	Calm
Glad	Proud	Relieved	Hopeful
Amused	Gratified	Comforted	In awe
Enthusiastic	Happy	Content	Wonder
Cheerful	Jubilant	Relaxed	
Jovial	Thrilled	Patient	
Delighted	Overjoyed	Tranquil	

Negative Emotions

Guilty	Disgusted	Outraged	Sad
Ashamed	Resentful	Intimidated	Hopeless
Humiliated	Contemptuous	Worried	Miserable
Embarrassed	Impatient	Surprised	Devastated
Regretful	Irritated	Fearful	
Envious	Angry	Panicked	
Jealous	Furious	Horrified	

Source: R. Fisher & D. Shapiro, *Beyond Reason* (New York: Penguin Books, 2005) at 13.

be difficult but impossible. However, the more often you tune in to your body and listen to what it is telling you, the easier and faster recognizing emotions will become. Do it right now. Is there tension in your upper back and neck as you bend over to read this book? How about your head? Do your legs feel fine or are the muscles in your calves clenched? How about your knees? Is there general muscle tension? How does your gut feel? Are you feeling anxious trying to get this chapter read in time for class? Excited by the new concepts? Bored? (I hope not!) So how long did that check take? About 30 seconds? By learning how your body reveals your inner emotional state, you will not only be more aware of what you are feeling but also be able to discover the onset of emotional states more quickly.

Another technique for becoming aware of your emotions is taking an emotional "temperature" check. Roger Fisher and Daniel Shapiro[28] suggest that you can do this by asking three questions during a negotiation.

Are your emotions

- **Out of control?** Past the boiling point. You are already saying things that are better left unsaid.
- **Risky?** Simmering. They are too hot to be safe for long.
- **Manageable?** Under control. You are both aware of them and able to keep them in check.

---

28   Fisher & Shapiro, *supra* note 20 at 148.

Figure 9.3   Hot and Cool Feelings

Hot Feelings	Cool Feelings
Rage, fury and anger	Annoyance and irritation
Despondency, despair, depression and pessimism	Sadness
Severe guilt, intense remorse	Regret
Self-worthlessness, self-hate	Self-disappointment
Severe hurt	Mild bruising
Anxiety, fear and panic	Concern

Source: S. Stein & H. Book, *The EQ Edge: Emotional Intelligence and Your Success* (Toronto: Stoddart Publishing, 2000) at 45.

Figure 9.4   Physical Signs and Feelings

Feelings	Physical Signs
Anger	Hands-on-hips posture, pounding heart, sweating and rapid breathing
Rage **Fury**	Clenched fists Cold-focused stare, loud and rapid speech
Depression **Despair** **Despondency**	Fatigue Weighted-down posture Slouching, staring into space, a slow, hesitant voice and frequent sighing
Anxiety	Restlessness, pounding heart, rapid breathing
Fear **Panic**	Aching muscles and headaches, tension in neck and shoulders

Source: S. Stein & H. Book, *The EQ Edge: Emotional Intelligence and Your Success* (Toronto: Stoddart Publishing, 2000) at 48.

If you are finding it hard to avoid berating the other negotiator or to concentrate on anything other than your emotions, then you are at least at the risky point.[29]

Perception and appraisal of one's own emotions are central to emotional intelligence. However, equally important in becoming emotionally intelligent is recognizing and dealing appropriately with the emotions of others.

---

29   *Ibid.*

Perception of Emotions in Others

There is a significant advantage to being able to accurately read emotional cues displayed by others during a negotiation. Such cues could well provide information about their reservation point, underlying interests, and constraints that might not otherwise be revealed in conversation. For example, a person might be agitated or display a strong negative emotion such as anger as she approaches her reservation point. A person might show signs of embarrassment when questions are asked about information that he does not want to reveal. People also provide important information on how they cope with such feelings. For example, a person may have an angry facial expression but a tight and controlled body posture. This disconnect may indicate unawareness, denial, or repression. Conversely, a person may have an angry facial expression together with a menacing posture and loud speech. In this case, the person may still be unaware of his feelings but is willing to express them.

It will come as no surprise that most information about emotion is transmitted non-verbally. What is surprising is that research on the general communication of information has found that only 7 percent of communication is verbal while the remainder—a huge 93 percent—is non-verbal.[30] These findings indicate that we get far more information from non-verbal language than we do from spoken words. However, since there is such a myriad of non-verbal information, it is often difficult to figure out what is important and what is just extraneous. Also, some of the popular literature on reading body language erroneously puts forward single and absolute interpretations of gestures—such as crossed arms always signal hostility—without taking into consideration the context of the gesture or the person's typical gestures.

Robert Bolton has developed several guidelines for interpreting non-verbal language that are simple, practical, and effective.[31] He suggests that we focus attention on the most helpful cues; read non-verbal language in context; note incongruities; and be aware of our own feelings and body language.

In terms of where to *focus attention*, most behavioural scientists agree that the face is the most important source of information about emotions. As noted by Paul Ekman and Wallace Friesen:

> The rapid facial signals are the primary system for expression of emotion. It is the face you search to know whether someone is angry, disgusted, afraid, sad etc. Words cannot always describe the feelings people have; often words are not adequate to express what you see in the look on someone's face at an emotional moment.[32]

---

30   R. Bolton, *People Skills: How to Assert Yourself, Listen to Others, and Resolve Conflicts* (New York: Simon & Schuster, 1979) at 78.

31   *Ibid.* at 80.

32   P. Ekman & W. Friesen, *Unmasking the Face: A Guide to Recognizing Emotions from Facial Clues* (Englewood Cliffs, NJ: Prentice-Hall, 1975) at 18.

We are remarkably accurate in our ability to perceive emotion in others by looking at their eyes and surrounding facial tissue, and it appears that we may be hard-wired for such perception.[33] Without any training, we are able to differentiate among many subtle emotions using only this facial area. Perhaps this is why advice about keeping a poker face and displaying no emotion during negotiations is so popular. One caution: when observing facial expressions of the other side, it is advisable to do so in a way that appears natural and non-threatening. You certainly don't want them to become anxious due to your surveillance of them.

An unexpected increase in non-verbal liveliness can also tell us what is important to a person. We have all been involved in conversations where we or the other person suddenly becomes animated, as if there has been an extra energy boost. Determining which topic was under discussion during a time of increased animation will reveal what matters to a person. This technique may be of particular assistance when determining underlying interests during a negotiation or in understanding a person more fully.

No single gesture ever stands alone; it usually forms part of a pattern. In addition, a gesture does not have the same meaning from one individual to another. Thus, gestures must be interpreted and understood *in the context of the situation*.[34] This context includes other body movements that are made at the time, the person's words at the time, and the typical gestures of that person. If a person seldom crosses her arms, when she does it could well mean that she is distancing herself from the topic under discussion or indicating hostility. However, if she tends to cross her arms all the time, especially when she is relaxed, then you will know when she is relaxed. Sudden changes, especially changes in the position of the torso, can convey important information. Sudden leaning forward or moving backward may indicate the level of interest in the discussion; however, it is important to take the individual's typical movements into account before drawing such conclusions.

Another guideline for interpreting non-verbal behaviour is to *note any incongruities* between the words spoken and the body language displayed. For example, shouting the words "I am not angry" while appearing red in the face and banging the table shows a big discrepancy. When there is such disconnect between the words spoken and the body language displayed, both messages are important. A person who bangs the table while denying anger is clearly conflicted about feeling angry and most likely unable to admit to such feelings.

Surprisingly, we can become better aware of what other people are feeling through our own feelings. There is new research indicating that the brain contains neurons, called *mirror neurons*, that respond in the same way to others' emotions as if we were feeling the emotions ourselves.[35] Scientists have postulated that these types of neurons underlie the human capacity for empathy. It is possible that mirror neurons might even be related to the unconscious activity of mirroring the actions of others when we are in sync with them during a conversation. In fact, therapists mirror the actions of patients intentionally to better understand what they may be feeling.

Emotions are contagious. Perhaps one reason some movie stars get paid incredible amounts is that they are able to make us feel good; when they smile, we smile. In a negotiation, if

---

33   Johnson, *supra* note 25 at 19.

34   Bolton, *supra* note 30 at 84.

35   D. Dobbs, "A Revealing Reflection" (2006) 17:2 Scientific American Mind 22.

another person is tense or anxious, we may also start feeling that way in response. Our reaction to the emotions of others may also explain how things can get emotional so quickly in a negotiation—we may "catch" a strong negative emotion by seeing it displayed by another person. The expression "he made me so mad" has new meaning based on these recent findings from the neurosciences. The idea that an emotion we feel may not even originate with us makes it even more important to be able to deal with strong negative emotions as they arise in a negotiation.

Dealing with Strong Negative Emotions

Negotiations, due to their nature, create and foster strong negative emotions. Where individuals meet to primarily promote their self-interests or where the past histories of the parties involved have been coloured by acrimony, it is not surprising that sometimes emotions are more powerful than facts in determining the course and outcome of negotiations. And, as indicated above, even if a strong negative emotion is not generated by us, the operation of mirror neurons may cause us to "catch" it if it is displayed by our counterpart. Not all emotions are triggered by the negotiation itself. Very recent research has shown that a negotiator's emotional state created by events unrelated to the negotiation, called *incidental* emotions, also affects that negotiator's behaviour and the negotiation outcome.[36]

The main assertion in this chapter thus far has been that emotion should not be ignored or suppressed because it has a very important role to play. However, emotional flooding—when specific, strong negative emotions overwhelm us[37]—can obstruct negotiations in several important ways: it can divert attention from substantive matters; reveal information that we would prefer to keep hidden (because it can be used to manipulate us by the other side); subordinate and disrupt our ability to think; and cause us to lose our temper, stumble over words, and/or neglect the substantive negotiation goals.[38] Suppressing emotion is not the answer. Doing so can lead to many unwanted consequences, some of which are similar to the disruptive effects of experiencing a strong negative emotion. Research indicates that suppressed emotion can lead to anxiety, impaired cognitive ability, reduced memory, a decrease in likeability, and greater competitive behaviour.[39] Suppressed emotion can also leak into an interaction through tone, non-verbal behaviour, and attitude.

So, how can you best handle strong negative emotions in a negotiation? It is important to (1) know your own personal *trigger points* and thus be able to anticipate when strong negative emotions may arise in you; (2) have *techniques and tools* to draw upon to proactively reduce or eliminate the triggers of strong negative emotions during a negotiation and help deal with strong negative emotions as they arise; and (3) *be able to assess* your emotions and their level of intensity as early as possible.

---

36 Lerner, *supra* note 3 at 3.

37 Neale, *supra* note 7.

38 D. Shapiro, "Untapped Power: Emotions in Negotiations" in A.K. Schneider & C. Honeyman, eds., *The Negotiator's Fieldbook: The Desk Reference for the Experienced Negotiator* (Washington, DC: ABA Section of Dispute Resolutions, 2006) 263 at 264.

39 *Ibid.* at 264; Neale, *supra* note 7 at 3.

Emotional Trigger Points

The two negative emotions that have been found to affect negotiations most often and most dramatically are anger and fear.[40] Thus, identifying negotiation situations and subjects that trigger anger and fear is a very important first step in learning to deal with such emotions. Anger can be triggered by violating rules[41] or assumptions[42] and by threats to our identity.[43] For example, if our assumptions about fairness, truthfulness, trust, or concession-making are violated, anger can be triggered. Once we recognize the assumptions that we are operating under, we can consider whether they are valid in the circumstances or not. Other triggers can include rudeness, time constraints, disregard for relationship, misrepresentation, excessive demands, the illegitimate exercise of another's authority, and challenges to a person's authority.[44]

Threats to our identity have the potential to disrupt our sense of self in the world or dash our ideas about who we think we are. Our identity comprises those stories we tell ourselves about who we are, and there are as many identities as there are people.[45] Negotiation seems to trigger several common identity issues, including *Am I competent? Am I fair? Am I a good person?* Threats to our identity are profoundly disturbing. They can easily knock us off balance and trigger strong negative emotions such as anger—even if we are unaware of the cause. The *Am I competent?* issue tends to be particularly important to lawyers—and can encompass concerns about being right, effective, and intelligent.

We cannot entirely protect ourselves against threats to our identity, just as we cannot eliminate our vulnerability. However, there are two ways to temper our reactions in the face of such threats. The first is to become aware of our particular identity issues (especially those that might come up during a negotiation), and the second is to avoid the all-or-nothing way of thinking about identity. For example, instead of saying "I'm either competent or incompetent, fair or unfair, good or evil," expand your thinking to include, "I can be both wrong and competent."[46]

Strong negative emotions can also be triggered by undesirable traits we see in others that we believe are not a part of us. These traits, or characteristics, make up our *shadow*. Since most of us are blind to our shadow, we strongly react to our undesirable characteristics in others.[47] In negotiations, the commonly held bias that we are cooperative and the other person is hostile and competitive[48] appears to be based on shadow projection. In other

---

40   R.S. Adler, B. Rosen & E.M. Silverstein, "Emotions in Negotiation: How to Manage Fear and Anger" (1998) 14:2 Negotiation Journal 161.

41   *Ibid.*

42   B. Gray, "Negotiating with Your Nemesis" (2003) 19 Negotiation Journal 299.

43   Stone, Patton & Heen, *supra* note 9 at 111.

44   Adler, Rosen & Silverstein, *supra* note 40.

45   Stone, Patton & Heen, *supra* note 9 at 112.

46   *Ibid.* at 114.

47   Gray, *supra* note 42 at 304.

48   Adler, Rosen & Silverstein, *supra* note 40.

words, this bias may arise due to the projection of our undesirable traits, or shadow, onto the other person in an unconscious attempt to keep from seeing it in ourselves. Shadow dynamics can impede negotiations because they trigger strong negative emotions and provide "hot buttons" for others to push. If you find yourself consistently overreacting to someone or to certain kinds of behaviour, try to identify what is triggering your response.[49] It just might be your shadow.

It is also possible to react negatively to another negotiator we have never met before based on his or her resemblance to someone who affected us emotionally in the past. Often this reaction occurs without our awareness of the resemblance, so this trigger point is particularly hard to identify and understand. If you have gone through all of the other types of trigger points and none of them seem applicable, it could be that you are dealing with a resemblance trigger. Figure 9.5 presents a checklist that may help you identify trigger points in a negotiation.

Figure 9.5 Trigger-Point Checklist

What Does It Involve?	Description
☐ **Violations of assumptions or rules**	Are my standards of fairness being violated? Is the common bias operating about my being cooperative and fair while the other party is hostile and competitive? What rule or assumption that I hold is being violated by the other's behaviour?
☐ **Identity issues**	Has something been raised that questions what I tell myself I am or hope to be, such as *Am I competent? Am I fair? Am I a good person?*
☐ **Shadow characteristics**	Is the other person demonstrating undesirable characteristics that I possess but will not admit to (dishonesty, incompetence, meanness, unfairness, etc.)?
☐ **Reminder of unpleasant past events or persons**	Does this situation remind me of a past unpleasant experience? Does the other person remind me of someone with whom I have had an unpleasant experience in the past?
☐ **Core concerns not being met**	Are my ideas, thoughts, and actions being devalued? Am I not being treated with respect but treated as an adversary? Is my freedom to make decisions being impaired? Am I being treated as inferior to others? Is my current role not personally fulfilling?

Note: This checklist can also be used to analyze the other side's strong negative emotions.

---

49   Gray, *supra* note 42 at 306.

Fear, the other emotion that most often affects negotiations, may be triggered by feeling unprepared or inadequate, being unable to deal with the other side, having a poor BATNA (best alternative to a negotiated agreement), or facing a more powerful opponent. Some people even suffer from fear of fear—that is, they fear the physical symptoms of fear. As with anger, the way to deal with fear involves being aware of it first and then using techniques to address it.

Techniques for Handling Strong Negative Emotions

It is important to note that even being aware of and recognizing our emotions may not be enough to control behaviour. Due to the way the human brain works, sometimes very strong negative emotions, such as extreme fear or rage, may lead us to act before we are even aware of the emotion. Also, most of our blood rushes to our extremities when we experience anger. So, although we are well prepared for a physical fight or for flight, our problem-solving abilities are not at their optimum, to say the least. Thus, it is ideal to be able to head off strong negative emotions before they arise; that is, to anticipate when they may arise and create an environment that will minimize their occurrence. If and when they do arise, it is important to be able to deal with them as early and as quickly as possible.

The various techniques and tools discussed below for dealing with strong negative emotions work well at different stages in the negotiation process. Some help deal with emotions when they arise during a negotiation, while others help anticipate and dissipate emotions even before they have the chance to arise.

During the Negotiation

Taking a Break

So, how do you control the strong negative emotions you feel and may act upon during a negotiation? Several techniques can help you immediately detach from the thoughts and events that are generating the emotion. Seeing the interaction from a distance allows calm rationality to prevail, and this gives you time to better analyze what is happening. The first group of techniques involves *mental pauses or breaks*:

- Say "let me think about that."
- Use an imaginary "pause button." Visualizing a big round red button and pressing it while you distance yourself from the immediate exchange will help you distance yourself mentally.
- Focus on physical sensations in the environment. Listen to the air flow in the room, feel the sensation of your body on the chair, your hand on the table, the position of words on a piece of paper. All of these will allow you to calm your mind.
- Think of a relaxing scene that you love and that touches you. It may be your backyard in the summer, a flower, your child's face, a beach. Any of these scenes will transport you away from the current situation.
- Adopt a relaxed position—find the tension in your body and relax it intentionally.

The second group of techniques involves *taking a physical break*, actually removing yourself from the negotiation:

- Take a break for coffee or lunch.
- Take a break to use the bathroom facilities.
- Halt the negotiations and schedule them for another time. You can preface this move by "I think this is a good time to take a break from negotiations."
- If you are negotiating on the phone, say that someone needs you urgently and that you will call them back. However, use this technique sparingly and only if you are unable to deal with strong negative emotions in other ways.

A break lets you step away and become a detached observer—to figure out what you are feeling and why. William Ury describes this technique as "going to the balcony."[50] As you relax and distance yourself emotionally, think about how to react constructively. Breathing techniques are very beneficial to achieving calm during both mental and physical breaks. Taking a deep breath in through your nose and letting the air out slowly through your lips will help you calm down. Similarly, taking a deep breath and letting the air out all at once, as if you were sighing, will also help you calm down. Deep breathing activates the parasympathetic part of the autonomic nervous system—the part you want activated during stress so that you can relax. However, be careful about using the second breathing technique around other people; they might think you are expressing frustration, despair, despondency, boredom, anxiety, or fatigue.

Changing Your Emotions

Emotions are not fixed—they are fluid and can be changed. Hot feelings, which are less adaptable and rational, can be changed to cool feelings, which are healthier and less volatile. Thus, one way to deal with a strong hot negative emotion is to change it into a weaker or cooler emotion. Since our feelings are related to our thoughts and beliefs, we can change our feelings by changing our thoughts and beliefs.[51] One simple way to change our thoughts about a feeling is to redefine it. For example, instead of labelling the emotion you are feeling as fury, identify it as irritation or annoyance instead. This small step can change how you perceive the emotion and consequently change how you feel it. Other examples include redefining depression as sadness, severe guilt as regret, and anxiety as concern.

Still another way to change an emotion is to look at the thoughts fuelling that emotion. Negotiators tend to have a bias that they are more cooperative than their counterparts and that such counterparts are more competitive and hostile.[52] Based on this bias, a strong negative emotion could be created by the thought that the other side is intentionally violating standards of fairness, standards that you are upholding to your detriment. You may even tell yourself that the violation is a personal slight. However, if you were aware of your thoughts and what you were telling yourself, you would be able to change the thoughts and stop the emotion from building momentum. You would be able to look at the situation more objectively and determine whether your assessment is accurate. In a calmer state the

---

50   W. Ury, *Getting Past No: Negotiating with Difficult People* (New York: Bantam Books, 1991) at 16.

51   Stein & Book, *supra* note 26 at 44.

52   Adler, Rosen & Silverstein, *supra* note 40.

behaviour of the other side, if unfair, could be addressed in a constructive manner using, perhaps, the communication techniques discussed below.

Using Communication Techniques

There are specific communication techniques that are particularly effective in defusing competitive verbal moves that are typically used to throw us off balance by evoking strong negative emotions. These moves can include challenging competence or expertise, demeaning ideas, criticizing style, and making threats.[53] These techniques are varied and include taking a break, naming the move, questioning the move, correcting the assertion with accurate information, and diverting the focus back to the substance in question. Examples of these techniques, or "turns," appear in figure 9.6. Active listening is yet another technique that works well to deal with a competitive move.

Another technique for minimizing strong negative emotions is expressing yourself assertively when others are acting aggressively toward you. Most people find it hard to be assertive and instead take a stance that is either too hard (aggressive) or too soft (submissive). Figure 9.7 presents examples of all three stances. The "too hard" stance involves a very strong position that does not take into account the other person's feelings or beliefs. In contrast, the "too soft" stance has no regard for the speaker's concerns or feelings. The "just right" (assertive) stance allows the facts, as viewed by the speaker, to be brought forward with an openness that both invites and allows the other party to respond.

Creating an assertive message can be difficult and, therefore, having a basic structure to work with is helpful. One that works well is the three-part assertive message put forward by Bolton.[54] The three-part message consists of (a) a non-judgmental description of behaviour, (b) disclosure of how you feel about the effect of the other's behaviour on you, and (c) a description of the concrete or tangible effect on you of such behaviour. For example, you may tell the other negotiator that setting the agenda without your input makes you feel unfairly treated because items that are important to you are not included. Or that when the other side is consistently late for the negotiations, you feel frustrated because of the time wasted while you wait for them. Figure 9.8 presents examples of assertive messages that use the three-part structure.

An assertive message allows for firmness without dominance and should satisfy the following six criteria:[55]

1. There is a high probability that the other person will alter the troublesome behaviour being dealt with.
2. There is a low probability that you will violate the other person's space.
3. There is little likelihood of diminishing the other person's self-esteem.
4. There is a low risk of damaging the relationship.
5. There is a low risk of diminishing motivation.
6. There is little likelihood that defensiveness will escalate to destructive levels.

---

53   D. Kolb, "Staying in the Game" Harvard Negotiation Newsletter (December 2003) at 3.

54   Bolton, *supra* note 30 at 140.

55   *Ibid.* at 142.

Figure 9.6   Examples of Turns

Turns	Examples
INTERRUPTING **Take a break**	"Let me think about that"/ "Let's take a break"/ "Let's get a coffee"
NAMING **Signal you recognize the move**	"You're questioning my credibility"/ "You're undermining my authority"
QUESTIONING **Question the substance of the statement or rephrase the attack by turning the description of your behaviour into a question**	"Unreasonable?"/ "Unfair?"
CORRECTING **Correct the accusation or implication**	"These are not my settlement figures, these are industry standards"/ "Here are the fees charged by others—our fees are competitive"
DIVERTING **Ignore the move and refocus on the problem**	"I would like to explore the concerns you have"/ "Let's discuss some other options"

Source: Based on the moves and turns set out in D. Kolb, "Staying in the Game" Harvard Negotiation Newsletter (December 2003).

Figure 9.7   The Three Stances

Issue	Stances
There are errors in the figures provided by the other side.	**Too soft:** "This is probably stupid, but these figures don't seem to add up to me." **Too hard:** "Are you trying to rip me off?" **Just right:** "Let's look at these numbers. There appear to be discrepancies we should look at."
The other side is not making any concessions on any issue.	**Too soft:** "I'm not sure that I have this right, but it seems to me that you have not made any concessions." **Too hard:** "What's with you? Don't you even know how to make concessions? Wasn't that in the 'Negotiation for Dummies' book?" **Just right:** "On several of the issues I have made concessions from my initial position. Please help me to understand why you are not also able to make concessions."

Source: Based on the Goldilocks Test from K. Patterson *et al.*, *Crucial Conversation Tools* (New York: McGraw Hill, 2002) at 133.

Figure 9.8   Examples of Three-Part Assertive Messages

Description of Behaviour	Disclosure of Feeling	Description of Tangible Effect
When you use my car and don't refill the gas tank	I feel unfairly treated	because I have to pay more money for gas.
When you borrow my tools and leave them out in the rain	I feel annoyed	because they become rusty and don't work well.
When you call me at work and talk at length	I feel tense	because I don't get all my work done on time.
When you do not put your dirty clothes in the hamper	I feel irritated	because it makes extra work for me when I do the wash.

Source: R. Bolton, *People Skills: How to Assert Yourself, Listen to Others, and Resolve Conflicts* (New York: Simon & Schuster, 1979) at 153.

Expressing yourself assertively will prevent emotions from building momentum and allow you to deal with bothersome behaviour or issues in a way that is both constructive and affirmative. In contrast, once emotions have built up, expressing them in inappropriate ways can be damaging to the relationship and counterproductive to achieving your negotiation goals. If you decide to express your emotions to the other side, express them appropriately. Don't vent, because venting may make the situation even worse. Be clear. Describe your feelings carefully. Don't attribute blame or judge—just share. Try to relate the emotional tone to the substantive issue. An important part of communicating about your emotions is tying your emotions to your negotiation goals; for example, expressing your frustration about the progress of the negotiation due to interests that are being ignored.

Emotion provides important information to you and the other side. If you are able to express emotion in a constructive way and at an appropriate time in the negotiation, rather than destroy or hurt the negotiation process, emotion can greatly enhance it.

Before the Negotiation Begins

Having techniques and tools to deal with strong negative emotions as they arise in a negotiation is important. However, Fisher and Shapiro assert that it is even more important to anticipate that strong negative emotions may arise and proactively stimulate positive emotions in a negotiation instead.[56] They propose that when negotiators address five core concerns—appreciation, affiliation, autonomy, status, and role—strong negative emotions can be anticipated (and, it is hoped, minimized). Fisher and Shapiro suggest that the core concerns be used as a *lens* to understand the emotions of each side and as a *lever* to stimulate positive emotions. Figure 9.9 presents the five core concerns and what happens when each is ignored or met.

---

56   Fisher & Shapiro, *supra* note 20 at 14.

Figure 9.9   The Five Core Concerns

Core Concerns	When the Concern Is Ignored ...	When the Concern Is Met ...
Appreciation	Your thoughts, feelings, or actions are devalued	Your thoughts, feelings, and actions are acknowledged as having merit
Affiliation	You are treated as an adversary and kept at a distance	You are treated as a colleague
Autonomy	Your freedom to make decisions is impinged upon	Others respect your freedom to decide important matters
Status	Your relative standing is treated as inferior to that of others	Your standing, where deserved, is given full recognition
Role	Your current role and its activities are not personally fulfilling	You so define your role and its activities that you find them fulfilling

Source: R. Fisher & D. Shapiro, *Beyond Reason* (New York: Penguin Books, 2005) at 17.

The central premise put forward by Fisher and Shapiro is that these five core concerns motivate people in a negotiation; when both sides feel their concerns are met, the relationship will be enhanced and the negotiation outcome will be improved. So, for example, to create a positive negotiation environment, you will want to be respectful and appreciative of the other party's ideas, interests, thoughts, and behaviour. As well, you will want to be respectful of the other side's autonomy—including their ability to make decisions.

Support for the five core concerns comes from research on words and phrases that trigger emotional responses. For example, labelling other people negatively and telling them what they should or should not do triggers the greatest number of emotional responses—the most typical one being anger.[57] Thus, during the negotiation planning stage, think about how to address the five core concerns and perhaps even create some key phrases to use during the negotiation.

Negotiating without a plan to deal with strong negative emotions has been compared to working in a hospital's emergency department without procedures and protocols in place for dealing with new patients.[58] Thus, it is important to find out which techniques and tools work best for you and are easiest to use. Experiment with them during uncomfortable conversations rather than waiting to try them out during a longer negotiation. Taking a break is always a good technique to use because it is easy to do; it allows you to stop reacting, and it permits you to become more analytical about what is happening. As part of your negotiation planning, list any responses, topics, behaviour, and attitudes that have triggered

---

57   H.A. Schroth, J. Bain-Chekal & D.F. Caldwell, "Sticks and Stones May Break Bones and Words Can Hurt Me: Words and Phrases That Trigger Emotions in Negotiations and Their Effects" (2006) 16 Int'l J. Confl. Mgmt 102.

58   Fisher & Shapiro, *supra* note 20 at 149.

strong negative emotions in the past during conversations or other negotiations. Try to ana-lyze whether your core identities or shadow characteristics were involved in your response. By doing this work, you will be able reduce the occurrence and strength of your emotional responses and, as a result, be better able to deal with them. Also, by becoming more aware of core concerns and trigger points, you may be better able to anticipate and reduce the chance of evoking strong negative emotions in others.

Using Emotion and Mood Strategically in Negotiations

Becoming an emotionally intelligent negotiator involves not only the awareness and regula-tion of emotion but also the creative and adaptive use of emotion. So, how do you use emotion strategically in a negotiation? As mentioned above, Fisher and Shapiro cogently argue for the use of the five core concerns as levers to create and enhance positive emotions in order to achieve a better negotiated outcome. Recent research has shown that both emotion and mood can have an effect on the behaviour of the negotiator experiencing them, on the other party perceiving them, on the relationship between the parties, and on the negotiated out-come. However, the strategic use of emotion raises significant ethical issues. See chapter 5 for more discussion on ethics in negotiation.

Thinking Inside the Box ...
Ethical Issues

Is the tactical manipulation of your own emotions or those of others in the pursuit of your negotiation goals ethical? Is faking anger or frustration similar to using a tactic such as misrepresentation of information? Or is it more like lying? What about creating the experience of an emotion in yourself to enhance your performance? Is that differ-ent from expressing an emotion in order to affect your counterpart's experience and behaviour? Does the purpose matter? Is it unethical when it is used for selfish or even nefarious ends but ethical when used to further joint gains? What about when it is used to enhance the relationship with the other party? What about the intentional triggering of strong negative emotions in others? Is that less ethical than fostering positive emotions in others?

Research Findings on Positive and Negative Emotions and Moods

Numerous researchers have examined the effects of positive and negative emotions and moods on various aspects of negotiation. A few definitions are needed at this point to understand the findings. *Positive emotions and moods* are those we experience as pleasant, and *negative emotions and moods* are those we experience as unpleasant. *Mood* refers to a more diffuse psychological state and is of a more enduring quality than emotions, which tend to be of high intensity, short duration, and directed at an object, person, or event.[59] The term *affect*, as used here, encompasses both mood and emotion. Researchers have examined affect in various ways, including how it can induce positive emotion and elevated moods in subjects and how it can be used to coach subjects to display a specific emotion. The influence of positive and negative affects has been found to be consistent for the most part, thus, the discussion that follows is based on this division.

POSITIVE AFFECT: MAKING FRIENDS AND INCREASING JOINT GAINS

The negotiator who displays positive affect has been shown to achieve greater cooperation and enhance the quality of the agreements reached. Specifically, the negotiator's positive emotional state or mood increases concession making,[60] stimulates creative problem solving,[61] increases joint gains,[62] reduces the use of contentious tactics,[63] increases preferences for cooperation, increases the use of cooperative negotiation strategies,[64] and increases the proposal of alternatives and suggested trade-offs.[65] Positive affect also has been shown to lead to better decisions and improved results for the negotiator displaying the affect.[66] Thus, the findings are consistent that negotiators who experience positive affect tend to be more cooperative, conciliatory, and creative. Not surprisingly, this cooperative, conciliatory, and creative behaviour has been found to result in higher joint gains on integrative negotiation tasks in numerous experiments.[67]

Until recently, research in this area has focused on the effect of emotional *experience* on the behaviour of the person feeling the emotion and the substantive outcome (intrapersonal effects) rather than the effect of one party's emotional *expression* on another's behaviour and the substantive outcome (interpersonal effects). Due to the varied and rich information

---

59   Van Kleef, De Dreu & Manstead, *supra* note 11.

60   R.A. Baron, "Environmentally Induced Positive Affect: Its Impact on Self-Efficacy, Task Performance, Negotiation, and Conflict" (1990) 20:5 Journal of Applied Social Psychology 368.

61   A.M. Isen, K.A. Daubman & G.P. Nowicki, "Positive Affect Facilitates Creative Problem Solving" (1987) 52 Journal of Personality and Social Psychology 1122.

62   K. Allred *et al.*, "The Influence of Anger and Compassion on Negotiation Performance" (1997) 70 Organizational Behavior and Human Decision Processes 175.

63   P.J. Carnevale & A.M. Isen, "The Influence of Positive Affect and Visual Access on the Discovery of Integrative Solutions in Bilateral Negotiation" (1986) 37:1 Organizational Behavior and Human Decision Processes 1.

64   J.P. Forgas, "On Feeling Good and Getting Your Way: Mood Effects on Negotiator Cognition and Behavior" (1998) 74 Journal of Personality and Social Psychology 565.

65   Kopelman, Rosette & Thompson, *supra* note 1.

66   Van Kleef, De Dreu & Manstead, *supra* note 11.

67   See Kopelman, Rosette & Thompson, *supra* note 1 for a review of studies.

that emotion conveys to others, the interpersonal effects of emotion are an important area of concern. In studies looking at such effects, participants were coached in displaying positive, negative, and neutral emotions. In three different types of situations, the expression of positive emotions was found to encourage the continuation of longer term relationships, help close deals in ultimatum situations, and allow the positive negotiator to get more concessions from the other party.[68]

In addition to obtaining a better substantive outcome, positive affect has also been found to increase the affective and relational satisfaction of the parties in a negotiation. Specifically, the display of positive affect encourages the continuation of longer term business relationships,[69] increases the report of a positive negotiation experience,[70] and increases the chance that an opponent will speak highly of the positive negotiator and portray that negotiator as fair and cooperative.[71] Perhaps an underlying basis for both increased joint gains and relational satisfaction is the trust that is created through the display of positive affect. The display of positive affect has been found to communicate one's trustworthiness and cooperativeness to others,[72] which, in turn, engenders more trust in a negotiation situation. Greater trust would correspondingly increase the degree to which interests are revealed and enhance the possibility for higher joint gains.

If experiencing and displaying positive emotions clearly helps reach substantive and relational goals, how then can you stimulate positive emotions in others? Researchers have induced elevated mood and positive emotions through humour, small gifts, pleasant scents, and positive performance feedback. Therefore, you may want to provide compliments and positive feedback to the other side during a negotiation as well as inject humour or jokes to create a more positive negotiating environment. Sales people often use the latter technique because making a joke typically puts people at ease and elevates their mood. People who are in a good mood are more likely to agree with you and buy what you are selling.

Meeting the five core concerns will also stimulate positive affect in others. For example, acknowledging the other person's thoughts or feelings as having merit or treating her like a respected colleague as opposed to an adversary will go far in creating a positive working environment for the negotiation. Positive emotions that have been found to promote the integrative process include excitement, enthusiasm, and happiness.[73] So, expressing these types of emotions will also help create positive feelings in the other party. To stimulate positive emotions in yourself just before starting a negotiation, try reading funny cartoons or think positive things about the negotiation. For example, think about the great facts you

---

68   *Ibid.*

69   *Ibid.*

70   M. Der Foo *et al.*, "Emotional Intelligence and Negotiation: The Tension Between Creating and Claiming Value" (2004) 15 Int'l J. Confl. Mgmt 411.

71   Kopelman, Rosette & Thompson, *supra* note 1.

72   C. Anderson & L.L. Thompson. "Affect from the Top Down: How Powerful Individual's Positive Affect Shapes Negotiations" (2004) 95 Organizational Behavior and Human Decision Processes 125 at 127.

73   Allred *et al.*, *supra* note 62.

have, the wonderful opportunity this is for you, the fabulous agreement that is possible, and the great relationship with the other side that will be created through this negotiation.

Although early research found that positive negotiators also realized higher individual gains on both integrative and distributive tasks than did negotiators in a neutral affect mental state,[74] more recent findings suggest that only negotiators displaying negative emotions realize higher individual gains.[75]

Negative Affect: Getting the Biggest Piece of the Pie

In contrast to the results of positive affect studies, negotiators experiencing negative affect have been shown to decrease initial offers, promote rejection of ultimatum offers, increase the use of competitive strategies, achieve fewer joint gains, refuse offers that served their economic interests, and decrease the desire to work together in the future.[76] These results consistently show that negotiators experiencing unpleasant affect tend to be more competitive and reluctant to make concessions. Anger, in particular, has been shown to cause bigger risk taking, more errors to be made, and greater financial loss in negotiations.[77] As such, many researchers have concluded that negative feelings have a negative impact on negotiations.

Advantages to using negative affect have been found in the research on *emotional expression of anger*. In face-to-face negotiations, anger was found to be every effective in extracting value where the other party perceived her options as weak.[78] This result appeared because a strategic display of anger communicates toughness, and more concessions are made to an opponent perceived as tough. Therefore, where there is a power imbalance, the negotiator with better alternatives can get an even bigger share of the negotiated resources by strategically expressing anger. The same effect was found when the negotiator's negative emotion was conveyed verbally. Subjects who thought they were facing a negative negotiator made larger concessions. Similarly, when participants were told about the other party's emotional state in a computer-mediated experiment, they conceded more to an angry opponent than to a happy one, but only when they were motivated to get a deal quickly.[79] Thus, greater individual gains have been obtained by expressions of anger both in face-to-face and computer-mediated negotiations, but only where other factors were operating as well. Despite the potential advantage of greater individual gain, such strategic use raises significant ethical issues.

These findings on negative affect highlight the need to be aware of our emotional states or we will negotiate under the influence of emotion—to our detriment. For example, experiencing negative affect may interfere significantly with carrying out a strategy that involves

---

74   Kopelman, Rosette & Thompson, *supra* note 1 at 83.

75   M. Sinaceur & L.Z. Tiedens, "Get Mad and Get More Than Even: When and Why Anger Expression Is Effective in Negotiations" (2006) 42 Journal of Experimental Social Psychology 314.

76   See Van Kleef, De Dreu & Manstead, *supra* note 11 for a review of studies.

77   Lerner, *supra* note 3.

78   Sinaceur & Tiedens, *supra* note 75.

79   *Ibid.*

creating value. On the other hand, it may enhance the execution of a claiming strategy. Since *experiencing* negative affect has been shown to interfere with clear thinking, the best approach is to *express the negative emotion* only and not experience it. Unfortunately, there is a fine line between expressing emotion and experiencing it; faking an emotion may in fact create it. So, when strategically expressing negative emotions, be careful that you do not start to experience such emotion. Another reason why strategically expressing negative emotions is risky business is that emotions are contagious—we can give them to others. For example, a negotiator who displays hostility may breed further hostility in the other side, which can lead the negotiation to spiral out of control. And, thus, what started out as a negotiation strategy to get higher individual gains could easily disrupt and possibly derail the entire negotiation. Clearly, it is far safer and more advantageous to employ a positive affect strategically.

Putting It All Together

The central premise of this chapter is that in order to become a truly skillful negotiator, it is important not only to be able to use cognitive strategies, tools, and techniques but also to be emotionally intelligent. The various skills, techniques, and tools relating to becoming a more emotionally intelligent negotiator have been discussed and follow, to a large extent, three broad dimensions of emotional intelligence: emotional awareness and perception (in self and others); regulation of emotion; and the use of emotion in creative, adaptive, and ethical ways. So, how then do you put together all of this information in preparing for and navigating a negotiation session?

At the negotiation planning stage, after you have determined your substantive goals and your strategy, emotion and mood can be used tactically to assist the process. If you are planning to use an integrative strategy and want to foster creativity, trust, and cooperation, you will want to create positive affect in yourself and others—by experiencing it, expressing it, and stimulating it in others. If the negotiation involves parties with whom you already have or wish to have a long-term relationship, you will want to employ positive affect. Techniques for creating positive affect include using the five core concerns as levers, displaying positive affect such as happiness, excitement, and enthusiasm, and elevating your mood by reading humorous cartoons and thinking positive thoughts about the negotiation before you come to the table. If the negotiation is entirely distributive, then you may wish to employ negative affect, especially where the other side wants a quick agreement or has weaker alternatives than you do. However, the expression of negative emotion is a risky business for many reasons. So, before deciding to employ negative affect for negotiation gain, it is best to be fully aware of the risks involved.

Immediately before the negotiation starts, check your mood. If you are in a low mood and you want to create positive affect, you will need to employ some of the techniques discussed above to elevate your mood. If you are already in an elevated mood and feeling good—then carry on. In contrast, if you intend to use competitive tactics only (and this would be a rare situation) and you are in an elevated mood, you may wish to think depressing thoughts before the negotiation.

To ensure a positive environment *at the beginning of the negotiation,* focus on the relationship with the other side and try not to be distracted by what they may do. If they do or say something that is adversarial, then take a break (mentally or physically) to focus on and accentuate the positive aspects of the relationship. Go through the five core concerns in your mind and find a way to get things back on a positive track. If their behaviour has been aggressive, you may want to use some communication techniques such as the three-part assertive message or some of Kolb's turns.[80]

During the negotiation, especially a contentious one, tune into your body periodically and do temperature checks. If you are experiencing strong negative emotions, take a break—either mentally or physically. During the break, you may want to use the techniques that change hot feelings into cooler ones. Once you are calmer and more detached, you can decide how to get the negotiation back on track. You may want to ask yourself how the other side is feeling. If you still want to foster a positive environment, use the tools and techniques that help with that. You may want to use communication techniques to respond in a constructive way to the aggressive moves of the other side. You may also want to take the time to assess whether the strong negative emotion was triggered by identity issues or shadow characteristics. During the negotiation session, be perceptive and watch for signs of emotion in the other person. Doing so can provide invaluable information.

At the end of the negotiation, especially where you want to promote positive future relationships, ensure that you leave the other side feeling good. Take time to foster good feelings and speak positively about the process and the result. Of course, you want to be truthful so you will do so only where the process and the results have been creative and integrative. Emphasize your pleasure in dealing with the other side. Remember that if they leave with good feelings, they will most likely speak highly of you and portray you as fair and reasonable.

Summary

Emotion is an integral part of negotiation. Thus, in order to become a truly skillful negotiator, it is important not only to employ cognitive skills and strategies but also to be emotionally intelligent. In this chapter, various skills, techniques, and tools for becoming a more emotionally intelligent negotiator are discussed. To a large extent, the discussions follow the broad dimensions of emotional intelligence involving emotional awareness and perception (in self and others); regulation of emotion; and the use of emotion in creative, adaptive, and ethical ways. *Emotional awareness* of our own feelings as well as those of others is key to becoming an emotionally intelligent negotiator. It is important to *deal with strong negative emotions* as they arise because negotiations tend to foster them, and while in their grip, clear thinking is difficult. The techniques and tools presented not only help keep negotiations on track during emotional upheaval but also help anticipate strong negative emotion and stimulate positive affect. The *creative and adaptive use of emotions* is also paramount, and current research on positive and negative affect is examined in light of how to use emotion and mood strategically in negotiations to achieve a desired outcome.

---

80   Kolb, *supra* note 53.

CHAPTER 10

The Essential Role of Communication in Negotiation

D. Paul Emond*

Introduction

This chapter describes and evaluates the important role that communication plays in negotiation.[1] A communication strategy and the ability to communicate effectively are the principal reasons for a successful negotiation. Conversely, an inability to communicate effectively is almost always the cause of failure in an unsuccessful negotiation. What makes communication just as or more important than other elements in a negotiation, such as planning, preparation, strategy, or tactics? The answer is that communication is more than an essential negotiation skill; it is the essence of a negotiation. It is not an "add on," nice-to-have skill used to enhance a negotiation, but rather an integral part of the very thing itself.

---

* The author wishes to recognize and thank Mark Andrew Wells for his important contribution in the research for and development of this chapter.

1 Much has been written about communication in a negotiation context. Students of the subject will want to review the very good treatment of the subject in the Selected Further Reading section at the end of this chapter.

In this chapter, after outlining the essential role of communication in negotiation, we explore the practical considerations of communication in a negotiation and ask, what is communication and how do negotiators communicate? Next we ask, what is the real purpose of communication in a negotiation? The short answer: it depends on the negotiator's style, where the parties are in a negotiation, and the extent to which the goals of principal and agent are aligned.[2] The purpose of the negotiation and, hence, of communication itself changes as the parties and their representatives move through the stages of a negotiation. Thus, it is important to understand those stages and how communication is used at each stage to further the negotiating goals of the parties. That leads to the next topic: what specific communication skills does an effective negotiator have? We discuss a number of key skills, profile the effective execution of each skill, and then examine some common mistakes negotiators make when employing that skill. Then, we turn to the negotiating context and examine briefly the role communication plays in a complex, multi-party negotiation in which communication is occurring between principal and representative, among members of a negotiation team, across the table, and between negotiating parties and their constituents.

Although the communication skills of the effective negotiator are the same regardless of context and whether the negotiator is a representative or the principal, how these skills are employed can vary dramatically.

Communication: Its Essential Role in Negotiation

Quintessentially, negotiation is communication.[3] This proposition is neither novel nor groundbreaking. Although the type of communication used and the role that it plays vary from negotiation to negotiation, communication remains the cornerstone of the process. However, to understand the relationship between negotiation and communication and the role that the latter plays in the former, we must first define each of these terms.

Negotiation has been defined in many ways. Herb Cohen, author of *You Can Negotiate Anything*, holds that negotiation is "the use of information and power to affect behaviour within a 'web of tension.'"[4] It is a "field of knowledge and endeavour that focuses on gaining

---

2   In this chapter the terms "principal" and "client," and the terms "representative" and "agent," are used interchangeably.

3   Definitions of negotiation frequently highlight the central role of communication. See D. Pruitt & P.J. Carnevale, *Negotiation in Social Conflict* (Buckingham, UK: Open University Press, 1993) at 154-63; "Negotiation," online: Wikipedia <http://en.wikipedia.org/wiki/Negotiation>— "Negotiation ... a discussion between two or more parties aimed at resolving incompatible goals"; D.A. Lax & J.K. Sebenius, *The Manager as Negotiator: Bargaining for Cooperation and Mutual Gain* (New York: Free Press, 1986)—"[N]egotiation [is] a process of potentially opportunistic interactions"; R. Fisher, W. Ury & B. Patton, *Getting to Yes: Negotiating Agreement Without Giving In*, 2d ed. (New York: Penguin, 1991)—"Negotiation is ... a back and forth communication designed to reach agreement."

4   H. Cohen, *You Can Negotiate Anything* (New York: Bantam Books, 1988) at 16.

favour of people from whom we want things."[5] Elsewhere, negotiation has been defined as the exchange of ideas with the intention of changing relationships.[6] All of these definitions underscore the requirements of a negotiation: there must be parties who come together in order to achieve a goal. However, either explicit or implicit in each of these definitions is the notion of an exchange of information. *Communication* can be defined as "the imparting or interchange of thoughts, opinions, or information by speech, writing, or signs."[7] It can also be thought of as "the passing of information in humans, animals, computers, or any other cognitive entity. Human communication refers to the social interaction of giving and receiving information for the purpose of not only understanding, but also facilitating social connection."[8]

When these definitions are juxtaposed, it becomes apparent that it is impossible to arrive at a negotiated agreement without some form of communication. For a negotiation to progress, negotiators must communicate to the other party their issues, interests, positions, and goals. This point suggests why communication is inextricably bound to negotiation. Many authors have noted this relationship. H. Peyton Young suggests that negotiation "is communication, direct or tacit, between individuals who are trying to forge an agreement for mutual benefit."[9] Another author contends that "negotiation depends on communication."[10] Moreover, because it occurs between individuals, negotiation can be considered an element of human behaviour.[11]

No matter how you conceptualize or define negotiation, you cannot avoid the conclusion that communication is not just an integral part of any negotiation framework, it is the essence of negotiation. Although the success of a negotiation may not derive from effective communication alone, negotiation failure is almost inevitably correlated with a failure to communicate effectively. Perhaps Roy Lewicki, David Saunders, and John Minton describe the nexus between negotiation and communication best: "communication is at the heart of the negotiating process. Although planning, preparation and strategizing are all key negotiation elements, communication is the central process by which these elements are enacted. Communication processes, both verbal and nonverbal, are critical to achieving goals, and to resolving conflicts."[12]

---

5   *Ibid.* at 15.

6   G.I. Nierenberg, *The Art of Negotiation: Psychological Strategies for Gaining Advantageous Bargains* (New York: Cornerstone Library, 1979) at 8.

7   "Communication," online: Webster's Dictionary <http://dictionary.reference.com/browse/communication>.

8   "Communication," online: Wikipedia <http://en.wikipedia.org/wiki/Communication>.

9   H.P. Young, "Negotiation Analysis" in H.P. Young, ed., *Negotiation Analysis* (Ann Arbor, MI: University of Michigan Press, 1991) 1.

10   Nierenberg, *supra* note 6.

11   *Ibid.*

12   R.J. Lewicki, D.M. Saunders & J.W. Minton, *Negotiation*, 3d ed. (Toronto: McGraw Hill, 1999) at 141.

Communication in the Context of a Negotiation

Communication has already been defined as an exchange of information between parties. However, this is only a cursory explanation. To better understand communication, we must delve deeper. In the context of negotiation, communication is, first and foremost, a human process that reflects the many characteristics of the negotiator. It is both interactive (a message usually elicits a response) and dynamic. The result is a dialogue, an exchange in which negotiators establish a rhythm of ask, counter ask, ask; or, present, respond, and present again. Response to and questions about what is received are both reactive (it is a reaction to the opinion expressed or question asked) and proactive (it is designed to elicit a particular response). Communication behaviours are learned—they are what have worked for negotiators in general, and what is working for a negotiator in a specific negotiation.

Briefly, then, communication is the art and science of sending a message from one person to another and, equally important, the art and science of receiving a message. For that to happen, the sender's message (thought) is encoded, most often in words, and then transmitted via a channel to the intended recipient, who in turn decodes the message.[13] The meaning of the message is found in the message itself and captured by the expression, "I mean what I say." But as we all know, what is said is sometimes not what is heard or understood. Words do not have a strict 1:1 correlation between sender and receiver. The same words can and often do mean different things to different people. Thus, while the encode–decode paradigm is frequently used to describe communication, it fails to capture the idea that communication is a human process and not merely a mechanical process. As a human process, it is important that the listener understands the intention that lies behind the speaker's message. But again, problems abound, particularly if the speaker's intention is contained in a non-literal message. One of the best examples of the divergence between a literal and intended message is Nikita Khrushchev's "threat" in 1956 to Western ambassadors.[14] Khrushchev's message was "obvious": a belligerent Soviet leader was quoted as saying "we will bury you," threatening the West. However, a more complete version of the quotation reads: "Whether you like it or not, history is on our side. We will bury you," which was meant to suggest that the Soviet Union would outlast the West and "*attend* your funeral" rather than "*cause* your funeral." In the absence of mutually shared knowledge, values, and ideologies (common ground), it is easy to misunderstand a non-literal statement. Khrushchev's intended message was not the received message.

---

13   In this way, a thought is encoded as a message, sent or transmitted over a channel to a receiver, who in turn decodes the message. The decoded message prompts a thought, which in turn is encoded as a message and transmitted across a channel to the original sender as a response. This model is best captured by E. Shannon and W. Weaver in their book *The Mathematical Theory of Communication* (Urbana, IL: University of Illinois Press, 1977).

14   This example was cited by R.M. Krauss & E. Morsella, "Communication in Conflict" in M. Deutsch & P.T. Coleman, eds., *The Handbook of Conflict Resolution* (San Francisco: Jossey-Bass, 2000) at 131-43.

The danger of misconstruing another's intention is especially high when the speaker uses non-literal meaning. It increases even more when the deeper meaning of the speaker's message is dependent upon cultural knowledge. Think of the phrase "Go ahead, make my day."[15] Unless both the speaker and listener share the same cultural background, the phrase is meaningless or, worse still, likely to be completely misinterpreted. The speaker can overcome these problems by sending messages that will lead to the desired interpretation on the recipient's part. How is this done? First, the speaker must imagine how her message will be received. The question is not "What do I mean by this?" but rather "How is my counterpart likely to understand what I am saying?" This means understanding one's message from the recipient's perspective and that, in turn, requires finding out what is and is not common ground. To do that, the speaker may have to enlarge her message. The listener must also search for the real message, and that means stepping out of the role of passive recipient and actively seeking the information needed to understand the meaning of the message. In this collaborative process, the speaker rephrases and expands the message; the listener raises questions and clarifies ambiguous declarations as each struggles to find the real meaning in the message.

Communication is even more problematic if a negotiator does not know what she (or her principal) wants, and the reasons that lie behind the wants, or if a negotiator is trying to mislead another party about those wants. In the first case the verbal messages sent will be confused and garbled, and in the second, the verbal and non-verbal messages will be contradictory. The garbled message stems from a confusion over the real goal of the negotiator— not simply what she is trying to achieve, but why she is trying to achieve a particular result. Inconsistent messages, on the other hand, occur because the verbal message will not usually be aligned with the non-verbal message. When a negotiator is trying to mislead the other side, words will say one thing while body language will usually say another. The recipient wonders, what is the real message? This problem was captured by Barbara Madonik.[16] How do you read visual and auditory cues, and how do you make sense of a communication when the auditory message (the spoken word) is not consistent with the visual message? Of the two messages, which one is authentic? As Madonik points out, it will almost always be the non-verbal message.

Similarly, problems can occur at the receiver's end of the communication. The sender's intention is important, but so too is the recipient's point of view. For the speaker to communicate effectively, he must imagine the point of view of the listener. If the speaker can accurately imagine the listener's point of view, especially in a complex negotiation, the message can be tailored to that point of view. But imagining another's point of view requires one to make assumptions about what the listener knows, and that is difficult, even if the two share a similar background. If there are no shared experiences, or if assumptions are clouded by stereotypes of the other, it is almost impossible.

Not only is communication an essential part of every negotiation, it is also a part of the process that is fraught with problems. As easy as "sending a message" to the other side may

---

15   An expression made famous by Clint Eastwood as Dirty Harry in the 1983 film *Sudden Impact*. Again, this example is cited in Krauss and Morsella, *ibid*.

16   B.G. Madonik, *I Hear What You Say, But What Are You Telling Me? The Strategic Use of Nonverbal Communication in Mediation* (San Francisco: Jossey-Bass, 2001).

appear to the novice negotiator, effective communication is a complex, difficult, and many-faceted process. The efficiency and accuracy of the communication process will depend on the sender's capacity to correctly encode a message and the recipient's ability to correctly decode the message, something that typically occurs only after a series of exchanges between the parties, especially if they do not know one another. Indeed, experienced negotiators will encourage frequent exchanges during the early stages of a negotiation to identify and correct communication errors.

How Do Negotiators Communicate?

Before looking in detail at how negotiators communicate and, specifically, the communication channels over which messages are sent and received, it is important to note how communication typically occurs. Face-to-face communication is used most frequently, although electronic communication is quickly making face-to-face communication less important, a matter we examine in more detail later in this section. When communicating face to face, a portion of the message is sent across an auditory channel (the verbal context), and a much larger portion is sent across a visual channel (the non-verbal context). The auditory channel can be further subdivided into two parts: the verbal context (the words spoken) and the vocal qualities of the speaker (the tone, pitch, tempo, pace, and volume of auditory communication). When one combines the communication that occurs over the visual channel (both facial expression and body language) with the communication sent by the vocal qualities over the auditory channel, the two represent 70 to 80 percent of the message. Add to that the body movement that is often used to enhance communication—the nod of the head, the hand gesture—and the non-verbal message increases to almost 90 percent.[17] In other words, it is not *what* a negotiator says that is important; it is *how* she says it.

The channels across which negotiators communicate often contribute to message failure. Face-to-face communication engages all channels: verbal (speech) as well as non-verbal (visual, auditory, and kinesthetic). And, while communicating over multiple channels provides many opportunities for messages to be sent, reinforced, and clarified, doing so can also result in miscommunication, a topic we'll examine in a moment. First, it is important to note that as channels are removed (for example, the visual channel is taken away when the negotiators communicate by phone), a negotiator's capacity to communicate is reduced. When a negotiator communicates over a single channel (print), as is the case when negotiations are conducted via email, the potential for miscommunication increases significantly, because the conduit over which a message is sent is rather impoverished. In other words, the potential for accurate communication is reduced as the number of channels over which the message is sent is reduced. Unless the spoken or print message is reinforced by visual, auditory, and kinesthetic messages, it is more likely that the message will be misinterpreted. There is, however, an advantage to using a single communication channel, namely, that there is less likelihood for inconsistent messages or messages that are inappropriately amplified or exaggerated by non-verbal communication. For those whose face gives away an attempt

---

17   A demonstration that begins with "let me show you" or "perhaps this will be clearer if I demonstrate" is an example of this form of non-verbal communication.

to bluff, the bluff is better sent via email than delivered at a face-to-face meeting. For those who have little to say or offer, the offer is best made face to face where it can be enhanced.

When negotiators communicate over multiple channels, the level of background noise increases so that the potential for miscommunication increases.[18] The children's game "broken telephone" provides a good example of the effects of noise along a channel. In the game, a message is passed along a "telephone wire" made up of several participants. After relatively few message exchanges, the initial message in the game becomes badly distorted, largely as a result of the "noise" along the route—the noise of extraneous information, wrong interpretations of what was said, unwarranted elaboration, too succinct summaries, distractions in the room, and so on. The more elaborate the channel (by *elaborate* we mean both the number of channels and the number of people involved in sending and receiving messages), the greater the noise; the greater the noise, the more likely the message will be distorted. This is a special problem for negotiators because while channels may add to the richness of the communication, they also "add to the noise." The more intermediaries that one adds to a negotiation, the more likely the message will be distorted. The dilemma that this creates for negotiators is this: the richer the channel, the fuller the message—something that is essential in a complex negotiation; but that, in turn, increases the noise level along the channel. The solution—and it's easier stated than implemented—is to maintain a favourable "signal-to-noise ratio." In other words, employ communication channels that are rich enough to convey the intended message, and yet not so complex that the noise drowns out or distorts the message. This solution suggests that simple, direct communication is always better. Taken too far, however, "simple" communication can become the source of the problems described above. That is, if a channel being used (email, for example) is not sufficiently rich to fully deliver a complex message, the result is that the message received is only a small portion of what the sender intended. Add to that the (mis)perceptions of the receiver when decoding "simple" print messages, and the problem of miscommunication is magnified.

The use of email in negotiation is growing, so it is worth examining the communication problems associated with it in more detail. It used to be that face-to-face negotiation was commonplace and that negotiation where both parties were not physically present in the same location and at the same time was rare. However, the information age has unequivocally altered the very course of human social interaction. Internet access and email usage are ubiquitous. Even the technology by which these forms of communication can be accessed has changed. No longer are individuals bound to a desktop computer. The Internet can be accessed through wireless devices such as laptops, handhelds, and cellphones. In the context of negotiation, technology has led to the proliferation of faceless communication: faceless or single-channel communication is now the norm rather than the exception.

What effects have these faceless communication channels had on the process and the outcomes of negotiation? First, it is important to note that electronic communication creates a context in which communicators "experience the other person as more distinct and unknown, and less salient and identifiable."[19] There is a complete absence of visual and social cues.

---

18   *Noise* simply refers to background distractions that take away from or distort the core message. Noise may relate to the channel (negotiations conducted in a noisy restaurant or via a poor telephone connection) or the message itself. Our focus in this section is on message noise.

19   L.L. Thompson, ed., *Negotiation Theory and Research* (New York: Psychology Press, 2006) at 149.

Faceless negotiation requires each party to interpret information being received from the other side, without the benefit of the elaboration that occurs over other communication channels:

> Visual cues convey information about the other person's facial expressions, gestures and posture. In addition, visual cues allow each person to see what the other person is looking at and doing. When I see that your attention is directed toward me, I am likely to feel more involved in the interaction, and vice versa. Being in the same place at the same time also gives rise to a sense of shared surroundings. Communicating via e-mail or IM (Instant Messaging), by contrast, often involves being in a room alone, for many minutes or even hours at a time. E-mail and IM are text based, so that communicators are unable to hear one another's voice, which eliminates cues derived from intonation and the timing of speech.[20]

Another feature of communication via email is the lack of co-temporality; "that is, when people communicate face to face, each person receives the other person's utterances at the time that they are spoken. By contrast, messages sent by e-mail are not typically read by the receiver at the same time they are sent, but often minutes, hours or even days later."[21] The result is that email communication reduces any social bond that would have been formed had the communication been face to face. The other party is perceived as less known and individualized, a stark contrast to how a person would be perceived, had the interaction been face to face.

Although "e-negotiations" have their advantages (convenience and less noise, to name two), they clearly have their disadvantages. One shortcoming is that email may not be the most appropriate channel given the subject matter, the stage of the negotiation, and the relationship between the parties. Negotiation is a complex, multi-stage process in which each stage plays a pivotal role in the communication between parties. As such, communication by some channels, such as email, may not be appropriate during the early stages of the negotiation, especially in complex multi-party negotiations where the need for the parties to connect with each other is greatest (especially if they are strangers). During the later stages of the negotiation, however, email communication may be most appropriate, because the lack of visual and auditory cues (distractions) forces the parties to focus on the substance of the message and the emerging agreement.

The channel(s) over which a message is sent determines, in part, the recipient's response. With email, people pay more attention to the message being disseminated, and less on the person sending the message. The impact of attending to the message can have implications for all stages of a negotiation, but particularly the later stage, when the focus is on persuading another. For example, a strong argument in a negotiation is more successful when made by telephone or via email rather than face to face, because the recipient's focus is on the message. On the other hand, a weak argument has a greater likelihood of success when a negotiator presents it face to face. Email encourages negotiators to focus on the quality and content of the positions taken or arguments advanced by the other party, whereas face-to-face negotiation leaves the parties more susceptible to being misled by the other through external and

---

20   *Ibid.* at 149-50.

21   *Ibid.* at 150.

peripheral factors. Said another way, a strong argument is more likely to be accepted when sent via mail; a weak argument is more likely to be accepted in a face-to-face encounter.

Knowing the potential communication pitfalls of e-negotiations is the first step to circumventing their effects on the negotiation process. We have suggested that the use of email may not be appropriate depending on the type and stage of negotiation, and the relationship between the parties. We have also suggested that negotiators must be alert to the advantages and disadvantages of communicating and negotiating via email. It is difficult if not impossible to create a blueprint that prescribes the ideal communication channel for negotiation. All negotiations are different. However, reflecting on the negotiation and the relationship between the parties before selecting a channel, such as email, can help the negotiator avoid some of the problems associated with e-negotiations. While face-to-face communication addresses many of the problems noted in e-negotiations, it creates, as noted above, other challenges.

There is, however, much that can be done to improve all forms of communication. Before we propose improvements, let us state again the obvious: in the context of negotiation, communication is a human process that reflects the many characteristics of the negotiator. It is also a collaborative process: meaning is created not only through the message sent and received but also through the many exchanges that take place between negotiators. While the starting point is words and how they are amplified by both the speaker's and listener's intention and point of view, the real message is only uncovered by the joint work of the negotiators.

Messages that are incomplete or distorted by background noise invite the recipient to "fill in" the missing information or the distorted message. This is how the recipient makes sense of the message sent. Unfortunately, "filled in" information is likely to further obscure and distort the message. The solution is for the sender to be redundant by stating and restating the same idea in different ways. The more ways an idea is expressed, the more likely it will be understood. This advice applies equally to the sender and the receiver: the former should look for alternative ways to express the same idea; the latter should keep asking for clarification and elaboration.

So the essential choice facing a negotiator is either a face-to-face or at least voice-to-voice interaction, or a faceless, voiceless print exchange. In some ways the disadvantages of one are the advantages of the other. In face-to-face negotiation, negotiators use several communication channels, thereby increasing both the richness of the message and the background noise. In faceless negotiation, negotiators eliminate the background noise but are confronted with the problem of a channel that may not be sufficiently rich to convey the whole message. Whatever the channel selected, sensitivity to the advantages and disadvantages of each, and the use of redundancy, will be essential if negotiators are to communicate effectively.

Factors That Influence Communication Goals in a Negotiation

Communication does not occur in the abstract. Nor is it happenstance or haphazard. Negotiators communicate for a reason, and, as a result, their communication is always purposeful. In the broadest sense, communication is designed to carry out a negotiation strategy, and that strategy normally reflects the style of the negotiator. It is also designed to accomplish very specific goals over the course of a negotiation. In this section, we first describe the two principal negotiating styles, the strategy and tactics that fit those styles best, and the type of communication that supports each strategy. Second, we explore how communication goals change as negotiators move through integrative and distributive parts of a negotiation. Third, we examine briefly the seven stages of a typical negotiation,[22] how a negotiator's objectives for each stage change, and the effect of that change on communication. Finally, we examine briefly the sometimes divergent goals of the representative negotiator and the represented party. In many ways, the negotiation and communication goals of the two are closely aligned, but in other respects they may be different. What impact does that have on communication and the negotiation?

Negotiation Style

Negotiators fall into two main types: competitive and cooperative.[23] A particularly adept negotiator can move from one style to another, depending on the negotiation style adopted by her counterpart. However, most negotiators have a preferred style and negotiate best within that style; they also use the communication strategy that is best aligned with that style most effectively. A cooperative negotiator's style is distinguished by moves *toward* the other side. As a result, the cooperative negotiator communicates to establish common ground, emphasizes shared values and objectives, and demonstrates a genuine interest in the other side. These goals are accomplished with a voice that is even-toned, reassuring, and sincere; and body language that includes frequent eye contact, and confident, self-assured smiles. In contrast, a competitive negotiator's style is distinguished by moves *against* the other side. The competitive negotiator communicates with threats, ridicule, sarcasm, and displays a general lack of interest, in both the other negotiator and the goals of the opposing client. The competitive negotiator's voice is loud, often confrontational, and generally dominating and controlling. Body language can send an equally confrontational message when arms are crossed, there is frequent head shaking, and there is a reluctance to make eye contact.

For the cooperative negotiator, discourse is best characterized as an exploration in search of a mutually acceptable solution. For the competitive negotiator, it is an argument involving the presentation and rationalization of one's position, combined with an attack on the other side's position. If the cooperative negotiator appeals to fairness and a win–win solution, the competitive negotiator appeals to logic and accepts the inevitability of a win–lose result.

When we look at the communication strategies and tactics designed to carry out the objectives of each negotiation style, the differences between the two are even more pronounced.

---

22   While the description of negotiation stages suggests that negotiations typically move in a linear and chronological fashion through each stage, the reader is reminded that this is a description of an ideal that is seldom seen in practice. Negotiations are messy, reflecting the push and pull of many factors and are likely to include loopbacks to earlier stages as the negotiations move forward.

23   G.R. Williams, "Style and Effectiveness in Negotiation" in L. Hall, *Negotiation: Strategies for Mutual Gain* (Newbury Park, CA: Sage, 1993).

The cooperative negotiator begins with realistic openings and reasonable demands; the competitive negotiator does just the opposite. The cooperative negotiator offers concessions to match and even exceed those of the other side; the competitive negotiator makes extreme demands, often escalating over time, with few and usually disproportionately small concessions. While one is prepared to share information and explain and seek to understand the other side's interests; the other releases information gradually and is disinclined to correct wrong perceptions, especially if the perception is advantageous to her and her client. One is upfront about needs, the other creates false issues. One makes fair, objective statements of facts; the other stretches and exaggerates the facts and is continually bluffing about her client's strengths, options, and interests. If open questioning, active listening, and reframing are the preferred communication tools of the cooperative negotiator, then leading questions, distortions, ridicule, and interrogations are the modus operandi of the competitive negotiator. The communication strategies of the two types of negotiator are very different, with each strategy designed to support very different goals for and approaches to negotiation.

Integrative and Distributive Bargaining

While the underlying communication goals are certainly influenced by the style or approach of the negotiator, where the parties are in the negotiations also affects what a negotiator is trying to achieve and how communication strategies are used to achieve these objectives. Negotiations typically move through two quite distinct and yet broad bargaining phases. The first is often described as integrative bargaining. During this phase, negotiators identify the interests and issues of each party, explore options for addressing those interests and needs, and then propose exchanges (often mutually beneficial[24]) that will meet those interests and needs. In this phase, communication tends to be exploratory (discovering each party's needs) and collaborative (determining what exchanges will best meet each party's needs). The goals of communication during this early phase are to establish a good rapport, understand interests, explore outcome options, and search for mutually beneficial exchanges. If mutually beneficial exchanges do not lead to full agreement (and usually they don't), then the negotiation typically moves on to a second phase, distributive bargaining—in which the gains of one party are losses for another. At this point, the goals of communication and indeed the communication itself change quite dramatically. Exploration, problem-solving, and collaborative communication strategies now give way to communication strategies that are designed to claim rather than create value. During this phase, even cooperative negotiators can find themselves using threats, demands, and "take it or leave it" offers as each side tries to win a larger piece of the proverbial negotiation pie. No longer are exchanges mutually beneficial; they are now individually beneficial. The negotiation moves from the potential for further win–win solutions (the hallmark of the integrative phase) to the prospect of a win–lose result, and this is certainly reflected in how negotiators communicate.

---

24 An exchange is mutually beneficial because the parties value things differently. Thus, a concession on something a party values less in return for a gain on something that the party values more is beneficial. If the other party valued the two items in such a way that the exchange was also beneficial, then the exchange is mutually beneficial.

Stages of a Negotiation

While most negotiations move from the value-creating tactics of the integrative bargaining phase to the claiming tactics of the distributive bargaining phase, these two general phases do not capture the many smaller, more discrete stages through which a typical negotiation progresses. In the same way that negotiation and communication strategies change as the negotiation moves from an integrative to a distributive phase, so too communication changes as a negotiation moves through these smaller, discrete stages. The description that follows assumes a "typical" seven-stage negotiation. As the negotiation moves from stage to stage, the way in which the parties communicate changes, with each change corresponding to a new goal or purpose.

A formal negotiation usually begins with an opening stage where negotiators attempt to create an environment that is conducive to achieving their outcome. From there, the negotiation moves to an educative stage where negotiators attempt to "learn" about the interests (goals) of the other side, and "teach" the other side about their interests. This stage often involves questions that pry into the positions that parties open with to learn what is "really" important. In the same vein, it also involves providing more information about one's own (or the client's) goals than what was disclosed at the opening of the negotiation. From here, negotiators typically move to a third stage in which interests are converted into issues, and this conversion process continues until each side is satisfied that they have a complete list of issues. At this point the negotiations move into the middle stages where, first, negotiators begin to prioritize issues. Once that is complete, the ensuing list typically becomes the agenda, which in turn structures and controls the subsequent discussions. The fifth stage provides the parties with an opportunity to generate, explore, and test proposals (options) for addressing each party's interests as they relate to the issues. From idea generation and testing, the typical negotiation then moves to a bargaining or exchange stage. This is the point at which the negotiation moves into the final or later stage. At this point in the negotiation, early exchanges are likely to be mutually beneficial and integrative; later ones are more likely to be individually beneficial and distributive. From here the parties move toward agreement and the drafting stage of the negotiation.

The Goal(s) of the Agents

The preceding discussion assumes that the goals of the representative negotiator (the agent) are fully aligned with those of the client, and that the communication strategies of one are supportive of the goals of the other. That may not be the case, and when it is not, it may lead to different communication strategies and the two communicating at cross purposes. This is a topic that is explored elsewhere in the text.[25] Suffice it to say, the circumstances that give rise to a divergence between the goals of the agent and principal are many and varied. They range from the way in which the agent is remunerated for his or her negotiation services to the reputation and professional responsibilities of the negotiator, particularly if she is a lawyer or an accountant, and required to adhere to a professional code of conduct. The point here is that the goals and responsibilities of the agent may be different from those

---

25   See parts II and III of this text.

of the principal, and this difference will have some effect on how an agent communicates on behalf of the principal.

The following list presents some of the potential differences between agent and principal and their impact on communication.

Difference	Impact on Communication
• Negotiation style	Differences in style are likely to lead to a "good cop, bad cop" communication strategy.

• Agent remuneration
  – Fee for success
  – Fee for time
	The first form of remuneration may lead to early concessions in search of a quick agreement; the second may lead to "endless" requests for additional information as the agent maximizes time spent on the negotiation.

• Reputational goals	The reputation and reputational goals of the two will lead to communication strategies best aligned with each goal.
• Professional responsibilities	An agent's membership in a professional association may limit or constrain the communication strategies used.

This section has argued that the way in which a negotiator communicates will be influenced by communication goals, and that these goals are influenced by such factors as the negotiating style of the negotiator; whether the negotiation is primarily integrative or distributive; and where the negotiators are in the negotiation (early, middle, or late stage). The goals of the agent may also be different from those of the client, and this may create some strain on the way in which one communicates on behalf of the other, with the agent pursuing one objective and communication strategy and the client another.

Having examined how negotiators communicate and the goals of that communication, it is now appropriate to examine the specific communication skills that negotiators employ.

The Communication Skills of an Effective Negotiator

The four principal communication tasks of negotiators are (1) gathering information; (2) conveying information; (3) guiding the negotiation; and (4) persuading another. While the particular communication skills that support a task may be used at any point in a negotiation, they are most effective when used with the task for which they were designed.

As noted earlier, communication skills generally correspond to certain steps or stages in a negotiation. The skills related to gathering and conveying information (questioning, listening, responding, and presenting) are used primarily during the early stages of a negotiation. Those related to guiding the negotiation (framing and reframing) are used during the middle stages. The skill related to persuading another (argument) is used most effectively during the later stages. Negotiators use communication skills whenever they think those skills will be most effective, and, hence, the correlation that is proposed here is by no means exact.

Before we examine the communication skills mentioned above, it is useful to consider these skills in the context of the language we use—whether it is the words we use to ask a question, express an idea, or make an argument. That context is one that is dominated by metaphors to the point that Deborah Tannen asserts, "We are what we speak."[26] How do we speak? As she and others have pointed out, we talk about things, especially topics at the negotiation table, as if it were a war. And the language of war that we use shapes our and the other side's perception of the issues faced by the parties. If you call it a *war*, if you describe negotiation as a *zero-sum game*, then that is what it becomes. "Language," according to Tannen, "invisibly molds our way of thinking about people, actions and the world around us."[27] And, having encouraged us to think about something one way, it becomes difficult to consider it another way. How questions are asked, presentations are made, and arguments put forward influences the reaction received. The challenge for effective negotiators is to choose metaphors and language appropriate for the negotiation and their negotiating goals, and that may mean analogizing the negotiation to performing a symphony rather than waging a war.

In the Early Stages

GATHERING INFORMATION

The key skills here are questioning, responding, and listening. A question prompts another to respond with an answer that conveys information. Listening, on the other hand, is designed to ensure that what is conveyed is received. Questioning is proactive in the sense that it prompts the speaker to speak and convey information; in contrast, listening is reactive and largely passive. Listening provides the receptacle into which information is deposited. However, the way in which listening occurs—either actively or passively—will generate more or less information, depending on the extent to which the listening encourages or discourages the speaker.

(i) Questioning

Good questions are never pointless. They have a purpose, and that purpose will reflect an underlying hypothesis that the questioner has of the negotiation or that fits a negotiation strategy. Questions are designed so that the questioner can learn something, deliver a message, create a tone or mood, or change the direction of the negotiation. This section assumes that the primary purpose of a question is to gather information (ideas, facts, opinions), while recognizing that a questioner may have other motives, including the desire to mislead the other party or frustrate the negotiation.

The most successful questioning strategy is one that is designed to gather information with general, open-ended questions that move, over time, to more specific and directed questions. Specific questions might be closed (they admit only a yes/no answer) or even leading (designed to explicitly confirm the hypothesis that lies behind the question). Leading

---

26   D. Tannen, *The Argument Culture—Stopping America's War on Words* (New York: Random House, 1998) at 7, 8.

27   *Ibid.* at 8.

questions should be used sparingly because they can be provocative and because they tend to close down the dialogue that good questions are meant to encourage. Effective questioning generally reflects a "T": the first open-ended questions create a fairly lengthy response that often identifies several issues that a negotiator subsequently investigates using a series of follow-up questions. Thus, a negotiator might start by asking, "what is your client trying to achieve?" or "describe your client's concerns or interests" or "can you elaborate on this?" As mentioned, a response to such questions will normally raise two or more issues, and each will invite further investigation, and that means more questions. The questioner then digs deeper into each issue with a series of follow-up questions, each designed to explore an issue in more detail and from multiple perspectives. As a result, the opening question produces a lengthy response that can be depicted by a horizontal line with several nodes, with each node representing an issue identified in the answer to the opening question:[28]

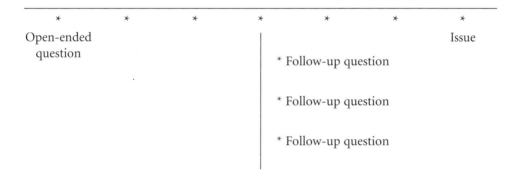

Seizing first on the middle node,[29] the questioner follows up with questions that may follow the chronology of the events related to that issue, or some other pattern of questioning. To flesh out a particular issue, a questioner needs several follow-up questions (five is a minimum, and more if the issue is complex).

One of the most common mistakes negotiators make is starting their questioning with far too specific questions (questions that are simply not open-ended enough) and, as a result, they miss opportunities to learn about the opposing party's other interests and issues. The result is that they have a relatively narrow view of the issues (for example, they focus on money) and their questions reflect that. If you think there is only one or two main issues and ask specific questions about those issues, you will never know what else may be at stake, or what other issues may be explored and whether an exploration of those issues might generate other options.

---

28   Another way to conceptualize questions is to imagine a funnel, with the first questions designed to explore the breadth of an issue and subsequent questions used to delve into the depth of an issue. Subsequent questions become ever more specific and focused, much as a funnel becomes narrower, the deeper you go.

29   Which node or issue a questioner follows up on first will depend on the questioner and her questioning strategy. What is important to note is that the questioner must follow up systematically on all issues in response to the open-ended question.

Another common mistake negotiators make is starting to form a theory of the negotiation and what a good result will look like on the basis of surprisingly little information. After one or two questions some negotiators suddenly think they know where the solution lies. This mistake is especially characteristic of "big picture" negotiators who are continually scanning the information gathered (however little) for trends and patterns. Undoubtedly, patterns do exist, but they seldom present themselves until a negotiator has identified all the issues and fully explored each issue, something that usually means asking five or more questions on each particular issue. By prematurely constructing a theory of a case and then pursuing questioning in light of that theory, there is little prospect of really understanding the case. Effective questioners ask many open-ended questions, seek confirmation that they have a complete picture of the negotiation, and then patiently and carefully construct a theory of the case (and verify its truthfulness), and, finally, explore by way of follow-up questions the opportunities presented by the information obtained.

There are other factors to keep in mind when questioning. Negotiators should keep their questions simple. Compound questions made up of two or more parts enable the other party to answer only one part of the question; and many questioners forget to pursue the unanswered part. Unless a question is fully and completely answered, there may well be need for a follow-up clarifying question on that point—"explain further," "elaborate in more detail," "expand," and so on. Some answers leave a questioner puzzled, even dismayed. In these circumstances it is necessary to seek justification, perhaps by asking for more facts or evidence. If there are apparent inconsistencies in the answers, it will be necessary to clarify by asking the other party to verify facts, information, or feelings that have been expressed. If an answer is implausible, it may be appropriate to conduct a reality check by asking, "The effect or the consequences of your answer is this. Is that what you intend?"

Another useful questioning technique is to ask linking questions. These questions begin with an explanation of an apparent connection that the questioner sees between topics, and then seek more information on the relationship between them. A series of questions are best punctuated with observations from the questioner on what she has heard and what that means for the negotiation, concluded by a summary of what she has learned. A good way to conclude questioning is to ask whether the questioner's summary is accurate and, if not, to clarify or expand as required.

• *An Example of Effective Questioning*

Begin with *open-ended questions*, ones that cannot be answered with a simple yes or no. These are questions on the who, what, when, where, and especially why,[30] and invariably provoke the other side to think and respond.

> Examples: Why are you taking that position in these discussions?
>
> What do you think of our offer?
>
> Who else will be affected by these negotiations?

---

30   Of the list of opening words for these types of questions, "why" questions are the most difficult to manage. They tend to be confrontational and promote judgmental, evaluative, and defensive responses. Remember, the purpose of questioning is not to prove a point (at least not in the

Follow up with planned questions, those that follow a specific sequence; then move on to directive questions and conclude with a combination of leading questions and gauging questions (questions designed to ascertain the other party's thinking or feeling about the negotiation).

Examples: Can you be more specific about that last point? If not, can you indicate when you expect the work will be completed? How soon after that can we take occupancy? What is the proposed rental rate per square foot just after the renovations are completed?

Don't you think our proposal is a fair offer?

What is your reaction to our proposal? Do you have any concerns with it? Can you provide more detail on that last point?

Note that these questions are all manageable. They invite a response—first in general terms, then in more specific terms. The questions don't shut down the discussion; they don't put the other party on the spot and encourage defensiveness; they aren't trick questions; and they certainly don't trigger an emotional and inappropriate response.

(ii) Listening

This is the reactive and largely passive[31] element of acquiring information. Having asked a question, it is now time for the questioner to hear (and see) the answer. For many, this is a chance to "sit back and listen." This is what good questions deserve—an attentive listener, one who is patient and doesn't interrupt. But there is more to listening than "simply" hearing what is said. Listening effectively means being alert to the opportunities to obtain more information than the initial question generated. Some types of listening evoke a much fuller response than others. What are the distinguishing characteristics of the effective listener?

The effective listener is someone who communicates interest and curiosity in a number of different ways. First, the listener is alert to both the verbal and non-verbal messages. She is focused on and engaged with the speaker. She is patient and gives the other time to speak. She is not uncomfortable with silence. She resists the temptation to interrupt and does not argue. She prefers eye contact to note taking, but if it is necessary to take notes, she asks the speaker to slow down or pause. She might preface that request by saying how important the speaker's point is and that she wants to make sure she records it accurately. She sets personal feelings about and reactions to the speaker aside. She displays curiosity rather than disinterest or frustration. She does not rehearse her response while the other person is speaking. She "tells" the speaker by her body language that she is genuinely interested. Eye contact, a nod of the head, an attentive and open posture, and appropriate facial expressions are the hallmarks of an engaged, active, and curious listener.

---

early stages), but rather to promote dialogue so that the parties can probe for underlying issues and test for understanding.

31 The active component of listening is often described as "active listening."

When it is appropriate to intervene, the active listener asks more questions, either to clarify what has been said or to follow up with additional open-ended questions to learn more about a topic. The listener neither evaluates what is said nor offers solutions. Instead, she empathizes with the speaker or the party the speaker represents. If she is confused or unclear about a point, she either asks for clarification or summarizes her understanding and asks the speaker if the summary is accurate and complete. She may repeat or paraphrase a key phrase or sentence to emphasize its importance and demonstrate that the message has been received. The effective listener is genuine and spontaneous, never superficial or formulaic in the questions asked. Finally, if the listener is surprised by a statement or an answer, she might repeat it and seek confirmation that this was indeed what was said. Questioning and listening roles are highly complementary.

The effective listener listens for both the spoken and the unspoken message. She listens for the substantive content and also for the unspoken, emotional components of what is being communicated. She listens and watches to see whether what is said is congruent with the non-verbal messages that are also being displayed. If not, she asks more questions as she attempts to identify the "real" message. Inconsistencies are best resolved in favour of the non-verbal message, as we discussed earlier. But rather than make assumptions about what is real, the effective communicator uses the apparent inconsistency between spoken words and non-verbal cues to explore the issues with more questions.

Michelle LeBaron[32] addresses a number of concerns that negotiators have expressed about active and highly engaged listening. First, negotiators complain that too many clarifying, confirming, and summarizing questions can feel artificial. Certainly, if the questioning is formulaic or overused, not only will it *feel* artificial, but also it will likely *be* artificial. It must be spontaneous, natural, and genuine. Related to the concern about artificiality is the worry that the practice can put the other party off. It can be irritating, even condescending, especially if the more common active listening techniques are overused. For active listening to be effective, it must become part of the normal cadence of conversation.

A second concern is that the speaker might conclude, incorrectly, that an active listener agrees with what is being said. During active listening, the listener must frame her comments clearly and convey to the speaker that while she understands what is being said, that does not mean she is in agreement.

A third concern is that active listening can be counterproductive and lead to less rather than more and better communication. For example, it would be hard to imagine a more provocative and inappropriate strategy than active listening when a speaker is angry. At this point in the "anger cycle," a wise and experienced listener will pass on the opportunity to find out more, or seek confirmation of her understanding of feelings and emotions. Both will have to wait for another time. Active listening at this stage in the negotiation is bound to make matters worse (that is, escalate conflict), not better.

Active listening also assumes that the listener can "read" the feelings that lie behind the substance of a message. This may not be the case, and making wrong assumptions and guesses about another negotiator's or party's feelings is likely to alienate the person questioned,

---

32   M. LeBaron, *Conflict Analysis and Resolution as Education: Culturally Sensitive Processes for Conflict Resolution* (Victoria, BC: University of Victoria Institute for Dispute Resolution, 1996).

especially if done repeatedly. This is especially important for the novice active listener—if you're not sure, then don't do it; if you've tried it and it is not working, then stop. In such circumstances, active listening will certainly be off-putting and likely do more harm than good. It is also fraught with danger in negotiations involving participants with different cultural backgrounds. Cultural differences will always make communication more difficult, but this is especially so with active listening. What is appropriate for one culture may be completely inappropriate for another.

CONVEYING INFORMATION

(i) Responding

Questions elicit responses, some of which are verbal and others non-verbal. The responder or speaker reacts to the question(s) asked and answers. Here again, answers play an important role in the communication that takes place between negotiators. How does one answer a question? Should it be answered at all? Should it be answered, but in a way that blocks the information requested? Should it be answered fully and completely, or narrowly and selectively? Should it be designed to mislead or obfuscate? Answers provide one of the key ways in which information (messages) is conveyed to another.

Answers, like questions, must be purposeful. There must be a good reason to answer, and that good reason will follow from questions such as, What, at this point in the negotiation, am I trying to achieve? What tone is appropriate? Is the time ripe to begin disclosing important or valuable, even confidential, information? Can I take that risk? Is there enough trust among negotiators to justify that response or that much disclosure? If not, what needs to be done to increase the trust level to the point at which a more fulsome response is appropriate? Should the disclosure be made conditionally, and, if so, what conditions should apply? Is it appropriate or necessary to use my answer to educate, to move the negotiation in a different or new direction? These are all important considerations when answering a question.

(ii) Presenting (Asserting)

Information is conveyed independent of the dialogue established through a series of questions and answers. A negotiator may, of course, present a position, make a demand, establish a fact, tell a story, make an assertion, or explain something. Presenting, like questioning, is proactive in the sense that the speaker takes control of and initiates the communication process. Presentations can be provocative in either a negative or positive way. A negative or competitive provocation will generally follow an assertion that is dominating, controlling, degrading, or humiliating. This type of presentation generally frustrates the flow of information and certainly stifles creativity. The recipient of the negative assertion becomes defensive, and once defensive, is not likely to respond to the assertion or participate in an exchange of information and ideas. A balanced or empathetic assertion, on the other hand, one that balances the self-interest of the presenter with the interest of the listener, will create a positive provocation and increase the flow of information by signalling to the other side that the presenter welcomes new ideas.

A presentation may be made orally or in writing. The channel used will likely be a function of the complexity of the negotiation: complex negotiations usually require a presentation in writing; simple negotiations are most likely facilitated with oral exchanges. Often a written presentation will follow with an oral elaboration of the points made in writing. In this way, the negotiator engages both main communication channels: the printed word, which encourages the recipient to focus on the substance of the message; and the oral presentation, which is usually designed to amplify and even exaggerate the strength of the message.

In the Middle Stages

Guiding the Negotiation

(i) Framing and Reframing

Framing is usually used to give the negotiation a direction or focus; reframing is usually used to give the negotiation a different direction or a new focus. It is designed to shift or change the paradigm adopted by a particular negotiator or indeed by all the other negotiating parties. The main focus of this section is on reframing because that is the more important and difficult skill. But first, the student should know that framing is about creating a perspective—often a perspective of what is important (a substantive frame), or of an ideal approach (a process frame), or of what the parties should aspire to (an aspiration frame). Framing occurs early in the middle stages of a negotiation and structures the discussion and bargaining that follows.

Reframing is used to change the initial frame or direction and comes later in the negotiation. Reframing may be done proactively and very simply by the person who controls the agenda, as in: "I'd like to move on to the next topic on the agenda and explore that or those issues." Or, "I think this discussion is no longer fruitful and it is time to move on ..." It can also be done by the person who is responding to a question or presentation. Under the guise of seeking clarification or simply attempting to "better understand" a question or statement, an effective negotiator can change directions through a reframe. This is the technique of giving a question or statement a slightly different emphasis or "spin," and, in doing so, moving a negotiation on to a new topic or, more often, to a new way of looking at an old topic. The types of movement provoked by a reframe include the following:

- movement toward a favourable outcome or away from an unfavourable outcome (gain–loss reframe)
- movement away from a past focus to a future focus
- movement away from a person or judgment focus to a problem focus
- movement from a position or blame focus to an interest focus

Reframing is a very powerful and effective skill, but it requires that a negotiator know the person with whom she is negotiating very well. For this reason it is also one of the most difficult communication skills to execute well. The following simple explanation will demonstrate both parts. Negotiators (and their principals) generally fall into two groups, those who are inclined to move toward an attractive outcome (a gain), and those who prefer to move away from an unattractive outcome (loss aversion). This may simply be another variation on the theme that people only respond to fear and greed. Movement toward a favourable outcome equates to greed; movement away from an unfavourable outcome equates to fear.

If a negotiator concludes, after testing different proposals, that those at the table are motivated primarily by fear, then movement will generally occur away from an undesirable result, rather than toward a desirable one. In such circumstances, it may be possible for a negotiator to generate the desired movement by framing proposals that highlight the unattractiveness of a particular result or by reframing answers in a way that emphasizes the undesirable consequences of no agreement, thereby encouraging movement "away from" rather than "toward."

A somewhat trivial example will serve to illustrate this last point. At a conference I attended recently,[33] a participant told the following story, which she claimed confirmed the negotiating effectiveness of children in general and her son in particular. Her family, she said, had a hard and fast rule: "no pets." The rule admitted no exceptions. Her son, however, successfully negotiated around this rule. How did he do that? By the way in which he framed the negotiation and subsequently reframed his mother's response. While the participant did not describe her son's negotiating prowess as framing and reframing, that is exactly what it was. First he sought permission to bring a boa constrictor home, knowing full well that the answer would be no. He made quite a spirited case in support of the proposed acquisition, and when that was unsuccessful, as he knew it would be, he asked "why not?" His mother offered a myriad of good reasons, each reflecting her repulsion for having a large snake in the house. The son then suggested that the boa constrictor could be managed in a way that would meet his mother's concerns. His mother wouldn't budge. At this point the son realized that he would have to reframe the negotiation in a way that moved them and his mother "away from" the dreaded boa constrictor. He did this by proposing a relatively benign pet, a turtle. The mother smiled at her son's ingenuity, but was still not persuaded. The turtle, like the snake, contravened the "no pet" rule, she asserted. The son's next step was to reframe the negotiation, again, this time in a way that changed his mother's rule focus to a problem-solving focus. What, he asked, were her concerns? Once he was able to demonstrate that the turtle was so benign that it did not offend any of her concerns, the problem was solved and he (as well as she) realized that he had been successful. At that point, like most good negotiators, he congratulated his mother on her win (she didn't allow him to get the snake he so "desperately" wanted), and went skipping off to his room to make plans for the arrival of the new addition to the family.

This story, of course, illustrates the power of asking why and then searching for options that meet your interests (a pet) and address the concerns of the other side. But it is even more instructive as a story that demonstrates the power of an appropriate frame and reframe. Had the son framed the negotiation so as to encourage his mother to move toward his desired outcome, she would have simply invoked the rule and he would not have been able to get around the rule. She would not likely have been moved by her son's glowing description of a pet turtle, and certainly would not have been attracted toward a decision that contravened a house rule. By framing the negotiation as a "flight from" the very unattractive option of a large snake, her son was successful in winning her support. Framing and reframing are essential communication skills that can be used successfully in any setting once you

---

33   Navigant Consulting, Women's Leadership Forum, Laguna Beach, California, 2007.

know whether your opponent is more likely to move away from an undesirable outcome or move toward a desirable one.[34]

A reframe is often used for purposes that are captured by the trilogy "neutralize, mutualize and generalize."[35] Remember, the negotiator who reframes is attempting to move the negotiation in a new, more productive direction. Thus, a negotiator will reframe the "stinging rebuke" to neutralize its effects. At the same time, the negotiator's reframe may highlight the mutuality of the concern. An assertion directed at one party can often be reframed to demonstrate that the problem belongs to all parties—it is a matter of mutual concern. Finally, the ability to reframe in a way that moves the negotiation from the specific to the general, from the narrow to the broad, and from the small to the big will often set the stage for a more creative exploration of options. One participant's demand for money may be reframed as a "need to address compensation." Another party's demand for retribution may be reframed as the search for a fair solution that respects a range of different goals. In each case, the reframe invites a discussion of other options not anticipated by the initial statement of interests.

In the Later Stages

PERSUADING ANOTHER

(i) Making a Good Argument

The power of a persuasive argument cannot be underestimated. It can be the communication skill that leads to the exchange that "seals the deal." On the other hand, a poorly placed argument, one that opens a negotiation or one that is used prematurely, will foreclose additional option generation and can put a quick end to an otherwise promising negotiation. Beginning a negotiation with a position, supported by a strong argument, is likely to do little more than provoke a counter-argument, and that, in turn, will lead to a counter–counter-argument. The result is a series of "good" arguments, but not a good result. Using

---

34   As "easy" as these reframes appear, the execution of the skill is difficult. It demands a spontaneous response—people don't have the luxury to try two or three reframes until they find one that works. They have only one opportunity, and that opportunity does not last long. A second challenge to those who hope to use reframes successfully is that reframing often comes at a difficult moment in the negotiation. An accusation has been made; the moment (and it is only a moment) for movement away from acrimony is now, but how should the statement be reframed? To be effective, the reframe must be appropriate, spontaneous, and seemingly effortless. This is one communication skill that requires practice away from the negotiation table. The price of not intervening with a reframe or intervening with a reframe that exacerbates the problem can be as high as a failed negotiation.

35   Bernie Mayer describes the following levels or purposes of reframing: detoxification reframing; definitional reframing; metaphoric reframing; and reframing to shift the conflict paradigm. Each illustrates the main function of reframing, and that is to change perspective to provoke movement. B. Mayer, *The Dynamics of Conflict Resolution* (San Francisco, CA: Jossey-Bass, 2000) at 134-39.

an argument when one should be asking a well-placed and well-timed question is not effective. By the same token, when it is time to justify a "final offer" with a good argument, no other communication skill will do.

Once interests are known, options have been generated and assessed, and bargaining begins, some back and forth among the parties will take place. But what is an appropriate exchange? What is the right exchange? Some will be obvious: a party can concede on issue A if the other side agrees to meet their interests on issue B. Other "exchanges" will be more difficult: we need a concession in one area, and have little or nothing to give in return. How are these "exchanges" made? What justifies them? What will persuade the other side to accept one's proposal? Informing the other side about the facts, the law, and the needs of the parties will be helpful, as will a strong presentation, but more is usually needed. That "more" is a good argument. From the other side of the table, the negotiator is faced with the opposite challenge: what arguments can I use to resist the proposed package? What arguments will support my counter-proposal? This is the point in the negotiation when argument becomes the key or dominant communication skill.

This section has highlighted a number of key communication skills. Each plays an important role in contributing to the success of a negotiation. Good questions and effective listening will open a flood of useful responses. Presentations, stories, and examples are at the heart of many negotiations. Done well, an assertion or story will create a positive response. Done poorly, an assertion will be seen as highly provocative and lead to a negative response. A well-placed reframe will redirect the negotiation and generate the movement needed to overcome a difficult moment or an impasse in the negotiation. And finally, arguments, like other key communication skills, are an essential part of the negotiator's communication tool box, and an essential step in a successful negotiation, provided they are not used prematurely.

Figure 10.1 summarizes the relationship between stages in a typical negotiation that correspond with communication skills.

How Does Context Affect Communication?

In one sense context does not matter. Negotiation is negotiation, and it does not matter whether the negotiation is simple or complex, whether the parties are represented or unrepresented, or indeed whether the parties are individuals or large organizations. The same principles apply and the same communication skills are required.

In another sense context *does* matter. There is a world of difference between a simple, one-on-one negotiation over a single issue and a complex, multi-party negotiation in which the parties are diverse and most, if not all, are represented by professional negotiators, such as lawyers. Of the two kinds of negotiation, the complex one is more challenging, particularly from the standpoint of representative negotiation and communication.[36] This section

---

36   The "simple," two-party, single-issue negotiation can also be challenging, particularly if the issue is highly emotional for the parties. In such cases, it may be appropriate for one or both parties to be represented in the negotiations by an agent. The combination of an emotional issue, personality differences between the parties, and the participation of representatives can make the so-called simple cases very complex.

Figure 10.1 The Stages of a Typical Negotiation and the Corresponding Communication Skills

Stages	Corresponding Communication Skills	Examples
Early Stages		
1. Opening (creating the negotiating environment)	Presenting, asserting, telling, storytelling, framing	Introductions followed by an outline of one's goals and how those goals might be met; demonstrating interest in the other side and its goals
2. Exploring interests (what is important and why)	Questioning, especially open-ended questions, listening, explaining (as an assertion or answer), seeking and providing clarification, confirming, understanding	• "Tell me more about …" • "What are you trying to achieve and why?" • "Why is that important?" • "Are there alternative approaches to that?" • "Explain your concerns."
3. Creating an issues list	Proposing, summarizing, further questioning, listening	• "Are these the issues?" • "Are there other issues that should be added to the list?"
Middle Stages		
4. Prioritizing issues (creating an agenda)	Framing and reframing Proposing, presenting	• "Let's move toward or away from …" • "Let's tackle the easy/hard issues first."
5. Generating and testing options to address the issues	Presenting ideas and options to address the issues	• "Would this work?" • "Have you thought about that?" • "What would happen if … ?"
Later Stages		
6. Proposing and making exchanges that are mutually or individually beneficial (bargaining)	Arguing, asserting, justifying	• "A fair or sensible trade-off is for us to concede that, in return for you accepting this." • "What do you need in return, if you were to accept this?" • "What can we offer you so that you'll accept this proposal?" • "Let me explain [argue] why my proposal makes sense for you and for me."
7. Agreement	Checking and confirming Asking for agreement Drafting the agreement document	• "I understand that we have agreed to this package [summarize]. Am I correct?" • "Is there anything else that needs to be addressed before we begin drafting our agreement?" • "Can we agree to this now, and return to the broader or more difficult issues at a later round of negotiations?"

focuses on two factors that contribute to complexity and create some special communication challenges. The first is the theme of this book and that is, how does the addition of a representative make a negotiation more complex and change the negotiation and its communication dynamics? The second factor relates to how the decision-making structure of the parties affects negotiation, particularly when there are many diverse parties involved.

The Agent–Principal Relationship in a Multi-party Negotiation

Parties who retain professional negotiators (agents) expect that representatives will generate superior negotiation outcomes. And so they should. Agents, or representatives, generally bring strong negotiating skills to the table, including the ability to communicate effectively. While the upside of agents is generally improved communication, there is also a downside. First, agents add to the background "noise," a topic we examined earlier. As a message passes through more and more people, the prospect that it will be inadvertently or intentionally distorted increases. Inadvertent message distortion occurs when the agent is unable to convey the principal's message to the other parties. Intentional message distortion, on the other hand, occurs when the goals of the agent are not congruent with those of the principal, and the agent misleads the other parties about the principal's goals. Agents can also change the dynamics of a negotiation, especially multi-party negotiations, in ways that may make communication particularly difficult. Let me illustrate this point by focusing on two psychological phenomena.

The first phenomenon is known as the *Abilene Paradox.*[37] It describes the group dynamic that sometimes occurs when many agents are negotiating on behalf of multiple parties and produce results that no single participant would consider appropriate, largely as a result of a breakdown in communication among the agents. Here is how it works. During a negotiation, coalitions tend to develop among the agents as they work together, and they, in turn, become susceptible to "groupthink." Groupthink occurs within the coalition because each agent makes moves and conveys information at the negotiating table designed to build confidence with other agents who are members of the coalition. Unfortunately, many of these confidence-building moves are inconsistent with the desires and beliefs of the agents' principals. Other agents act and react to the information communicated by these moves, and that ultimately leads to collective decisions and actions that are contrary to their principals' instructions. Agents become frustrated with this result and begin to blame each other. The problem is, how can the lock of groupthink be broken? No one is prepared to stop the process because each is fearful of betraying the group (and possible ostracism by the group), and that fear is greater than the fear of betraying one's principal. The result is that each agent continues down a path that leads to further alienation from the principal and the principal's goals. The solution requires one or more agents to recognize the phenomenon, and then change the communication pattern that led to the groupthink. That means confronting the other agents; telling them that the group may be making a decision that is contrary to the best

---

37   J.B. Harvey, *The Abilene Paradox and Other Meditations on Management* (Lexington, MA: Lexington Books, 1988).

interests of their principals (hopefully with support from the principal). This will either lead to a rapid refocusing of the group in a new direction or, at the least, some intrinsic psychological satisfaction for the agent who confronts the others. It is best, of course, to avoid the phenomenon, and that requires agents to be aware of it and ensure that they do not embrace groupthink at the expense of their principals' goals.

The second phenomenon is known as *Adam's Paradox*,[38] and it too afflicts agents, especially those who occupy a boundary-role position on behalf of their organization in a multi-party negotiation. These agents, who are psychologically and physically distant from their principal and yet enjoy some considerable amount of influence at the negotiating table, must build a rapport with other agents who occupy a similar position, and at the same time be aware of their principal's instructions. This is not an easy task. The distance between agent and principal, combined with the close proximity among agents at the negotiating table, accentuates the agent's detachment from the principal. As the two become more detached, the principal becomes more suspicious of the agent and more inclined to monitor the agent's behaviour. The agent interprets the principal's increased monitoring as a sign that their relationship is weakening. At the same time, congeniality, and especially increased collegiality, among agents leads the principal to become even more suspicious of the agent, and the agent more detached from the principal.

The problem, however, is more than simply one of the close proximity of the agents, which is a natural phenomenon when people work together over long periods of time and is often the case in complex negotiations. One of the tasks of each agent is to change the priorities of the other agents at the negotiating table. Each agent attempts to influence the others. The give and take of a typical negotiation means that agents will be receptive to some of the suggestions of other agents, and, over time, receptivity will lead agents to attempt to alter the initial preferences and priorities of their principals. In the search for an acceptable result, the agent may propose to the principal that the matter be settled with a solution that is less than optimal from the principal's perspective. At this point, the agent's loyalty is clearly suspect and the principal will monitor the agent even more closely. To demonstrate loyalty to the principal, the agent will begin to interpret the principal's instructions narrowly and rigidly, and this will inevitably lead to positional bargaining and a reduction in bargaining effectiveness. As bargaining effectiveness declines, so too does the agent's ability to achieve results that are even close to optimal. This confirms the principal's earlier belief that the agent is not bargaining effectively on behalf of the principal.

The solution is to redress the root cause of the problem, namely, a failure of the agent and principal to communicate effectively. When agents are introduced into a negotiation, the need for close and continuous communication between agent and principal increases dramatically. Their failure to communicate leads to the cycle of distrust described above, namely, suspicion and distrust, followed by close monitoring, ineffective bargaining, and finally more distrust. The only escape from Adam's Paradox is for the agent and principal to meet frequently and for the agent to report not only on the general progress of the negotiation but also on the specific proposals made; the agent should also continually seek

---

38   J.S. Adams, "The Structure and Dynamics of Behavior in Organizational Boundary Roles" in M. Dunnitte, ed., *Handbook of Industrial and Organizational Psychology*, 3d ed. (New York: John Wiley & Sons, 1983) at 1175.

instructions on how best to proceed. Similarly, the principal must continually instruct, evaluate, and re-instruct the agent.

When agents represent principals in multi-party negotiations, the communication challenges are considerable. Not only do agents add to the noise that distorts the principal's message, but also they are susceptible to falling into communication patterns with the other agents that can further frustrate the goals of the principal. Whether it is the groupthink of the Abilene Paradox or the cycle of distrust of Adam's Paradox, the solution to problems created by these phenomena is the same: ongoing, honest, and effective communication between principal and agent.

The Different Decision-Making Approaches of the Parties in a Multi-party Negotiation[39]

The goal of the agent is not to reach agreement with the other parties, but rather to reach an agreement that will be ratified by the party (such as an organization) that she represents. As noted above, there is always the danger that agents will be captured by the negotiation process and become aligned with the other agents at the negotiating table. Better communication between the agent and principal will counteract this tendency, but what does "better communication" mean when the parties represented are different—different in the way in which represented parties make decisions and different in their relationship to their constituencies? These differences don't change the need for good communication skills. Good communication skills are essential, irrespective of party or organizational differences. What these organizational differences do mean is that the level of communication, the frequency of communication, and the time frame over which the communication occurs will vary quite dramatically from party to party, and it is essential that the agents and their principals understand these differences. If not, these differences are likely to lead to a breakdown in communication and, ultimately, in the negotiation.

Let's look at a complex, multi-party negotiation in which there are four distinct types of parties: a government agency or ministry; a First Nation; a corporation; and a non-governmental organization (NGO). There could be others, including individuals, but a brief look at the different decision-making structures and communication styles of these four parties will highlight the communication challenges that arise in this type of negotiation. The distinguishing characteristics of each type of party are noted below. Bear in mind that what is noted here are general characteristics only.

Government Agency or Ministry:
- Decision making is hierarchical, with authority passed down from above.
- Issues in the negotiation are likely to cross agency lines, complicating the ability of an agent to represent "government" and complicating the ratification process, especially if the agencies are not coordinated under a single authority.

---

39   The following draws on material prepared by Gerald Cormick. See G. Cormick, "Negotiating as a Representative" in *Using ADR to Resolve Complex Public Policy Disputes*, course material (2001) Osgoode Hall Law School, York University.

- Political authorities outside the hierarchy may intervene.
- The ratification process may be multi-tiered, involving both the agency and, for politically important matters, an elected authority such as a council, minister, or cabinet.
- Depending on the seniority of the representative and his or her access to key decision makers, changes in position and ratification of agreement are likely to be very time-consuming.

First Nation:

- Decision making is consensual, notwithstanding the appearance of a hierarchical structure.
- The representative negotiator may be a non-member, selected for her expertise, not for her standing within the First Nation community.
- Time is not "of the essence." First Nations prefer consensus-building to ensure a right decision, rather than hurrying negotiations toward a timely decision.
- First Nations require more time to modify positions and ratify agreements than other parties.

Corporation:

- Decision making is hierarchical, with authority passed down from above.
- Although complex negotiations will invariably cross departmental lines, the seniority of the representative and the level of authority conferred make it easier for that person to negotiate with authority.
- When faced with opposition, corporations tend to adopt a siege mentality, seeing others as inherently unreasonable and, as a result, can become suspicious of changes proposed by others.
- Corporations come to the table well prepared, with detailed internal positions on all issues. This degree of preparation can make modification difficult, especially if the corporation has a narrow view of its goals.
- Because "time is money" for corporations, they are structured so that their representatives can move swiftly, whether they are obtaining corporate approval for changes or ratification of tentative agreements.

Non-governmental Organization (NGO):

- Decision making is "messy." While most NGOs have a flat, or from-the-bottom-up authority structure, those at the top have control over information and how it is dispersed.
- The raison d'être of many NGOs is advocacy for a particular purpose.
- Representatives are not likely to have authority to make the accommodations necessary to reach an agreement. This phenomenon becomes even more pronounced if the NGO's fundraising strategy emphasizes the different values of the other parties to the negotiation.
- Ratification will often require formal approval by a membership whose involvement in the issues is as an avocation rather than a vocation.

- Representatives may be volunteers, rather than paid staff or professionals.
- NGOs may enter a negotiation as a coalition, further complicating and delaying the decision-making process.

Differences among these negotiating parties create a real strain on the negotiation process. Different parties have different ratification processes, something that must be communicated to and respected by others at the outset of the negotiation. The timelines of the organizational parties are very different: what appears to one party as the unreasonable or strategic delay of an NGO may simply be a function of the decision-making structure of that organization. The aggressive, "let's decide now" stance of a corporate participant will be viewed with equal suspicion, until others recognize the constraints under which that party is operating. Elected decision-makers pose a special challenge: the agreement that is reached at the negotiation table at which government is a party may be little more than a recommendation to an elected body (such as Cabinet) and Cabinet will decide in a way that may or may not respect the negotiated outcome. A related problem is the propensity of elected bodies to "tinker" with tentative agreements by making some adjustments to carefully crafted deals that can cause a package of provisions to become unravelled. None of these challenges are fatal, if the ratification process of each party is clearly communicated to the other parties at the outset.

In each case, the solution to the problem is more frequent and better communication. Each agent must communicate to the other agents how the organization she represents is structured; how decisions are made; how negotiating instructions are revised; how proposals are assessed; and how tentative agreements are ratified. Agents must alert those who they represent to these differences, and urge them to respect these differences. Agents must also keep their party fully informed of developments at the table, and developments that are occurring between other agents and the organizations that they represent. Parties are different. If the differences are well known and respected by all parties, the suspicion and bad faith that emanates from ignorance about others will subside.

And so, context does matter. When agents are involved in complex, multi-party negotiations, and the parties are very different, the communication challenges are significant. Or, to put the point a little differently, if the negotiating agents are not aware of the challenges or lack the practice skills or knowledge required to address the challenges, the likelihood of a successful result is low indeed.

Final Considerations

This chapter began with the proposition that communication is the essence of negotiation and, as a result, plays a key role in the success or failure of every negotiation. We began by noting some of the challenges of communicating in a negotiation context, and then focused on how negotiators actually communicate. How do they send and receive messages? Over what channel are messages best sent? What are the consequences when a negotiator attempts to communicate over a channel that is inappropriate for the negotiations in general? For the message in particular? We examined briefly how communication is enhanced when the communication activity is aligned with the most appropriate channel, and we noted as well how the communication goals of the negotiator are influenced by the negotiator's style and the stage of the negotiation. We also noted how communication strategy changes as the negotiators move through the various stages of a negotiation. Then, we examined the specific communication skills of the effective negotiator and argued again that particular skills are best utilized during the stage(s) of a negotiation where that skill will advance the negotiation. Finally, we looked at the communication challenges faced by representative negotiators in complex, multi-party negotiations where the parties are differently constituted. A sensitivity to difference—by both agent and principal—is essential, if the factors that lead to communication failure are to be overcome.

As the student of negotiation reflects on his or her role as a representative negotiator, it is important to remember that communication plays a key role in achieving success at the bargaining table.

Selected Further Reading

C.B. Craver, *Effective Legal Negotiation and Settlement*, 5th ed. (Newark, NJ: LexisNexis, 2005) at 34-70.

J.P. Folger, M.S. Poole & R.K. Stutman, *Working Through Conflict: Strategies for Relationships, Groups, and Organizations*, 3d ed. (New York: Longman, 1997) at 69-94.

M.J. Gelfand & J.M. Brett, eds., *The Handbook of Negotiation and Culture* (Stanford, CA: Stanford University Press, 2004) at c. 6.

R.J. Lewicki *et al.*, *Negotiation: Readings, Exercises, and Cases*, 4th ed. (Boston: McGraw-Hill/Irwin, 2003) at 256-63, 141-81.

A.L. Sillars & W.W. Wilmot, "Communication Strategies in Conflict and Mediation" in J.A. Daly & J.M. Wiemann, eds., *Strategic Interpersonal Communication* (Hillsdale, NJ: Laurence Erlbaum Associates, 1994).

M.L. Spangle & M.W. Isenhart, *Negotiation: Communication for Diverse Settings* (Thousand Oaks, CA: Sage Publishing, 2003) at 3-7, 27-32, 136-37, 117-40.

CHAPTER 11

Critiques of Settlement Advocacy

Andrew Pirie

Introduction

The Purpose of Critiques of Settlement Advocacy

The critiques of advocating for settlement in all cases ("settlement advocacy") presented in this chapter are not intended to deter or discourage lawyers, business people, or others from engaging in representative negotiation. Such a goal would be impractical. As many know from their experience and as the preceding chapters in this book make clear, negotiation is used extensively and is prevalent not only in legal and business settings but also in virtually every other area of social endeavour.

Parties to a dispute or individuals interested in a common venture often use negotiation to reach an agreement. We also know that almost all civil lawsuits in Canada, the United States, and many other countries are settled by negotiation or through negotiation-assisted processes such as mediation or judicial dispute resolution. Also, many disputes or problems that do not make it to the litigation stage—and there are many—are settled consensually by negotiation. Neighbours talk over fences about concerns, business people resolve issues in boardrooms, and people in general make decisions in conversations over the Internet. Practically speaking, negotiated settlements are the norm in dispute resolution.

Rather than discourage the use of negotiation, the purpose of the critiques of settlement advocacy is to contribute to important decision-making processes. Negotiation and representative negotiation are common in the lives of lawyers, business people, and indeed most everyone. The critiques of settlement advocacy are intended to strengthen both types of negotiation by (1) exposing the weaknesses in negotiation ideas and practices, and (2) ensuring that these weaknesses are factored into the decision about whether or not to use negotiation. When and how, if at all, should negotiation be used? The critiques of settlement advocacy help lawyers assess whether negotiation will be practical and effective for the situation rather than counterproductive.

The Links to Ethical Responsibilities

The critiques of settlement advocacy are not intended to diminish the substantial ethical responsibilities that are imposed on all legal professionals when they represent clients. Through codes of professional conduct, lawyers have an ethical and professional duty to advise and encourage clients to settle disputes. While lawyers are advocates and as such are required to resolutely represent their clients, the adversarial role that requires lawyers to raise every issue, advance every argument, ask every question that advances his or her client's case, and obtain for the client every remedy or defence authorized by law is tempered by the ethical duty to settle whenever it is reasonable to do so. Professional legal representation includes an ethical obligation to settle.

Consider the specific language used in the *Canadian Bar Association Code of Professional Conduct*:

Chapter III Advising Clients

Compromise or Settlement

6. The lawyer should advise or encourage the client to compromise or settle a dispute whenever possible on a reasonable basis and should discourage the client from commencing or continuing useless legal proceedings.

Chapter IX The Lawyer as Advocate

Encouraging Settlements and Alternative Dispute Resolution

8. Whenever the case can be settled reasonably, the lawyer should advise and encourage the client to do so rather than commence or continue legal proceedings.[1]

The guideline that directs lawyers to "advise or encourage the client to compromise or settle" obviously refers to the negotiation process. While the above ethical stipulations provide lawyers with some discretion—"whenever possible on a reasonable basis," "whenever the case can be settled reasonably"—the ethical mandate to settle is clear. It would be the rarest of situations where it would not be reasonable to consider a negotiated settlement. While settlement on a reasonable basis might be or appear to be difficult in certain instances, ethics mandates that at least an effort to settle be made. These conclusions about considering and using negotiation are particularly true when the lawyers for all sides to the dispute are operating under the same ethical principles respecting the direction to settle.

---

1   Canadian Bar Association, *Canadian Bar Association Code of Professional Conduct* (CBA, 2006) at 12, 61.

Some codes of professional conduct for the legal profession go a step further. The *Canadian Bar Association Code of Professional Conduct* also requires the lawyer to

> consider the use of alternative dispute resolution (ADR) for every dispute and, if appropriate, the lawyer should inform the client of the ADR options and, if so instructed, take steps to pursue those options.[2]

The ethical requirement to consider the use of alternative dispute resolution (ADR) for every dispute and to pursue ADR options if appropriate also would, at the very least, require the lawyer to discuss the possibility of using negotiation with his or her client. Such a discussion would include the lawyer thoroughly explaining to the client the advantages as well as the disadvantages of using negotiation in order to determine whether this settlement process is appropriate and should be pursued. While not mandating the use of negotiation, the ethical requirement to "consider" settlement "for every dispute" through ADR processes such as mediation and negotiation again clearly spells out the preference for settlement being promulgated in these ethical rules.

Rather than diminish the ethical responsibility to consider and encourage settlement whenever possible, the critiques of settlement advocacy enrich the dispute resolution decision-making process. When a lawyer exercises the ethical mandate to consider whether negotiation is appropriate and possible, the critiques of settlement advocacy ensure that he or she carefully examines both the advantages and disadvantages of negotiation. A professional and ethical approach to negotiation necessarily involves a full understanding of the criticisms of settlement.

The Critiques of Settlement Advocacy

The critiques of settlement advocacy are meant to inspire a closer and more critical examination of negotiation and its use. In a critical examination of negotiation, the main questions are as follows: What are the downsides associated with negotiation? What should be the response to these downsides? Is rejection of negotiation ever appropriate in light of its widespread use and the ethical requirements around its practice? What other responses, apart from rejecting negotiation, would not only address the downsides but also improve the negotiation process?

The critiques of settlement advocacy are also meant to encourage a more effective, better informed, and more professional practice of negotiation. By understanding, analyzing, and responding to these critiques in relation to their impact on the practices and policies of representative negotiation, it is hoped that negotiation practices can become even better.

The critiques of settlement advocacy are presented under the following four headings:

- Being Against Settlement
- Economic Efficiency Versus Quality Justice
- A Move Away from Progressive Legal Rights
- Searching for a Constant Negotiating Paradigm

---

2 *Ibid.* at 61.

Being Against Settlement
Against Settlement

This section examines the classic critique of settlement advocacy expressed by Owen Fiss in "Against Settlement."[3] It also reviews Trevor Farrow's concerns about the democratic perils that may follow the privatization of dispute practices through negotiation.[4]

Fiss theorizes that the institutionalization of settlement or settlement advocacy is highly problematic for several reasons. First, the inevitable disparity in resources between parties to disputes necessarily results in settlement victims—parties who are disadvantaged in the settlement process due to inequalities in bargaining resources. Fiss gives the example of a poorer party who is forced to settle because she does not have adequate resources to finance the litigation or needs the damages immediately. The other party to the litigation takes advantage of these disparities by offering to settle for much less than is fair, knowing the indigent party cannot continue to an adjudicated result. Second, Fiss suggests that the widespread diversion of cases from the courtroom into private settlement settings, such as representative negotiations, would deprive our courts, and particularly our appellate courts, of sufficient numbers of cases from which to make and advance the law. Important precedents would be lost. Parties might settle while leaving justice undone. For example, what if *Donoghue v. Stevenson*, the leading Commonwealth case on negligence law, had been settled before the House of Lords was able to articulate the "neighbour" principle? What if the lawyers and their clients in an important *Charter of Rights and Freedoms* case in Canada had successfully concluded a deal, to everyone's mutual satisfaction, that not only settled the case but also included in the negotiated agreement, as is quite common, an enforceable contractual provision requiring the parties to keep all details of the agreement strictly confidential? The confidentiality clause would prevent any publicity that might encourage other claimants who are in a similar situation from coming forward, minimize publicity that might damage reputations or balance sheets, and otherwise keep the outcome of the *Charter* case completely private. Fiss posits that the widespread encouragement of private settlement would rob the courts of a fundamental public role—that of advancing developments in the law through publicly created precedents.

As you read the following excerpt from "Against Settlement," consider the idea, based on recent empirical evidence in Canada, the United States, and other common-law countries, that we are experiencing a phenomenon known as the "vanishing trial."[5] While Fiss only speculated in 1984 that the number of court cases would decline, this supposition has actually materialized not only in trial courts but also in appellate courts. While not extinct, the number of civil trials and appellate court hearings is dramatically down. Accordingly, will

---

3   O.M. Fiss, "Against Settlement" (1984) 93 Yale L.J. 1073.

4   T.C.W. Farrow, "Privatizing Our Public Civil Justice System" (2006) 9 News and Views on Civil Justice Reform 16.

5   See *e.g.* M. Galanter, "The Vanishing Trial: An Examination of Trials and Related Matters in Federal and State Courts" (2004) 1 Journal of Empirical Legal Studies 459; online: <http://www.marcgalanter.net/Documents/declineoftrials.htm>.

settlement advocacy diminish the role of the courts, undermine a key element of the rule of law, and cause other grave implications for the credibility of the entire legal system?

As you read the Fiss excerpt, think about responses that can be made to Fiss's arguments against settlement. Fiss acknowledges that being against settlement does not mean that parties should be forced to litigate, since that disposition would not only distort the adjudicative process but also interfere with the autonomy of the parties. Is the correct response to Fiss only the acquisition of the understanding that when parties settle society gets less and the parties get less than some ideal outcome that would be imposed by the courts?

Owen M. Fiss
"Against Settlement"
(1984) 93 Yale L.J. 1073, footnotes omitted

In a recent report to the Harvard Overseers, Derek Bok called for a new direction in legal education. He decried "the familiar tilt in the law curriculum toward preparing students for legal combat," and asked instead that law schools train their students "for the gentler arts of reconciliation and accommodation." He sought to turn our attention from the courts to "new voluntary mechanism" for resolving disputes. In doing so, Bok echoed themes that have long been associated with the Chief Justice, and that have become a rallying point for the organized bar and the source of a new movement in the law. This movement is the subject of a new professional journal, newly formed section of the American Association of Law Schools, and several well-funded institutes. It has even received its own acronym—ADR (Alternative Dispute Resolution).

The movement promises to reduce the amount of litigation initiated, and accordingly the bulk of its proposals are devoted to negotiation and mediation prior to suit. But the interest in the so-called "gentler arts" has not been so confined. It extends to ongoing litigation as well, and the advocates of ADR have sought new ways to facilitate and perhaps even pressure parties into settling pending cases. Just last year, Rule 16 of the Federal Rules of Civil Procedure was amended to strengthen the hand of the trial judge in brokering settlements: The "facilitation of settlement" became an explicit purpose of pre-trial conferences, and participants were officially invited, if that is the proper word, to consider "the possibility of settlement or the use of extrajudicial procedures to resolve the dispute." Now the Advisory Committee on Civil Rules is proposing to amend Rule 68 to sharpen the incentives for settlement: Under this amendment, a party who rejects a settlement offer and then receives a judgment less favorable than that offer must pay the attorney's fees of the other party. This amendment would effect a major change in the traditional American rule, under which each party pays his or her own attorney's fees. It would also be at odds with a number of statutes that seek to facilitate certain types of civil litigation by providing attorney's fees to plaintiffs if they win, without imposing liability for the attorney's fees of their adversaries if they lose.

The advocates of ADR are led to support such measures and to exalt the idea of settlement more generally because they view adjudication as a process to resolve disputes. They act as though courts arose to resolve quarrels between neighbors who had reached an impasse and turned to a stranger for help. Courts are seen as an institutionalization of the stranger and adjudication is viewed as the process by which the stranger exercises power. The very fact that the neighbors have turned to someone else to resolve their dispute signifies a breakdown in their social relations; the advocates of ADR acknowledge this, but nonetheless hope that the neighbors will be able to reach agreement before the stranger renders judgment. Settlement is that agreement. It is a truce more than a true reconciliation, but it seems preferable to judgment because it rests on the consent of both parties and avoids the cost of a lengthy trial.

In my view, however, this account of adjudication and the case for settlement rest on questionable premises. I do not believe that settlement as a generic practice is preferable to judgment or should be institutionalized on a wholesale and indiscriminate basis. It should be treated instead as a highly problematic technique for streamlining dockets. Settlement is for me the civil analogue of plea bargaining: Consent is often coerced; the bargain may be struck by someone without authority; the absence of a trial and judgment renders subsequent judicial involvement troublesome; and although dockets are trimmed, justice may not be done. Like plea bargaining, settlement is a capitulation to the conditions of mass society and should be neither encouraged nor praised.

The Imbalance of Power

By viewing the lawsuit as a quarrel between two neighbors, the dispute-resolution story that underlies ADR implicitly asks us to assume a rough equality between the contending parties. It treats settlement as the anticipation of the outcome of trial and assumes that the terms of settlement are simply a product of the parties' predictions of that outcome. In truth, however, settlement is also a function of the resources available to each party to finance the litigation, and those resources are frequently distributed unequally. Many lawsuits do not involve a property dispute between two neighbors, or between AT&T and the government (to update the story), but rather concern a struggle between a member of a racial minority and a municipal police department over alleged brutality, or a claim by a worker against a large corporation over work-related injuries. In these cases, the distribution of financial resources, or the ability of one party to pass along its costs, will invariably infect the bargaining process, and the settlement will be at odds with a conception of justice that seeks to make the wealth of the parties irrelevant.

The disparities in resources between the parties can influence the settlement in three ways. First, the poorer party may be less able to amass and analyze the information needed to predict the outcome of the litigation, and thus be disadvantaged in the bargaining process. Second, he may need the damages he seeks immediately and thus be induced to settle as a way of accelerating payment, even though he realizes he would get less now than he might if he awaited judgment. All plaintiffs want their damages immediately, but an indigent plaintiff may be exploited by a rich defendant because his need is so great that the defendant can force him to accept a sum that is less than the ordinary present value of the judgment. Third, the poorer party might be forced to settle because he does not have the resources to finance the litigation, to cover either his own projected expenses, such as his lawyer's time, or the expenses his opponent can impose through the manipulation of procedural mechanisms such as discovery. It might seem that settlement benefits the plaintiff by allowing him to avoid the costs of litigation, but this is not so. The defendant can anticipate the plaintiff's costs if the case were to be tried fully and decrease his offer by that amount. The indigent plaintiff is a victim of the costs of litigation even if he settles.

There are exceptions. Seemingly rich defendants may sometimes be subject to financial pressures that make them as anxious to settle as indigent plaintiffs. But I doubt that these circumstances occur with any great frequency. I also doubt that institutional arrangements such as contingent fees or the provision of legal services to the poor will in fact equalize resources between contending parties: The contingent fee does not equalize resources; it only makes an indigent plaintiff vulnerable to the willingness of the private bar to invest in his case. In effect, the ability to exploit the plaintiff's lack of resources has been transferred from rich defendants to lawyers who insist upon a hefty slice of the plaintiff's recovery as their fee. These lawyers, moreover, will only work for contingent fees in certain kinds of cases, such as personal-injury suits. And the contingent fee is of no avail when the defendant is the disadvantaged party. Governmental subsidies for legal services have a broader potential, but in the civil domain the battle for these subsidies was hard-fought, and they are in fact extremely limited, especially when it comes to cases that seek systemic reform of government practices.

Of course, imbalances of power can distort judgment as well: Resources influence the quality of presentation, which in turn has an important bearing on who wins and the terms of victory. We count, however, on the guiding presence of the judge, who can employ a number of measures to lessen the impact of distributional inequalities. He can, for example, supplement the parties' presentations by asking questions, calling his own witnesses, and inviting other persons and institutions to participate as amici. These measures are likely to make only a small contribution toward moderating the influence of distributional inequalities, but should not be ignored for that reason. Not even these small steps are possible with settlement. There is, moreover, a critical difference between a process like settlement, which is based on bargaining and accepts inequalities of wealth as an integral and legitimate component of the process, and a process like judgment, which knowingly struggles against those inequalities. Judgment aspires to an autonomy from distributional inequalities, and it gathers much of its appeal from this aspiration.

The Absence of Authoritative Consent

The argument for settlement presupposes that the contestants are individuals. These individuals speak for themselves and should be bound by the rules they generate. In many situations, however, individuals are ensnared in contractual relationships that impair their autonomy: Lawyers or insurance companies might, for example, agree to settlements that are in their interests but are not in the best interests of their clients, and to which their clients would not agree if the choice were still theirs. But a deeper and more intractable problem arises from the fact that many parties are not individuals but rather organizations or groups. We do not know who is entitled to speak for these entities and to give the consent upon which so much of the appeal of settlement depends.

Some organizations, such as corporations or unions, have formal procedures for identifying the persons who are authorized to speak for them. But these procedures are imperfect: They are designed to facilitate transactions between the organization and outsiders, rather than to insure that the members of the organization in fact agree with a particular decision. Nor do they eliminate conflicts of interests. The chief executive officer of a corporation may settle a suit to prevent embarrassing disclosures about his managerial policies, but such disclosures might well be in the interest of the shareholders. The president of a union may agree to a settlement as a way of preserving his power within the organization; for that very reason, he may not risk the dangers entailed in consulting the rank and file or in subjecting the settlement to ratification by the membership. Moreover, the representational procedures found in corporations, unions, or other private formal organizations are not universal. Much contemporary litigation, especially in the federal courts, involves governmental agencies, and the procedures in those organizations for generating authoritative consent are far cruder than those in the corporate context. We are left to wonder, for example, whether the attorney general should be able to bind all state officials, some of whom are elected and thus have an independent mandate from the people, or even whether the incumbent attorney general should be able to bind his successors.

These problems become even more pronounced when we turn from organizations and consider the fact that much contemporary litigation involves even more nebulous social entities, namely, groups. Some of these groups, such as ethnic or racial minorities, inmates of prisons, or residents of institutions for mentally retarded people, may have an identity or existence that transcends the lawsuit, but they do not have any formal organizational structure and therefore lack any procedures for generating authoritative consent. The absence of such a procedure is even more pronounced in cases involving a group, such as the purchasers of Cuisinarts between 1972 and 1982, which is constructed solely in order to create funds large enough to make it financially attractive for lawyers to handle the case.

The Federal Rules of Civil Procedure require that groups have a "representative"; this representative purports to speak on behalf of the group, but he receives his power by the most questionable of all elective procedures—self-appointment or, if we are dealing with a defendant class, appointment by an adversary. The rules contemplate notice to the members of the group about the pendency of the action and the claims of the representative, but it is difficult to believe that notice could reach all members of the group, or that it could cure the defects in the procedures by which the representative gets his power. The forces that discourage most members of the group from stepping forward to initiate suits will also discourage them from responding to whatever notice may reach them. The sponsors of the amendment to Rule 68 recognize the nature of class actions and exempt them from its special procedures. But this exemption does little more than create an incentive for casting all civil litigation as class actions, with their attendant procedural complexities, and leaves the problem of generating authoritative consent for organizational parties unsolved. The new Rule 16 does not even recognize the problem.

Going to judgment does not altogether eliminate the risk of unauthorized action, any more than it eliminates the distortions arising from disparities in resources. The case presented by the representative of a group or an organization admittedly will influence the outcome of the suit, and that outcome will bind those who might also be bound by a settlement. On the other hand, judgment does not ask as much from the so-called representatives. There is a conceptual and normative distance between what the representatives do and say and what the court eventually decides, because the judge tests those statements and actions against independent procedural and substantive standards. The authority of judgment arises from the law, not from the statements or actions of the putative representatives, and thus we allow judgment to bind persons not directly involved in the litigation even when we are reluctant to have settlement do so.

The procedures that have been devised for policing the settlement process when groups or organizations are involved have not eliminated the difficulties of generating authoritative consent. Some of these procedures provide a substantive standard for the approval of the settlement and do not even consider the issue of consent. A case in point is the Tunney Act. The Act establishes procedures for giving outsiders notice of a proposed settlement in a government antitrust suit and requires the judge to decide whether a settlement proposed by the Department of Justice is in "the public interest." This statute implicitly acknowledges the difficulty of determining who is entitled to speak for the United States in some authoritative fashion and yet provides the judge with virtually no guidance in making this determination or in deciding whether to approve the settlement. The public-interest standard in fact seems to invite the consideration of such nonjudicial factors as popular sentiment and the efficient allocation of prosecutorial resources.

Other policing mechanisms, such as Rule 23, which governs class actions, make no effort to articulate a substantive standard for approving settlements, but instead entrust the whole matter to the judge. In such cases, the judge's approval theoretically should turn on whether the group consents, but determining whether such consent exists is often impossible, since true consent consists of nothing less than the expressed unanimity of all the members of a group, which might number in the hundreds of thousands and be scattered across the United States. The judge's approval instead turns on how close or far the proposed settlement is from what he imagines would be the judgment obtained after suit. The basis for approving a settlement, contrary to what the dispute-resolution story suggests, is therefore not consent but rather the settlement's approximation to judgment. This might appear to remove my objection to settlement, except that the judgment being used as a measure of the settlement is very odd indeed: It has never in fact been entered, but only imagined. It has been constructed without benefit of a full trial, and at a time when the judge can no longer count on the thorough presentation promised by the adversary system. The contending parties have struck a bargain, and have every interest in defending the settlement and in convincing the judge that it is in accord with the law.

The Lack of a Foundation for Continuing Judicial Involvement

The dispute-resolution story trivializes the remedial dimensions of lawsuits and mistakenly assumes judgment to be the end of the process. It supposes that the judge's duty is to declare which neighbor is right and which wrong, and that this declaration will end the judge's involvement (save in that most exceptional situation where it is also necessary for him to issue a writ directing the sheriff to execute the declaration). Under these assumptions, settlement appears as an almost perfect substitute for judgment, for it too can declare the parties' rights. Often, however, judgment is not the end of a lawsuit but only the beginning. The involvement of the court may continue almost indefinitely. In these cases, settlement cannot provide an adequate basis for that necessary continuing involvement, and thus is no substitute for judgment.

The parties may sometimes be locked in combat with one another and view the lawsuit as only one phase in a long continuing struggle. The entry of judgment will then not end the struggle, but rather change its terms and the balance of power. One of the parties will invariably return to the court and again ask for its assistance, not so much because conditions have changed, but because the conditions that preceded the lawsuit have unfortunately not changed. This often occurs in domestic-relations cases, where the divorce decree represents only the opening salvo in an endless series of skirmishes over custody and support.

The structural reform cases that play such a prominent role on the federal docket provide another occasion for continuing judicial involvement. In these cases, courts seek to safeguard public values by restructuring large-scale bureaucratic organizations. The task is enormous, and our knowledge of how to restructure on-going bureaucratic organizations is limited. As a consequence, courts must oversee and manage the remedial process for a long time—maybe forever. This, I fear, is true of most school desegregation cases, some of which have been pending for twenty or thirty years. It is also true of antitrust cases that seek divestiture or reorganization of an industry.

The drive for settlement knows no bounds and can result in a consent decree even in the kinds of cases I have just mentioned, that is, even when a court finds itself embroiled in a continuing struggle between the parties or must reform a bureaucratic organization. The parties may be ignorant of the difficulties ahead or optimistic about the future, or they may simply believe that they can get more favorable terms through a bargained-for agreement. Soon, however, the inevitable happens: One party returns to court and asks the judge to modify the decree, either to make it more effective or less stringent. But the judge is at a loss: He has no basis for assessing the request. He cannot, to use Cardozo's somewhat melodramatic formula, easily decide whether the "dangers, once substantial, have become attenuated to a shadow," because, by definition, he never knew the dangers.

The allure of settlement in large part derives from the fact that it avoids the need for a trial. Settlement must thus occur before the trial is complete and the judge has entered findings of fact and conclusions of law. As a consequence, the judge confronted with a request for modification of a consent decree must retrospectively reconstruct the situation as it existed at the time the decree was entered, and decide whether conditions today have sufficiently changed to warrant a modification in that decree. In the Meat Packers litigation, for example, where a consent decree governed the industry for almost half a century, the judge confronted with a request for modification in 1960 had to reconstruct the "danger" that had existed at the time of the entry of the decree in 1920 in order to determine whether the danger had in fact become a "shadow." Such an inquiry borders on the absurd, and is likely to dissipate whatever savings in judicial resources the initial settlement may have produced.

Settlement also impedes vigorous enforcement, which sometimes requires use of the contempt power. As a formal matter, contempt is available to punish violations of a consent decree. But courts hesitate to use that power to enforce decrees that rest solely on consent, especially when enforcement is aimed at high public officials, as became evident in the Willowbrook deinstitutionalization case and the recent Chicago desegregation case. Courts do not see a mere bargain between the parties as a sufficient foundation for the exercise of their coercive powers.

Sometimes the agreement between the parties extends beyond the terms of the decree and includes stipulated "findings of fact" and "conclusions of law," but even then an adequate foundation for a strong use of the judicial power is lacking. Given the underlying purpose of settlement—to avoid trial—the so-called "findings" and "conclusions" are necessarily the products of a bargain between the parties rather than of a trial and an independent judicial judgment. Of course, a plaintiff is free to drop a lawsuit altogether (provided that the interests of certain other persons are not compromised), and a defendant can offer something in return, but that bargained-for arrangement more closely resembles a contract than an injunction. It raises a question which has already been answered whenever an injunction is issued, namely, whether the judicial power should be used to enforce it. Even assuming that the consent is freely given and authoritative, the bargain is at best contractual and does not contain the kind of enforcement commitment already embodied in a decree that is the product of a trial and the judgment of a court.

Justice Rather Than Peace

The dispute-resolution story makes settlement appear as a perfect substitute for judgment, as we just saw, by trivializing the remedial dimensions of a lawsuit, and also by reducing the social function of the lawsuit to one of resolving private disputes: In that story, settlement appears to achieve exactly the same purpose as judgment—peace between the parties— but at considerably less expense to society. The two quarreling neighbors turn to a court in order to resolve their dispute, and society makes courts available because it wants to aid in the achievement of their private ends or to secure the peace.

In my view, however, the purpose of adjudication should be understood in broader terms. Adjudication uses public resources, and employs not strangers chosen by the parties but public officials chosen by a process in which the public participates. These officials, like members of the legislative and executive branches, possess a power that has been defined and conferred by public law, not by private agreement. Their job is not to maximize the ends of private parties, nor simply to secure the peace, but to explicate and give force to the values embodied in authoritative texts such as the Constitution and statutes: to interpret those values and to bring reality into accord with them. This duty is not discharged when the parties settle.

In our political system, courts are reactive institutions. They do not search out interpretive occasions, but instead wait for others to bring matters to their attention. They also rely for the most part on others to investigate and present the law and facts. A settlement will thereby deprive a court of the occasion, and perhaps even the ability, to render an interpretation. A court cannot proceed (or not proceed very far) in the face of a settlement. To be against settlement is not to urge that parties be "forced" to litigate, since that would interfere with their autonomy and distort the adjudicative process; the parties will be inclined to make the court believe that their bargain is justice. To be against settlement is only to suggest that when the parties settle, society gets less than what appears, and for a price it does not know it is paying. Parties might settle while leaving justice undone. The settlement of a school suit might secure the peace, but not racial equality. Although the parties are prepared to live under the terms they bargained for, and although such peaceful coexistence may be a necessary precondition of justice, and itself a state of affairs to be valued, it is not justice itself. To settle for something means to accept less than some ideal.

I recognize that judges often announce settlements not with a sense of frustration or disappointment, as my account of adjudication might suggest, but with a sigh of relief. But this sigh should be seen for precisely what it is: It is not a recognition that a job is done, nor an acknowledgment that a job need not be done because justice has been secured. It is instead based on another sentiment altogether, namely, that another case has been "moved along," which is true whether or not justice has been done or even needs to be done. Or the sigh might be based on the fact that the agony of judgment has been avoided.

There is, of course, sometimes a value to avoidance, not just to the judge, who is thereby relieved of the need to make or enforce a hard decision, but also to society, which sometimes thrives by masking its basic contradictions. But will settlement result in avoidance when it is most appropriate? Other familiar avoidance devices, such as certiorari, at least promise a devotion to public ends, but settlement is controlled by the litigants, and is subject to their private motivations and all the vagaries of the bargaining process. There are also dangers to avoidance, and these may well outweigh any imagined benefits. Partisans of ADR—Chief Justice Burger, or even President Bok—may begin with a certain satisfaction with the status quo. But when one sees injustices that cry out for correction—as Congress did when it endorsed the concept of the private attorney general and as the Court of another era did when it sought to enhance access to the courts—the value of avoidance diminishes and the agony of judgment becomes a necessity. Someone has to confront the betrayal of our deepest ideals and be prepared to turn the world upside down to bring those ideals to fruition.

The Real Divide

To all this, one can readily imagine a simple response by way of confession and avoidance: We are not talking about *those* lawsuits. Advocates of ADR might insist that my account of adjudication, in contrast to the one implied by the dispute-resolution story, focuses on a rather narrow category of lawsuits. They could argue that while settlement may have only the most limited appeal with respect to those cases, I have not spoken to the "typical" case. My response is twofold.

First, even as a purely quantitative matter, I doubt that the number of cases I am referring to is trivial. My universe includes those cases in which there are significant distributional inequalities; those in which it is difficult to generate authoritative consent because organizations or social groups are parties or because the power to settle is vested in autonomous agents; those in which the court must continue to supervise the parties after judgment; and those in which justice needs to be done, or to put it more modestly, where there is a genuine social need for an authoritative interpretation of law. I imagine that the number of cases that satisfy one of these four criteria is considerable; in contrast to the kind of case portrayed in the dispute-resolution story, they probably dominate the docket of a modern court system.

Second, it demands a certain kind of myopia to be concerned only with the number of cases, as though all cases are equal simply because the clerk of the court assigns each a single docket number. All cases are not equal. The Los Angeles desegregation case, to take one example, is not equal to the allegedly more typical suit involving a property dispute or an automobile accident. The desegregation suit consumes more resources, affects more people, and provokes far greater challenges to the judicial power. The settlement movement must introduce a qualitative perspective; it must speak to these more "significant" cases, and demonstrate the propriety of settling them. Otherwise it will soon be seen as an irrelevance, dealing with trivia rather than responding to the very conditions that give the movement its greatest sway and saliency.

Nor would sorting cases into "two tracks," one for settlement, and another for judgment, avoid my objections. Settling automobile cases and leaving discrimination or antitrust cases for judgment might remove a large number of cases from the dockets, but the dockets will nevertheless remain burdened with the cases that consume the most judicial resources and represent the most controversial exercises of the judicial power. A "two track" strategy would drain the argument for settlement of much of its appeal. I also doubt whether the "two track" strategy can be sensibly implemented. It is impossible to formulate adequate criteria for prospectively sorting cases. The problems of settlement are not tied to the subject matter of the suit, but instead stem from factors that are harder to identify, such as the wealth of the parties, the likely post-judgment history of the suit, or the need for an authoritative interpretation of law. The authors of the amendment to Rule 68 make a gesture toward a "two track" strategy by exempting class actions and shareholder derivative suits, and by allowing the judge to refrain from awarding attorney's fees when it is "unjustified under all of the circumstances." But these gestures are cramped and ill-conceived, and are likely to increase the workload of the courts by giving rise to yet another set of issues to litigate. It is, moreover, hard to see how these problems can be avoided. Many of the factors that lead a society to bring social relationships that otherwise seem wholly private (e.g., marriage) within the jurisdiction of a court, such as imbalances of power or the interests of third parties, are also likely to make settlement problematic. Settlement is a poor substitute for judgment; it is an even poorer substitute for the withdrawal of jurisdiction.

For these reasons, I remain highly skeptical of a "two track" strategy, and would resist it. But the more important point to note is that the draftsmen of Rule 68 are the exception. There is no hint of a "two track" strategy in Rule 16. In fact, most ADR advocates make no effort to distinguish between different types of cases or to suggest that "the gentler arts of reconciliation and accommodation" might be particularly appropriate for one type of case but not for another. They lump all cases together. This suggests that what divides me from the partisans of ADR is not that we are concerned with different universes of cases, that Derek Bok, for example, focuses on boundary quarrels while I see only desegregation suits. I suspect instead that what divides us is much deeper and stems from our understanding of the purpose of the civil law suit and its place in society. It is a difference in outlook.

Someone like Bok sees adjudication in essentially private terms: The purpose of lawsuits and the civil courts is to resolve disputes, and the amount of litigation we encounter is evidence of the needlessly combative and quarrelsome character of Americans. Or as Bok put it, using a more diplomatic idiom: "At bottom, ours is a society built on individualism, competition, and success." I, on the other hand, see adjudication in more public terms: Civil litigation is an institutional arrangement for using state power to bring a recalcitrant reality closer to our chosen ideals. We turn to the courts because we need to, not because of some quirk in our personalities. We train our students in the tougher arts so that they may help secure all that the law promises, not because we want them to become gladiators or because we take a special pleasure in combat.

To conceive of the civil lawsuit in public terms as America does might be unique. I am willing to assume that no other country—including Japan, Bok's new paragon—has a case like *Brown v. Board of Education* in which the judicial power is used to eradicate the caste structure. I am willing to assume that no other country conceives of law and uses law in quite the way we do. But this should be a source of pride rather than shame. What is unique is not the problem, that we live short of our ideals, but that we alone among the nations of the world seem willing to do something about it. Adjudication American-style is not a reflection of our combativeness but rather a tribute to our inventiveness and perhaps even more to our commitment.

The Perils of Private Civil Justice

The following excerpt from Trevor Farrow, "Privatizing Our Public Civil Justice System," adds to the critiques of settlement advocacy put forward by Fiss. In this excerpt, Farrow argues that there is often more at stake in representative negotiations than simply the direct interests of the negotiating clients and their representatives. For example, in a negotiation between the federal government and a sector of female employees over the issue of pay equity or in a negotiation involving Aboriginal and non-aboriginal governments, outcomes will have a significant and lasting impact on broad public interests. Do private settlement and the consequential avoidance of public scrutiny associated with negotiations adversely affect democracy at a fundamental level? If we discard the public scrutiny associated with open court procedures, the application of previously decided cases to the facts of the current case, and the publication of precedents to guide future public behaviour, do we rob a free and democratic society of a pillar of its existence?

Trevor C.W. Farrow

"Privatizing Our Public Civil Justice System"

(2006) 9 News & Views on Civil Justice Reform 16, footnotes omitted

At every level of the system—starting with the federal government itself—a strong preference is being voiced for getting cases out of the public stream and into a typically private, or at least confidential, alternative stream. Small claims courts, provincial superior courts, the Federal Court, and provincial and federal administrative tribunals have all developed alternatives to traditional, more formal investigation and hearing processes. These are in addition to the already available informal private tools of negotiation, mediation and arbitration typically available outside of a formal court or tribunal setting.

There are many stated benefits to this trend of privatization. In terms of the formal court or tribunal-connected tools, the overwhelming justification for their promotion is system efficiency: backlog reduction and savings of time, money and other resources. In terms of Alternative Dispute Resolution (ADR) tools generally, proponents point to advantages including reduced costs and delays, the ability to choose laws, procedures and judges and the potential to maintain relationships. Typically the most important advantage, however, is the ability to avoid public scrutiny. When a dispute involves the private rights of A v. B, and further, when two "consenting adults" (including corporations) have chosen to move their dispute off the busy docket of our public court system and into the private boardroom of an arbitrator or mediator, current views suggest that justice is being served. The argument is that the resolution of disputes—like other goods and services—should not be deprived of the benefits of freedom of movement and contract in efficiency-seeking, innovative and expanding market economy.

These purported benefits, however, do not come without costs. Without public scrutiny—through open court processes, the publication of precedents and the application of case law to the facts to be adjudicated—there is a real danger that parties, particularly those with power, will increasingly use this privatizing system in order to circumvent public policies, accountability and notions of basic procedural fairness.

These procedural concerns are clearly significant. In addition, however, there is a more fundamental concern at issue: democracy—and in particular, the way in which we regulate ourselves in democratic, common law communities.

Law Making in a Democracy

Law in a democratic society is primarily made through the tools of legislation and adjudication. Recognizing that adjudication plays an ordering role in society both in terms of resolving individual disputes and, more broadly, modifying societal behaviour, both public and private processes of adjudication count as lawmaking tools.

There is normally no issue as to the democratic legitimacy of the typical legislative process. Further, in terms of adjudication, contrary to the concerns of "judicial activism" critics, decisions made in open court, by appointed judges, pursuant to fair procedural regimes, also, in my view, usually accord with constitutional principals characterized by democratic notions of transparency, accountability and the rule of law. Where a democracy deficit comes into play, however, is not in open court with "activist" judges, but rather when the important societal ordering tool of adjudication goes underground to private arenas, without the guarantee of the rule of law badges of procedural fairness, transparency and independence of the decision maker. When decisions are made in these private circumstances, we often do not know what they are. And in any event, to the extent that we do know (which knowledge brings the broader behaviour modification element of adjudication into play), we typically have no record or guarantee of the fairness of the procedural or substantive legal regimes that were employed to reach a given result. What we are doing with our increasing reliance on ADR, then, is privatizing a significant way in which we make law and order our public and private affairs.

So why are we so acquiescent and even seemingly disinterested in the current move to privatize the adjudicative aspects of our law-making tools? That, in my view, is the democracy deficit with which we should be concerned. With limited exceptions, we expect public hearings, precedent and transparency in traditional court proceedings. Why then— other than for efficiency and privacy interest preferences—are we so deferential to the concern of privacy when it comes to the use of alternative dispute resolution tools?

Reclaiming the Rule of Law in Dispute Resolution Practices

In opposition to those who relegate public procedures honouring basic rule of law values to the background in favour of modern, consensually-based private dispute resolution regimes, I argue for increased transparency and accountability in current and emerging approaches to dispute resolution. The potential strengths of dispute resolution alternatives, particularly in free market economies must, of course, be recognized. When carefully crafted, however, such mechanisms can effectively secure rule of law values, while still facilitating many of the efficiency and accessibility goals of more privatized dispute resolution processes. But when it comes to a conflict between cost saving and efficiency on the one hand and transparent procedural justice on the other—particularly in cases involving issues of public interest—the latter must always trump.

There is no more important topic in law than the procedural rules by which our democratic system operates. Important parts of that system are the processes by which disputes are resolved. Without sound, accountable, yet creative dispute resolution processes, we potentially jeopardize individual rights, together with collective democratic values. In my view, current trends of privatization in the context of dispute resolution processes, are potentially putting those rights and values at risk. As such, we need to question our current trend of privileging the private over the public. And in any event, if we are going to continue experimenting with privatized civil justice—and it is likely that we will (and in some cases should)—we should only do so with full disclosure to the public regarding the rationalizations for, and implications of, these tools. To date, the public is largely unaware of the aggressive and systematic privatization of its public civil justice system. The resulting democratic deficit jeopardizes one of the foundational tenets of our civil justice system and our common law system of governance as a whole.

What other concerns does Farrow's critique raise about privatization? Much like the critiques made of privatizing education and health care in Canada, will the active encouragement of settlement as a desirable justice policy goal ultimately encourage the emergence of a separate system of private justice? Examples already exist of for-profit private courts or chambers where entrepreneurs not only offer adjudicative services, often staffed by retired judges, but also provide comprehensive dispute resolution services, including services to help parties negotiate their own resolutions to disputes. While public justice through the courts may still exist, will advocating for settlements through private means such as negotiation and mediation have adverse impacts on the public justice system? Will access to private justice only be available to those who can afford it? Will a fully developed private justice system with an emphasis on private settlement take away needed attention, resources, credibility, and importance from the public justice system, particularly the courts? Will the promotion of settlement ultimately result in a market-driven model of justice where access to all parts of the system is on a profit-driven fee-for-service basis with no or limited public or collective support?

In a private justice system, how would *justice* be defined? Would a private justice system create inequalities in the way justice is defined and dispensed? What would prevent private justice providers from adopting norms and "laws" that are promulgated as fair and just within the private system but that conflict with and perhaps contradict more widely accepted norms and laws in the public justice system? If negotiations take place in the shadow of the law, what would "law's shadow" comprise in a private justice system?

Economic Efficiency Versus Quality Justice

The History of ADR

An appreciation of the economic efficiency versus quality justice critique first requires an understanding of the history of ADR, because settlement advocacy has its genesis in the ADR movement.

While the full history of ADR can be found elsewhere,[6] ADR's background is steeped in settlement. The expression *alternative dispute resolution* emerged out of popular dissatisfaction with the administration of justice in the United States in the 1970s. This dissatisfaction

---

6   See for an overview A. Pirie, *Alternative Dispute Resolution: Skills, Science, and the Law* (Toronto: Irwin Law, 2000).

related to a number of serious concerns directed at court adjudication. Citing a need to avoid the undue costs and delays of court adjudication, ADR focused on informal justice and consensual methods of dispute resolution. Negotiation and assisted negotiation processes such as mediation initially attracted the most attention. Under ADR, settlement was the preferred outcome and negotiation was the dispute resolution process of choice. Consensual dispute resolution processes became alternatives to court adjudication.

ADR pressed the legal profession to look beyond the adversarial arena of the courtroom and the dominant image of the lawyer "as a knight in shining armor whose courtroom lance strikes down all obstacles."[7] It drew upon informal and private methods of dispute resolution from other cultures and experiences in dispute resolution in international settings as well as in labour relations. Naturally, negotiation and mediation, where a third-party mediator assists disputants to negotiate an outcome, were processes of much interest. The literature on negotiation and mediation flourished, and much attention was directed at a remarkable book by Roger Fisher and William Ury entitled *Getting to Yes: Negotiating Agreement Without Giving In.*[8]

Initially, ADR attracted criticism and hostility because it was a direct response to failings in the formal justice system, was becoming the norm rather than an alternative, and was considered better to boot. Its primary critics were those in the legal community whose court-centred procedures and structures were under attack. In the early 1980s, the harshest criticism was reserved for mediation, a process that was new and unfamiliar to most lawyers at the time. Former Chief Justice Allan MacEachern of the British Columbia Supreme Court "put the boots" to ADR, saying that

> ADR is often supported by well-intentioned people who, for a variety of reasons, are anxious to reorganize society and procedures of courts with naïve, theoretical concepts of humanity and efficiency ... society's decent people need the no-nonsense, straightforward procedures of courtroom litigation to fight unreasonable claims and not the "soft" procedures ADR offers.[9]

These criticisms did not put an end to ADR. It continued to grow in popularity, partly because its proponents educated those in the legal profession about ADR and located ADR within a problem-solving framework. Rather than view ADR as standing in isolation from the courts, a 1989 Canadian Bar Association Task Force on Alternative Dispute Resolution,[10] following similar developments in the United States, urged lawyers and others working with disputes to see their primary function as problem solving. If problem solving was the overriding function of a lawyer or the general mission of lawyering, ADR just provided other ways that lawyers could use to solve their clients' problems. Rather than separate ADR from traditional court procedures, the legal problem solver would evaluate the entire continuum

---

7   W. Burger, "Isn't There a Better Way?" (1982) 68 A.B.A. J. 274 at 275, the annual report on the state of the judiciary to the American Bar Association.

8   R. Fisher & W. Ury, *Getting to Yes: Negotiating Agreement Without Giving In* (Boston: Houghton Mifflin, 1981).

9   A. MacEachern, "Chief Justice Puts Boots to ADR" *Lawyers Weekly* (October 26, 1989).

10 Canadian Bar Association Task Force on Alternative Dispute Resolution, *Alternative Dispute Resolution: A Canadian Perspective* (Ottawa: CBA, 1989).

of dispute resolution techniques, skills, and resources and choose the most appropriate steps to resolve a dispute or conclude a transaction. ADR was not a movement to be resisted but an expression of the legal profession's continuing professional and ethical commitment to fair, effective, and accessible dispute resolution.

Framed in this manner, ADR flourished. A 1996 Canadian Bar Association Task Force on Systems of Civil Justice[11] affirmed the problem-solving orientation of lawyers in Canada and defined ADR as "involving a range of processes for resolving disputes," excluding only a trial or hearing. The task force specifically called for dispute resolution techniques (avoiding the baggage of the "alternative" moniker) to be promoted "not as alternatives to the civil justice system but as integral components of it." ADR even penetrated the courts. Pretrial conferences where judges had long-helped parties prepare for trial turned into settlement conferences where judges, essentially acting as mediators, helped parties negotiate solutions to their claims short of trial through judicial dispute resolution (JDR).

While ADR has now come to comprise all methods of dispute resolution, what has not changed over time is ADR's encouragement of and advocacy for settlement. Whether taking place inside or outside the courts, settlement by consensus lies at the heart of the modern ADR movement. Negotiation still remains the key consensual process. Whether practised by representatives, assisted by mediators in a range of mediation settings, or used directly by the parties themselves, negotiation stands front and centre with its goal of settlement or compromise.

On its face, the ADR movement, with its settlement ideal through negotiation, seems to make sense. But behind the modern rise in popularity of ADR is a complex political phenomenon composed of fundamental contradictions. Critics have asked why this emphasis on settlement happened at all, particularly when parallel justice reform movements were observed. Observing the cyclical nature of discontent with the courts and the resulting reforms characterized as informal justice, community justice, delegalization, deinstitutionalization, and now the development of alternative dispute resolution, critics have begun to look more closely at the newest reform movement. Since ADR is not a "new" development, what is behind the current surge in interest in private settlement? The answer lies in the goals of ADR.

The Goals of ADR: A Move to Economic Efficiency

Advocates of settlement assert that ADR has many laudable goals. According to Stephen Goldberg, Frank Sander, and Nancy Rogers,[12] ADR seeks to

- decrease court caseloads and expenses
- reduce the parties' expenses and time
- provide speedy settlement of those disputes that are disruptive to the community or the lives of the parties' families

---

11   Canadian Bar Association Task Force on Systems of Civil Justice, *Report of the Task Force on Systems of Civil Justice* (Ottawa: CBA, 1996).

12   S.B. Goldberg, F.E.A. Sander & N.H. Rogers, *Dispute Resolution: Negotiation, Mediation, and Other Processes* (New York: Aspen Law and Business, 1999) at 8.

- improve public satisfaction with the justice system
- encourage resolutions that are suited to the parties' needs
- increase voluntary compliance with resolutions
- restore the influence of neighbourhood and community values and the cohesiveness of communities
- provide accessible forums to people with disputes
- teach the public to try more effective processes than violence or litigation for settling disputes

Specific ADR programs have their own goals. Court-annexed programs seek to decrease court dockets, speed up the pace of cases, increase litigants' satisfaction with the court system, and lower recidivism. Neighbourhood justice centres, where local residents in conflict go and negotiate solutions themselves, strive to improve communications, strengthen communities, and be cost effective. Business leaders have pledged allegiance to ADR to reduce the costs associated with litigation and preserve ongoing relationships. Government has supported ADR to reduce the public cost of litigation.

The rationale for supporting ADR has been categorized according to economic and non-economic claims. Quantitative-efficiency claims consider ADR as cheaper and faster. Qualitative-justice claims consider ADR as better. In other words, ADR has production goals (the ability to do more with less) and quality goals (the ability to encompass values apart from time, cost, and institutional convenience). It is clear that different constituencies pursue ADR for different reasons. It is also clear that cheaper and faster do not always equate with better.

Quantitative-efficiency claims explain that the reason for ADR's promotion of settlement is economic efficiency. According to these claims, settlement is less expensive than dispute resolution in the courts. Settling a case before trial or before other expensive pretrial processes such as examinations for discovery results in enormous savings of lawyer fees and other associated legal costs. In addition to legal costs, the ancillary costs of prolonging disputes also can be saved. The business executive's valuable time is spared. She no longer has to be available for consultation and instructions to lawyers. Nor does she need to schedule time away from work to prepare for and attend a lengthy examination for discovery, be available to go to court, or be called as a witness at a trial. Other costs that often accompany a lengthy conflict are those imposed on the lives of friends, families, and other third parties associated with the dispute; these costs are avoided by settlement. Settlement also can improve the efficiency of the courts by reducing court dockets and freeing up judges' time and other court resources. Settlement allows court administrators to reallocate resources to other cases so that the overall efficiency of the system is improved.

Quantitative efficiency also includes time savings. Negotiated solutions can be reached more quickly than resolutions through the courts. As compared with the traditional and often slow pace of the litigation process, where cases may not get to trial for months or even years, settlement through negotiation can take place much earlier. Accordingly, many ADR initiatives provide for the early evaluation of cases so that parties can focus at the outset on negotiating what is really at issue. Mandatory mediation programs prevent parties from proceeding past a certain point in a lawsuit until good faith efforts have been made to negotiate a settlement with the help of a neutral third party—the mediator. Time is money and settlements made early save money.

Qualitative-justice claims behind ADR's emergence and its encouragement of settlement point in a different direction. According to these claims, settlement by negotiation can be qualitatively better than resolution through the courts for several reasons. First, in a settlement setting, the parties are empowered to make their own decisions. Rather than having a third-party judge or arbitrator impose a decision, the parties themselves take responsibility for the agreement. This empowerment strengthens individual autonomy and lessens dependency on external institutions. Second, the empowerment to make one's own decision about what to do in a dispute situation will lead to greater individual satisfaction not only with the outcome but also with the process itself. Third, negotiated settlements will be long-lasting. The endurance of negotiated settlements is based on the parties' ownership of their decision. Rather than having a stranger impose a decision (such as you must pay $12,000 per month in maintenance in a family-law case or you are liable for all the damages suffered in the motor vehicle accident in a personal injury case), voluntary settlements will be followed and complied with by the parties because it is the parties themselves who have agreed to the terms. It is their agreement. Fourth, ongoing relationships will be preserved through settlement. If the settlement process does not follow a highly adversarial approach but takes a principled or problem-solving approach that focuses on a mutually satisfactory, or win–win, solution, it is likely that any relationship between the disputants after the settlement will remain strong and intact. Finally, the settlement process will be transformative for individuals and society because it shows the disputing parties how to resolve future differences. Going through a settlement process enables individual disputants and even the communities they are part of to experience change and growth, particularly in terms of how they view others in dispute settings.

Has Economic Efficiency Vanquished Quality Justice?

While the pursuit and achievement of the above broad-ranging ADR goals seems to make sense, some have questioned whether market goals, particularly the reduction of litigation costs and delays, have come to dominate our thinking about the main goals of ADR and settlement. This is not to say that economic efficiency in dispute resolution should or could be ignored in a market economy. The concern is that the quality-justice goal that also inspired the ADR movement has been ignored or marginalized. Quality-justice ideals such as relationship building or educating disputants on the other side's point of view seem to have become less important because they do not easily fit with either the win–lose philosophy of adjudicative processes or the economic efficiency model of dispute resolution. It may be that the goals of economic efficiency and quality justice are incompatible. Directing disputes into time-saving processes such as negotiation may create injustice if the speedier disposition of cases through private negotiation removes traditional procedural safeguards that are available in the courts. In 1991 Carrie Menkel-Meadow concluded that efficiency had become the more prominent concern behind settlement advocacy, although "the quality of justice proponents came first in very recent history."[13]

---

13   C. Menkel-Meadow, "Pursuing Settlement in an Adversary Culture: A Tale of Innovation Co-opted or the Law of ADR" (1991) 19 Fla. St. U.L. Rev. 1 at 2.

The concern that settlement advocacy is now mainly about economic efficiency finds support in other disciplinary analyses. Locating ADR and its focus on settlement within an economic structure fits with Max Weber's sociological analysis of the relationship between law and capitalism.[14] Weber saw a direct link between the economic rationality embodied in capitalism—the pursuit of self-interest through the rational calculation of means and ends, and the particular type of legal rationality best able to sustain the capitalist economic order. In an emerging capitalist society, formal legal institutions and guaranteed legal rights ensure the predictability necessary for market activity. The legitimacy of this formal legal order is based on a belief in the rightness of a logically formal or gapless system of law in which judges apply abstract rules to individual cases to reach correct decisions. However, with a capitalist order firmly entrenched, the legitimacy provided by the ideology of formal justice alone is no longer required. With the formal justice system under attack as too rigid, slow, and inequitable, what arises from the anti-formalistic tendencies of modern legal development is not law reform to serve all ends that underlie the disenchantment with formal law such as social justice ends. What does arise is the increasing rationalization of law finely tuned to the rationality of advanced capitalism. Accordingly, Weber saw the emergence of special procedures "to eliminate the formalities of normal legal procedures for the sake of a settlement that would be both expeditious and better adapted to the concrete case" and "the general acceptance of law as an instrumental mechanism that facilitates compromise between conflicting interests."[15] ADR provides these "special procedures" and particularistic laws. Its focus on settlement could be seen as a capitalistic enterprise, a rationalization of the rigidities and arbitrariness of formal justice.

Accordingly, what may be missing in promoting or advocating for settlement is a concern for quality justice. Consider lawyer negotiators sitting down to work out a solution to a dispute between a liability insurer and a person who suffered serious personal injuries in a motor vehicle accident and is now confined to a wheelchair. These types of representative negotiations in personal injury cases are common. There is a lot of money at stake and no one would argue that we don't want the negotiation process to be economically efficient. But if resorting to negotiation to achieve a settlement that is economically efficient is the overarching goal, will other aspects of the dispute be ignored or marginalized? How is the emotional well-being of the plaintiff handled in the negotiation? Will time be available to address the non-monetary issues that likely exist between the plaintiff whose life has been changed forever and the negligent driver or the insurer who has offended the plaintiff with an unrealistic settlement offer? In a long-standing neighbour dispute around noise, would resorting to representative negotiation be successful if the main motivation was simply to help the parties avoid court costs and settle quickly without paying much attention to the future of their relationship? In complex treaty claims and other contentious matters, would representative negotiators for Aboriginal and non-Aboriginal governments ever reach a resolution if their focus is primarily on how much land, money, and other resources get redistributed? Surely negotiations that do not take account of the colonial experience and the severance

---

14   For an overview of Weber's work, see A. Kronman, *Max Weber* (London: Edward Arnold, 1983).

15   S. Ewing, "Formal Justice and the Spirit of Capitalism: Max Weber's Sociology of Law" (1987) 21 Law & Soc'y Rev. 509.

of trust experienced by First Nation peoples have no chance of success even if the negotiation process is carefully designed to be as fast and as inexpensive as possible.

On close examination, are economic factors the primary forces at play in determining the shape and form of new approaches to dispute resolution that encourage settlement? Are the encouragement of settlement and the search for the best theory and practice of representative negotiation actually just enterprises of a modern capitalist state? Is settlement advocacy mainly designed to correct the economic imbalances and inefficiencies in our formal dispute-resolution systems? Is the emphasis on interest-based, or integrative, negotiation in reality the promotion of an economic model of bargaining and one that ignores or has difficulty quantifying important non-economic factors?

If economic goals dominate developments in negotiation structure and practice, the concern is that qualitative matters that would be essential to be factored into a negotiation process might be excluded. Repairing an ongoing relationship and addressing how disputants could deal with each other in future disputes or responding to emotional scars caused by an act of discrimination are left out of negotiation sessions because they take too much time. These non-economic considerations, which actually lie behind the dispute and the goal of achieving a truly just result, cannot be easily quantified. Yet, isn't it precisely these qualitative matters that must be addressed in addition to economic efficiency and that should inform a reasoned consideration and use of negotiation?

Richard Abel recognizes the quandary of achieving both economic efficiency and quality justice through ADR. He suggests that informal justice processes like negotiation should not be repudiated because they do offer benefits to disputants:

> Yet if the goals of informal justice are contradictory and if it is incapable of realizing them because of contradictions inherent in advanced capitalism, informalism should not simplistically be repudiated as merely an evil to be resisted, or be dismissed as a marginal phenomenon that can safely be ignored. It is advocated by reformers and embraced by disputants precisely because it expresses values that deservedly elicit broad allegiance: the preference for harmony over conflict, for mechanisms that offer equal access to the many rather than unequal privilege to the few, that operate quickly and cheaply, that permit all citizens to participate in decision making rather than limiting authority to "professionals," that are familiar rather than esoteric, that strive for and achieve substantive justice rather than frustrating it in the name of form.[16]

A Move Away from Progressive Legal Rights

Integrative and Distributive Bargaining

ADR certainly has created renewed interest in many aspects of the negotiation process. We now more readily realize that people bring various conflict styles to a negotiation. Researchers have analyzed the tactics of a variety of negotiators to better understand which actions could be most effective. They discovered that some negotiators make unrealistic opening offers to maximize gains. Others engage in *Boulewarism*—a take-it-or-leave-it tactic. Feigned withdrawals could also be part of a negotiator's moves. Cross-cultural differences have also

---

16   R.L. Abel, *The Politics of Informal Justice* (New York: Academic Press, 1982) at 310.

been noted among negotiators. For example, in certain cultures, crossing the legs and point-ing the foot on the crossed leg directly at another person is viewed as threatening. In others, avoiding direct eye contact is a sign of respect rather than a sign that a person is hiding something. ADR focuses considerable attention on the intricacies of negotiation.

One aspect of negotiation that has not only attracted considerable attention but also become a dominant feature of negotiation research and practice is negotiating strategy. Research on negotiation strategy recognizes that a negotiator or representative negotiator takes either an integrative or distributive approach to bargaining (see chapters 3 and 4). Often the distinction between these strategies has been characterized as the difference between win–win and win–lose negotiation strategies, between interest-based bargaining and positional bargaining, between cooperation and competition, or between collaborative and adversarial approaches to problem solving. Leonard Riskin and James Westbrook explain this distinction according to the last characterization as follows:

> The adversarial orientation is grounded upon the assumption that there is a limited resource— such as money, golf balls, or lima beans—and the parties must decide whether and how to divide it. In such a situation, the parties' interests conflict; what one gains, the other must lose. An adversarial orientation naturally fosters strategies designed to uncover as much as possible about the other side's situation and simultaneously mislead the other side as to your own situ-ation. Until recently, the adversarial orientation has been the basis for most of the writing about negotiation by lawyers as well as most of the popular writing about negotiation.
>
> The problem solving orientation is quite different. It seeks to meet the underlying needs of all parties to the dispute or transaction, and, accordingly, tends to produce strategies designed to promote the disclosure and relevance of these underlying needs. The recommended tech-niques include those intended to increase the number of issues for bargaining or to "expand the pie" before dividing it.[17]

Getting to Yes

In *Getting to Yes*, Fisher and Ury advocate that the integrative approach to bargaining can optimize negotiation outcomes:

> Consider the story of two men quarreling in the library. One wants the window open and the other wants it closed. They bicker back and forth about how much to leave it open; a crack, halfway, three quarters of the way. No solution satisfies them both.
>
> Enter the librarian. She asks one why he wants the window open. "To get some fresh air." She asks the other why he wants it closed. "To avoid a draft." After thinking a minute, she opens wide a window in the next room, bringing in fresh air without a draft.[18]

By focusing on the underlying needs or interests of the parties in the library—a need for fresh air, a need to avoid drafts, and a common need for a comfortable reading environ-ment—the librarian identifies a creative solution that satisfies all interests. Rather than be

---

17   L.L. Riskin & J.E. Westbrook, *Dispute Resolution and Lawyers* (St. Paul, MN: West Publishing, 1987) at 116.

18   Fisher & Ury, *supra* note 8 at 41.

immobilized and frustrated at an impasse with stark conflicting positions—the window is either closed or open in varying degrees—the men agree upon a mutually acceptable solution that meets both parties' needs.

Similar interest-based analyses can be undertaken for more complex problems. By identifying underlying interests, negotiators can develop mutually acceptable solutions that satisfy the parties' important needs. For example, a defendant feels that his financial status and reputation would be threatened if his case goes to court and a large damage award is made against him. A confidential settlement for a reasonable dollar amount could respond to the defendant's concerns. In another example, a manager in a commercial dispute determines that a settlement may undermine her credibility in the eyes of her employees if they feel she is too soft in settling or giving in too easily. A letter from the other side to the employees (posted in the workroom) that applauds the competence of the manager in the negotiations and extols the benefits of a settlement could eliminate the manager's concern.

ADR has, by and large, strongly favoured the integrative, interest-based, problem-solving, collaborative, win–win approach. And why not? Who would argue against a negotiation process that encourages parties to work collaboratively together, to identify their underlying interests, and to develop creative win–win solutions? The alternative has often been portrayed as a nasty, costly, and long fight that would harm long-term relationships, result in winners and losers, and produce agreements that might not be long-lasting.

Shifting Away from Progressive Legal Rights

There is no question that ADR's emphasis on interests versus positions has been positive for disputants. Still, some critics have raised concerns that interest-based bargaining ignores the harsh reality of most bargaining situations.[19] That reality, they argue, is that most disputes are inherently distributive. Ultimately, negotiators need to agree on a distribution of resources. Whether the insurance company pays $1.5 million to settle or $750,000—the bargaining range based on best estimates of what a court would do if the case went to trial—depends not on interests but on hard adversarial bargaining.

Other critics have raised a more problematic concern: that interest-based bargaining is a regressive shift away from the public litigation that achieved progressive legal rights victories in the 1960s and 1970s. They believe that ADR has pulled attention from legal rights and given it to individual interests. By de-emphasizing legal rights and emphasizing party interests, ADR depoliticizes law. Susan Silbey and Austin Sarat describe this shift:

> ADR advances a non-rights based conception of the juridical subject … eschewing rights, ADR proponents deploy the discourse of interests and needs. They re-conceptualize the person from a carrier of rights to a subject with needs and problems, and in the process hope to move the legal field from a terrain of authoritative decision-making where force is deployed to an arena of integrative bargaining and therapeutic negotiation.[20]

---

19   J. White, "The Pros and Cons of 'Getting to Yes'" (1984) 34 J. Legal Educ. 115.

20   For an analysis of this change in emphasis, see S. Silbey & A. Sarat, "Dispute Processing in Law and Legal Scholarship: From Institutional Critique to the Reconstruction of the Juridical Subject" (1989) 66 Denv. U.L. Rev. 437 at 479.

Reframing disputes from rights-oriented problems to interpersonal or psychological-based problems reflects Fiss's critiques against settlement. Encouraging settlement advocacy through negotiation not only moves disputes out of the courts but also moves the resulting private settlements away from legal rights. In the interest-based bargaining scenarios preferred by ADR, discussions of legal rights are replaced with collaborative bargaining over packages of personal interests that are traded back and forth to arrive at a settlement.

The alienation of legal rights in dispute resolution can be particularly problematic to individuals or groups in society who are struggling to assert or advance their legal rights, perhaps under an equity umbrella. The important needs of these individuals and groups may be addressed in private negotiation, but any related advancement in social change is stalled. A negotiation process that emphasizes the satisfaction of interests raises concerns not only about individual harm and exploitation but also about the perpetuation of systemic inequalities.[21]

Consider a single mother of colour who claims that she has been discriminated against when a landlord refused to let her rent an apartment. Her lawyer advises her that she has a good chance of succeeding in a formal complaint under human rights legislation because her rights have been violated. Let's say the mother seeks a resolution through an interest-based bargaining scenario. Her interests could be identified as substantive (a need for housing), psychological (the embarrassment of facing discrimination), and procedural (the desire to deal with matters quickly). The landlord's interests could be identified as financial (wanting to avoid expensive proceedings) and reputational (wanting to maintain its reputation). A negotiated settlement that gives the mother an apartment quickly, an apology from the landlord, an agreement by the landlord to post anti-discrimination posters (for a time) in the apartment building, and an agreement by the mother to keep things quiet may meet all needs. However, legal rights and past behaviour are effectively jettisoned in favour of a forward-looking negotiation process that is mutually satisfying.

Searching for a Constant Negotiation Paradigm

Negotiation and Socio-economic and Political Conditions

This critique begins with several questions. These questions juxtapose the idea of a search for a constant theoretical understanding of negotiation, representative or otherwise, with the idea that negotiation is much too complex and omnipresent to be captured in such a way. In other words, is it possible to argue for a type of superiority in negotiation theory and practice, or are the ideas and practices of negotiation around the world or even in Canada too complex and diverse to be contained in one model of the process? Is it possible

---

21   There is a large body of literature that is critical of moving private disputes into private negotiation or mediation settings that is not only based on the disappearance of legal rights discussed above but also based on related grounds around lack of formality, absence of accountability, and important serious concerns about power imbalances due to violence, abuse, and fear. For an introduction to these critiques, see Pirie, *supra* note 6 at 189.

to conceptualize representative negotiation within clearly agreed-upon parameters? Is searching for a compact description of how best to represent people in negotiation possible and helpful? Or, is the best we can hope for a project that can only create another image of negotiation to add to the many that we already have? While contributing to theoretical understandings and perhaps even influencing the behaviour of some negotiators, does negotiation defy such an encapsulation?

The analysis of negotiation contained in this book is certainly not an isolated effort. As previously mentioned, the emergence of ADR spawned an appetite for a great deal of intellectual inquiry into negotiation theories and practices. The excerpt below from Menkel-Meadow, "Why Hasn't the World Gotten to Yes? An Appreciation and Some Reflections"[22] provides a recent and rich retrospective on the research and writing, both applied and practical, that has gone into negotiation over the last two decades. The breadth and depth of the work on negotiation is remarkable, and this book on negotiation can easily be added to the list.

Menkel-Meadow chronicles a number of multidisciplinary studies of negotiation. From the groundbreaking work of Mary Parker Follett in the 1920s to Richard Walton and Robert McKersie's development of the basic model of integrative, interest-based bargaining for labour relations in the 1960s, to John Nash's economic consideration of cooperative and competitive games, to Fisher and Ury's immensely popular *Getting to Yes* in 1981 and its many spin-offs, to Raiffa's reflections on the art and science of negotiation, the list goes on and on. Missing is mention of the work by pioneers like Fred Zemans and Neil Gold, who led the study of negotiation in the Canadian law school curriculum. Menkel-Meadow also responds to critics who saw problems with failing to address the relevance of culture, gender, differing substantive contexts, and the emotional or non-rational aspects in negotiation. She documents the enormous influences of writers from social psychology, anthropology, political science, and philosophy to the present understanding of negotiation. The enormity of it all takes your breath away.

Menkel-Meadow asks the question: "So, with all this intellectual ferment and practical activity, why has the world not been more successful at 'getting to yes'?"[23] Her response raises yet another daunting challenge for those who advocate for settlement. Menkel-Meadow proposes that those who research and write about settlement through negotiation, and particularly those who work to expand and adapt the hallmarks of integrative bargaining explored in *Getting to Yes*, may have been

> naïve about the social structural conditions under which integrative negotiation can most optimally occur. So, while social psychologists and game theorists look at strategic interactive behaviour at the individual, dyadic, or group level, I wonder whether we negotiation theorists need to spend more time on the macro questions surrounding our work: under what socio-economic and political conditions can we actually get to yes by negotiating fairly, equitably, and wisely to achieve joint and mutual gains with those we negotiate with?[24]

---

22   C. Menkel-Meadow, "Why Hasn't the World Gotten to Yes? An Appreciation and Some Reflections" (2006) 22 Negotiation Journal 485.

23   *Ibid.* at 497.

24   *Ibid.* at 499.

As you read the extract from Menkel-Meadow, consider what challenges her comments pose for advocates of settlement. How would you respond to these challenges?

Carrie Menkel-Meadow
"Why Hasn't the World Gotten to Yes?
An Appreciation and Some Reflections"
(2006) 22 Negotiation Journal 485, footnotes omitted

A Revolutionary Agenda

Some years ago at a conference of negotiation teachers sponsored by the Program on Negotiation at Harvard Law School and the Hewlett Foundation, Roger Fisher, speaking with some regret, remarked that he had hoped to change the world with the publication of *Getting to Yes* (Fisher and Ury 1981; Fisher, Ury, and Patton 1991). Yet, he said, the ways in which both world leaders and ordinary people had interacted with each other when in conflict seemed to have changed so little.

I rose to remind him that *Getting to Yes* had been published in more than thirty different languages, had sold millions of copies (and, as of this writing, is in its fortieth printing), and had revolutionized how negotiation is taught in law schools, business, public policy and planning, and in international relations and government departments. (Many of these places, in fact, had never even taught negotiation before the book's publication.) In addition, thousands of lawyers, diplomats, business people, labor negotiators, managers, and educators around the world have been trained in the book's concepts of "interest-based" bargaining, to think about "interests, not positions," to "separate the people from the problem," to "invent options for mutual gain," and to "use objective criteria" to productively resolve their disputes and conflicts. These have become the four golden rules of principled negotiation and *Getting to Yes* has become the canon.

Students of the book's authors, Roger Fisher, Bill Ury, and Bruce Patton, have learned not only these four methods of approaching others with the goal of improving the prospects of both parties via their negotiation. They have also mastered the "seven elements" of problem solving: learning how to diagnose and frame a problem, how to brainstorm multiple possible solutions, how to decide what information is necessary to develop solutions, and how to choose, implement, and evaluate actions taken. In negotiation classes throughout the world, students consider what they "did well" or what they would "do differently next time" as they navigate the experiential and behavioral components of the *Getting to Yes* conceptual frameworks, learning to improve behavior through on-going self-reflection and by constantly reapplying conceptual templates to the messiness and chaos of human communications and interactions.

In additional books, "spin-offs" of *Getting to Yes*, the authors have expanded the principles and elements to human relationships (*Getting Together: Building Relationships as We Negotiate* 1989); international relations (*Beyond Machiavelli: Tools for Coping with Conflict* by Fisher, Kopelman, and Schneider 1994); preparing for negotiation (*Getting Ready to Negotiate* by Fisher and Ertel 1995); designing systems of dispute resolution (*Getting Disputes Resolved: Designing Systems to Cut the Cost of Conflict* by Ury, Brett, and Goldberg 1988); dealing with difficult people (*Getting Past No: Negotiating with Difficult*

People by Ury 1991) or difficult issues (*Difficult Conversations: How to Discuss What Matters Most* by Stone, Patton, and Heen 1999); leadership (*Getting It Done: How to Lead When You Are Not in Charge* by Fisher and Sharp 1999); and most recently, emotions (*Beyond Reason: Using Emotions as You Negotiate* by Fisher and Shapiro 2005). All of these books were coauthored or heavily influenced by Fisher, Ury, and Patton, working with an ever-expanding group of the next generation of negotiation theorists, teachers, and practitioners.

The *Getting to Yes* influence has extended to the production of new theories, many books and articles, laboratory and empirical studies of actual or simulated negotiation behavior, and countless applications of the basic interest-based or principled model of negotiation for mutual gain in actual negotiations, both dyadic and multipartied.

Getting to Yes did not create a field *per se*, because others had gone before and were the sources of many of the book's insights. Notable among these sources were Boston educator Mary Parker Follett, who in the 1920s had developed important ideas about constructive and integrative conflict resolution, and Richard Walton and Robert McKersie (1965), who developed the basic model of integrative, interest-based bargaining for labor relations in the 1960s. The authors of *Getting to Yes* also drew on the many constituent disciplines of negotiation theory and practice, including economics, game theory, psychology, anthropology, political science, sociology, decision sciences, communications, and planning, to name some, but not all, of the bodies of knowledge that have contributed ideas or "memes" (cultural genes) about negotiation. However, the publication of *Getting to Yes* heralded the birth of a newly invigorated interdisciplinary, behavioral, and conceptual field, whose theorists and practitioners hoped, as Roger has said, "to change the world" through ideas, teaching, and action.

In this retrospective essay, I seek to appreciate and celebrate the achievement of *Getting to Yes* and its progeny, to explore the ideas it has contributed to what we know and what we do, and to consider the new frontiers of knowledge that are being explored in its name. In addition, I will reflect on what was *missing* in the original conceptions (some of which has been added in more recent work) and on what remains to be done. Finally—and, more poignantly—I will take up Roger Fisher's question of why the world has not changed enough so that we explore every situation of conflict as an opportunity to get to some kind of "Yes" with the others we are involved with. Whether lamenting the absence of world peace or more constructive ordinary human interaction, I fear that ideas of adversarialism, competition for seemingly scarce resources, individual or national maximization strategies, so-called "clashes" of competing interests and cultures, and vested interests in competitive habits—rather than cooperation or collaboration—continue to thrive and to blunt the great vision of human potential that lies at the heart of *Getting to Yes*. Why this is so should be one of the most important subjects in the study of human interaction.

Roots and Sources: Intellectual Convergences
This essay is a personal appreciation as well as my attempt to both assess and advance the intellectual and practical impact of a body of work aimed at changing intellectual and behavioral worldviews (or paradigms, if you prefer the now trite reference to the work of Thomas Kuhn [1962]). What produces paradigm shifts, or more modestly, new ideas or conceptions of human reality? Moreover, what allows them to take hold or not at particular moments in time?

Consider my first encounter with *Getting to Yes*. It was 1982 and I had just completed the first draft of my own attempt to transform the adversarial mindset with which lawyers approach legal disputes, a work titled *Toward Another View of Legal Negotiation: The Structure of Problem Solving* (see Menkel-Meadow 1984). I was in a bookstore in Manhattan, visiting my hometown from my academic home three thousand miles away in "touchy-feely" California. I spotted a new book whose cover announced in bold green letters that one can "negotiate agreement without giving in."

I began to read and my professional self felt a knot in her stomach—the advantage of thinking that you are writing something new (or non-case-oriented in law) is that you cannot, in law review terms, be intellectually or legally "preempted." I read the four principles of "principled negotiation" as Fisher and Ury articulated them and saw an amazing likeness to my own "problem-solving" conception of negotiation, involving consideration of "needs and interests" not legal positions, a search for "creative solutions" that "meet the needs of all parties" by "expanding resources" and an attempt to persuade competitive individual maximizers—whose lawyer ethics require negotiators to be zealous advocates, to instead "focus on solving the underlying problem of both parties." In the important four maxims of *Getting to Yes*, I saw an elegant, pithy, and compressed template, distilled from thousands of words and ideas from the "shoulders of giants" who had gone before (Merton 1993).

I also began to see some places where I differed from this spare but wise text. No "separating the people from the problem" for me—the people *are* too often the problem to be solved—and negotiation is more like a set of simultaneous equations that require a focus both on the substantive problem and on the human relations problems (now conceptualized by other negotiation theorists as "the negotiation across the table" and "behind the table" [Mnookin, Peppet, and Tulumello 2000]). And, while the pithy, elegant spareness of the prose aspires to universal or generalizable principles of negotiation, I wondered how "insisting on and using objective criteria" can function in legal negotiations where both parties appeal to "objective" legal principles as they seek settlements of contested lawsuits or argue about the appropriate language for an administrative regulation.

However, with my new book in hand and remembering Thomas Kuhn's shifting paradigms, I emerged from the bookstore with the knot in my stomach loosened, believing that I was witnessing a particular, propitious, and exciting moment of human insight. What I had been thinking and studying on the West Coast at the University of California, I discovered, was simultaneously being explored in Cambridge, Massachusetts, and in other places, and by those in countless other disciplines outside of the law.

A Cultural Convergence

This was a moment of important intellectual and cultural convergence! As it was with the important studies of the structure of DNA or the origin of AIDS that were conducted simultaneously in different laboratories thousands of miles apart, so it was with the development of ideas of negotiation and alternative dispute resolution in the early 1980s: no one theorist or researcher dreams or thinks alone. Ideas are the products of their time; searches for solutions to historically contingent human problems.

I was not alone—others were thinking that people could do things more effectively by trying to meet the needs of others, as well as themselves, by getting the other side to say "yes" to their propositions, by looking for ways to give those on the other side of a negotiation what they want. And, I knew, there was grand theory, known as game theory, to support this iconoclastic notion in the law. (I had read the theories of John Nash, who was later awarded the Nobel Prize in economics, of equilibria in both competitive and cooperative two-party and multiparty "games" [Nash 1953, 1950].) Then, just a few months later, Howard Raiffa published a masterful text that explained both the math (the science) and the human dimension (the art) of applying game theoretic notions to problems of human communication and coordination (Raiffa 1982).

So why were Roger Fisher, Bill Ury, Bruce Patton, Howard Raiffa, Thomas Schelling, Mary Rowe, Frank Sander, Lawrence Susskind, Deborah Kolb, Jeff Rubin, James Sebenius, Michael Wheeler and others, like me, thinking some of the same things at the same time—that new models of negotiated behavior were necessary? To slightly revise Shakespeare, the answers lie not only in us but also in our cultures (Breslin and Rubin 1991).

Roger Fisher has often spoken of the inspiration for his *Getting to Yes* ideas: from his earlier work for the Justice Department where he argued cases before the Supreme Court and from his experience of losing friends in World War II. Witnessing the waste of war and unnecessary death and destruction, as well as the impoverished rigidity of adversarial argument, he thought that there must be a better way for nations and people to live with each other.

Out of that same era comes much of the theory that informed conventional models of negotiation—whether analyzing the two-sided alliances of World War II or the Cold War, an entire generation of scientists studied and theorized, mostly through simulation, how people behave under conditions of uncertainty, poor or nonexistent communication, and apparently divergent values and goals. And so, theories of mostly competitive and individual self-interest and maximization were developed, to be tested in laboratories under simulated conditions, to provide "real-world," as well as academic, guidance about how to negotiate with others (presumed adversaries). In the law (Menkel-Meadow 2004), which was my professional discipline as well as Roger Fisher's, these dominant models of competition, assumed scarce resources, and divergent goals and values meshed nicely with the American adversarial legal system and its centuries-old institutions of conflict resolution that were designed to produce winners and losers (Menkel-Meadow 2006).

For Bill Ury, on the other hand, whose discipline is anthropology, no one human form of interaction could possibly be so universal, and he had witnessed and participated in other ways of solving problems and resolving conflicts (Ury 2000).

The legal system was experiencing attacks from all sides, with U.S. Supreme Court chief justice Warren Burger decrying the cost, waste, and delay of the American court system, and community activists and consumers demanding greater participation in decision making, lawmaking, and governance. These critiques and demands for change cast doubt on the effectiveness of bilateral binary forms of adversarial and command dispute resolution in both litigation and negotiation. In 1976, Harvard Law School professor Frank Sander … had argued for more institutional variety in formal legal dispute resolution (Sander 1976) so that different institutional arrangements might be available for different kinds of disputes.

In my own case, I had litigated a series of successful public interest lawsuits challenging prisons, discriminatory employment practices, and state welfare systems that had failed to solve the underlying problems of my clients and their interest groups, and I began to search other fields for guidance on different approaches to legal problem solving (Menkel-

Meadow 1983). Dissatisfied with the brittle labor arbitration outcomes in the mining industry, Stephen Goldberg at Northwestern University had begun to focus on a more mediational model of negotiation in grievance cases and eventually developed a systemic approach to changing conflict resolution culture. Gary Lowenthal was examining similar issues in the criminal justice system (Lowenthal 1982). Hotly contested environmental cases that consumed years of litigation and stalled both conservation and development projects led environmentalists like Larry Susskind and Gail Bingham to focus on more flexible, participatory, and consensual modes of dispute resolution.

Clearly, the stars were aligning, and something in the culture was converging. Theorists and practitioners of negotiation and conflict resolution from a variety of disciplines were dissatisfied enough with the dominant paradigms and practices to rebel and to develop "new" ideas and prescriptions about how people might more effectively interact to solve problems.

Of course, as I noted earlier, the negotiation approaches introduced to wider audiences in the early 1980s were not entirely new. They were derived from earlier work by such practitioner-theorists as Follett (1995) and, more recently, political scientists and psychologists such as William Zartman (Zartman and Berman 1982) and Morton Deutsch (1973), who had studied processes of human coordination in other domains and had begun to develop taxonomies of such different forms of both individual and group behavior as cooperation and competition, and integrative and distributive forms of bargaining.

Another important observation: the approaches suggested by those who supported "integrative," "principled," or "problem-solving" negotiation were optimistic, not pessimistic, differing in that way radically from the worldview of the Cold War generation of scholars. The modern flowering of negotiation theory precedes the collapse of the Berlin Wall and the end of the Cold War by nearly a decade. And the canon that comprises *Getting to Yes* and other pioneering works from the same era contained positive and prescriptive social theory. Their authors believed they could teach to the best in people, not the worst. An abiding American optimism, attached to classic American pragmatism, characterized these works in their belief that new ideas could be harnessed to new techniques with the power to transform human behavior and solve social dilemmas. This represented a marked departure from the more pessimistic theories of human behavior that ruled several disciplines at the time, including law and economics, which measures human behavior by self-interested "utilities" and "transaction costs," or Oliver Wendell Holmes' "bad man" theory of jurisprudence that invoked the law and reason to curb man's instinct to take advantage of others if unconstrained. One can also draw a link between these ideas and the positive, progressive, and participatory methods of education being developed at many American universities in the 1970s and 1980s, which included clinical legal education programs and the use of simulations and case studies in business and policy schools.

Although *Getting to Yes* espoused no particular political theory and, in Roger Fisher's words, was written with the idea of giving advice to "both sides" of any dispute, it was seen by some as promoting particular agendas—world peace, the human potential movement, the destruction of the legal profession as we know it, "soft" compromise or agreements to bargain with the devil—and thus raised the ire of those who continued to see the world as dark, competitive, and brutish (White 1984).

In the second edition, in an appended section that attempts to deal with some of the questions and criticisms leveled at "principled negotiation," the authors confess: "[W]e do think that, in addition to providing a good all-round method for getting what you want in a negotiation, principled negotiation can help make the world a better place. It promotes understanding among people, whether they be parent and child, worker and manager, or Arab and Israeli. … The more a problem-solving approach to negotiation becomes the norm in dealing with differences among individuals and nations, the lower will be the costs of conflict. And beyond such social benefits, you may find that using this approach serves values of caring and justice in a way that is personally satisfying" (Fisher, Ury, and Patton 1991: 154–155). Therefore, *Getting to Yes* does indeed aim to improve the world at the global, local, and personal levels.

Stated simply, the basic core ideas of *Getting to Yes*, derived from the social scientists and practitioners who inspired the authors, are that by *determining* what parties' interests and needs actually are, rather than assuming what they are, we can search for ways to craft a solution to a problem by looking for *complementary*, not competing, goals, needs, or desires (Homans 1974). We can then search for *new resources* or *expanded options* and use principles of merit or agreed-upon standards to find solutions, which can often be *creative* (better than what parties would have come up with on their own), sometimes *contingent* (to be revisited as conditions change), and more *legitimate* because they are mutually arrived at, rather than commanded by the law or other powerful institutions or acquiesced in through the force of power.

Among the most important contributions of *Getting to Yes* was the focus on "joint" or mutual, rather than individual, gain. The mindset of many conventional negotiators, as well as most popular books about negotiating at the time, was to focus on helping the negotiator get what he or she wanted by overpowering or persuading the other side (Cohen 1980). To think of *Getting to Yes* in deep philosophical terms, it turned negotiation into a deontological Kantian project of treating all people as ends, not means, for mutual benefit, not self-interested Hobbesian coexistence. So negotiators are always to have "both" or "all" sides (or "counterpart or partners," as Jonathan Cohen [2003] terms them) in mind when negotiating, not just themselves or their own constituencies. And negotiations should be evaluated by how wise, efficient, and relationship-enhancing they are (Fisher, Ury, and Patton, 1991: 4) *for all parties.*

At a practical level, *Getting to Yes* also operationalized the teachings of social psychologists and some political scientists. Learn what other people care about, as George Homans (1974) and Abraham Maslow (1970) recommended. Ask for reasons that go behind stated positions and seek to rationally persuade those you are working with, as Jurgen Habermas (1989) suggested. Think of new ideas; do not be overly restricted by old ways and precedents; use "friction" to create new possibilities like music from the friction of a bow on a violin, as Mary Parker Follett (1995) advocated. "Integrate" the needs and interests of all parties, rather than see them as necessarily in opposition, according to the recommendations of Follett (1995) and Walton and McKersie (1965). Develop a plan in advance, but be open to "brainstorming" new ideas without overly critical or premature evaluation. These principles of action, "theories-for-use" (in Donald Schön's [1983] terms), are potentially so universal and helpful—has always bothered me that this pithy distillation of thousands of years of scholarship on human behavior is often only found in the "business" (or "communication" or "management" or "marketing") sections of our local bookstores. Why not in "world affairs," "psychology," "law," "philosophy," or certainly, "current affairs"?

Moving Forward: What Was Missing and What Has Been Added

The publication of *Getting to Yes* helped provide a needed text for courses in conflict resolution in many different fields. At the same time, the financial support of the Hewlett Foundation helped found several important interdisciplinary theory centers on negotiation and dispute resolution. In addition, the ideas of *Getting to Yes* were both further developed and criticized in the two decades that followed.

Early critics—and I was one of them—accused the book of aiming at impossible or inaccurate universal levels of generalization by making assumptions about nonscarcity (White 1984), or by failing to address the relevance of culture (Avruch 2000; Brett 2001), gender (Kolb and Coolidge 1991, Menkel-Meadow 2000), and different substantive contexts of negotiation (Menkel-Meadow 2001). Others criticized its failure to focus on the emotional or nonrational aspects of negotiation, for assuming equal bargaining power among and between negotiators, for failing to address the issues of serious inequalities of bargaining endowments (Grillo 1991), and for being focused exclusively on dyadic and relatively simple, rather than multiparty, or complex, negotiations.

In the years that have followed publication of *Getting to Yes*, much work has been done by its authors, their colleagues, and an international array of scholars and practitioners to enrich, supplement, and expand on the ideas, concepts, and frameworks necessary to study and perform "successful" negotiations, as well as to study, empirically, the conditions under which we are more or less likely to "get to yes."

Lengthier and more rigorous analysis of negotiation problems produced taxonomies and classifications of negotiation types. Howard Raiffa, exploring negotiation from mathematical and decision-making perspectives, made the concept of Pareto-optimality accessible to many negotiators, pointing out that there were often many points on the frontier of possible settlements that would make both parties better off. Raiffa also focused on the differences between descriptive and prescriptive approaches to negotiation analysis and asked negotiation analysts to think about whether their advice to negotiators would be the same or different if advising only one side of a bargaining exercise or both, illuminating the way in which strategic thinking depends on what it is being used for.

David Lax and James Sebenius (1986), fresh from involvement in such complex real-world negotiations as those that crafted the Law of Sea, coined the term "negotiator's dilemma" to describe the likelihood that opportunities for creative problem solving, value creation, and integrative bargaining coexist with opportunistic efforts to "claim value" in every negotiation. Negotiators, they argued, must then choose when and how to engage in both collaborative and competitive strategies in interaction with other parties making similar choices. Their work on the negotiator's dilemma expanded on the strategic dilemmas of conflict developed earlier by Thomas Schelling (1960) as part of his theories of conflict action, a work that was recognized last year with a Nobel Prize in economics. Their work also paralleled the research of social psychologists Kurt Lewin and Morton Deutsch who mapped two basic human responses to conflict: competition and cooperation (Deutsch 1973, 2000).

At the University of Michigan, Robert Axelrod's (1984) compelling work on *The Evolution of Cooperation* used a computer-driven Prisoner's Dilemma game to explore strategies of relative cooperation, with measured opportunities for revenge and forgiveness. This work has implications not just for negotiation, but for evolutionary biology as well: how and why do traits of cooperation and trust appear in organisms if competition and survival of the fittest is indeed the way species evolve? These questions continue to be examined by those who hold more optimistic explanations of human adaptive behavior.

Assisted negotiation (mediation) and the roles of third parties became a booming area for both teaching and study beginning in the 1980s (Kolb and Associates 1994). Other theorists and practitioners developed the field even further to examine complex public policy disputes of environmental, budgetary, and community issues (Susskind, McKearnan, and Thomas-Larmer 1999). Much, but not all of this work, was done in the physical shadow of Fisher, Ury, Patton, and the Program on Negotiation at Harvard Law School that was their home base. Family and community mediation programs were strongest in California, where they provided opportunities for empirical evaluation of the effectiveness of consensual agreements (Friedman 1993; Merry and Milner 1993; Pearson and Thoennes 1989) and also for trenchant critiques of the "accommodation" or "harmony" culture (Grillo 1991; Nader 1993), which questioned whether it was not sometimes necessary to stay in conflict and fight for important reforms.

At Stanford, a multidisciplinary group of scholars, working in social and cognitive psychology, law, economics, and political theory, building on earlier studies of social and psychological processes in negotiation (Rubin and Brown 1975), created a rigorous and organized research program to study why people more often "get to no," culminating in the important *Barriers to Conflict Resolution* (Arrow et al. 1995). From the work of these scholars came another important general question that itself has spawned hundreds of studies: if "getting to yes" makes so much sense, why do so many barriers to reaching agreement remain so powerful? If integrative bargaining is rational *and* economically efficient, why do we not engage in it more often?

In departments of psychology, economics, and schools of law and business, researchers began to study the important behavioral questions underlying *Getting to Yes*. Under what conditions do people cooperate or compete? How much information do people really process or hear during tense strategic interactions? Max Bazerman and Margaret Neale (1993) at Northwestern University, explored the "rationality" of negotiation, while Amos Tversky, Lee Ross, and Daniel Kahneman (also a Nobel prize winner) explored the "distortions" in human behavior, the "heuristics" or shortcuts in human thought and behavior processes that fail objective, empirical, and verifiable tests of rationality. Lee Ross's (1995) observation that parties in a negotiation literally cannot hear each other and "reactively devalue" what others say, simply because of the structural opposition inherent in their roles (parent–child, spouse–spouse, teacher–student, boss–employee, etc.), empirically justified the use of third-party mediators who are needed to clean out the "noise" or at least "neutralize" the information.

Others have labeled the intellectual developments of the late twentieth century as the "interpretative or hermeneutic turn." In negotiation studies, I have always thought of this work as the "heuristic cognitive bias turn." For at least fifteen years now, negotiation scholars in a variety of disciplines have theorized, modeled, and tested how cognitive distortions get in the way of reaching wise and fair negotiated settlements by looking at such phenomena as primacy, recency, loss and risk aversion, the winner's curse, reactive devaluation, and endowment effects. (See Korobkin and Guthrie 2004; Mnookin 1993; Rachlinski 1996 for some summaries of this research.)

This work continues to flourish and provide us with many insights, although I sometimes wonder—as I think of Roger Fisher's desire to provide practical and useful advice to negotiators—how much information about distorted decision making can one negotiator handle or correct? So, while these inquiries are analytically rich and intellectually fascinating, I sometimes wonder if too much attention to the details of "bad" reasoning gets in the way of using the simpler, if more positive, principles of "principled negotiation."

As intellectual developments in the rest of the academy challenged universalism, *Getting to Yes*, as well as the growth of the mediation field and the whole alternative dispute resolution movement, were interrogated for assuming that all negotiators are equal, share a common culture, and generally seek the same ends. I remember my own intellectual vertigo, when, at a conference on Gender and Negotiation at the Program on Negotiation in 1995, a number of scholars launched a "feminist" critique of *Getting to Yes* for being instrumental (focused on utilitarian "interests," not human needs), unconcerned with power imbalances in negotiation, ignoring important principles of justice that affected those outside of the parties' own consensual universe, and for making assumptions that by any standard or principle could be "objective."

How could I, a feminist teaching women's studies, reconcile my feminist critique with my faith in the four principles of problem-solving negotiation? What could be unfeminist about meeting people's needs and trying to solve problems? Deborah Kolb (1991), Kolb and Williams (2003), and others (Babcock and Laschever 2003) took on these important questions; and, in the last decade, research on whether the theory itself is gendered, or whether the practice of negotiation depends on certain patterned demographics (gender, race, class, age, nationality, ethnicity) has flourished, although in my view, the answers to these controversial questions remain unresolved (Menkel-Meadow 2000).

More recently, scholars and practitioners of negotiation have worked with psychotherapists, musicians, and actors to explore the components of behavioral improvisation and to understand how we choose to behave or "intervene" when trying to enact our concepts of what makes for good negotiation (Balachandra 2005). So negotiation "principles," once thought of in recipe-like prescriptive terms, now take on the dilemma of modern chaos theory: can we construct order out of the spontaneous and interactive interactions of random human beings trying to make something happen together? Is negotiation like jazz (requiring flexibility and creativity) or is it more akin to war planning or puzzle solving (methodical, logical, and strategic)?

And, in an effort to respond to some of their earlier critics who bemoaned the absence of discussion of the "human dimension" in trying to get to yes with someone else who does not want to, Roger Fisher, with Daniel Shapiro (2005), has joined a growing group of negotiation scholars studying the role of emotions and mood in affecting negotiation behaviors and outcomes (Freshman, Hayes, and Feldman 2002; Reilly 2005; Ryan 2006).

These lines of inquiry, then, focus both on the interpersonal communication aspects of negotiation, such as Kolb's (2004) analysis of "moves and turns" in conversation to meet, challenge, or deflect status put-downs as well as the larger structural issues, that is, asking under what conditions can negotiators achieve good results, or what inhospitable conditions reduce good thinking or make resource expansion unlikely. Such questions have expanded our ideas about where we negotiate, when we negotiate, and what we can negotiate for.

Applications of this more recent work, both critical and expansionary, have expanded examinations of negotiation processes into new realms:

- administrative rule making or "reg-neg" (regulation-negotiation);
- organizational problem solving through ombudsmanship;
- public policy decision making; and
- deliberative democracy (see *Dispute Resolution Magazine* 2006).

These new uses of problem-solving negotiation build on the earlier applications of *Getting to Yes* principles in practices such as

- the convening of mediation and settlement conferences in courts all over the U.S.;
- the development of mediation programs in primary and secondary schools (peer mediation for problem solving);
- the adaptation of more participatory meeting management styles (Susskind and Cruikshank 2006); and
- the famous use of the "one-text procedure" outlined in *Getting to Yes* at the Camp David peace talks (under both Presidents Jimmy Carter and Bill Clinton).

Getting to Yes was written as generic advice for negotiations in a wide variety of human endeavors. More recently, negotiation scholars and practitioners have begun to look at whether negotiation in *dispute* settings (litigation, political battles, and international diplomacy) differs from negotiation in *deal* settings, such as many classic business transactions where new entities and relationships are being established (such as contract negotiations, mergers and acquisitions, and property transfers). And, with growing sophistication about context, negotiation may be thought of and practiced differently when it occurs among such "repeat players" as friends, spouses, colleagues, organizations with established business relationships, and powerful nations than it is in "one-off" buyer–seller encounters. And so "getting to yes" has become more nuanced and complex, less of a "unified field theory" than when the book was initially published (Schneider and Honeyman 2006).

The Way Forward: The Continuing Legacy of *Getting to Yes*
So, with all of this intellectual ferment and practical activity, why has the world not been more successful at "getting to yes"?

The legacy of *Getting to Yes* operates on several different levels. It functions on the ideational or theoretical level; that is, what ideas did it give us? It also functions on the practical level: do we achieve more consensual and better-executed settlements than we used to? Is this a good model of negotiation to teach people? Finally, the book's legacy has a moral dimension: should we continue to try to "get to yes" with those whom we have profound disagreements with or whom we are trying to make something new with?

At the level of ideas, *Getting to Yes* was nothing short of a plea for a major cultural change. To focus on underlying interests and to approach another party in a negotiation with the idea of forging a joint agreement that would meet the needs of both parties was—and, I am afraid, still is—countercultural to the way in which most parties approach negotiations. Rather than thinking of the other side as someone to be bested, *Getting to Yes* asks us to think about seeing the other party as a partner in creating new entities, new or better relationships, or new resources, even if we are in disagreement (or worse, engaged in litigation or war) with the other party.

Getting to Yes provided some of the techniques for trying to achieve this (brainstorming, one-text procedures, side-by-side planning), and subsequent scholarship and popular writing provided more. Lax and Sebenius (1986), for example, wrote about the analytics of trading, and making contingent and sequential agreements. More recently, negotiation scholars have broadened the intellectual agenda to consider under what conditions integrative or principled bargaining will be mostly likely to succeed, whether negotiation is best studied as a rational process of thinking and planning or a more chaotic human behavioral improvisational art, and under what circumstances negotiation is the best process to use and which circumstances are better suited to a different process.

In the last two decades, teachers of negotiation from varied disciplines have created thousands of simulations to be used in teaching particular techniques (listening, brainstorming, trading for differences, value creation, resource expansion, dovetailing differential goals) in arenas as diverse as management, international relations, environmental studies, public policy, labor relations, and all areas of litigation. (See, e.g., Menkel-Meadow, Schneider, and Love 2006.) Periodically, we meet and exchange research findings and pedagogical ideas. And, over the years, we have implemented efforts to bring theorists and practitioners together to bridge the theory–practice divide (Volpe and Chandler 2001; Cheldelin et al. 2002). And, although there has been spirited debate about the times when negotiation is *not* appropriate or right (see, e.g., Mnookin 2003), most of us do all this believing that "getting to yes" is a morally good thing to do.

But, as Roger Fisher asked several years ago, if all of this *is* such a good idea, why have these ideas not had a greater cultural impact or more of an effect on international relations, in the media, in the schoolyard, our universities, workplaces, or in Congress? Is there something in human nature that prevents us from seeing those opposite us at a negotiation table as a partner with whom we might create a joint venture, or, at the very least, an agreement to stop disagreeing? Are we socialized in a competitive society to consider "the other" as an antagonist? Is the world really one of scarce resources that makes sharing or making new things virtually impossible? Does the larger *zeitgeist* in which we live (Cold War, economic boom and bust, globalization, the War on Terror) affect how we conceptualize the world and what we do? Is *Getting to Yes* and its progeny a product of its time or a more universal expression of what might be possible, of what might be achieved?

These difficult questions merit deep exploration. We must ask to what extent the *Getting to Yes* model is situated in a larger culture over which it has attempted to exercise some influence and to what extent it is a product of a particular time as Mary Parker Follett (the 1920s) and the game theorists (1940s–1960s) were of theirs? I also wonder why the negotiation theorists, teachers, and practitioners among us are not more often consultants to nations in conflict, to litigants in dispute, to government agencies. Moreover, when we have had these opportunities, what have we learned about our own effectiveness?

I am reminded of Michael Ignatieff's (1995) eloquent lament in the introduction to his book *Blood and Belonging* in which he expressed the hope that the fall of the Berlin Wall and the Soviet state signaled the dawn of an era of cosmopolitanism, to be characterized by an appreciation for cultural differences within a world of peaceful exchange and democratic governance. But as ethnic wars broke out in rapidly disintegrating nation-states, Ignatieff wrote that he learned an important lesson: that some degree of nation-state security and economic self-sufficiency is necessary to prevent the scarcity and suspicion that breed the fear and insecurity that lead to death and destruction.

When I think of *Getting to Yes* and the world of integrative negotiation that I too have embraced, I wonder sometimes if we have been naïve about the social structural conditions under which integrative negotiation can most optimally occur. So, while social psychologists and game theorists look at strategic and interactive behavior at the individual, dyadic, or group level, I wonder whether we negotiation theorists need to spend more time on the macro questions surrounding our work: under what socioeconomic and political conditions can we actually get to yes by negotiating fairly, equitably, and wisely to achieve joint and mutual gain with those we negotiate with? What do we owe to others—both those inside and outside our negotiations—when we negotiate (Menkel-Meadow and Wheeler 2004)? Should we work to "get to yes" only for the parties inside a negotiation or should we think about how what we do affects the rest of the world?

How can we fully evaluate what *Getting to Yes* and the rest of us negotiation theorist-practitioners have accomplished? Certainly, the academy has been affected; additional courses and degree programs in conflict resolution have been launched every year since 1981, and legions of new books and articles on the subject have been published. Increasingly, children have been taught to "use your words" in school-based conflict resolution and peer mediation programs. More and more workplaces offer ombuds or other internal grievance systems for conflict prevention and resolution, which are sometimes called organizational dispute resolution or internal dispute resolution.

For all the criticism leveled against court-based mediation and settlement programs, most state and federal courts now require some effort at conciliatory processes before parties can engage in the full adversarial tilt of trial. More and more divorcing couples seek mediated, rather than litigated, resolution of their changed family situations. And a new breed of lawyers seeks to resolve disputes through collaborative, not competitive, techniques (Tesler 2001). Despite the current War on Terror and fighting in the Middle East, the Dayton Accords and the Oslo Accords exemplify the use of negotiation and mediation-based principles in international diplomacy and violence reduction.

Negotiation principles are now explicitly discussed in transactional work (contracting, entity creation) and governmental and policy decision making. Some might argue that negotiation and conflict resolution theory is part of the backbone or foundation of recent efforts to enhance deliberative democracy in our own nation, as well as abroad.

Perhaps most importantly, many of us have discovered that friends, acquaintances, and colleagues from outside our areas of expertise will sometimes display an awareness of the principles of *Getting to Yes*; in the midst of a disagreement and in an unlikely place, we will sometimes discover someone who "speaks our language." These ideas are increasingly well exposed, and some of my students and younger colleagues report that in many settings (childcare, sports teams, schools), one can expect people to solve problems and approach each other differently than they did, say thirty years ago.

Of course, we can all rattle off a list of places in which this thinking has *not* taken hold—from Columbine High School and all the other tragic school shootings in the U.S.

to the horrifically violent ethnic conflicts that continue to rage around the world. And, many of us have met lawyers, as well as real estate, entertainment, and sports brokers and agents who still prefer to "shoot first, talk later" or who continue to act as if the world is only made up of scarce resources. Clearly, there are groups of people who have vested interests in perpetuating conflict and adversarial and competitive approaches to its resolution. We must study further the incentives and disincentives for choosing particular approaches to conflict and problem solving, and their costs and benefits in both the long and short run.

I still believe firmly in the four core principles and the seven elements of *Getting to Yes* as they have been developed over the years. And I believe that "small is beautiful" and "local is global." We should all keep working to teach and practice "getting to yes" wherever we happen to be. But I also think that for those of us who seek to make the world a better, more peaceful place through negotiation ("as long as they are talking, they are not killing"), we owe it to Roger Fisher, Bill Ury, and Bruce Patton to rigorously explore when and how getting to yes can be made more possible in the world. In short, it is time for us to rigorously study those situations of success (where and when the tenets of *Getting to Yes* have worked) and failure (what has not worked in particular settings and why). And, of course, each of us should ask ourselves every day, what have we done today to get to yes (or not) in our own lives?

For many of us, *Getting to Yes* either signaled the beginning or was a development in the middle of our life journey to help bring people, groups, and nations together productively. Twenty-five years later, we have a rich research and teaching agenda, with more complex questions posed and more real-world situations to study. I want to thank Roger Fisher, Bill Ury, and Bruce Patton for giving us this powerful tool for teaching, this rich text for contemplating—I personally own five copies, including an autographed first edition—as the rest of us continue to work to get the rest of the world to see it is better to reach agreement (without giving in!) than to fight.

Negotiation and the Uncertainty of Culture

At one level, the response of negotiation proponents, as Menkel-Meadow urges, is to continue to rigorously explore, as this book does and others have before, "when and how getting to yes can be made more possible in the world." The varied adaptations of "getting to yes" through this ongoing work will yield more nuance and more complexity. Answers will be formulated not only to the critiques raised in this chapter but also, as is implied, to the macro-questions Menkel-Meadow asks.

On the other hand, Menkel-Meadow's concern does raise a dilemma. If the project involves the search for a superior negotiating universe or a constant negotiation pattern or paradigm, bounded in some ways by the core principles or elements of *Getting to Yes* as they have been developed over the years, is this universe discoverable at all?

The dilemma behind addressing Menkel-Meadow's concern arises in part because of the cultural complications already raised in this book. However skillfully adapted or disguised, are world views about "getting to yes" adaptable or practical in a culturally diverse world where in some societies the idea of interests or needs in dispute settings may have no easy translation? Despite cultural sensitivity and increased awareness about diversity in disputes, are "getting to yes" ideas essentially Western or Eurocentric constructs? Is the process of identifying important bundles of interests or needs (for representative negotiators and their clients), attaching utility to them, and working together in some process designed to create mutually satisfying solutions actually an efficiency-maximizing process that mimics Pareto efficient or optimal exchanges? Can work in negotiation that relies on such Western concepts apply widely across the divergent experiences of individuals, communities, and countries?

Consider whether you could sell, in book form or otherwise, the ideas of representative negotiation contained herein to Aboriginal negotiators representing First Nations who are trying to reach agreements with non-Aboriginal negotiators representing non-Aboriginal governments in treaty settings. Similarly, consider whether business people from Japan would buy the adapted ideas of "getting to yes" in a negotiation setting involving the pricing of raw log exports from British Columbia to companies in their own country. In both of these examples, would any negotiation model or process make sense except models or processes finely tuned to the experiences of the divergent characteristics of all constituencies involved in these negotiations? How could we hope to possibly articulate a coherent version of such a negotiation model or process?

Negotiation and the Uncertainty of Social Structural Conditions

Apart from the uncertainty that culture, broadly defined, imposes, uncertainty also arises when we consider social structural conditions—the socio-economic and economic conditions that Menkel-Meadow asserts require more study. These fields of study are in themselves enormous. Where do we start? Is the problem that there are too many starting points?

Paul Wangerin provides one starting point.[25] He explores the relationship between political and economic systems and our understanding of dispute resolution (including negotiation) and how disputes get settled. He describes two competing conceptions regarding the nature of human beings and the social institutions they form—classic liberalism and civic humanism:

> A full picture of the notion of classic liberalism, a picture that is essentially a mirror of civic humanism described earlier, can now be seen. First, proponents of classical liberalism suggest that science itself has established that human beings are, by nature, self-interested and competitive. (Proponents of civic humanism, it should be recalled, insist that science demonstrates that human beings are by nature, cooperative and altruistic.) Second, proponents of classical liberalism argue that the self-interest and competitive instincts of individual people are good things rather than bad, at least from an overall social perspective. This is so, these people believe, because the use of these instincts in a "check and balance" fashion eliminated the need for all powerful governments. (Civic humanism, of course, seeks to root out self interest and competition.) Third, proponents of classical liberalism believe that social institutions should encourage

---

25   P.T. Wangerin, "The Political and Economic Roots of the 'Adversary System' of Justice and 'Alternative Dispute Resolution'" (1994) 9 Ohio St. J. Disp. Resol. 203.

people to engage in competitive activities that involve markets, such as activities that employ reciprocal self interest. (Again, civic humanists have no interest in these things.) Finally, classic liberalism requires information processing to be done in a decentralized manner. (Civic humanists, it should be recalled, do not have problems with centralized power.)[26]

Rather than discuss dispute resolution systems in a vacuum, Wangerin points to the relationship between dispute resolution (including negotiation) and social structures. He makes direct links between the adversarial system of disputing and the competitiveness and self-interest of classic liberalism and alternative approaches to disputing and the intrinsically cooperative, communitarian, and altruistic character of civic humanism. Attacks against the adversarial system, he surmises, are the direct result of increasing dissatisfaction with classic liberalism and an increasing attraction to civic humanism.

The problem is, however, what is the nature of human beings that shape social systems? Wangerin sees great uncertainty. He notes that science shows "humans—like other animals—are highly variable … likely to show contradictory traits."[27] Accordingly,

> The first requisite for a rigorous scientific approach to human nature is … willingness to abandon the belief that answers are either/or: [o]ur behaviour can be both innate and acquired; both cooperative and competitive; both similar to that of other species and uniquely human.[28]

Wangerin notes that social scientists like Morton Deutsch also have attempted to determine whether human beings are, by nature, cooperative and altruistic or competitive and self-interested. Although Deutsch's work does suggest that social institutions that encourage cooperative and altruistic behaviour do work better in connection with dispute resolution than social institutions that encourage competitive and self-interested behaviour, it says nothing about the nature of human beings themselves.

The end result for settlement advocacy surely is uncertainty, particularly when the deep exploration of the social structural conditions that Menkel-Meadow calls for is actually done. In the real world, social structures are hardly stable. Perhaps this is due to the uncertainty of the human condition that Wangerin explores. However, if it is the socio-economic and political conditions that actually inform negotiation theories and practices and if these conditions are inherently unpredictable or in flux, how can negotiation theories and practices be framed in light of such great uncertainty? What if negotiation is not a rational process of thinking and planning but a chaotic human behavioural improvisational art?

Uncertainty should not deter attempts to better understand how to negotiate for the reasons mentioned in the opening of this chapter. Negotiation is a pervasive practice. Attempting to understand its complexity and to know when it is better to reach agreement (without giving in!) than to fight makes sense. However, the uncertainty of it all does create enormous challenges about where to start. Menkel-Meadow's exhortations to look closely at social structural conditions (and, by necessary implication, human nature) rather than

---

26   *Ibid.* at 221.

27   *Ibid.* at 236.

28   *Ibid.*

seek a unified field theory will not only add to the rich multidisciplinary work on negotiation but also reflect the truly complex nature of a seemingly simple process—a back-and-forth communication designed to reach agreement.

Notes and Questions

1. You represent a woman who claims she was assaulted by an ex-boyfriend. The personal injuries are serious and long-lasting. The boyfriend denies the allegation and provides an alibi defence. The police investigate. Crown counsel decides there is not enough evidence to warrant criminal charges in all the circumstances because there is no reasonable chance of conviction. The woman's lawyer provides an opinion that there is a good chance—say 65 percent—that a civil judgment could be obtained even given the alibi evidence. Damages after trial could approximate $200,000. The ex-boyfriend's lawyer calls you and says his client is interested in seeing if a negotiated settlement could be reached and suggests taking an integrative approach to the problem. Based on your readings of the critique of settlement advocacy, what do you say to the other lawyer?

2. Do you agree with the critique that economic interests lie behind many developments in negotiation practices, perhaps even the new ideas contained in this book? If so what steps or measures need to be taken by representative negotiators to ensure the values Richard Abel describes in *The Politics of Informal Justice* that he says deserve "broad allegiance" get factored into negotiation practices?

Selected Further Reading

L. Babcock & S. Laschever, *Women Don't Ask: Negotiation and the Gender Divide* (Princeton, NJ: Princeton University Press, 2003).

D. Luban, "Settlements and the Erosion of the Public Realm" (1995) 83 Geo. L.J. 2619.

C. Menkel-Meadow, "Whose Dispute Is It Anyway? A Philosophical and Democratic Defence of Settlement" (1995) 83 Geo. L.J. 2663.

R. Mnookin, "When Not to Negotiate: A Negotiation Imperialist Reflects on Appropriate Limits" (2003) 74 U. Colo. L. Rev. 1077.

A.K. Schneider & C. Honeyman, *The Field Guide to Negotiation* (Washington, DC: ABA Press, 2006).

Index

Acknowledgments

Page 52: Excerpt from GETTING TO YES 2/e by Roger Fisher, William Ury and Bruce Patton. Copyright © 1981, 1991 by Roger Fisher and William Ury. Reprinted by permission of Houghton Mifflin Company. All rights reserved.

Page 84: © John Lande, 1996. http://www.law.missouri.edu/lande.

Page 91: © The New Yorker Collection 2006 Leo Cullum from cartoonbank.com. All rights reserved.

Page 111: Reprinted by permission of the publisher from "Ethical and Moral Issues" in THE ART AND SCIENCE OF NEGOTIATION: HOW TO RESOLVE CONFLICTS AND GET THE BEST OUT OF BARGAINING by Howard Raiffa, pp. 344-349, Cambridge, Mass.: The Belknap Press of Harvard University Press, Copyright © 1982 by the President and Fellows of Harvard College.

Page 116: "Bargaining with the Devil Without Losing Your Soul," from BARGAINING FOR ADVANTAGE by G. Richard Shell, copyright © 1999 by G. Richard Shell. Used by permission of Viking Penguin, a division of Penguin Group (USA) Inc.

Pages 105 and 106: Excerpted from *Negotiator's Fieldbook*, 2006, edited by Andrea Kupfer Schneider and Christopher Honeyman, published by the American Bar Association Section of Dispute Resolution. Copyright © 2006 by the American Bar Association. Reprinted with permission.

Page 107: © 2003 McGraw-Hill/Irwin. Reproduced with the permission of The McGraw-Hill Companies.

Page 166: CP/Hamilton Spectator/Barry Gray.

Page 179: © 1998 Michael Coyle.

Page 198: © Aspasia Tsaoussis. Reprinted by permission of the author.

Page 224: "A Landscape of Sometimes Hard-to-Find Feelings," from DIFFICULT CONVERSATIONS by Douglas Stone, Bruce M. Patton, and Sheila Heen, copyright © 1999 by Douglas Stone, Bruce M. Patton & Sheila Heen. Used by permission of Viking Penguin, a division of Penguin Group (USA) Inc.

Pages 225 and 237: From BEYOND REASON by Roger Fisher and Daniel L. Shapiro, copyright © 2005 by Roger Fisher & Daniel L. Shapiro. Used by permission of Viking Penguin, a division of Penguin Group (USA) Inc.

Page 226: Reprinted with permission.

Page 236: Reprinted with the permission of Scribner, an imprint of Simon & Schuster Adult Publishing Group, from PEOPLE SKILLS by Robert Bolton. Copyright © 1979 by Simon & Schuster, Inc. All rights reserved.